Rodale's Complete GARDEN PROBLEM SOLVER

Rodale's Complete GARDEN PROBLEM SOLVER

INSTANT ANSWERS TO THE MOST COMMON GARDENING QUESTIONS

Delilah Smittle, Editor

Contributing Writers: Dayna S. Lane, Cheryl Long, Barbara Pleasant, Sally Roth, and Sarah Wolfgang-Heffner

Rodale Press, Inc.
Emmaus, Pennsylvania

We're happy to hear from you.

For questions or comments concerning the editorial content of this book, please write to:

Rodale Press, Inc.
Book Readers' Service
33 East Minor Street
Emmaus, PA 18098

For more information about Rodale Press and the books and magazines we publish, visit our World Wide Web site at:

http://www.rodalepress.com

Editor: **Delilah Smittle**
Cover Designer: **Nancy Smola Biltcliff**
Cover Illustrator: **Douglas Schneider**
Interior Book Designer: **Diane Ness Shaw**
Interior Illustrator (plants): **Maureen A. Logan**
Interior Illustrator (insects and diseases):
  Thomas C. Quirk Jr.
Copy Editor: **Barbara McIntosh Webb**
Editorial Assistance: **Susan L. Nickol and
  Jodi Rehl**
Manufacturing Coordinator: **Melinda Rizzo**
Indexer: **Lina B. Burton**

Rodale Home and Garden Books
Vice President and Editorial Director:
  Margaret J. Lydic
Managing Editor, Garden Books:
  Ellen Phillips
Art Director: Paula Jaworski
Associate Art Director: Mary Ellen Fanelli
Studio Manager: Leslie M. Keefe
Copy Director: Dolores Plikaitis
Office Manager: Karen Earl-Braymer

Library of Congress Cataloging-in-Publication Data
Rodale's complete garden problem solver ;
    instant answers to the most common gardening questions / Delilah Smittle, editor ;
    contributing writers, Dayna S. Lane ... [et al.].
      p. cm.
    Includes bibliographical references and index.
    ISBN 0–87596–774–4 (hardcover; acid-free paper)
    1. Garden pests—Control—Handbooks, manuals, etc. 2. Plant diseases—Handbooks, manuals, etc. 3. Organic gardening—Handbooks, manuals, etc. I. Smittle, Delilah. II. Lane, Dayna S. III. Rodale Press.
SB974.R64 1997
635—dc21   97–4795

Distributed in the book trade by St. Martin's Press

2 4 6 8 10 9 7 5 3   hardcover

Contents

How to Use This Book vi

Vegetables 1

Herbs 91

Fruits and Nuts 123

Flowers 187

The Pest Finder 329

The Disease Finder 332

Sources 334

Recommended Reading . . 335

Index 336

USDA Plant Hardiness
  Zone Map 346

How to Use This Book

Rodale's Complete Garden Problem Solver is the most complete, up-to-date, and easiest-to-use reference for warding off whatever ails your garden. We have filled it with all-new expert advice to give you the best organic techniques for fighting and preventing pests, diseases, and other problems that attack your garden.

This problem solver is designed so you can find instant solutions to your gardening problems—all in one handy volume. We organized it so that the answers to your gardening problems are literally right at your fingertips.

COLORFUL SECTIONS HELP YOU SOLVE PROBLEMS INSTANTLY

If you turn *Rodale's Complete Garden Problem Solver* on its edge, the first thing you will see are four distinct stripes of color: green for vegetables, yellow for herbs, blue for fruits and nuts, and red for flowers. Simply open the book to whatever the right color is for the section you need. You'll never have to turn from one part of the book to another.

Plant-by-plant entries are alphabetical within each color-coded section. We've listed the plants by their common names first to make them extra easy to find. Each entry describes a plant's potential problems and then gives solutions—all in the same place. The first solution you see is always the first thing you should do. These quick fixes are followed by long-term solutions aimed at keeping the problem from returning.

NOW TRY THIS

See for yourself how the *Problem Solver* works. First, turn to the section featuring the plant you're having a problem with. Next, skim through the lists of that plant's common problems to find out whether the culprit is an insect, a disease, or some other cause (like air pollution or a nutrient deficiency). Then check the information listed under "Cause" to identify the source and "What to Do" to control it. Then try the other solutions to make sure it is gone for good.

STOP PROBLEMS BEFORE THEY START

It's important to remember that a trouble-free garden is a healthy garden. The solutions recommended in *Rodale's Complete Garden Problem Solver* tell you not only how to keep pests and diseases off your plants but also how to build balanced, disease-resistant soil and how to grow healthy plants. You'll find the names of the best pest- and disease-resistant varieties to grow. You'll learn how to stop pests before they damage plants, by using proven techniques like making and setting out barriers and repellents, making simple and effective traps, and companion planting. All of the solutions here are up-to-the-minute, tested, organic controls that are used by professionals who garden organically.

SPECIAL FEATURES MAKE THIS PROBLEM SOLVER EVEN EASIER TO USE

Rodale's Complete Garden Problem Solver is so handy that you can even carry it into the garden to help you identify problems on the spot. Most plant entries are accompanied by a colorful drawing of the plant and the pests that plague it. The accurate drawings of pests and diseases are oversized to help you identify even the smallest critter you see.

Two handy tables at the back of the book make it easy to see solutions at a glance for the most commonly encountered pests and diseases that trouble your plants. The USDA Plant Hardiness Zone map on page 346 will help you to see whether plants that you want to grow will survive and prosper in your climate. "Sources" on page 334 gives you a list of mail-order sources for all of the special tools, treatments, and organic controls recommended in the book.

This handy, one-volume guide gives you everything you need to combat garden pests, diseases, and the whims of Mother Nature. Enjoy a bountiful harvest with the help of *Rodale's Complete Garden Problem Solver*.

Vegetables

Asparagus 2
Bean 4
Beet......................8
Broccoli 10
Brussels Sprouts......12
Cabbage.................14
Chinese Cabbage....18
Carrot....................20
Cauliflower.............22
Celery....................24
Corn 26
Cucumber 30
Eggplant 34
Garlic.....................36
Kale 38
Kohlrabi 40
Leek......................42
Lettuce 44
Melon....................46

Okra 48
Onion 50
Parsnip 52
Pea 54
Pepper...................56
Potato 60
Radish 64
Rhubarb 66
Rutabaga...............68
Spinach 70
Summer Squash......72
Sweet Potato 74
Swiss Chard...........76
Tomato..................78
Turnip...................84
Watermelon 86
Winter Squash
   and Pumpkin......88

1

Asparagus

(Asparagus officinalis)

 Asparagus Pests

PROBLEM: As spears emerge in spring, some curl. Others are cut off at the soil's surface. Some remain healthy.

CAUSE: Cutworms (Family Noctuidae). The larvae of several species of night-flying moths, cutworms are gray or dull brown caterpillars, 1 to 2 inches long. Cutworms feed on your asparagus seedlings at night and hide in soil or mulch during the day.

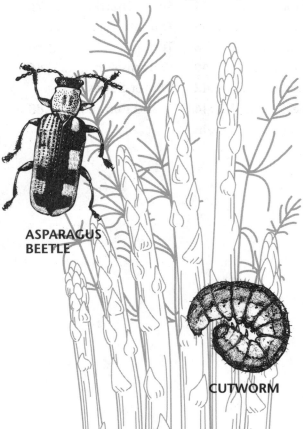

ASPARAGUS BEETLE

CUTWORM

WHAT TO DO:
• Handpick.
• Apply beneficial nematodes (*Steinernema carpocapsae* and *Heterorhabditis heliothidis*), which you can purchase from mail-order suppliers. Live nematodes are shipped suspended in gels or sponges. Follow label instructions for application, and release nematodes when pest larvae are present.

PROBLEM: Spears have vertical wrinkles and are partially cut beneath the soil. Tiny white worms are inside stems.

CAUSE: Asparagus miners (*Ophiomyia simplex*). These asparagus-eating pests are white worms about $\frac{3}{16}$ inch long. The adults are small black flies, less than $\frac{1}{6}$ inch long.

WHAT TO DO:
• Destroy infected spears.
• Use floating row covers to exclude flies. Cover the plants with these synthetic, spun-bonded fabrics, and bury the edges of the row cover in the soil. Place row covers over the planting and bury the edges in the soil.
• Clean up garden debris in winter.

PROBLEM: Spears show scars and brown areas on tips. Some leaves are missing, and dark stains are on plants.

CAUSE: Asparagus beetles (*Crioceris asparagi*). These pests are $\frac{1}{4}$-inch-long, shiny black beetles with bright yellow and red markings. Adults feed on spear tips. The white larvae, which are $\frac{1}{3}$ inch long with black heads, eat the leaves.

WHAT TO DO:
• Handpick.
• Attract beneficial insects, like lady beetles and tiny wasps, by planting small-flowered nectar plants, including yarrow, dill, and Queen-Anne's-lace.
• Birds eat these pests.
• Clean up garden debris in winter.

PROBLEM: In midspring, needle-like leaves look pale and bleached; small, pear-shaped insects are on them.

CAUSE: Aphids (Family Aphididae). Aphids are soft-bodied, $\frac{1}{16}$- to $\frac{3}{8}$-inch-long insects ranging in color from pale tan to light green to nearly black. They damage leaves and stems by sucking plant juices. But even a large infestation won't do serious damage unless it persists for more than two weeks.

WHAT TO DO:
• Wash aphids off plants with a strong stream of water.
• Use insecticidal soap, following label directions.
• Attract beneficial insects, like lady beetles and lacewings, by planting small-flowered nectar plants, including alyssum, scabiosa, yarrow, dill, and Queen-Anne's-lace. Give the beneficials time to bring the aphids under control.

 Asparagus Diseases

PROBLEM: Elongated, reddish orange blisters, like small, raised scratches, appear on stems or the needle-like leaves.

CAUSE: Rust (*Puccinia asparagi*). At first the spots of this fungal disease are reddish orange and leave a brick red trail of dust if rubbed with a damp paper towel. The disease spreads rapidly during rainy weather or when dew causes the asparagus plants to remain wet for long periods of time.

WHAT TO DO:
• Clean up garden debris in winter.
• Plant rust-resistant varieties of asparagus, such as 'California 500', 'Jersey Giant', and 'Jersey King'.

PROBLEM: When spears break through the ground in spring, some are spindly and weak. Their leaves turn yellow.

CAUSE: Fusarium wilt, also called root rot (*Fusarium* spp.). One or more fungi cause this disease. The disease fungi live in soil and cause asparagus roots to rot. The plants look increasingly feeble as summer progresses, with the fernlike branches on each plant turning yellow. Damage made by asparagus miners (see opposite page) gives root rot an easy entry into the plants. Root rot also can develop in poorly drained soil or where the soil's pH is too acidic.

WHAT TO DO:
• Raise soil alkalinity to pH 6.5 to 7.5 by adding lime to the soil.
• Control asparagus miners.

PROBLEM: In warm, humid climates, gray or tan oval spots with red borders appear on lower leaves and spread up.

CAUSE: Cercospora leaf spot (*Cercospora asparagi*). This disease is also known as needle-blight or cercospora blight. It is a fungal infection that carries over from year to year in dead asparagus tissue. Affected leaves wither and drop. Infected asparagus will come back the following spring but may be weakened and need extra fertilizer and water to regain strength.

WHAT TO DO:
• Use drip irrigation rather than overhead watering.
• Clean up garden debris in winter.

Bean

(Phaseolus spp.)

 Bean Pests

PROBLEM: Seedlings vanish overnight, or else you find them the next morning, lying on the soil's surface.

CAUSE: Cutworms (Family Noctuidae). These pests are the larvae of several species of moths. Cutworms are gray or dull brown caterpillars that grow from 1 to 2 inches long. The caterpillars feed on bean plants at night and hide in the soil during the day.

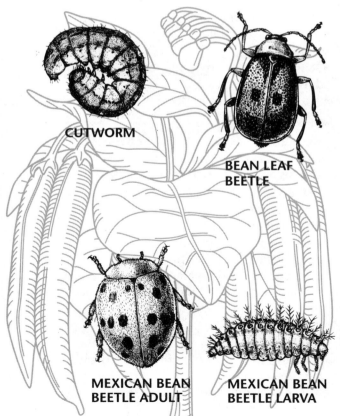

CUTWORM

BEAN LEAF BEETLE

MEXICAN BEAN BEETLE ADULT

MEXICAN BEAN BEETLE LARVA

WHAT TO DO:
• Make cutworm collars to keep cutworms from reaching your seedlings. Use shears to cut 2- to 3-inch-long sections from paper-towel tubes or aluminum cans. Place the short tubes over small seedlings as soon as they sprout.
• Handpick.
• Apply beneficial nematodes (*Steinernema carpocapsae* and *Heterorhabditis heliothidis*), which you can purchase from mail-order suppliers. Live nematodes are shipped suspended in gels or sponges. Follow label instructions for application, and release nematodes when pest larvae are present.

PROBLEM: Bean leaves develop small, translucent patches that gradually skeletonize, consisting mostly of veins.

CAUSE: Mexican bean beetles (*Epilachna varivestis*). These pest larvae are ⅓-inch-long, yellow-orange, spiny grubs. They feed on bean leaves by rasping tissues from the backs of leaves. Adult bean beetles look like ¼-inch-long, dusty lady beetles.

WHAT TO DO:
• Handpick beetles and larvae.
• Apply neem (azadirachtin). This botanical pesticide repels and poisons insect pests without harming beneficials, plus it retards pest-insect growth. Neem also protects plants from diseases by inhibiting the development of plant pathogens. The pesticide, which is extracted from seeds of the neem tree (*Azadirachta indica*), a native tree of India and Africa, is nearly nontoxic to mammals and is biodegradable. Follow label directions for mixing and applying neem products.

PROBLEM: The edges of your bean leaves are curling downward. They are bleached-out green or yellow-green.

CAUSE: Leafhoppers (Family Cicadellidae). Leafhoppers suck plant juices from bean leaves. The pests are wedge-shaped, brown or green insects that are about ⅒ inch long. Leafhoppers can be hard to see because they usually hop away as you approach them.

WHAT TO DO:
• Wash leafhoppers off plants with a strong stream of water.
• Use insecticidal soap, following label directions.

PROBLEM: The leaves of your bean plants have round holes about ¼ inch in diameter scattered across them.

CAUSE: Bean leaf beetles (*Cerotoma trifurcata*). These pests are ¼-inch-long, dark yellow or red adult beetles with black dots on their backs. The pests attack beans in two ways. The beetles eat bean leaves; then they lay eggs near the soil, which hatch into ⅓-inch-long white worms that eat bean roots.

WHAT TO DO:
• Handpick adults.
• Appy beneficial nematodes (*Steinernema carpocapsae* and *Heterorhabditis heliothidis*), which mail-order suppliers ship live, suspended in gels or sponges. Follow label instructions, and release nematodes when pest larvae are present.

PROBLEM: Smooth-edged holes suddenly appear in the leaves of your bean plants, but you can see no insects.

CAUSE: Slugs (Order Stylommatophora). Garden slugs are usually gray and look like snails without shells. They may be from ¼ to 4 inches long, and they produce a sticky slime wherever they go. Small slugs crawl up bean stems to feed after dark. By morning, the slugs hide in the soil, in mulch, or under plant debris.

WHAT TO DO:
• Handpick.
• Make beer traps from recycled cans sunk to the brim in soil and filled with yeasty beer. Create a roof over the trap to provide shade so the spot remains cool and moist. Attracted by the scent of beer, the slugs will fall into the trap and drown.
• Apply diatomaceous earth (DE) to the soil. This abrasive dust is made of fossilized shells, called diatoms, that penetrate the pests' skin as they crawl over DE. Wear a dust mask to avoid inhaling particles. Apply DE when bean plants are wet with dew.

 Bean Diseases

PROBLEM: Leaves are crinkled and brittle. They have patches of yellow and dark green.

CAUSES: Bean mosaic virus and other viruses are to blame. Once viruses invade bean plants, they interfere with the plants' genetic blueprint for growth. Affected plants will have tightly clustered flowers that yield few beans. Viruses are usually spread by aphids, which introduce diseases to plants as they feed. Pole beans may outgrow the problem, but bush beans seldom resume normal growth once they are infected.

WHAT TO DO:
• Remove and destroy infected plants.
• Do not save seeds of infected plants.
• Plant resistant varieties, such as 'Goldcrop', 'Provider', 'Roma Z', and 'Sungold'.

PROBLEM: Dark-colored spots up to ½ inch in diameter develop on bean pods during periods of cool, damp weather.

CAUSE: Anthracnose (*Colletotrichum* spp.). The leaves of affected bean plants are usually free of spots, but the leaf veins on the backs of the lowest, oldest leaves turn dark, and the stems may also darken. These symptoms indicate the fungal disease anthracnose. It thrives in cool, rainy weather and is spread by wind or rain. The disease carries over from season to season in soil or on infected bean seeds.

WHAT TO DO:
• Space plants widely for good air circulation.
• Compost plant debris.
• Plant healthy seeds.

PROBLEM: In midsummer, small, irregular yellow spots with deposits of red dust in the center form on older leaves.

CAUSE: Rust (*Uromyces phaseoli* var. *typica*). This fungal disease spreads quickly when its dusty-orange spores are blown or carried to damp bean leaves.

WHAT TO DO:
• Use succession planting. Start the same plant at two- or three-week intervals to stagger the harvest.
• Stay out of the patch when leaves are wet.
• Rotate crops. Simply avoid growing a bean crop in the same spot each year to minimize the spread of this disease.
• Clean up the garden, and compost plant debris.

PROBLEM: Bean plants grow slowly, they wilt on hot days, and the leaves shrivel and die.

CAUSES: Root-rot fungal diseases. The following fungal diseases, fairly easy to diagnose, along with several other, harder-to-diagnose diseases with similar symptoms, can cause bean roots to rot and the roots and the stem at the soil line to feel hollow.

Pythium root rot (*Pythium* spp.). This fungal disease causes most of the roots to disappear, leaving behind little more than a single, shriveled, dark taproot.

Fusarium root rot, also known as dry rot (*Fusarium solani* f. *phaseoli*). This disease causes the damaged tissues of bean plants just below the soil line to look dry and shriveled. The top of the roots look woody, brown, and cracked. Sometimes, affected bean plants attempt to grow small roots just beneath the surface of the soil and at the very bottom of the older, main roots. In between, there is a woody section with vertical wrinkles and cracks.

Rhizoctonia root rot (*Rhizoctonia solani*). Bean plants affected by this fungal disease lose their roots. Rhizoctonia root rot causes young seedlings to rot very quickly. When this type of root rot infects older beans, you will see reddish brown, sunken places on the main root, and almost all of the small roots will rot. If you cut open the stem of a bean plant infected with the Rhizoctonia root rot, you will see red streaks inside it.

WHAT TO DO:
• Incorporate compost into the soil to improve soil drainage and to introduce disease-fighting soil organisms.
• Rotate crops. If you don't grow beans in the same spot each year, rhizoctonia fungi will die out.

PROBLEM: Small, rust-colored, angular or round polka dots form on leaves. The backs of leaves may be fuzzy.

CAUSE: Cercospora leaf spot (*Cercospora* spp.). As the disease progresses, the centers drop out of the leaf spots, and the leaves shrivel and then drop. The disease carries over from year to year in soil and in dead bean plants.

WHAT TO DO:
- Compost plant debris.
- Avoid overhead irrigation; water at the soil level.
- Improve soil drainage.
- Rotate crops. Simply avoid growing a crop in the same spot each year.

PROBLEM: In wet weather, bush bean pods close to the ground begin to rot. They develop a gray, powdery mold.

CAUSE: Gray mold, also know as botrytis (*Botrytis cinerea*). This fungus lives on dead and dying bean plants. The disease is present in the soil but seldom causes problems unless the weather remains very damp for extended periods of time.

WHAT TO DO:
- Mulch the soil's surface.
- Pick beans as they ripen.
- Clean up plant debris and compost it.
- Allow the soil to dry out between waterings.

PROBLEM: In late summer, old bean plants develop gray or white powdery patches on leaves.

CAUSE: Powdery mildew (*Erysiphe polygoni*). As this fungal disease progresses, the leaf area beneath the patches on the backs of the leaves dies and turns tan. If new leaves do emerge, they may be small and curled, and they may also turn yellow and wither. The pods of affected bean plants are small and misshapen. The strain of this fungal disease that infects beans will not spread to other garden crops.

WHAT TO DO:
- Rotate crops. Simply avoid growing the same crop in the same spot each year.
- Space plants widely to encourage air circulation.
- Pick and destroy infected leaves.

- Use succession planting. Start the same plant at two- or three-week intervals to stagger the harvest.

 Other Problems

PROBLEM: Seemingly healthy plants blossom, but only a few pods, only partially filled with beans, are produced.

CAUSE: Heat stress caused by temperatures above 85°F causes bean blossoms to fail. This can be discouraging with bush bean varieties that bloom heavily only once a season. Some bush beans can tolerate the heat better than others, and lima beans hardly ever have this problem. Pole beans bloom over a longer period of time, and they get more chances to produce beans during cooler periods throughout the season.

WHAT TO DO:
- Plant bush beans early in the season and again in late summer.
- Choose indeterminate varieties like 'Provider', or plant any variety of pole bean.

PROBLEM: Your bean plants are missing, or they are chewed and partially eaten, and the pods are missing.

CAUSE: Animals. Grazing animals, including deer, raccoons, woodchucks, rabbits, squirrels, chipmunks, and other rodents, will eat bean plants and pods if they can get into your garden.

WHAT TO DO:
- Pick bean pods and leaves that touch the soil. This will deter small rodents, which can reach only low-hanging parts of plants.
- Repel them with human hair. Stuff hair into mesh bags or old stockings, and place near plants. Replace the hair every few weeks.

Beet

(Beta vulgaris)

Beet Pests

PROBLEM: Small, pale tan or yellow patches appear on beet leaves, and the affected leaves may be slightly curled.

CAUSE: Aphids (Family Aphididae). These wedge-shaped, ¹⁄₁₆- to ³⁄₈-inch-long insects cling to the backs of leaves. Their sticky secretions, called honeydew, can attract ants and encourage the growth of mold. Aphids can also transfer plant viruses as they feed.

WHAT TO DO:
• Wash aphids off with a stream of water.
• Use insecticidal soap as directed on label.
• Pour boiling water into entry holes of ant-hills that are not adjacent to plant roots.
• Tolerate light infestations.

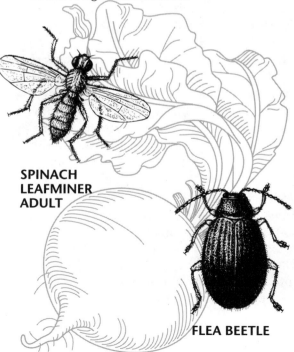

SPINACH LEAFMINER ADULT

FLEA BEETLE

PROBLEM: Light tan, meandering lines beneath the surface of leaves make the leaves look as if they were scribbled on.

CAUSE: Spinach leafminers (*Pegomya hyoscyami*). Leafminers are the minute, translucent, pale green larvae of a ¹⁄₈-inch-long black or black-and-yellow fly. The larvae emerge from eggs laid on the backs of leaves. The larvae feed on the inner tissues of beet leaves, where they are protected by the leaf surfaces. After one to three weeks, larvae drop to the soil to pupate.

WHAT TO DO:
• Use floating row covers to exclude insect pests. Cover the plants with these spun-bonded fabrics, and bury the edges in soil.

PROBLEM: Small, circular holes appear in beet leaves. Some don't penetrate the leaves but look like tan pinpricks.

CAUSE: Flea beetles (Family Chrysomelidae). Approach quietly and you can see the ¹⁄₁₀-inch-long, bronze, brown, or black beetles on both sides of the beet leaves. The holes they make can become entry points for diseases.

WHAT TO DO:
• Use floating row covers to exclude insect pests. Cover the plants with these spun-bonded fabrics, and bury the edges in soil.

PROBLEM: You see ½- to 1½-inch-long, pale green caterpillars with dark stripes eating your beet leaves.

CAUSE: Armyworms (Family Noctuidae). Armyworms can destroy young plants. These caterpillar pests are the night-feeding larvae of gray moths with white dotted wings.

WHAT TO DO:
• Apply BTK. "BT" stands for *Bacillus thuringiensis*, an insect-stomach poison that kills caterpillars without harming beneficial insects. *B.t.* var. *kurstaki* (BTK) kills armyworms. Follow label directions to spray a solution of BTK on plants where young pests are feeding.

 Beet Diseases

PROBLEM: Beet seedlings fall over soon after sprouting. When you pull up a plant, you see rotten roots.
CAUSE: Root rot. This is a joint attack on beet roots by several soil fungi, including *Pythium ultimum* and *Rhizoctonia solani*. Affected mature beets have small roots with holes and cracks in them.
WHAT TO DO:
• Improve soil drainage.
• Mulch plants with compost.
• Rotate plants annually to minimize disease.

PROBLEM: Your beet plants have unusual, knobby-looking roots with corky patches on their skins.
CAUSE: Scab (*Streptomyces scabies*). Infected beet roots are small and woody and may sprout a fuzz of hairy roots. Unless plants already have several healthy leaves, the distorted new ones will slow their growth. This soil-dwelling fungus flourishes in acidic soil and can be encouraged by applying fresh manure to the garden soil.
WHAT TO DO:
• Raise soil pH above 5.5, preferably close to the neutral 7.0, by incorporating lime into the soil.
• Rotate beets with crops other than potatoes, which are also susceptible. Simply alternate beets and potatoes with other plants annually to minimize problems.

PROBLEM: Beet leaves have clusters of circular to oval spots with gray or brown centers and red-brown borders.
CAUSE: Cercospora leaf spot *(Cercospora beticola)*. The spots quickly increase in warm, humid weather. This fungal disease is most active during summer. It persists from year to year in dead plants.
WHAT TO DO:
• Remove plant debris.
• Mulch beets to keep spore-laden mud from splashing onto the plants.
• Plant beets with wide spacing for better air circulation.

 Other Problems

PROBLEM: Leaves are small and slow to appear. Older leaves gradually turn yellow and droop. Roots are small.
CAUSES: Shortage of nitrogen, shortage of water. Beets require a lot of nitrogen, especially when temperatures are in the 60s and 70s and the plants are growing rapidly.
WHAT TO DO:
• Apply a fast-acting, high-nitrogen fertilizer, such as fish emulsion, once a week until you see noticeable improvement.

PROBLEM: New leaves turn brown or black. Roots have cork-textured dead tissue, hard black spots, and cracks.
CAUSE: Boron deficiency. This soil nutrient disorder occurs in ground that is too alkaline for growing beets properly, that has excessive calcium, or that receives too little water.
WHAT TO DO:
• Water beets regularly.
• Acidify the soil as needed with organic matter or sulfur.

Broccoli

(*Brassica oleracea,* Botrytis group)

 ## Broccoli Pests

PROBLEM: Velvety-textured green caterpillars with yellow stripes on their sides are eating your broccoli leaves.

CAUSE: Imported cabbageworms (*Artogeia rapae*). These ½- to 1½-inch-long caterpillars are the larvae of cabbage white butterflies. The butterflies have black-tipped and spotted, white wings and a wingspan of 1½ inches. The butterflies appear early in the spring to lay eggs on broccoli and related plants.

WHAT TO DO:
• Handpick.
• Apply *Bacillus thuringiensis* var. *kurstaki* (BTK).

PROBLEM: Pale-green caterpillars are eating broccoli florets. When they move, their bodies rise up to create a loop.

CAUSE: Cabbage loopers (*Trichoplusia ni*). These are the larvae of gray moths with wing markings that make them look like tree bark. Cabbage looper caterpillars emerge later in spring than imported cabbageworms and are lighter green. They have white stripes on their sides. When they move, they show the classic inchworm posture, with the middle of their bodies raised up to create a loop.

WHAT TO DO:
• Handpick.
• Apply *Bacillus thuringiensis* var. *kurstaki* (BTK), a bacterial stomach poison that kills caterpillars, including cabbage loopers. BTK is most effective before pests tunnel into plants. Follow label directions to apply.
• Make your landscape inviting to birds, which eat cabbage loopers.

PROBLEM: Broccoli leaves are pale and slightly wilted. Clusters of tiny insects cling to stems and backs of the leaves.

CAUSE: Cabbage aphids (*Brevicoryne brassicae*). These soft-bodied, pear-shaped insects are ¹⁄₁₆ to ³⁄₈ inch long. Aphids damage leaves and stems by sucking plant juices.

WHAT TO DO:
• Handpick.
• Knock aphids from plants with a strong stream of water.
• Wipe leaves with a wet cotton swab.
• Use insecticidal soap as directed on label.

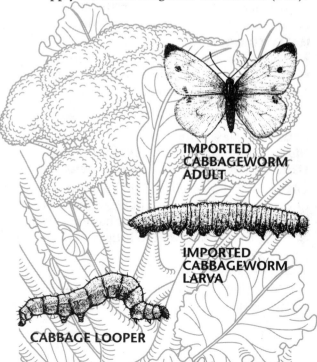

IMPORTED CABBAGEWORM ADULT

IMPORTED CABBAGEWORM LARVA

CABBAGE LOOPER

PROBLEM: Soon after broccoli seedlings are set out, they begin to wilt and die over two to three days.

CAUSE: Cabbage maggots (*Delia radicum*). These white maggots are the same size and shape as grains of rice. The adult cabbage maggots, ¼-inch-long gray flies, lay their eggs at the base of the plants. The larvae feed below ground.

WHAT TO DO:
• Destroy plant debris.
• Use floating row cover to exclude flies. Cover plants with these synthetic, spun-bonded fabrics and bury the edges in the soil.
• Apply diatomaceous earth (DE), an abrasive dust that penetrates the pests' skin, to the soil.
• Apply beneficial nematodes (*Steinernema carpocapsae* and *Heterorhabditis heliothidis*), which are shipped live, suspended in gels or sponges, from mail-order suppliers. Follow instructions; apply when pests are present.

 Broccoli Diseases

PROBLEM: Broccoli seedlings suddenly fall over and die. Their stems darken at the soil line.

CAUSE: Damping-off (*Pythium* spp. and *Rhizoctonia solani*). Fungi cause this common disease. Stem injuries are likely sites of infection; but because the disease-causing fungi live in soil, roots are also vulnerable.

WHAT TO DO:
• Use sterile seed-starting mix.
• Start seeds in clean containers.
• Provide ample spacing between plants for better air circulation.

PROBLEM: Leaves of your broccoli plants become wilted and slightly yellow. The plants look sickly.

CAUSES: There are two soilborne, fungal diseases that cause these symptoms.

Clubroot (*Plasmodiophora brassicae*). Clubroot causes wilting to worsen gradually over one to two weeks. Symptoms are most severe on warm, sunny days. Infected roots have thick, knobby galls.

Fusarium yellows *(Fusarium oxysporum f. conglutinans).* Suspect this disease if you see no galls, but roots are skinny and lacking root hairs. If you cut through the stem at the base of the plant, you'll see a dark, circular ring about ¼ inch from the wall.

WHAT TO DO:
• Raise soil pH to 7.0 or above by adding lime to the soil.
• Compost infected plants in a separate heap.
• Improve soil drainage.
• Rotate crops.

PROBLEM: The upper sides of broccoli leaves show brown spots, and the backs of leaves have patches of mold.

CAUSE: Downy mildew (*Peronospora parasitica*). Cool, damp conditions cause this unsightly but rarely fatal fungal disease.

WHAT TO DO:
• Control weeds.
• Drench soil with fermented compost tea.
• Plant tolerant varieties, such as 'Arcadia', 'Eureka', 'Everest', and 'Patriot'.

 Other Problems

PROBLEM: The mature heads of your broccoli plants are small and have large, hollow areas in their main stems.

CAUSE: Boron or potassium deficiency in the soil can cause the disease. Dry soil, warm weather, or damp weather aggravates it.

WHAT TO DO:
• Raise soil pH to 6.0 or higher by adding lime.
• Drench the soil around the plants with liquid seaweed solution or compost tea every few weeks to provide needed nutrients.

Brussels Sprouts

(*Brassica oleracea*, Gemmifera group)

 Brussels Sprouts Pests

PROBLEM: Small, dark caterpillars, usually less than 1 inch long, are eating seedlings set out in late summer.

CAUSE: Fall armyworms (*Spodoptera frugiperda*). These caterpillars are the night-feeding larvae of gray moths with a white dot on each wing. The adult moths can lay more than 500 eggs a week on lower plant leaves. Armyworms become less numerous as nights become cooler, and they usually disappear after the first frost.

WHAT TO DO:
• Handpick.
• Apply BTK, *Bacillus thuringiensis* var. *kurstaki,* which kills armyworms. BTK is most effective when pests are young and before they tunnel into plants. Follow label directions to spray a solution of BTK on plants as soon as eggs begin to hatch or where young pests are feeding.

PROBLEM: Velvety-textured, green caterpillars with yellow stripes are eating your brussels sprouts leaves.

CAUSE: Imported cabbageworms (*Artogeia rapae*). These ½- to 1½-inch-long caterpillars are the larvae of cabbage white butterflies. The butterflies have black-tipped and spotted, white wings and a wingspan of 1½ inches. These are among the first butterflies to lay eggs in the spring. Their eggs hatch into tiny, ¼-inch-long, yellow-green caterpillars that turn green as they begin to feed. Eventually the caterpillars grow to 1½ inches long. The largest of these caterpillars have pale yellow stripes along their sides. They can eat entire young brussels sprouts seedlings, but they only eat holes in older leaves.

WHAT TO DO:
• Handpick.
• Apply *Bacillus thuringiensis* var. *kurstaki* (BTK). Follow label directions.
• Companion plant with radishes.

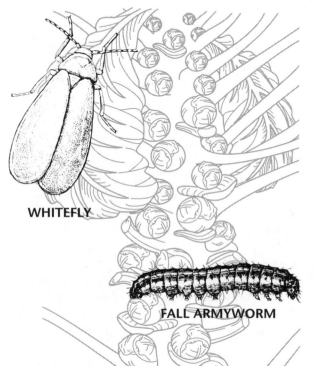

WHITEFLY

FALL ARMYWORM

PROBLEM: White, flying insects $\frac{1}{20}$ inch long are on the backs of leaves. They fly away when you approach.

CAUSE: Whiteflies (Family Aleyrodidae). When these pests are numerous, infested leaves may wilt slightly on sunny days and become lighter in color. Whiteflies lay yellowish eggs the size of a pinpoint on the backs of brussels sprouts leaves, which hatch into $\frac{1}{20}$-inch-long, translucent nymphs. Both the nymphs and adult flies are sucking insects that weaken plants when they feed in large numbers. You are most likely to see them in late summer while the weather remains warm and young brussels sprouts seedlings planted for fall harvest are struggling to grow. Whiteflies usually disappear after the first frost.

WHAT TO DO:
• Gather adults with a hand-held, rechargeable vacuum.
• Use insecticidal soap, following label directions.
• Attract beneficial insects, like lady beetles and tiny wasps, by planting small-flowered nectar plants, including yarrow, dill, and Queen-Anne's-lace.

 Brussels Sprouts Diseases

PROBLEM: After several hard freezes, the leaves at the top of your plants darken, wilt, and develop a gray mold.

CAUSE: Downy mildew (*Peronospora parasitica*). This fungal disease moves in when young leaves have freeze damage. The tender top leaves where ice or snow accumulates are most often damaged and most affected. Dry weather may make the mold disappear, leaving the cluster of leaves brown and wilted.

WHAT TO DO:
• Cut off and dispose of damaged leaves.
• Use floating row covers to protect plants from temperature fluctuations. Cover the plants with these synthetic, spunbonded fabrics, and bury the edges of the row cover in the soil.
• Clean up garden debris in winter.

 Other Problems

PROBLEM: Sprouts are small and loose. They have conical shapes instead of being round as they should be.

CAUSE: Too much warm weather can make brussels sprouts eager to flower, and the first sign of flower formation is the elongation of the sprouts. Sprouts crowded by many leaves may also fail to plump up until they are overripe.

WHAT TO DO:
• Snap off leaves surrounding sprouts when the sprouts are the diameter of a dime.
• Plant brussels sprouts either early in the spring or else late enough in the season to allow time for them to mature in cold weather.

OCCASIONAL PROBLEMS: Several of the pests and diseases that infect broccoli and cabbage can also become a problem for brussels sprouts because all of these vegetables are members of the same plant family (Cruciferae). The problems listed above are the most common ones for garden-grown brussels sprouts. But if you see problems you cannot identify, refer to the following pests and diseases: Cabbage loopers (*Trichoplusia ni*), listed under "Broccoli" on page 10. Cabbage aphids (*Brevicoryne brassicae*), listed under "Broccoli." Cabbage maggots (*Delia radicum*), listed under "Broccoli." Black leg (*Phoma lingam*), listed under "Cabbage" on page 14. Black rot (*Xanthomonas campestris*), listed under "Cabbage." Clubroot (*Plasmodiophora brassicae*), listed under "Broccoli."

Cabbage

(*Brassica oleracea*, Capitata group)

 Cabbage Pests

PROBLEM: Velvet-textured green caterpillars are eating cabbage leaves and leaving dark-green excrement.

CAUSE: Imported cabbageworms (*Artogeia rapae*). These caterpillars are the larvae of cabbage white butterflies. The butterflies have black-tipped and spotted, white wings and wingspans of 1½ inches. These are among the first butterflies to lay eggs on cabbage and related plants in the spring. Their eggs hatch into tiny ¼-inch-long, yellow-green caterpillars that turn green as they begin to feed. Eventually the caterpillars grow to 1½ inches long. The largest of these caterpillars have pale yellow stripes along their sides.

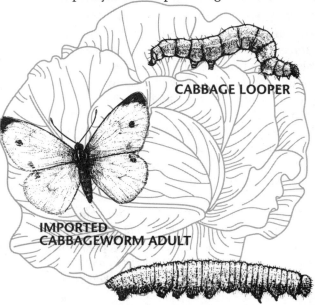

CABBAGE LOOPER

IMPORTED CABBAGEWORM ADULT

IMPORTED CABBAGEWORM LARVA

They can eat entire young seedlings, but they only eat holes in the older leaves. On plants where you find one caterpillar, you usually find several more along with small, yellowish eggs scattered on the backs of the leaves. When infestations are severe, cabbage heads will have small holes where the caterpillars have entered to feed inside the head. You can also see this pest in late summer on cabbage grown for winter harvest; but as fall days become shorter, the cabbageworms become less numerous.

WHAT TO DO:
• Handpick.
• Apply BTK. "BT" stands for *Bacillus thuringiensis*, an insect-stomach poison that kills caterpillars without harming beneficial insects. *B.t.* var. *kurstaki* (BTK) kills cabbageworms. BTK is most effective when pests are young and before they tunnel into plants. Follow label directions to spray a solution of BTK on plants when eggs begin to hatch or where young pests are feeding.
• Companion plant cabbages with radishes, and let the radishes flower to attract beneficial insects to the garden.

PROBLEM: Smooth-skinned, green caterpillars are eating your cabbage leaves, leaving holes in no particular pattern.

CAUSE: Cabbage loopers (*Trichoplusia ni*). These caterpillars are the larvae of mottled, gray-brown moths with wingspans of 1½ inches. Their coloring and their V-shaped, silvery wing markings make the moths blend in with tree bark. Their larvae are frequent visitors to cabbage and other members of the Brassica family, such as broccoli. The caterpillars differ from the imported cabbageworms in several ways. They emerge a little later in spring and are a slightly lighter shade of green with white stripes (rather than yellow ones) along their sides. Their skin has a satiny rather than fuzzy texture, and they have no legs along the middle of their bodies. These caterpillars may attempt to "hide" by lying flat against leaves and leaf veins. But when they move, they show the classic inchworm posture, with the middle of their bodies raised up into a loop. The eggs and young hatchlings of these caterpillars look similar to those of imported cabbageworms, although they tend to be more green than imported cabbageworm eggs and hatchlings.

WHAT TO DO:
• Use floating row covers to exclude insect pests. Cover plants and bury the edges of the row cover in the soil.
• Handpick.
• Apply BTK. "BT" stands for *Bacillus thuringiensis*, an insect-stomach poison that kills caterpillars without harming beneficial insects. *B.t.* var. *kurstaki* (BTK) kills cabbage loopers. BTK is most effective when pests are young and before they tunnel into plants. Follow label directions to spray a solution of BTK on plants when eggs begin to hatch or where young pests are feeding.
• Since cabbage loopers usually do not appear until late spring, wasps, birds, and other predators feed on the loopers.

PROBLEM: In early to midspring, young cabbage plants grow slowly. They wilt slightly on sunny days.
CAUSE: Cabbage aphids (*Brevicoryne brassicae*). Aphids are a common spring insect on cabbage seedlings. These soft-bodied, pear-shaped insects are $\frac{1}{16}$ to $\frac{3}{8}$ inch long.

Clusters of them cling to cabbage stems and to the backs of cabbage leaves. Aphids damage leaves and stems by sucking the plant juices. Their sticky secretions, called honeydew, can encourage the growth of mold, and aphids can transfer plant viruses as they feed. These pests are most numerous on the tender young stems and leaves of developing cabbages.

WHAT TO DO:
• Handpick.
• Knock aphids off cabbage plants with a strong stream of water.
• Use insecticidal soap, following label directions.

PROBLEM: A few weeks after seedlings are set out, they suddenly wilt, then die over a period of two to three days.
CAUSE: Cabbage maggots (*Delia radicum*). These maggots are the larvae of $\frac{1}{4}$-inch-long gray flies. They feed on cabbage roots and the stem just below the soil line. Cabbage maggots will attack mature plants, but they cause the most damage to tender, young plants. You will find the dead seedlings lying on the ground, with their stems still attached to the roots. When you pull up the plants, you may see the little white maggots. They are about the size and shape of a grain of rice, and you may see them fall away from the roots and onto the surrounding soil as you lift the plants.

WHAT TO DO:
• Destroy plant debris.
• Use floating row covers to exclude flies and other insect pests. Cover the planting with these synthetic, spunbonded fabrics, and bury the edges in the soil.
• Apply beneficial nematodes (*Steinernema carpocapsae* and *Heterorhabditis heliothidis*). Mail-order suppliers ship the nematodes live, suspended in gels or sponges.
• Clean up garden debris in winter.

PROBLEM: Colorful bugs are eating cabbage leaves, causing them to become blotched with yellow and white.

CAUSE: Harlequin bugs (*Murgantia histrionica*). These pests are so colorful that you will see the bugs before you see the damage. Look for shield-shaped, shiny black and orange insects, ½ inch long, with black antennae and a black hind end. Harlequin bugs puncture aboveground plant parts and suck sap from them. You will rarely see these pests until early summer, when they seek out cabbages left in the garden after warm weather arrives. On hot days you can find them all over cabbage plants.

WHAT TO DO:
• Handpick.
• Grow early-maturing varieties, such as 'Salarite'. Early cultivars will allow you to harvest cabbages before hot weather and harlequin bugs arrive.

PROBLEM: You see ½- to 1½-inch-long, smooth, pale-green caterpillars with dark stripes eating cabbage leaves.

CAUSE: Armyworms (Family Noctuidae). these serious caterpillar pests can destroy young plants. They are the night-feeding larvae of gray moths with a white dot on each wing.

WHAT TO DO:
• Apply BTK. "BT" stands for *Bacillus thuringiensis*, an insect-stomach poison that kills caterpillars without harming beneficial insects. *B.t* var. *kurstaki* (BTK) kills armyworms. Spray when pests are feeding.

 Cabbage Diseases

PROBLEM: Cabbage plants grow slowly; leaves are pale yellow; neither water nor fertilizer perks the plants up.

CAUSE: Fusarium yellows (*Fusarium oxysporum* f. *conglutinans*). This fungal disease lives in the soil and enters cabbage through its roots, clogging the stems and veins so that moisture and nutrients cannot flow to the leaves. In warm weather the symptoms become worse. The outer leaves turn yellow, wilt, turn brown, and eventually fall. If you cut a head of cabbage from an infected plant, you will see a dark ring inside the main stem, about ¼ inch from the outer stem wall.

WHAT TO DO:
• Pick and destroy infected leaves.
• Improve soil drainage.
• Space plants widely to encourage air circulation.
• Rotate crops. Avoid growing cabbage or related plants in the same spot each year.
• Plant resistant varieties, such as 'Gourmet', 'Stonehead', and 'Vantage'.

PROBLEM: Brown, wedge-shaped spots develop along margins of older leaves and run together to make a margin.

CAUSE: Black rot (*Xanthomonas campestris*). This is a disease of bacterial origin. If you break off and inspect a badly spotted leaf, you will see a dark streak running through the base of the main leaf vein. If the plants are old enough to develop heads, the infection may be worse on one side of the head than the other, giving the cabbage plants a lopsided look. Eventually, the cabbage heads will rot. Growing contaminated plants or seeds can bring this disease into your garden. When it is present, black rot quickly spreads to other cabbage plants via splashing rain drops. Luckily, the combined efforts of seed producers and bedding-plant growers have greatly reduced the prevalence of this disease.

WHAT TO DO:
• Pick and destroy infected plants.

• Space plants widely to encourage adequate air circulation.
• Plant healthy seeds.
• Rotate crops. Avoid growing cabbages in the same spot each year.
• Pick up garden debris and compost it.

PROBLEM: Leaves are gray-green and show ringlike spots that are larger and more numerous in damp weather.

CAUSE: Alternaria leaf spot (*Alternaria* spp.). This fungal disease travels on infected seeds, and it lives from year to year in dead cabbage plants and plant debris left in the garden over winter. The disease progresses with time, so that the spots spread across the entire cabbage head and are especially noticeable on the outer leaves of the heads.

WHAT TO DO:
• Pick and destroy infected leaves and plants.
• Compost plant debris.
• Plant healthy seeds.
• Space plants widely to encourage air circulation.

PROBLEM: Dark, sunken spots on the base of the main stems cut off moisture to leaves, which then begin to wilt.

CAUSE: Black leg (*Phoma lingam*). This fungal disease gradually girdles the main stem of cabbage plants. It is a serious disease that can be fatal if left untreated. Looking for the black specks within the larger leaf spots of infected cabbages is the best way to positively diagnose this disease. You may also see large, brown, angular spots on leaves between the leaf veins. Use a magnifying glass to check for tiny black specks within the larger brown spots of infected plants. This fungus can persist in soil for two to three years. It can also infect several cabbage cousins, including broccoli, brussels sprouts, and cauliflower.

WHAT TO DO:
• Pick and destroy infected plants.
• Remove and compost plant debris at the end of the growing season.
• Plant healthy seeds.
• Space plants widely, when planting, to encourage air circulation.

 Other Problems

PROBLEM: The heads of your cabbages suddenly split open as if they are being cracked apart like eggshells.

CAUSE: Dry soil conditions that suddenly change to wet while plants are growing, as when a heavy, soaking rain follows a period of drought, cause the problem. Under these conditions, the inner leaves of cabbage heads take up more water than the outer leaves, and their rapid expansion causes the outer leaves to split apart.

WHAT TO DO:
• Maintain even soil moisture throughout the growing season by watering cabbage plants regularly.
• Mulch the soil around cabbage plants to help reduce evaporation of moisture and conserve soil moisture.

OCCASIONAL PROBLEMS: Several of the pests and diseases that infect broccoli and brussels sprouts can also become a problem for cabbage, since all three of these vegetables are members of the same plant family (Cruciferae). If you see cabbage problems you cannot identify, refer to the following pests and diseases listed elsewhere in this book: Whiteflies (Family Aleyrodidae), listed under "Brussels Sprouts" on page 12. Damping-off (caused by several species of fungi), listed under "Broccoli" on page 10. Clubroot (*Plasmodiophora brassicae*), listed under "Broccoli."

Chinese Cabbage

(*Brassica rapa,* Pekinensis group) and Other Asian Greens

Chinese Cabbage Pests

PROBLEM: Plant leaves show many little circular holes. Some are so tiny that they look like tan pinpricks.

CAUSE: Flea beetles (Family Chrysomelidae). When you approach the plants quietly, you may see the 1/10-inch-long bronze, brown, or black beetles on either side of the leaves. The beetles on the leaves will quickly jump away when you approach them. These common

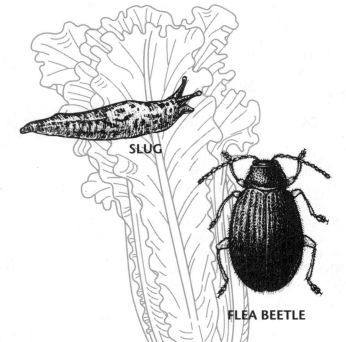

SLUG

FLEA BEETLE

Chinese cabbage pests are especially active in late spring and early summer. Their feeding seldom kills plants, but the holes may become entry points for diseases. Their population ordinarily decreases after midsummer.

WHAT TO DO:

• Use floating row covers to exclude feeding insects. Cover oriental greens during early summer with these synthetic, spunbonded fabrics, and bury the fabrics' edges in the soil.

PROBLEM: The rib sections of the leaves show elongated, sunken, and hollow spots that gradually turn brown.

CAUSE: Slugs (Order Stylommatophora). These relatives of clams and mussels find the leaves of Chinese cabbage and related greens very palatable. Garden slugs are usually gray and look like snails without shells. They may be from 1/4 to 4 inches long and will leave a sticky slime on your fingers if you touch them. Slugs crawl up the stems of their victims after dark, or if the weather is very cloudy, they may start their trek just before nightfall. This explains why you may find more damaged areas toward the base of the plants than near the leaf tips. Before morning, the slugs climb down and find shelter between the closely spaced leaves of Chinese cabbage and those of its relatives. You may also find a few napping under plant debris on the ground.

WHAT TO DO:
- Tolerate light damage.
- Handpick.
- Make beer traps from recycled cans sunk to the brim in soil and filled with yeasty beer. Attracted by the scent of beer, the slugs will fall into the trap and drown.
- Apply diatomaceous earth (DE). This abrasive dust is made of fossilized shells called diatoms that penetrate the pests' skin as they crawl over DE. Wear a dust mask to avoid inhaling it. Apply DE when plants are wet.

Chinese Cabbage Diseases

PROBLEM: The old leaves close to the ground, or those at the tops of the plants, are tan or have white patches.

CAUSE: Downy mildew (*Peronospora parasitica*). Cool, damp weather encourages this fungal disease. The tops of the plants, where rain and dew accumulate, are where you will see the most damage. If you look on the backs of the leaves opposite the discolored patches, you will see gray fuzz.

WHAT TO DO:
- Harvest plants when they mature.
- Remove diseased growth when you see signs of infection.
- Plant resistant varieties such as 'Blues' and 'China Pride'.

Other Problems

PROBLEM: Seedlings started indoors are thin and lanky, and they are falling over onto the ground.

CAUSE: Too little light. Chinese cabbage seedlings that have not had enough light after germinating will grow long, thin and limp. Transplant them into deeper containers filled with sterile potting mix. When repot-

ting, bury the threadlike lower stem in sterile potting mix to help hold the plant upright. After transplanting, move the pots outdoors into bright light for stockier growth.

WHAT TO DO:
- Keep seedlings started indoors within 2 inches of a high-intensity grow light to promote stocky growth, until they are big enough to move outdoors.
- If you choose to start seeds in the stronger light of the sun, start them early in a cold frame or direct-seed them in garden beds after danger of frost has passed.

PROBLEM: Instead of growing into dense heads, the leaves of your Chinese cabbage plants remain loose.

CAUSE: Bolting, which is the process a mature plant goes through when it flowers and sets seed. From the center of the loose and drooping leaves you will see a flowerstalk shoot up. When you set out transplants more than eight weeks old in late spring, as the days get longer and warmer, the plants are at high risk for bolting. Bolting is seldom a problem for fall-planted oriental greens.

WHAT TO DO:
- Set out young seedlings in early spring.
- Set out Chinese cabbage and related plants in late summer to allow time for them to mature for fall harvesting.

OCCASIONAL PROBLEMS: Several of the pests and diseases that attack regular cabbage and radishes can become a problem for Chinese cabbage and related plants because they are all members of the cabbage family (Family Cruciferae). The problems listed above are the most common ones for Chinese cabbage and other Asian greens. If you see problems you cannot identify, refer to the pests and diseases listed under "Cabbage" on page 14 and under "Radish" on page 64.

Carrot

(Daucus carota var. *sativus)*

Carrot Pests

PROBLEM: Carrots stop growing. The leaves look pale and droop. The roots are riddled with rust red tunnels.

CAUSE: Carrot rust fly larvae (*Psila rosae*). These maggots are ⅓ inch long. They feed on roots before pupating into metallic, greenish black flies about ¼ inch long.

WHAT TO DO:

• Use floating row covers to exclude feeding insects. Cover the plants and bury the edges of the row cover in the soil.

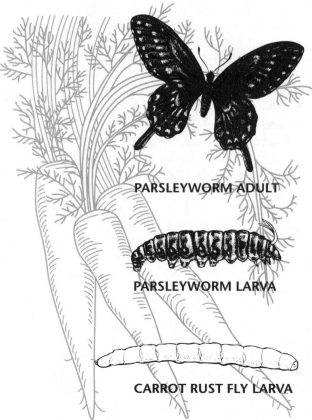

PARSLEYWORM ADULT

PARSLEYWORM LARVA

CARROT RUST FLY LARVA

• Time planting so that carrots will mature before maggots hatch.

• Plant resistant varieties, such as 'Fly Away'.

PROBLEM: Many carrot leaves are suddenly missing. Others have little more left of them than the main leaf veins.

CAUSE: Parsleyworms *(Papilio polyxenes)*. These 1- to 2-inch-long, green caterpillars are the larvae of eastern black swallowtail butterflies. Consider sharing carrot tops with them.

WHAT TO DO:

• Use floating row covers to exclude insects. Cover the plants and bury the edges of the row cover in the soil.

• Handpick.

PROBLEM: Leaves begin to shrivel and dry, and close inspection reveals that the lowest 1 inch of the stem is hollow.

CAUSE: Carrot weevil larvae (*Listronotus oregonensis*). These white grubs are the larvae of hard-shelled, brown weevils about ⅕ inch long.The adult weevils lay their eggs on leaf stems, and the emerging larvae eat their way into the carrot roots.

WHAT TO DO:

• Use floating row covers to exclude insects. Cover the plants with these synthetic, spun-bonded fabrics, and bury the edges of the row cover in the soil.

• Remove plant debris.

PROBLEM: You notice random holes in the carrot roots you harvest, but the plants show no distress above ground.

CAUSE: Wireworms (Family Elateridae).

These root-eating pests are the larvae of slender click beetles. The adults are ⅓- to ¾-inch-long, brown or black beetles with grooved wings that make a clicking noise when they flip from their backs to their feet.

WHAT TO DO:
• Cultivate soil to expose wireworms to birds, which will eagerly eat them.
• Bury raw potato or carrot pieces several inches deep and dig them up every few days to collect larvae that feed on them.

 ## Carrot Diseases

PROBLEM: Numerous dark brown to black spots appear on older leaves. The affected leaves shrivel and bend.

CAUSE: Alternaria leaf blight (*Alternaria dauci*). This fungal disease spreads by wind and raindrops when carrot leaves are wet. The fungal spores overwinter in plant debris and on the soil.

WHAT TO DO:
• Rotate crops. Avoid growing carrots in the same spot each year.
• Space plants widely for air circulation.
• Plant tolerant varieties, like 'Bolero' and 'Cheyenne'.
• Plant carrots in raised beds.

PROBLEM: Brown to gray speckles appear on leaves and stems. Entire leaves turn yellow, then brown, and die.

CAUSE: Cercospora leaf blight (*Cercospora carotae*). This fungus travels on wind and in rain. It is most active in warm weather.

WHAT TO DO:
• Rotate crops. Avoid growing carrots in the same spot each year.
• Space plants widely for air circulation.
• Pick and destroy infected leaves.
• Plant carrots in raised beds.

PROBLEM: New leaves that grow from the center of the plants are small, with yellow or red tips. Some are bunched.

CAUSE: Aster yellows. This is a disease caused by a viruslike organism called a mycoplasma that enters holes made in leaves by aster leafhoppers (*Macrosteles quadrilineatus*).

WHAT TO DO:
• Wash leafhoppers off plants with a strong stream of water.
• Apply insecticidal soap as directed.
• Destroy infected leaves and roots.

PROBLEM: Plants grow slowly. Roots are stubby and may have forked tips and round nodules.

CAUSE: Root-knot nematodes (*Meloidogyne* spp.). These microscopic worms live in the soil and are common in sandy soils and warm climates. Root-knot nematodes are most active when temperatures are warm.

WHAT TO DO:
• Solarize the soil. Clear plastic sheeting placed over bare soil for three to four weeks kills pests and weed seeds. After removing the plastic, plant crops as usual.
• Rotate crops. Avoid growing carrots in the same spot each year.

 ## Other Problems

PROBLEM: You notice that some carrots develop long cracks in their sides just as they begin to reach mature size.

CAUSE: Fluctuating soil moisture. Carrot roots can crack when they plump up during a period of rainy weather that follows a dry spell.

WHAT TO DO:
• Water carrots regularly during dry spells.
• Mulch.
• Grow fast-maturing varieties, such as the 'Nantes' types.
• Dig carrots as they ripen.

Cauliflower

(Brassica oleracea, Botrytis group)

 Cauliflower Pests

PROBLEM: Cauliflower roots have holes and tunnels in them. Tunnels are lined with slime and maggots.

CAUSE: Cabbage maggots (*Delia radicum*). These maggots are less than ½ inch long. They are the larvae of ¼-inch-long, gray flies that look like houseflies. The flies lay their eggs around the base of cauliflower plants.

WHAT TO DO:
• Weed regularly.
• Cultivate the soil shallowly to expose maggots to predators, such as birds.
• Apply beneficial nematodes (*Steinernema carpocapsae* and *Heterorhabditis heliothidis*), which you can purchase from mail-order suppliers. Live nematodes are shipped suspended in gels or sponges. Follow label instructions for application.
• Apply diatomaceous earth (DE) to the soil. This abrasive dust is made of fossilized shells called diatoms that penetrate pests' skin as they crawl over DE.

PROBLEM: Velvety green caterpillars are eating your cauliflower leaves and are leaving behind green excrement.

CAUSE: Imported cabbageworms (*Artogeia rapae*). These caterpillars are the larvae of cabbage white butterflies. The butterflies have black-tipped and spotted white wings and wingspans of 1½ inches. The largest of the caterpillars have faint yellow stripes along their sides. The adults are among the first butterflies to lay eggs on cauliflowers in the spring. The yellowish eggs hatch into tiny, yellowish caterpillars that turn green as they begin to feed. As late-season days become shorter, the cabbageworms become less numerous.

WHAT TO DO:
• Handpick.
• Attract beneficial insects with small-flowered nectar plants, such as dill and Queen-Anne's-lace.
• Companion plant cauliflower with radishes.
• Apply BTK. *Bacillus thuringiensis* var. *kurstaki* (BTK) is a stomach poison that kills imported cabbageworms. Follow label directions to spray a solution of BTK on plants when eggs begin to hatch or where young pests are feeding.

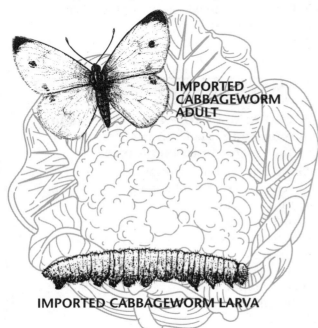

IMPORTED CABBAGEWORM ADULT

IMPORTED CABBAGEWORM LARVA

Cauliflower Diseases

PROBLEM: Dark-colored, sunken spots are on the base of the main stem. The leaves begin to wilt.

CAUSE: Black leg (*Phoma lingam*). This fungal disease gradually girdles the main stem of plants. In time it can be fatal. Looking for black specks within the larger leaf spots is the best way to positively diagnose this disease. You may also see large, brown, angular spots between the veins of leaves. This fungus can persist in soil for two to three years.

WHAT TO DO:
• Pick and destroy infected plants.
• Remove and compost plant debris.
• Plant healthy seeds.
• Space plants widely for good air circulation.

PROBLEM: As cauliflower heads form, they show grayish black patches in the small spaces between florets.

CAUSE: Downy mildew (*Peronospora destructor*). Cool, damp weather encourages this common fungal disease. It is unsightly but seldom life-threatening.

WHAT TO DO:
• Harvest cauliflower heads as they mature. When harvesting, discard damaged sections of the heads.
• Plant cauliflower in sunny, fertile soil with a near-neutral acidity, or pH (6.0 to 6.8).
• Mulch to keep the roots cool and moist.

 Other Problems

PROBLEM: Cauliflower heads begin to turn from white to green as they mature, but they look fine otherwise.

CAUSE: Too much sunlight. Overexposure causes the white heads of cauliflower to develop chlorophyll and turn green.

WHAT TO DO:
• Grow cauliflower in spring and fall, when the weather is cool.
• Blanch heads. Either bend a few large leaves down over the heads until they break or use clothespins to pin the leaves together.
• Harvest heads as they ripen. In cool weather, blanched heads will stay in good condition on the plants for several days, but in warm weather you should cut them from the plants promptly.

PROBLEM: Cauliflower heads are very small and have a grainy texture. Instead of being white, heads are tan.

CAUSE: Temperature extremes or over-ripening. Exposure to very cold or very warm weather causes cauliflower heads to be small and poorly textured. Brownish, discolored heads are usually overripe.

WHAT TO DO:
• Use a cloche, which is a dome of plastic, glass, or fabric. When placed over tender plants, it shields them from the elements.
• Grow early-maturing varieties, such as 'Snow Crown' and 'Cashmere'.
• Time planting to avoid extremely hot or cold temperatures.
• Harvest as the heads mature.

OCCASIONAL PROBLEMS: If you see problems you cannot identify, refer to the following: Cabbage looper (*Trichoplusia ni*), listed under "Broccoli" on page 10. Fall armyworms (*Spodoptera frugiperda*), listed under "Brussels Sprouts" on page 12. Harlequin bugs (*Murgantia histrionica*), listed under "Cabbage" on page 14. Whiteflies (Family Aleyrodidae), listed under "Brussels Sprouts." Black rot (*Xanthomonas campestris*), listed under "Cabbage." Damping-off (caused by several fungi), listed under "Broccoli."

Celery

(Apium graveolens var. *dulce)*

Celery Pests

PROBLEM: Celery stops growing. The leaves look pale and droop. The roots are riddled with rust red tunnels.

CAUSE: Carrot rust fly larvae (*Psila rosae*). These pests are maggots less than ⅓ inch long. They feed on celery roots for three to four weeks before pupating into metallic, greenish black flies about ¼ inch long.

WHAT TO DO:
• Use floating row covers to exclude rust flies. Cover the plants with these synthetic, spun-bonded fabrics, and bury the edges of the row cover in the soil.
• Time planting so that celery matures before maggots hatch.

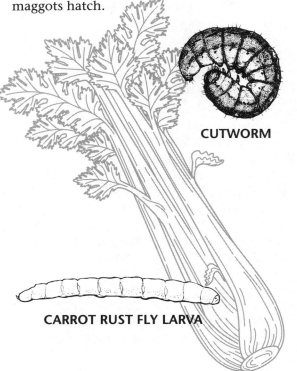

CUTWORM

CARROT RUST FLY LARVA

PROBLEM: Seedlings disappear overnight. You find some lying on the ground, severed at the roots.

CAUSE: Cutworms (Family Noctuidae). The larvae of several species of night-flying moths, cutworms are gray or dull brown caterpillars, 1 to 2 inches long. Cutworms are active only at night. Young plants are easy victims, and since celery seedlings remain small for several weeks, they are vulnerable to cutworms.

WHAT TO DO:
• Handpick.
• Apply beneficial nematodes (*Steinernema carpocapsae* and *Heterorhabditis heliothidis*), which you can purchase from mail-order suppliers. Live nematodes are shipped suspended in gels or sponges. Follow label instructions for application, and release nematodes when pest larvae are present.
• Use cutworm collars to prevent cutworms and other crawling pests from reaching your seedlings. To make these collars, use shears to cut 2- to 3-inch-long sections from paper-towel tubes or tin cans. Then place the tubes over small seedlings as soon as they sprout.

Celery Diseases

PROBLEM: Plants grow normally for a while, then get discolored patches that slowly rot. Stalks taste bitter.

CAUSE: Soft rot (*Erwinia carotovora* var. *carotovora*). Soilborne bacteria cause soft rot in celery. As the disease progresses, leaves turn yellow or light green. Leaves wilt on warm days, and the stalks develop a bitter flavor.

WHAT TO DO:
• Pull diseased plants and compost them separately.
• Compost garden debris.
• Plant healthy seeds.
• Rotate plantings. Alternating other plants with celery annually protects the soil from pests and diseases. For optimum results, move crops in three-year rotations.
• Space plants far enough apart for good air circulation.

 Other Problems

PROBLEM: Tips of young leaves in the centers of plants appear bruised and wet. They turn brown and rot.

CAUSE: Black heart. Black heart is the common name for a nutritional disorder. It combines a soil-calcium deficiency with high levels of soil potassium, leading to these symptoms in celery plants. Dry weather increases the symptoms.

WHAT TO DO:
• Test the soil and enrich it by incorporating compost and any missing minerals prior to planting.

PROBLEM: Plants have plenty of crisp stalks, but they are much more slender than stalks offered by grocery stores.

CAUSE: Unrestricted access to light. Garden-grown celery exposed to full sun looks different than commercially grown celery, but there is nothing wrong with it. The stalks of garden-grown celery are a darker shade of green and have a concentrated, intense celery flavor. To produce the kind of celery stalks sold in stores, commercial growers hill the soil up around the celery plants as they grow to deprive the stalks of light in order to make them a light green color.

WHAT TO DO:
• Accept your celery as it grows.
• Mulch plants. A deep mulch of straw tucked around the celery stalks will lighten their color.

PROBLEM: Despite good growing conditions, the celery in your garden just doesn't seem to thrive.

CAUSE: Lack of chilling. Celery requires a longer period of cool weather than most cool-season crops. With a good head start, it makes a fine vegetable for the spring or fall garden. You can buy seedlings or grow your own, but either way it's important to let celery enjoy every day of cool weather your climate has to offer.

WHAT TO DO:
• Mulch celery plants in order to keep their roots constantly cool and moist.
• Harvest outer stalks, one at a time. Taking a few stalks at a time will prolong the harvest.
• Plant in full sun.
• Grow celery in rich soil that holds moisture well.
• Rotate crops. Alternating plants annually protects the soil from pests and diseases. Always rotate celery with vegetables other than carrots.

OCCASIONAL PROBLEMS: Several of the pests and diseases that infect carrots can also become a problem for celery because both vegetables are members of the same plant family (Family Apiaceae). The problems listed above are the most common ones for garden-grown celery. If you see celery problems that you cannot identify, refer to the following pests and diseases listed elsewhere in this book: Parsleyworms (*Papilio polyxenes*), listed under "Carrot" on page 20. Root-knot nematodes (*Meloidogyne* spp.), listed under "Carrot."

Corn

(Zea mays)

 Corn Pests

PROBLEM: Large sections of your corn patch show no seed germination. Seeds or seedlings lie on the soil's surface.

CAUSES: Birds and mice. These pests find tender sprouting corn seeds and seedlings delicious. Seed-eating birds raid the corn patch during the day, while mice conduct their thievery at night.

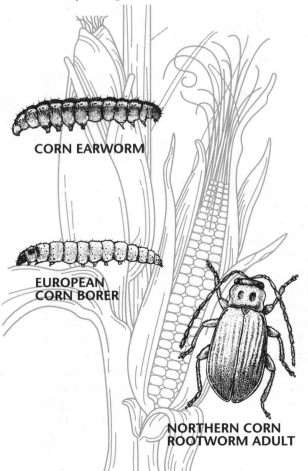

CORN EARWORM

EUROPEAN CORN BORER

NORTHERN CORN ROOTWORM ADULT

WHAT TO DO:
• Noisy, moving bird-scare devices are sometimes effective.
• Cover seeded patches of ground with chicken wire until the plants are up and growing well.

PROBLEM: Two weeks after germination, something fells seedlings. You find them where they fall or elsewhere.

CAUSE: Cutworms (Family Noctuidae). These pests are the larvae of several species of night-flying moths with wingspans of 1½ inches. The larvae are gray or dull brown caterpillars 1 to 2 inches long. They feed on plants at night and hide in the soil during the day. The damage stops as quickly as it started, and symptoms disappear altogether by the time the plants are two weeks old.

WHAT TO DO:
• Handpick.
• Apply beneficial nematodes. You can purchase beneficial nematodes (*Steinernema carpocapsae* and *Heterorhabditis heliothidis*) from mail-order suppliers. Live nematodes are shipped suspended in gels or sponges. Follow label instructions for application, and release nematodes when pest larvae are present.
• Seed thickly to compensate for early losses. Thin the remaining seedlings as necessary after cutworms are no longer a problem.

PROBLEM: Small holes appear in the stalks of young corn plants, and slimy material is piled outside the holes.

CAUSE: European corn borers (*Ostrinia nubilalis*). These pests are the larvae of pale beige, night-flying moths with 1-inch wingspans. The females have zigzag wing patterns, and the males have darker gray wings. These moths lay masses of overlapping white or tan eggs on the backs of leaves of young corn plants in early summer. The 1-inch-long larvae are gray or beige, segmented caterpillars with brown dots on each segment. The larvae feed on corn for three or four weeks. The pests overwinter in dead cornstalks left in the field.

WHAT TO DO:
• Handpick.
• Knock caterpillars off plants with a strong stream of water.
• Time plantings to avoid hatching caterpillars.
• Remove plant debris.
• Apply BTK. "BT" stands for *Bacillus thuringiensis*, an insect-stomach poison that kills caterpillars without harming beneficial insects. *B.t.* var. *kurstaki* (BTK) kills corn borers.

PROBLEM: Corn plants and ears appear healthy, but brown or green caterpillars with striped backs are on ear tips.

CAUSE: Corn earworms (*Helicoverpa zea*). These caterpillars are the larvae of grayish brown moths. One of the frustrating aspects of these pests is that the adult moths lay over a thousand eggs, one at a time, on corn silks just as the ears are forming. You will find the ½- to 2-inch-long caterpillars have eaten up the corn silk right around the tips of the ears, and may also eat some kernels.

WHAT TO DO:
• Apply vegetable oil to ear tips.
• Spray BTK, or sprinkle BTK granules into ear tips. *Bacillus thuringiensis* var. *kurstaki* (BTK) is a stomach poison that kills corn earworms.

PROBLEM: Corn germinates and grows normally until the plants are about a foot tall or have tassels, then stops.

CAUSES: Corn rootworms (*Diabrotica* spp.). These pests are the larvae of two species of small beetle. If you examine the roots and the lowest section of the stem, you may find that either structure has holes bored through it by caterpillars. They hollow out large roots and eat small ones.

In northern areas the adult beetles (*Diabrotica longicornis*) are ¼ inch long and yellow-green and are seldom seen except in fall, after the ½-inch-long, wrinkled, white larvae pupate into adults. In warmer climates, spotted cucumber beetles (*Diabrotica undecimpunctata* var. *howardi*), which are yellow and black beetles, are the culprit. The corn-eating larvae, called southern corn rootworms, are white, ¾-inch-long, segmented caterpillars with brown patches on the first and last segments.

WHAT TO DO:
• Apply beneficial nematodes (*Steinernema carpocapsae* and *Heterorhabditis heliothidis*), which you can purchase from mail-order suppliers. Live nematodes are shipped suspended in gels or sponges. Follow label instructions for application, and release nematodes when pest larvae are present.
• Rotate crops. Avoid growing a crop of corn in the same spot each year. Three-year rotations are best.

PROBLEM: Corn grows until it is a few inches tall, then growth stops and leaves turn yellow or reddish.

CAUSES: Ants (Family Formicidae) and aphids (Family Aphididae). Aphids are soft-bodied, pear-shaped insects that are ¹⁄₁₆ to ⅜ inch long. They damage leaves and stems by sucking plant juices. Ants take care of aphids by protecting aphid eggs through winter and by carrying young aphids to corn plants so they can feed. In return, the ants consume the sticky, sweet "honeydew" produced by aphids.

WHAT TO DO:
- Rotate plants. Avoid growing corn in the same spot each year.
- Pour boiling water into entry holes of ant-hills that are not adjacent to plant roots.

 Corn Diseases

PROBLEM: The leaves of young plants have yellow streaks that turn brown. Stems darken at their bases.

CAUSE: Stewart's bacterial wilt (*Erwinia stewartii*). Flea beetles spread this bacterial disease to corn. The disease is potentially deadly for young plants; in order for the plants to become infected, disease-carrying flea beetles must survive winter. This disease is therefore more prevalent following warm winters.

WHAT TO DO:
- Plant resistant varieties, such as 'Ambrosia', 'Sensor', 'Silver Queen', and 'Tuxedo'.

PROBLEM: Gray-green spots, usually ½ inch wide and from 1 to 6 inches long, appear on corn leaves and run together.

CAUSE: Northern corn leaf blight (*Helminthosporium turcicum*). This fungal disease spreads from one corn plant to another when leaves remain damp for long periods of time. The fungus thrives at temperatures between 65°F and 77°F and is most often seen in the North. Northern corn leaf blight weakens plants, but they can still produce a good crop.

WHAT TO DO:
- Plant tolerant varieties, such as 'Crisp 'n Sweet', 'Pegasus', and 'Sensor'.
- Turn under or compost crop residue.

PROBLEM: Tan spots about ¼ inch wide and less than ¾ inch long, with reddish brown borders, appear on corn leaves.

CAUSE: Southern corn leaf blight (*Helminthosporium maydis*). This fungal disease is similar to the northern corn leaf blight described above. Southern corn leaf blight also requires damp weather to spread, but it thrives in temperatures between 68° and 90°F.

WHAT TO DO:
- Plant resistant varieties, such as 'Maxim' and 'Silver Queen'.
- Turn under or compost crop residue.

PROBLEM: You notice gray galls popping out of ears of corn and sometimes out of corn stems and tassels as well.

CAUSE: Corn smut (*Ustilago maydis*). This fungal disease can live in the soil from year to year and is prevalent when summers are hot and dry. Holes made in plants by insects, hail, and windblown sand are entry points for the disease that ruins the ears of corn.

WHAT TO DO:
- Collect and destroy infected ears.

PROBLEM: Small yellowish spots with cinnamon brown centers appear on both sides of corn leaves.

CAUSE: Rust (*Puccinia* spp.). This fungal disease can spread rapidly in rainy weather or when heavy dews keep plants wet. Ears from infected plants are edible.

WHAT TO DO:
- Remove plants from the garden after harvesting ears.
- Compost crop residue.
- Plant resistant varieties, such as 'Delectable', 'Lancelot', and 'Seneca Horizon'.

PROBLEM: Plants grow normally at first, and then new leaves begin appearing close together at the tops.

CAUSE: Maize dwarf mosaic virus. The sap-sucking insects called aphids transmit this viral disease to corn plants. The background color of affected leaves is a shade lighter than normal, and leaves are streaked with dark green. Instead of producing two or three leafy tufts that might develop into ears, infected plants produce a half-dozen of the leafy tufts.

WHAT TO DO:
• Plant corn early, because the virus is most prevalent from midsummer to the end of the season.
• Plant resistant varieties, such as 'Crisp 'n Sweet', 'Snow White', 'Spring Rush', and 'Sundance'.

PROBLEM: Healthy corn suddenly produces yellow leaves with reddish edges. The older leaves remain green.

CAUSE: Maize chlorotic dwarf virus. Feeding leafhoppers transmit this viral disease to corn. Tassels on the diseased plants may develop, but good ears never appear.

WHAT TO DO:
• Plant corn early because the virus is most prevalent from midsummer to the end of the season.
• Plant resistant varieties, such as 'Sundance', 'Snow White','Spring Rush', and 'Crisp 'n Sweet'.

 ## Other Problems

PROBLEM: Despite good conditions, the germination of your corn plants is less than half of the seeds planted.

CAUSE: Seeds rotted. Dig into the soil with your fingers to unearth ungerminated seeds. If they look gray or black, they are rotting.

WHAT TO DO:
• Sow seed when soil is warm.
• Soak seeds in clean water for a day before planting them.

PROBLEM: Healthy corn plants blow over in a strong storm. They continue to grow, but stalks become crooked.

CAUSE: Lodging. This term indicates the worrisome posture, but as long as pollen gets to the corn silks, lodged plants can be productive.

WHAT TO DO:
• Hand-pollinate to assure productivity of lodged corn plants.

PROBLEM: Ears fill partially with kernels; some areas contain no kernels. Kernels may have several rows missing.

CAUSE: Poor pollination. This is a common problem in small plantings of sweet corn.

WHAT TO DO:
• Hand-pollinate.
• Grow corn in a block, rather than in a row, to increase chances of pollination by wind.

PROBLEM: You notice that the leaves of your corn plants are narrow and pale green, and the plants grow slowly.

CAUSE: Nitrogen deficiency. Most sweet corn requires very high levels of nitrogen in the soil.

WHAT TO DO:
• Topdress with manure, and drench the soil with fish emulsion solution.

PROBLEM: Young corn plants show purplish color on leaf edges. The plants grow slowly and wilt during the day.

CAUSE: Phosphorus deficiency in the soil. Some varieties show purple in leaves naturally, so this symptom is not always a sign of trouble. Have your soil tested to be sure.

WHAT TO DO:
• Work compost into the soil.
• Sow seed when soil warms up, because the condition worsens in cool soil.

Cucumber

(Cucumis sativus)

 Cucumber Pests

PROBLEM: When seedlings break through the ground, some become severed from their roots at the soil.

CAUSE: Cutworms (Family Noctuidae). These pests are the larvae of several species of night-flying moths with wingspans of 1½ inches. The larvae are gray or dull brown, 1- to 2-inch-long caterpillars that are active only at night. Frequently a single cutworm will kill a seedling or two for several days.

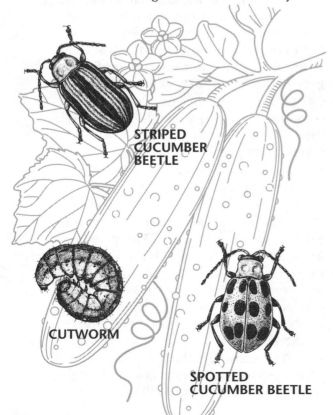

STRIPED CUCUMBER BEETLE

CUTWORM

SPOTTED CUCUMBER BEETLE

The seedlings are usually lying on the soil's surface, but they may disappear altogether.

WHAT TO DO:

• Sow extra seeds. Cutworm damage is usually spotty with cucumbers. Simply sowing extra seeds and letting the cutworms help you thin them to proper spacing is an easy form of insurance.

• Handpick.

• Apply beneficial nematodes (*Steinernema carpocapsae* and *Heterorhabditis heliothidis*), which you can purchase from mail-order suppliers. Live nematodes are shipped suspended in gels or sponges. Follow label instructions for application, and release nematodes when pest larvae are present.

• Use cutworm collars to prevent cutworms and other crawling pests from reaching your seedlings. To make these collars, use shears to cut 2- to 3-inch-long sections from paper-towel tubes or tin cans. Place these short tubes over small seedlings as soon as they sprout.

PROBLEM: Seedlings show slight wilting and puckering of seedling leaves. The plants are slow to develop true leaves.

CAUSE: Squash bugs (*Anasa tristis*). These ⅝-inch-long, brownish bugs have orange-speckled, flat backs shaped like shields. They lay shiny eggs on the backs of leaves that start out yellow and turn to red before hatching into gray, powdery-looking nymphs. Both adults and nymphs suck plant juices from cucumber seedlings, either by attacking the stem or by feeding on the backs of the seedling leaves.

WHAT TO DO:
- Use floating row covers to exclude insect pests. Cover the plants with these synthetic, spunbonded fabrics, and bury the edges of the row cover in the soil.
- Handpick.

PROBLEM: Small ragged holes are in cucumber leaves; unless plants are seedlings, you do not see much damage.

CAUSE: Striped cucumber beetles (*Acalymma vittatum*). These pests damage cucumbers by chewing on leaves, stems, and roots. As they penetrate plant tissues, the beetles can transmit viral diseases and bacterial wilt (*Erwinia tracheiphila*). You may see the ¼- to ⅓-inch-long yellow or greenish yellow beetles with black stripes down their backs on your cucumber plants. Early in the morning, you will almost certainly find these beetles hiding in cucumber blossoms. If you place small boards on the ground around your cucumbers, you will likely find them hiding under the boards early in the day. As cucumber fruits develop, these little beetles may eat away little patches of the skin, but they don't make holes in the fruits.

WHAT TO DO:
- Handpick.
- Use floating row covers to exclude cucumber beetles, exclude animal pests, and protect against temperature fluctuations. Cover the plants with these synthetic, spunbonded fabrics, and bury the edges of the row cover in the soil.

PROBLEM: Small, ragged-chewed spots are in cucumber leaves. You see yellow beetles with black spots on their backs.

CAUSE: Spotted cucumber beetles (*Diabrotica undecimpunctata* var. *howardi*). Like striped cucumber beetles, spotted cucumber beetles chew on leaves, stems, and roots and can transmit bacterial wilt (*Pseudomonas solanacearum*) and plant viruses as they feed. In addition to being spotted, they are slightly larger than striped cucumber beetles.

WHAT TO DO:
- Handpick.
- Use floating row covers to exclude feeding insects, such as spotted cucumber beetles. Cover the plants with these synthetic, spunbonded fabrics, and bury the edges of the row cover in the soil.
- Plant nonbitter varieties, which are less appealing to spotted cucumber beetles than the bitter varieties.

PROBLEM: During warm summer weather, adjoining leaves wilt on sunny days. The wilting worsens.

CAUSE: Squash vine borers (*Melittia cucurbitae*). These caterpillars are the larvae of slender moths with wingspans of 1 to 1½ inches. The moths look almost like wasps, with olive brown front wings, clear hind wings, and a black-ringed red abdomen. Their eggs hatch into white caterpillars called borers that are from ½ to 1 inch long and have dark heads. The larvae overwinter in the soil.

WHAT TO DO:
- Time plantings early enough so that cucumbers can mature and be strong enough to survive attacks.
- Use floating row covers to exclude feeding insects. Cover the plants with these synthetic, spunbonded fabrics, and bury the edges of the row cover in the soil.

 Cucumber Diseases

PROBLEM: Angular gray or tan spots appear between the leaf veins, and the centers dry out and turn into holes.

CAUSE: Angular leaf spot (*Pseudomonas syringae* pv. *lachrymans*). This bacterial disease travels on seeds and persists from year to year in plant debris. When there are a lot of these spots on cucumber leaves, there also may be a disturbing symptom on the fruits—small, sunken spots that quickly cause the entire fruit to rot.

WHAT TO DO:
• Destroy diseased plants.
• Remove plant debris.
• Plant healthy seeds.
• Plant disease-resistant varieties of cucumbers, such as 'Fanfare', 'Little Leaf', 'Superset', and 'Sweet Slice'.

PROBLEM: Cucumber leaves are grayish and show ringlike brown spots that increase in size and number over time.

CAUSE: Alternaria blight (*Alternaria cucumerina*). This fungal disease travels on infected seeds and lives from year to year in dead cucumber tissue.

WHAT TO DO:
• Pick and destroy infected leaves and plants.
• Compost plant debris.
• Space plants widely to encourage air circulation.
• Plant healthy seeds.

PROBLEM: Pale, yellowish leaf spots rapidly enlarge and turn dark brown. When the interiors dry, they shatter.

CAUSE: Anthracnose (*Colletotrichum lagenarium*). This fungal disease thrives in cool, rainy weather, and the spores spread from plant to plant in blowing wind or rain. Anthracnose carries over from season to season in the soil or on seeds. If you discover that these leaf spots are present, examine the stems to see if there are dark spots there as well. Finally, look for dark-colored, sunken spots on the cucumbers. In the center of these soft, depressed places on the fruits, you may see a pale pink liquid leaking from the fruits. The flavor of affected cucumbers will be bland or bitter.

WHAT TO DO:
• Space plants widely for good air circulation.
• Compost plant debris.
• Plant healthy seeds.
• Plant resistant varieties such as 'Fanfare', 'Orient Express', and 'Sweet Slice'.

PROBLEM: Plants appear healthy until part of a vine suddenly wilts. Wilting worsens, and the whole plant soon dies.

CAUSE: Bacterial wilt (*Erwinia tracheiphila*). This bacterial disease spreads from plant to plant by feeding cucumber beetles. When a cucumber plant is infected, the disease spreads rapidly no matter what you do. The wilted sections of vine may perk up, but within a few days, more wilting develops. As the wilting worsens, the plant's recovery declines. Within four to eight days, the whole plant wilts and eventually dies.

WHAT TO DO:
• Use floating row covers to exclude insects. Cover the plants with these synthetic, spun-bonded fabrics, and bury the edges of the row cover in the soil.

PROBLEM: The upper sides of cucumber leaves show brown spots. The backs of leaves have patches of mold.

CAUSE: Downy mildew (*Peronospora cubensis*). Cool, damp conditions encourage this common fungal disease. It is unsightly but rarely life-threatening.

WHAT TO DO:
• Control weeds.
• Drench the soil with fermented compost tea to introduce disease-fighting organisms.

PROBLEM: Leaves appear dusted with a white powder that resists being rubbed off with your finger.

CAUSES: Powdery mildew (*Erysiphe cichoracearum; Sphaerotheca puliginea*). This is a disfiguring fungal disease that attacks leaf tissues, but not the fruits, of cucumber plants. Powdery mildew is rarely fatal.

WHAT TO DO:
• Plant resistant varieties. Modern hybrids and improved open-pollinated varieties are all resistant.
•Space plants widely for adequate air circulation.

PROBLEM: Leaves are brittle, thick, and mottled with yellow and dark green. The plants seem to be dying.

CAUSE: Cucumber mosaic virus. Feeding insects spread this common plant virus. The same dappled color pattern that the leaves take on also appears on the cucumber fruits, which also become misshapen. Some cucumber plants can become infected while others show no symptoms.

WHAT TO DO:
• Pull out diseased plants.
• Cover plants with floating row covers to exclude insect pests, and bury the edges of the row cover in the soil.
• Plant disease-resistant varieties of cucumbers, such as 'Comet', 'Fanfare', 'Jazzer', and 'Sweet Slice'.

 Other Problems

PROBLEM: The blossom ends of fruits are small and shriveled. The stem ends appear normal. Fruits are misshapen.

CAUSE: Inadequate pollination. This problem develops when insufficient pollen is available for female flowers.

WHAT TO DO:
• Hand-pollinate.
• Plant self-pollinating varieties, such as 'Jazzer' and 'Sweet Slice'.
• Grow more cucumber plants.

PROBLEM: Your cucumber plants look healthy and the fruits look and taste fine, but the fruits are misshapen.

CAUSE: Contact with solid surfaces. When cucumbers rest on the ground or against a fence, their weight can cause them to develop odd shapes. The exceptions are long-fruited oriental and Armenian cucumbers, which always curl.

WHAT TO DO:
• Grow varieties that produce short cucumbers that do not reach the soil.
• Grow cucumbers on a trellis.

PROBLEM: Your cucumber plants look healthy, and the fruits look normal, but they taste bitter.

CAUSE: Moisture stress. Insufficient soil moisture while fruits are developing leads to bitter-tasting cucumbers. There could also be other reasons. Serious stress induced by pests or diseases can cause cucumbers to lose flavor. Nutrient deficiencies in the soil can lead to bitter-tasting fruits; but if you provide cucumbers with modest amounts of compost, this should not be a problem.

WHAT TO DO:
• Enrich the soil with compost before planting.
• Plant nonbitter-tasting varieties of cucumbers, such as 'Jazzer' and 'Sweet Success', which cucumber beetles find less attractive than bitter types.
• Handpick.
• Keep the soil evenly moist while plants are growing.

Eggplant

(Solanum melongena var. esculentum)

 Eggplant Pests

PROBLEM: In early summer, slender, dark beetles about 1 inch long swarm over eggplants and eat the leaves.

CAUSE: Blister beetles (Family Meloidae). They are called blister beetles because their bodies contain an oil that can cause blisters if you touch them with your bare skin. The beetles have long abdomens with striped edges along their wing covers and have a lighter-colored head that can swivel around. The adults lay their eggs in midsummer underground in grasshopper egg burrows. The main diet for blister beetle larvae is grasshopper eggs. Adult blister beetles feed on plants for less than six weeks.

WHAT TO DO:
• Tolerate light damage.
• Handpick with gloved hands.
• Collect beetles with a hand-held vacuum.
• Use floating row covers to exclude beetles. Cover the plants with these synthetic, spunbonded fabrics, and bury the edges of the row cover in the soil.

PROBLEM: Eggplant leaves show many little holes. Some don't penetrate the leaf and just look like tan pinpricks.

CAUSES: Flea beetles (Family Chrysomelidae). When you approach the plants quietly, you may see the 1/10-inch-long bronze, brown, or black beetles on either side of the leaves. The beetles on the leaves will quickly jump away when you approach them. These common eggplant pests are especially active in late spring and early summer. Their feeding seldom kills plants, but the holes may become entry points for diseases. Flea beetles become more manageable after midsummer because the population ordinarily decreases as the season progresses.

WHAT TO DO:
• Use floating row covers to exclude feeding insects, such as flea beetles. Cover the plants with these synthetic, spunbonded fabrics, and bury the edges of the row cover in the soil. Protect eggplants this way during early summer.

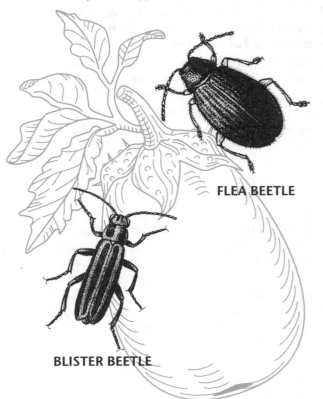

FLEA BEETLE

BLISTER BEETLE

Eggplant Diseases

PROBLEM: Numerous dark brown to black spots appear on older leaves. The affected leaves shrivel and bend over.

CAUSE: Early blight *(Alternaria solani)*. This fungal disease spreads in wind and raindrops.

WHAT TO DO:
• Rotate crops. Avoid growing eggplants in the same spot each year.
• Space plants widely to encourage air circulation.
• Plant eggplants in raised beds.

PROBLEM: During warm summers, eggplant leaves and stems develop brown-edged, tan spots.

CAUSE: Phomopsis blight *(Phomopsis vexans)*. This fungal disease travels on seeds and lives in dead plant material left in the soil. It ordinarily only develops in cool climates on infected seedlings. As the disease progresses, older leaves that have many spots turn entirely yellow and die. When these spots develop on the stems of young plants, the plants may die quickly. If infected plants can develop fruits, the fruits will develop large, circular sunken spots. Then they will begin to rot.

WHAT TO DO:
• Pull up and destroy infected plants.
• Plant resistant varieties, such as 'Florida Market'.

PROBLEM: Seedlings show little evidence of new growth. They die after a few weeks in the garden.

CAUSE: Verticillium wilt *(Verticillium albo-atrum)*. This a soilborne fungal disease. In addition to getting a slow start in life, diseased plants may have other unusual characteristics. Young plants may grow normally for a while. Then their growth slows down, and new leaves are noticeably smaller. The older leaves slowly shrivel, turn from yellow to brown, and drop. Verticillium wilt is most common in the country's midsection, and it can build up to damaging levels in most parts of the country, but it rarely occurs in very hot climates.

WHAT TO DO:
• Pull up and dispose of infected plants.
• Space plants widely to allow for adequate air circulation.
• Grow plants in containers filled with sterilized soil.

 ## Other Problems

PROBLEM: The fruits of your eggplants are bitter tasting. They have an overabundance of seeds.

CAUSES: Overripe fruits. Green-skinned eggplants usually become bitter if you pick them after they are no longer young and tender. Except for green eggplants, light skin color is associated with mild, sweet flavor.

Poor growing conditions. Bitter flavor also develops in unseasonably cool temperatures.

WHAT TO DO:
• Harvest young eggplant fruits. If the seeds are fully formed, the eggplant is too mature for optimum flavor.
• Time plantings so that eggplants grow during the warmer months of the season.

OCCASIONAL PROBLEMS: The problems listed above are the most common ones for garden-grown eggplant, but you might also refer to the following pests and diseases: Potato leafhoppers *(Empoasca fabae)*, listed under "Potato" on page 60. Southern blight *(Sclerotium rolfsii)*, listed under "Pepper" on page 56. Bacterial wilt *(Pseudomonas solanacearum)*, listed under "Tomato" on page 78.

Garlic

(Allium sativum)

Garlic Pests

PROBLEM: Plants grow slowly. Outer leaves may be wilted, shriveled, and brown. New leaves are small and weak.

CAUSE: Onion maggots (*Delia antiqua*). These maggots are the larvae of ¼-inch-long, pale gray onion maggot flies. The flies emerge in spring and lay eggs around the base of garlic plants and other members of the onion family. The eggs hatch into root-eating maggots. If you pull up an affected plant, you may find these ⅓-inch-long, white worms feeding on the roots. If they are absent from the roots, look for them in the soil near the plant, and also look for them on the clove you planted (called a mother clove).

Another way to detect these pests is to submerge the garlic root and surrounding soil in water. Any pests hiding in the soil will float. These maggots can also hollow out garlic bulbs, killing mature garlic plants. They can even ruin cloves in storage. The maggots are most active in the garden during cool, wet weather.

WHAT TO DO:

• Use floating row covers to exclude onion maggot flies. Cover the plants with these synthetic, spunbonded fabrics, and bury the edges of the row cover in the soil.

• Apply beneficial nematodes (*Steinernema carpocapsae* and *Heterorhabditis heliothidis*), which you can purchase from mail-order suppliers. Live nematodes are shipped suspended in gels or sponges. Follow label instructions for application, and release nematodes when pest larvae are present.

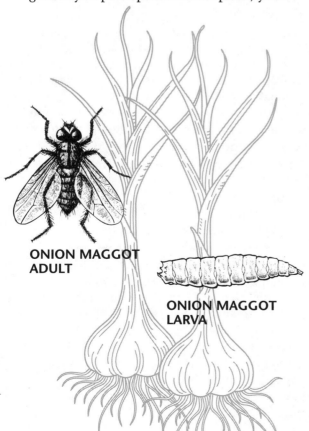

ONION MAGGOT ADULT

ONION MAGGOT LARVA

Garlic Diseases

PROBLEM: A few shoots emerge in spring, then die back. Fallen plants are spotted with blue-green mold.

CAUSE: Blue mold rot (*Penicillium* spp.). This fungal disease invades garlic cloves and causes them to rot in the soil, roots and all, before they can be harvested.

WHAT TO DO:

• Rotate crops. Simply avoid growing garlic

plants in the same spot each year.
• Plant healthy garlic cloves.
• Take care not to bruise or cut cloves when planting.
• Air dry garlic cloves. After you dig the bulbs in fall, let the garlic bulbs air dry for several days before storing them.

PROBLEM: **Tips of leaves turn yellow, and the yellowing gradually spreads downward toward the plants' crowns.**

CAUSE: White rot (*Sclerotium cepivorum*). This fungal disease lives in the soil and can infect all members of the onion family. White rot thrives in cool, damp, and poorly drained soil. Affected plants pull easily from the soil because most of their roots are rotten. The cloves (or bulbs on older plants) may be covered with white, fluffy mold dotted with black specks.

WHAT TO DO:
• Improve soil drainage.
• Rotate crops. Avoid growing a crop in the same spot each year.
• Grow garlic in raised beds.
• Air dry garlic cloves. After you dig the bulbs in fall, let the garlic bulbs air dry for several days before storing them.

 Other Problems

PROBLEM: **Garlic plants begin to flower soon after you plant them, and then they die back without producing bulbs.**

CAUSE: Bolting, which is the process a mature plant goes through when it flowers and sets seed. Garlic often bolts when you plant it in spring instead of in fall. The plants flower naturally in spring as the days grow longer and warmer. If the planted cloves have not had all winter to grow a good root system, they cannot store up food reserves in bulbs before they flower and set seed.

WHAT TO DO:
• Plant garlic cloves in fall (October in the North, November in the South).
• Let fall-planted cloves overwinter in the soil, and plan to harvest them the following season after the plants bloom and the bulbs ripen.

PROBLEM: **In spite of healthy-looking plants, garlic cloves you harvest taste bland or lack a garlicky flavor.**

CAUSE: Sulfur deficiency in the soil. This soil mineral deficiency can cause garlic to lose its characteristic flavor punch. Test your soil to determine for certain whether this deficiency is the problem, and amend the soil as needed to correct it.

WHAT TO DO:
• Enrich soil with plenty of compost before planting garlic cloves.
• Test the soil in planting beds, and add any missing minerals that are detected.

PROBLEM: **Harvested garlic bulbs have too much flavor. They taste very hot and have a flavor that is almost bitter.**

CAUSE: Too little rain or irrigation water in early summer. While the underground bulbs are forming, a drought can keep the garlic cloves from plumping up properly, robbing them of their undertone of juicy sweetness.

WHAT TO DO:
• Water as needed to keep the soil from drying out while your garlic is actively growing.
• Water deeply at least once a week during dry spring weather.
• Mulch. In cold climates, mulch over the row with 3 inches of straw or other organic mulch.
• Pinch off the flowerstalks when they appear in late spring.

Kale

(*Brassica oleracea*, Acephala group)

Kale Pests

PROBLEM: Pale-green caterpillars are eating kale plants. When they move, their bodies rise into a loop.

CAUSE: Cabbage loopers (*Trichoplusia ni*). These are the larvae of gray moths with wing markings that make them look like tree bark. The cabbage looper caterpillars emerge late in spring and are a light shade of green, with white stripes on their sides. When they move, they show the classic inchworm posture, with the middle of their bodies raised up to create a loop.

WHAT TO DO:
• Handpick.
• Apply *Bacillus thuringiensis* var. *kurstaki* (BTK), a stomach poison that kills cabbage loopers. BTK is most effective before pests tunnel into plants. Follow label directions to apply.
• Attract birds, which eat cabbage loopers.

PROBLEM: Velvety-textured caterpillars, the same color as young kale leaves, eat leaves and leave excrement.

CAUSE: Imported cabbageworms (*Artogeia rapae*). These caterpillars are the larvae of cabbage white butterflies. The butterflies have black-tipped and spotted white wings and a wingspan of 1½ inches. The largest of their caterpillar larvae have faint yellow stripes down their sides and grow to 1½ inches long. On the leaf backs, you can see very small yellowish eggs and some immature, small, yellow-green caterpillars. Kale grown in spring may become heavily infested with cabbageworms, but fall-grown plants easily outgrow the damage.

WHAT TO DO:
• Handpick.
• Attract beneficial insects with small-flowered nectar plants, such as dill and Queen-Anne's-lace.
• Companion plant kale with radishes.
• Apply *Bacillus thuringiensis* var. *kurstaki* (BTK), a stomach poison that kills imported cabbageworms.

PROBLEM: Soon after you set out kale seedlings for fall harvest, you discover tiny white insects clinging to the leaves.

CAUSE: Whiteflies (Family Aleyrodidae). You can often see these tiny flies swarming in white clouds when the weather remains

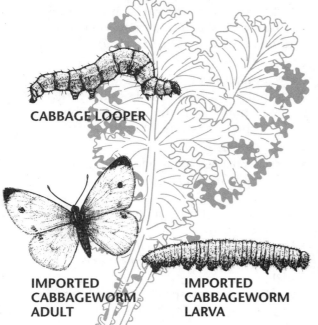

CABBAGE LOOPER

IMPORTED CABBAGEWORM ADULT

IMPORTED CABBAGEWORM LARVA

warm and kale seedlings planted for fall harvest are struggling to grow. Whiteflies suck juices from tender plant leaves and stems, and they leave behind a sticky honeydew that can attract a black sooty mold. The little flies usually disappear after the first frost.

WHAT TO DO:
• Gather adults with a rechargeable vacuum.
• Apply insecticidal soap as directed.
• Cover the plants with floating row covers to exclude feeding insects. Bury the edges of the row covers in the soil.
• Encourage beneficial insects, like lady beetles and tiny wasps, by planting small-flowered nectar plants, including dill and yarrow.

PROBLEM: Brown-and-orange-striped caterpillars, less than 1 inch long, eat kale leaves in late summer or early fall.

CAUSE: Fall armyworms (*Spodoptera frugiperda*). These caterpillars are the night-feeding larvae of gray moths. The moths have a white dot on each wing and have wingspans of 1½ inches. Armyworms can destroy young plants, but if the plants' central growing tips remain intact, they can recover quickly. These pests usually disappear after the first frost.

WHAT TO DO:
• Handpick.
• Apply BTK. "BT" stands for *Bacillus thuringiensis*, an insect-stomach poison that kills caterpillars without harming beneficial insects. *B.t.* var. *kurstaki* (BTK) kills armyworms.

PROBLEM: In early spring, you find crown and growing tips of fall-planted kale covered with tiny green insects.

CAUSE: Cabbage aphids (*Brevicoryne brassicae*). These soft-bodied, pear-shaped insects are ¹⁄₁₆ to ³⁄₈ inch long. Aphids damage leaves and stems by sucking plant juices.

WHAT TO DO:
• Handpick.

• Snap off and destroy infested growing tips.
• Knock aphids from plants with a strong stream of water.

 Kale Diseases

PROBLEM: Seedlings fall over and die when they have fewer than three true leaves. Stems darken at the soil.

CAUSE: Damping-off. Several species of fungi can cause this common disease of kale and other seedlings. Stem injuries are likely sites of infection; but because the fungi live in soil, roots are also vulnerable.

WHAT TO DO:
• Use sterile seed-starting mix and pots.
• Keep seedlings within 2 inches of a plant light if seeds are started indoors.

PROBLEM: Following periods of cool, damp weather, upper surfaces of topmost leaves get brownish gray patches.

CAUSE: Downy mildew (*Peronospora parasitica*). Cool, damp conditions encourage this common, disfiguring fungal disease.

WHAT TO DO:
• Pinch off and dispose of affected leaves.
• Control weeds to improve light penetration and air circulation.
• Drench the soil with fermented compost tea.

 Other Problems

PROBLEM: The leaves of your kale plants look healthy but lack sweetness and have an unpleasantly strong flavor.

CAUSE: Bad weather or old age. Kale leaves develop sugars in response to temperatures below about 40°F and also lose their flavor when they pass the point of ripeness.

WHAT TO DO:
• Timed planting. Either plant kale in early spring, or plant it late in the growing season.

Kohlrabi

(Brassica oleracea, Gongylodes group)

 Kohlrabi Pests

PROBLEM: Pale-green caterpillars are eating your kohlrabi. When they move, their bodies raise up to create a loop.

CAUSE: Cabbage loopers (*Trichoplusia ni*). These are the larvae of gray moths with wing markings that make them look like tree bark. The cabbage looper caterpillars emerge later in spring than imported cabbageworms and are a lighter shade of green, with white stripes on their sides. When they move, they show the classic inchworm posture, with the middle of their bodies raised up to create a loop.

WHAT TO DO:
• Handpick.
• Apply *Bacillus thuringiensis* var. *kurstaki* (BTK), a stomach poison that kills cabbage loopers. BTK is most effective before pests tunnel into plants. Follow label directions to apply.
• Attract birds, which eat cabbage loopers.

PROBLEM: Small, dark caterpillars, usually less than 1 inch long, eat kohlrabi grown in the fall.

CAUSE: Fall armyworms (*Spodoptera frugiperda*). These caterpillars are the night-feeding larvae of gray moths with a white dot on each wing. The adult moths can lay more than 500 eggs a week on lower plant leaves, so where you see a few larvae, there will likely be many more. These caterpillars are much more common some years than in others, and sometimes you can see them in spring.

WHAT TO DO:
• Handpick.
• Apply *Bacillus thuringiensis* (BT), an insect-stomach poison that kills caterpillars without harming beneficial insects. Follow directions and apply when pests are present.

PROBLEM: Velvety-textured, green caterpillars are eating holes in kohlrabi leaves and leaving trails of excrement.

CAUSE: Imported cabbageworms (*Artogeia rapae*). These caterpillars are the larvae of cab-

FALL ARMYWORM

CABBAGE LOOPER

IMPORTED CABBAGEWORM LARVA

bage white butterflies. These common butterflies have black-tipped and spotted white wings and wingspans of 1½ inches. They are among the first butterflies to lay eggs on kohlrabi leaves in spring. Eggs hatch into tiny, yellowish caterpillars that turn green as they begin to feed. Frequently these caterpillars travel along the central leaf veins, where they are difficult to see. Their camouflage is less effective on kohlrabi varieties that have purplish green leaves. The largest caterpillars have faint yellow stripes down their sides and grow to 1½ inches long. On the leaf backs, you can find very small yellowish eggs scattered about singly, and perhaps some very small, slender, newly hatched yellowish caterpillars as well. As late-season days become shorter, cabbageworms become less numerous.

WHAT TO DO:
• Handpick.
• Attract beneficial insects with small-flowered nectar plants, such as dill.
• Companion plant kohlrabi with radishes.
• Apply *Bacillus thuringiensis* var. *kurstaki* (BTK), a stomach poison that kills imported cabbageworms.

 Kohlrabi Diseases

PROBLEM: Young seedlings fall over and die when they have less than three true leaves. Stems darken at the soil.

CAUSE: Damping-off (*Pythium* spp. and *Rhizoctonia solani*). Several different species of soilborne fungi can cause this common disease of kohlrabi and other seedlings. Stem injuries are likely sites of infection, but because the fungi live in soil, roots are also vulnerable. When you pull up the seedling, you find nothing more than a single dark stringy root. In kohlrabi, damping-off is more common with seedlings grown in containers indoors than with those that sprout from di-

rect-sown seeds. If seedlings struggle to get enough light, they will grow long and leggy. These weakened seedlings have tender, easily bruised stems. As seedlings grow older, they develop resistance.

WHAT TO DO:
• Use sterile seed-starting mix. Start seeds in clean containers.
• Provide strong light for seeds started indoors. Place the upper leaves within 2 to 4 inches of fluorescent lights, and lower the plants as they grow to maintain the spacing between leaf tips and light tubes.

 Other Problems

PROBLEM: Plants grow slowly and the bulbs are small. The skin and interior of the bulbs are tough and woody.

CAUSE: Insufficient water. Drought during the plants' growing cycle slows the growth of kohlrabi, making both aboveground plant parts and the bulbs scrawny and fibrous.

WHAT TO DO:
• Mulch.
• Water as needed to keep the soil moist during development. Plants require a constant supply of soil moisture to promote the development of plump, juicy bulbs.

OCCASIONAL PROBLEMS: Several of the pests and diseases that infect kohlrabi also affect vegetables that are members of the same plant family (Family Cruciferae). The problems listed above are the most common ones for garden-grown kohlrabi. If you see problems you cannot identify, refer to the following pests and diseases listed elsewhere in this book: Whiteflies (Family Aleyrodidae), listed under "Brussels Sprouts" on page 12. Fusarium yellows (*Fusarium oxysporum* f. *conglutinans*), listed under "Cabbage" on page 14.

Leek

(Allium ampeloprasum, Porrum group) and Bunching Onions (*A. fistulosum*)

Leek Pests

PROBLEM: Leek leaves have pale streaks and small white blotches. Tips turn dry and shrivel. Plants die back.

CAUSE: Thrips (Order Thysanoptera). These pests are tiny, $\frac{1}{50}$- to $\frac{1}{25}$-inch-long winged insects that are yellowish, brown, or black. When thrips feed in large numbers, they draw so much sap from leek plants that the plants cannot grow and the leaves begin to turn brown and die back.

WHAT TO DO:
• Spray infested plants with insecticidal soap.
• Control weeds to allow light and air to reach leek plants.

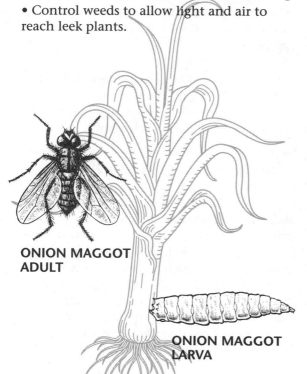

ONION MAGGOT ADULT

ONION MAGGOT LARVA

PROBLEM: The bases of leek and scallion plants, just above the roots, are riddled with small holes.

CAUSE: Onion maggots (*Delia antiqua*). These maggots are the larvae of $\frac{1}{4}$-inch-long, pale gray onion maggot flies. The flies emerge in spring and lay eggs around the base of onion-family members. When the eggs hatch, the larvae enter the plants' roots through the main stem, causing the leaves to turn yellow and wilt as the unseen pests destroy the main stem. Onion maggots are most common where summers are rainy and in commercial onion-growing areas.

WHAT TO DO:
• Use floating row covers to exclude insect pests. Cover the plants with these synthetic, spunbonded fabrics, and bury the edges of the row cover in the soil.
• Apply beneficial nematodes (*Steinernema carpocapsae* and *Heterorhabditis heliothidis*), which you can purchase from mail-order suppliers. Live nematodes are shipped suspended in gels or sponges. Follow instructions for application, and release nematodes when pest larvae are present.

Leek Diseases

PROBLEM: Plants grow slowly, but the leaves remain green. They have only a few stringy, pinkish brown roots.

CAUSE: Pink root (*Pyrenochaeta terrestris*). This fungal disease can live in the soil for many years. Infected plants usually continue to grow, but they never reach full size.

WHAT TO DO:

• Compost plant debris.

• Plant resistant scallion varieties, such as 'Long White Summer Bunching' and 'Tokyo Long White'.

• Rotate crops. Simply avoid growing a crop in the same spot each year to minimize disease.

• Solarize the soil. Clear plastic sheeting placed over bare soil for three to four weeks uses the sun's energy to heat the soil enough to kill most pests and weed seeds in the top few inches of soil. After removing the plastic, plant crops as usual.

PROBLEM: Your leek and scallion plants suddenly wilt and die, and you find that the roots have rotted.

CAUSE: Fusarium basal rot, also called root rot (*Fusarium oxysporum* f. *cepae,* and other forms). One or more fungi cause this disease, which makes the roots of leeks rot. Often the first clue to the disease is that plants appear to stop growing, and the leaves begin to wilt slowly. Root rot also can develop in poorly drained soil or where the pH is too acidic. This disease is rarely caused by a single fungus but rather by several that build up in the soil.

WHAT TO DO:

• Grow leeks and scallions in raised beds.

• Rotate crops.

• Plant resistant scallion varieties, such as 'Long White Summer Bunching'.

 Other Problems

PROBLEM: The weather and growing conditions are good, but your leek and scallion plants rot soon after planting.

CAUSE: Deep planting. Planting leeks and scallions with the base of the green leaves below the soil line can cause them to rot. Only the white shank section of these and other onion relatives can defend itself against soilborne molds.

WHAT TO DO:

• Make sure the green portions of the leaves are above ground.

• Plant them in raised beds or rows if you want to grow leeks and scallions over winter so that they will be easier to harvest and resist rotting.

PROBLEM: Soon after you've blanched leeks to make the shanks light colored, they stop growing and begin to rot.

CAUSE: Premature blanching. Blanching is the process of hilling up soil around the white part (shank) of leeks. This technique is widely used to make the tender white shanks grow unusually long. But burying the shanks of young leeks that are only the thickness of a pencil can induce rot.

WHAT TO DO:

• For blanching to work properly, plant leeks in a shallow trench. Fill the trench around them with 1 inch of soil each week, beginning when the leek shanks are about ½ inch in diameter.

• Wrap shanks loosely with paper before hilling to keep grit out of the leaves and to protect the plants from soilborne diseases that could cause them to rot.

• In warm climates, set leeks out in fall and harvest them in late spring. In northern areas it's best to plant them in spring for fall harvest.

OCCASIONAL PROBLEMS: The problems listed above are the most common ones for leeks and scallions. If you see a problem you cannot identify, refer to the following disease: Smut (*Urocystis* spp.), or other problems listed under "Onion" on page 50.

Lettuce

(*Lactuca sativa*)

 Lettuce Pests

PROBLEM: As leaves emerge in spring, some are cut off at the soil's surface overnight, but some remain healthy.

CAUSE: Cutworms (Family Noctuidae). The larvae of several species of night-flying moths, cutworms are gray or dull brown caterpillars that are 1 to 2 inches long. Cutworms feed at night and hide in soil or mulch during the day. The damage usually lasts for about three weeks.

WHAT TO DO:
• Handpick.
• Use cutworm collars to prevent cutworms and other crawling pests from reaching your seedlings. To make these collars, use shears to cut 2- to 3-inch-long sections from paper-towel tubes or tin cans. Place these over small seedlings as soon as they sprout.

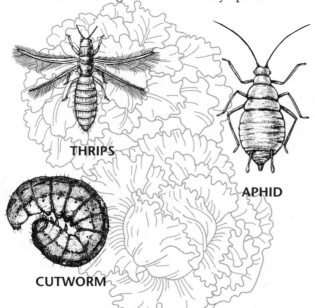

THRIPS

APHID

CUTWORM

• Apply beneficial nematodes (*Steinernema carpocapsae* and *Heterorhabditis heliothidis*), which you can purchase from mail-order suppliers. Live nematodes are shipped suspended in gels or sponges; apply as directed.

PROBLEM: You see many insects, smaller than a pinhead, on lettuce leaves; they may have brown patches.

CAUSES: Aphids (Family Aphididae); thrips (Order Thysanoptera); leafhoppers (Family Cicadellidae). These tiny insects all cause slight damage to lettuce leaves, but they can transmit potentially fatal viral diseases as they feed.

Aphids are 1/16- to 3/8-inch-long, soft-bodied, pear-shaped insects.

Thrips are 1/50- to 1/25-inch-long winged insects that are yellowish, brown, or black.

Leafhoppers are wedge-shaped brown or green insects only 1/10 inch to 1/2 inch long.

WHAT TO DO:
• Knock the insects off lettuce plants with a strong spray of water.
• Apply insecticidal soap.

 Lettuce Diseases

PROBLEM: Young seedlings fall over and wilt. You can see a darkened section of stem at the soil line.

CAUSE: Damping-off (*Pythium* spp.). Several different species of fungi cause this common seedling disease. Plants with a long stem are more prone to damping-off than stocky plants.

WHAT TO DO:
• Use sterile seed-starting mix and pots.

• Grow seedlings within 2 inches of strong fluorescent light, or direct sow outdoors.

PROBLEM: Healthy seedlings with several true leaves suddenly turn slimy, wilt, and die. They have fuzzy mold.

CAUSE: Botrytis *(Botrytis cinerea)*. This fungal disease, also known as gray mold, is present in most gardens but rarely affects lettuce unless the weather is very rainy.

WHAT TO DO:
• Dispose of infected plants.
• Drench survivors with baking soda spray or fermented compost tea. Make a spray solution by dissolving 1 teaspoon of baking soda in 1 quart warm water. Add 1 teaspoon of liquid biodegradable or insecticidal soap to make a solution that sticks to leaves.
• Grow upright-growing varieties, such as romaine types of lettuce.
• Space plants widely to encourage air circulation.

PROBLEM: Older leaves close to the ground are brown and slimy, then dry out. Head lettuce is most susceptible.

CAUSE: Bottom rot *(Rhizoctonia solani)*. Damp weather and soil beneath the leaves are ideal conditions for this fungal disease, which lives in the soil. These symptoms are rarely seen on upright-growing types, such as romaine lettuce.

WHAT TO DO:
• Plant leaf lettuce.
• Space plants widely for air circulation.

PROBLEM: Plants grow slowly. New leaves are small and crinkled. Leaves may have yellow and brown streaks.

CAUSES: Lettuce mosaic virus and cucumber mosaic virus. Feeding insects, such as aphids, spread these diseases, as do infected seeds. These viruses are rare in home gardens.

WHAT TO DO:
• Plant healthy seeds.
• Dispose of affected plants.
• Use floating row covers to exclude feeding insects. Cover the plants with these synthetic, spunbonded fabrics, and bury the edges of the row cover in the soil.

 Other Problems

PROBLEM: Instead of developing crisp, tight centers, plants grow upward and the leaves have a bitter flavor.

CAUSE: Bolting, which is the process a plant goes through when it flowers and sets seeds. Lettuce plants bolt naturally when they mature, especially when they mature in early summer, when days become longer and warmer.

WHAT TO DO:
• Harvest lettuce promptly.
• Use succession planting. Start the same plant at two- or three-week intervals to stagger the harvest.
• Plant in late summer for fall harvest.

PROBLEM: Leaf tips or edges are dry and brown and may be slightly curled. Dark spots mar veins of old leaves.

CAUSE: Tipburn. This nutritional disorder is encouraged by hot weather and dry soil. When hot weather increases the plants' need for water and the soil is dry, lettuce plants develop an acute but temporary calcium deficiency. The inner leaves will remain perfectly edible.

WHAT TO DO:
• Water as needed to keep the soil evenly moist.
• Mulch.
• Time planting of lettuce early or late in the season so that it won't mature during the heat of summer.

Melon

(Cucumis melo)

 Melon Pests

PROBLEM: Small, circular holes appear in leaves. Some don't penetrate the leaf but just look like tan pinpricks.

CAUSE: Flea beetles (Family Chrysomelidae). Approach quietly to see ⅒-inch-long bronze, brown, or black beetles on either side of the leaves. The feeding holes made by flea beetles may become entry points for a variety of plant diseases.

WHAT TO DO:

• Use floating row covers to exclude flea beetles. Cover the plants with these synthetic, spunbonded fabrics, and bury the edges of the row cover in the soil.

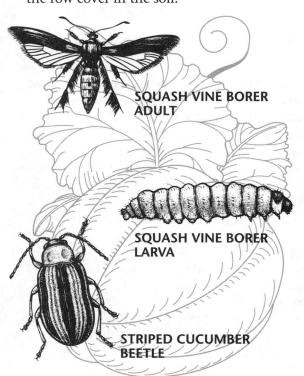

SQUASH VINE BORER ADULT

SQUASH VINE BORER LARVA

STRIPED CUCUMBER BEETLE

PROBLEM: During warm summer weather, adjoining leaves wilt on sunny days. The wilting steadily worsens.

CAUSE: Squash vine borers (*Melittia cucurbitae*). These caterpillars are the larvae of slender moths with wingspans of 1 to 1½ inches. The moths look almost like wasps, with olive brown front wings, clear hind wings, and red abdomen with black rings. The moths lay very small eggs on the largest stems of melons. The eggs hatch into plump, white caterpillars called borers. The white borers are from ½ to 1 inch long and have dark heads. The larvae overwinter in the soil.

WHAT TO DO:

• Time planting of melons early enough for them to mature and be strong enough to survive attacks.

• Use floating row covers to exclude feeding insects and animals and protect against temperature fluctuations. Cover the plants with these synthetic, spunbonded fabrics, and bury the edges of the row cover in the soil.

PROBLEM: Small, ragged spots appear in leaves; but unless the plants are seedlings, there is no extensive damage.

CAUSE: Striped cucumber beetles (*Acalymma vittatum*) or spotted cucumber beetles (*Diabrotica undecimpunctata* var. *howardi*). The culprits are ¼- to ⅓-inch-long, yellow or greenish yellow beetles with black stripes, or black spots on their backs. Their feeding damage is usually minor, but cucumber beetles transmit the fatal disease bacterial wilt (*Erwinia tracheiphila*).

WHAT TO DO:
• Handpick.
• Use floating row covers to exclude beetles. Cover the plants with these synthetic, spun-bonded fabrics, and bury the edges of the row cover in the soil.

 Melon Diseases

PROBLEM: Plants appear healthy, until suddenly you notice sections of vine wilt. Within a week plants die.
CAUSE: Bacterial wilt (*Erwinia tracheiphila*). This bacterial disease is spread from plant to plant via feeding cucumber beetles. Once the bacterium gets inside a melon plant, it multiplies very rapidly; so pruning off wilted parts has no impact on the disease.

WHAT TO DO:
• Use floating row covers to exclude feeding insects. Cover the plants with these synthetic, spunbonded fabrics, and bury the edges of the row cover in the soil.

PROBLEM: Leaves have a white, powdery coat that resists removal. Fruits are not sweet and have little flavor.
CAUSE: Powdery mildew (*Erysiphe cichoracearum*). This fungal disease is anchored in leaf tissues and ruins fruit flavor.

WHAT TO DO:
• Pick and destroy infected leaves.
• Rotate crops. Simply avoid growing a crop in the same spot each year.
• Space plants widely for good air circulation.
• Plant resistant varieties, such as 'Ambrosia' and 'Athena'.

PROBLEM: Small, circular brown spots appear on leaves and slowly expand until they are ½ inch in diameter.

CAUSE: Alternaria blight (*Alternaria cucumerina*). This common fungal disease usually infects melons after they produce fruits. It can shorten the plants' productive life by weakening them.

WHAT TO DO:
• Employ good cultural practices.
• Use succession planting. Start the same plant at two- to three-week intervals to stagger the harvest.

PROBLEM: Immature green melons develop dry, corky patches that start out ½ inch in diameter and expand.
CAUSE: Scab (*Cladosporium cucumerinum*). This fungal disease can be transmitted by infected seeds and can live from year to year on dead plants and garden debris. This disease is most common late in the season, when nights become cool and damp.

WHAT TO DO:
• Compost plant debris.
• Rotate crops. Simply avoid growing a crop in the same spot each year.

PROBLEM: Melon plants show yellowing and curling leaves with dark green patches and curled edges.
CAUSE: Mosaic viruses. Viruses that cause the splotchy, discolored leaves described above are spread from plant to plant by sap-sucking insect pests and are introduced to the garden on infected seeds. The disease causes new growth to be small and stunted, usually leading to plant death.

WHAT TO DO:
• Use floating row covers to exclude insects. Cover the plants and bury the edges of the row cover in the soil.
• Pull up and destroy infected plants to prevent spreading the disease.

Okra

(Abelmoschus esculentus)

 Okra Pests

PROBLEM: Leaves have large holes in them. The holes go all the way through and have clean edges. New holes keep appearing overnight.

CAUSE: Night-flying and daytime beetles. Many species of night-flying beetles eat holes in okra leaves. The copper and blue-green,

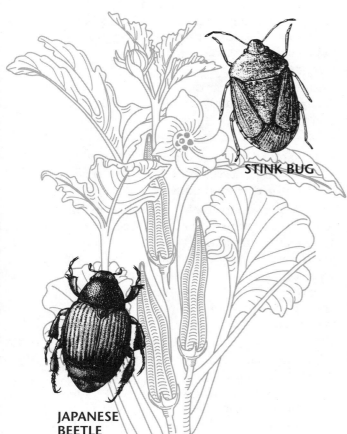

STINK BUG

JAPANESE BEETLE

½-inch-long Japanese beetles (*Popillia japonica*) often join the okra-eating party during the day. The damage these beetles cause is usually moderate. If young plants are attacked, you will need to intervene. After plants are more than 15 inches high, they often grow so rapidly that protective measures are not needed.

WHAT TO DO:
• Handpick beetles.
• Use floating row covers to exclude beetles and other feeding and egg-laying insects. Cover the plants with these synthetic, spun-bonded fabrics, and bury the edges of the row cover in the soil.
• Apply milky disease spores to nearby grassy areas. This insecticide is a combination of spores of *Bacillus popilliae* and *B. lentimorbus*. The soil-dwelling grubs die after eating the spores.

PROBLEM: Okra pods have small bumps on them, and there also may be little bumps on plant leaves and stems.

CAUSE: Stink bugs (Family Pentatomidae). These ½-inch-long, gray or green bugs with flat, shield-shaped backs sink their mouthparts into okra pods to suck out plant juices. Stink bugs often feed on okra in late summer. The bumps are the evidence of this feeding. Even so, the affected pods are fine to eat, bumps and all.

WHAT TO DO:
• Tolerate light damage.
• Handpick.
• Collect stink bugs with a hand-held, rechargeable vacuum.

Okra Diseases

PROBLEM: Your okra plants grow very slowly, and the leaves droop on hot days, even when the soil is moist.

CAUSE: Root-knot nematodes (*Meloidogyne* spp.). These microscopic soil-dwelling worms enter plants through the roots and cause diseaselike symptoms. If you dig up an affected plant, you will find many round galls attached to the root hairs. Most of the galls are the size of peas, but they may be as large as a nickel. Okra is so susceptible to root-knot nematodes that it is often used as a test crop to see if root-knot nematodes are present in soil where other crops are grown. Root-knot nematodes are most common in sandy soils in warm climates where the ground does not freeze hard in winter. They are much more active in summer than in winter.

WHAT TO DO:
• Solarize the soil. Clear plastic sheeting placed over bare soil for three to four weeks uses the sun's energy to heat the soil enough to kill most nematodes in the top few inches of soil. After removing the plastic, plant crops as usual.
• Incorporate chitin, a soil additive made from the shells of shellfish. Chitin provides nitrogen and potassium as it breaks down, and then it creates conditions that encourage beneficial soil organisms.
• Rotate plantings with marigolds (*Tagetes* spp.*)*, and turn the marigold plants under at the end of the season. Marigolds have a nematode-inhibiting effect on the soil.

PROBLEM: Blossoms have white, brown, or purple mold. The mold is speckled with thousands of tiny black dots.

CAUSE: Blossom blight (*Choanephora cucurbitarum*). This fungal disease appears when weather conditions are extremely damp. The mold disappears when dry weather returns.

WHAT TO DO:
• Pick and dispose of blighted blossoms.
• Space plants widely for optimum air circulation.

PROBLEM: Mature plants suddenly wilt, affecting the whole plant. The stem's base rots, and plants die within days.

CAUSE: Southern blight (*Sclerotium rolfsii*). This fungal disease is most common in warm climates, like that of southern states. Southern blight often strikes one or two plants, while others in the okra patch are unaffected. The fungi can live in soil for many years.

WHAT TO DO:
• Add compost to the bed before planting okra.
• Pull up and destroy infected plants.
• Disinfect tools with rubbing alcohol and clean hands after working with infected plants, to keep from spreading the disease.
• Space plants widely when planting, or thin to encourage adequate air circulation.
• Rotate plants. Avoid planting okra in the same plot two years in a row, or for longer periods, if possible.

 Other Problems

PROBLEM: Even though the growing conditions are good, fewer than half the seeds you planted have sprouted.

CAUSE: Poor germination. There are several possible causes for poor germination. It can be caused by planting old seeds, planting good seeds in soil that is too cold, or letting the soil dry out before the seeds can sprout.

WHAT TO DO:
• Plant fresh seeds.
• Sow seeds in warm soil.
• Presoak seeds overnight before planting them.

Onion

(Allium cepa)

Onion Pests

PROBLEM: Small holes are riddling onion stems just below the soil line. The tops of the bulbs have holes in them.

CAUSE: Onion maggots (*Delia antiqua*). These maggots are the larvae of ¼-inch-long, pale gray onion maggot flies. The flies emerge in spring and lay eggs around the base of onion plants and other members of the onion family. The eggs hatch into the ⅓-inch-long, root-eating maggots. Small onion bulbs may be eaten entirely from the inside out.

WHAT TO DO:
• Use floating row covers to exclude feeding insects. Cover the plants with these synthetic, spunbonded fabrics, and bury the edges of the row cover in the soil.
• Apply beneficial nematodes (*Steinernema carpocapsae* and *Heterorhabditis heliothidis*), which you can purchase from mail-order suppliers. Live nematodes are shipped suspended in gels or sponges. Follow label instructions for application, and release nematodes when pest larvae are present.
• Rotate crops. Simply avoid growing a crop in the same spot each year.

PROBLEM: Onion leaves develop short, light-colored streaks and small white blotches. Leaf tips turn dry and shrivel.

CAUSE: Thrips (Order Thysanoptera). These pests are tiny, 1/50- to 1/25-inch-long winged insects that are yellowish, brown, or black. When onion thrips feed in large numbers, they draw so much sap from plant leaves that the plants cannot grow.

WHAT TO DO:
• Spray infested plants with insecticidal soap.
• Control weeds to allow light and air to reach onion plants.

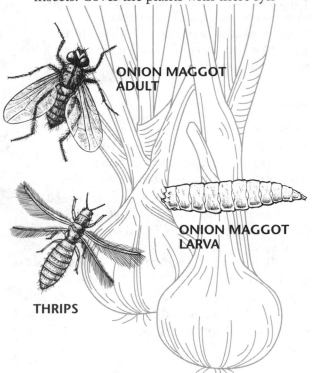

ONION MAGGOT ADULT

ONION MAGGOT LARVA

THRIPS

Onion Diseases

PROBLEM: Onion plants grow slowly but show no other obvious symptoms. The roots are pinkish brown.

CAUSE: Pink root (*Pyrenochaeta terrestris*). The spores of this fungal disease can live in the soil for many years. Infected plants usually continue to grow, but they never reach full size; if they produce bulbs, the bulbs will be disappointingly small.

WHAT TO DO:
• Compost plant debris.
• Plant tolerant varieties, such as 'Legacy', 'Nordic', and 'Texas Grano 1015Y'.
• Rotate crops. Simply avoid growing a crop in the same spot each year to minimize disease.

PROBLEM: Gray streaks appear in onion leaves. As streaks grow and develop powdery spores, leaves die.
CAUSES: Smut (*Urocystis* spp.). This fungal disease is unique in that it infects young onion tissues but not older plants. So you can safely grow onions from sets or from sturdy transplants in smut-infested soil. Smut is most active in cool soil.
WHAT TO DO:
• Plant disease-free onion sets or plants.

PROBLEM: Small white spots turn into slimy, dark purple blotches on onion leaves and flower stalks.
CAUSE: Purple blotch (*Alternaria porri*). This is a fungal disease that infects only onions. The leaves above these spots turn yellow and twisted, and then they die. As the disease progresses, the spots enlarge and become more numerous. The disease spreads quickly in warm, damp weather.
WHAT TO DO:
• Rotate crops. Simply avoid growing a crop in the same spot each year.
• Space plants widely to encourage air circulation.
• Plant healthy seeds.
• Compost onion tops after harvesting.

PROBLEM: Plants suddenly wilt and die; and when you dig them up, you find rotten roots.
CAUSE: Fusarium basal rot, also called root rot (*Fusarium oxysporum* f. *cepae* and other

forms). One or more fungi that live in soil cause many of the plants' roots to rot. Root rot also can develop in poorly drained soil.
WHAT TO DO:
• Destroy infected plants.
• Plant resistant or tolerant varieties, such as 'Legacy' and 'Texas Grano 1015Y'.
• Grow disease-free plants in well-drained, raised beds in a new location.

 Other Problems

PROBLEM: Onions develop a flowerstalk in late spring, when plants barely mature, then fail to grow large bulbs.
CAUSE: Premature flowering. Onions flower too early when the plants are exposed to cold weather when they are very young. Hot, dry conditions in early summer can also favor flowering at the cost of bulb formation.
WHAT TO DO:
• Time planting of onion sets for either late spring, when the soil has warmed, or late enough in the season so that they will mature in mild fall temperatures.

PROBLEM: The onions you harvest are extremely pungent, and the bulbs are small, tight, and marginally juicy.
CAUSES: Hot temperatures and dry soil. Onion variety, soil fertility, and the amount of water the plants get while they are growing are all factors that affect flavor. The largest, mildest onions grow in soils that contain no sulfur. Poor growing conditions can cause onions to be extra spicy. On the plus side, pungent onions often store very well, and their flavor becomes much sweeter after cooking.
WHAT TO DO:
• Plant in fertile soil.
• Provide plenty of water as bulbs expand.

Parsnip

(Pastinaca sativa)

 Parsnip Pests

PROBLEM: Parsnips stop growing. The leaves look pale and droop. Roots are riddled with rust red tunnels.

CAUSE: Carrot rust fly larvae (*Psila rosae*). The maggots, less than ⅓ inch long, feed on parsnip roots three to four weeks before pupating into greenish black flies ¼ inch long.

WHAT TO DO:
• Use floating row covers to protect plants from feeding insects. Cover the plants with these synthetic, spunbonded fabrics, and bury the edges of the row cover in the soil.
• Time planting so that parsnips will mature before carrot rust fly maggots hatch.

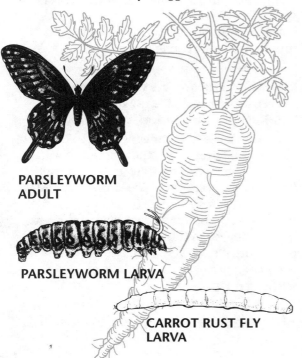

PARSLEYWORM ADULT

PARSLEYWORM LARVA

CARROT RUST FLY LARVA

PROBLEM: Clusters of parsnip leaves are missing, stripped off by fat green caterpillars with yellow, dotted bands.

CAUSE: Parsleyworms (*Papilio polyxenes*). These 1- to 2-inch-long caterpillars are the larvae of eastern black swallowtail butterflies. Because the butterflies are so pretty and parsnip tops are so vigorous, you may want to allow one or two parsleyworms to feed on a selected plant. However, parsnips that lose many leaves to these worms will be small and weakly flavored (compared to those that mature with a full set of leaves).

WHAT TO DO:
• Handpick.
• Use floating row covers to exclude feeding insects. Cover the plants with these synthetic, spunbonded fabrics, and bury the edges of the row cover in the soil.

PROBLEM: Parsnips left in the ground through winter flower in spring. The flowerheads can be covered in webs.

CAUSE: Parsnip webworms (*Depressaria pastinacella*). These caterpillars are larvae of gray moths with wingspans of ¾ inch. Webworms are most common in northern areas, where they favor the mature flowerheads of angelica (*Angelica archangelica*) and Queen-Anne's-lace (*Daucus carota* var. *carota*) along with parsnip flowers. Inside the webs they spin, ¼- to ¾-inch-long, yellow-green, segmented caterpillars with black stripes and three black spots on each segment are busily eating the parsnip flowerheads. Somewhat slow to germinate and grow, parsnips require patience on the part of the gardener. Roots that mature in cool weather tend to have the best flavor.

WHAT TO DO:
• Snip off and dispose of affected flower clusters.
• Remove weeds from your garden.
• Mulch.
• Let parsnips stay in the ground until after the first fall freeze, to improve their flavor.

 ## Parsnip Diseases

PROBLEM: New leaves that grow from the center of the plants are bunched and small, with yellow or red tips.

CAUSE: Aster yellows. This is a disease caused by a viruslike organism called a mycoplasma. Aster yellows spreads by entering feeding holes made in leaves and stems by aster leafhoppers (*Macrosteles quadrilineatus*) and other leafhoppers.

WHAT TO DO:
• Wash leafhoppers off parsnip plants with a strong stream of water.
• Apply insecticidal soap as directed.
• Destroy infected leaves and roots.

PROBLEM: Brown scabby spots develop on roots, especially near the shoulders. They are dark and sunken.

CAUSE: Canker and leaf spot (*Itersonilia perplexans*). This is a fungal disease unique to parsnips and it lives from year to year in dead plant residue left in the garden. You seldom see this disease outside the Northeast.

WHAT TO DO:
• Remove plant debris from the garden.
• Rotate crops. Simply avoid planting parsnips in the same place more often than once every four years.
• Dig compost into soil after harvesting parsnips.

 ## Other Problems

PROBLEM: Few parsnip seedlings germinate from a sowing, even though growing conditions are good.

CAUSE: Seed viability was poor. Parsnips' seeds are notoriously bad keepers.

WHAT TO DO:
• Sow fresh seed every year.
• If you want to try to save seeds for a later sowing, keep them in your refrigerator in a tightly sealed jar.

PROBLEM: Your parsnip roots are unusually hairy looking, and many of them have forked tips.

CAUSE: Too much soil nitrogen. Parsnip roots grow well and look their best when the soil is deeply worked and not allowed to compact. Parsnips resent manure or other nitrogen-rich fertilizers worked into the soil before planting.

WHAT TO DO:
• Don't fertilize parsnips with manure or other high-nitrogen fertilizers.

PROBLEM: The middle of roots, especially the portions near the shoulders, have dark, hollow holes in the cores.

CAUSE: Heart rot. This problem is caused by a boron deficiency in the garden soil where the parsnips grow.

WHAT TO DO:
• Amend soil with compost.
• Apply seaweed solution. Spray aboveground plant parts with a seaweed solution every three weeks while the plants are growing.
• Check soil pH and amend as needed to keep near neutral (7.0).

Pea

(*Pisum sativum* and varieties)

 Pea Pests

PROBLEM: Seed germination is sparse. You find some seedlings lying on top of the soil. Others are missing altogether.

CAUSE: Mice or birds. Both of these pests eat pea seeds in the early spring, when other food supplies are scant. Birds sometimes also eat young seedlings or clip tender leaves from the older plants.

WHAT TO DO:
• Cover seeded beds with chicken wire.
• Use bird netting to protect seedlings and young plants.

CUTWORM

BIRD

PROBLEM: Peas germinate and grow normally, then disappear overnight. Some lie on the soil. Others disappear.

CAUSE: Cutworms (Family Noctuidae). These pests are the larvae of several species of night-flying moths with wingspans of about 1½ inches. Cutworms are 1- to 2-inch-long, gray or dull brown caterpillars. The caterpillars hide in the soil during the day and come out at night to eat pea seedlings and the leaves of older plants.

WHAT TO DO:
• Handpick.
• Apply beneficial nematodes (*Steinernema carpocapsae* and *Heterorhabditis heliothidis*), which you can purchase from mail-order suppliers. Live nematodes are shipped suspended in gels or sponges. Follow label instructions for application, and release nematodes when pest larvae are present.
• Plant early to give the plants a chance to mature before cutworms become active.

PROBLEM: Pea plants grow normally for a while, then new growth slows and top leaves appear pale and bleached.

CAUSE: Aphids (Family Aphididae). These common pea pests are soft-bodied, wedge-shaped, ⅛-inch-long insects ranging in color from pale tan to light green to nearly black. Aphids weaken the plants by sucking their juices. Aphids also create entry points for viral diseases by damaging plant tissues as they feed. Pea aphids usually congregate on tender new growth, and a plant that hosts a few pea aphids quickly becomes heavily infested as the aphids multiply.

WHAT TO DO:
• Use insecticidal soap, following label directions.
• Grow the types that aphids ignore. It is not uncommon for one pea variety to be infested while others have no aphids at all.

Pea Diseases

PROBLEM: Pea plants grow slowly or not at all. Older leaves wilt and turn yellow or brown. Roots are darkened.

CAUSE: Root rot. Several strains of soil-dwelling fungi cause this problem. Root rot seldom develops when peas are planted where no peas have been grown for four years. It takes one to two seasons for the fungi populations to increase to damaging levels.

WHAT TO DO:
• Rotate crops. Simply avoid growing a crop of peas in the same spot each year.
• Pick and destroy infected leaves.

PROBLEM: Leaves develop white, powdery deposits, and the problem can quickly spread to stems and pods.

CAUSE: Powdery mildew (*Erysiphe polygoni*). This fungal disease causes infected plants to grow slowly. The peas within the pods may turn gray or brown and lack flavor.

WHAT TO DO:
• Plant resistant varieties, such as 'Cascadia' snap pea, 'Knight' and 'Patriot' shell peas, and 'Oregon Giant' snow pea.

PROBLEM: Yellowish patches appear on leaf tops. Leaf backs develop translucent white blisters or ridges.

CAUSE: Pea enation mosaic. This viral disease is most prevalent where peas are grown commercially. Feeding aphids can spread mosaic to peas in late spring and early summer. New leaves and any pods that infected plants produce will be small and distorted. Once infected, pea plants cannot recover.

WHAT TO DO:
• Plant resistant varieties, such as 'Cascadia' snap pea, 'Maestro' and 'Olympia' shell peas, and 'Oregon Giant' snow pea.

PROBLEM: Pea flowers are compressed in unusual-looking clusters. Leaves are small, curled and have pale veins.

CAUSE: Pea stunt. This viral disease is also called red clover vein mosaic virus. This disease spreads from clover to peas by sap-sucking aphids as they feed. Infected pea plants will produce few pods.

WHAT TO DO:
• Use insecticidal soap, following directions.
• Encourage beneficial insects, like lady beetles and lacewings, by planting small-flowered nectar plants, including yarrow, dill, and Queen-Anne's-lace.
• Wash aphids off plants with a strong stream of water.

Other Problems

PROBLEM: Pea plants grow well and produce numerous flowers, but the plants produce very few pods.

CAUSE: Adverse weather conditions. Hot weather or too much rain can cause pea flowers to drop. In hot weather, plants may stop flowering altogether. Wet weather stress may be more temporary, because new flowers often pop out when dry weather returns.

WHAT TO DO:
• Plant them in early spring, so you can harvest them before the hottest part of summer.
• Improve soil drainage.
• Plant peas in raised beds.

Pepper

(Capsicum annuum var. *annuum)*

Pepper Pests

PROBLEM: In early summer, slender, dark beetles about 1 inch long swarm over plants and eagerly eat the leaves.

CAUSE: Blister beetles (Family Meloidae). These are so named because their bodies contain an oil that can cause a blister if you touch a crushed beetle with bare skin. The beetles have long abdomens with striped edges along their wing covers and a lighter-colored head that can swivel around. The adults lay their eggs in midsummer underground in grasshopper egg burrows. The main diet for blister beetle larvae is grasshopper eggs. Adult blister beetles feed on plants for less than six weeks in summer.

WHAT TO DO:
• Handpick with gloved hands.
• Collect beetles with a hand-held vacuum.
• Use floating row covers to protect plants from feeding insects, such as blister beetles, and from hungry animals and temperature fluctuations. Cover the plants with these synthetic, spunbonded fabrics, and bury the edges of the row cover in the soil at the edges of the planting.

PROBLEM: Within days after setting seedlings out, some are felled. Older plants lose lower leaves overnight.

CAUSE: Cutworms (Family Noctuidae). The larvae of several species of night-flying moths, cutworms are gray or dull brown caterpillars with wingspans of 1½ inches. The larvae of the cutworm moths are 1 to 2 inches long. These caterpillars are active at night and hide in the soil during the day. Cutworms attack plants by curling around the stem of a pepper seedling at the soil line and eating through it, often leaving the top of the plant behind, lying on the ground. If the stems of seedlings are sturdy enough, cutworms may climb them and consume the tender leaves.

WHAT TO DO:
• Stake seedlings. When setting out peppers, shove a slender stick into the ground alongside the main stem. If a cutworm tries to girdle the stem, it will be foiled by the sturdy stick.
• Use cutworm collars to prevent cutworms from reaching your seedlings. To make these collars, use tin shears to cut 2- to 3-inch-long sections from paper-towel tubes or from tin

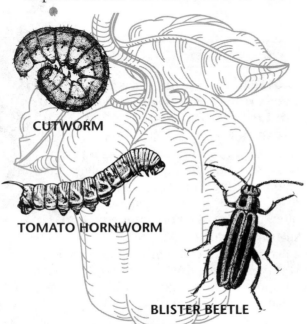

CUTWORM

TOMATO HORNWORM

BLISTER BEETLE

cans. Place these barriers over small seedlings when transplanting or as seedlings emerge from the soil.

• Apply beneficial nematodes (*Steinernema carpocapsae* and *Heterorhabditis heliothidis*), which you can purchase from mail-order suppliers. Live nematodes are shipped suspended in gels or sponges. Follow label instructions for application, and release nematodes when pest larvae are present.

PROBLEM: Large holes are eaten from the edges to the central leaf veins in the leaves in the upper third of plants.

CAUSE: Tomato hornworms (*Manduca quinquemaculata*). These 1- to 4-inch-long, bright green caterpillars have eight diagonal white stripes on their sides and a fleshy, pointed, black "horn" on their tail ends. The caterpillars are the larvae of the large hummingbird moth. These moths are easily recognized: They have fuzzy, orange abdomens, narrow wings, and wingspans of 4 to 5 inches. The moths scatter their eggs about pepper plants, tomatoes, and other closely related plants. The larvae hatch to feed on the plants' leaves until they are quite fat and 3 to 4 inches long, then they pupate into the adult moths.

WHAT TO DO:
• Handpick.
• Apply BTK. "BT" stands for *Bacillus thuringiensis*, an insect-stomach poison that kills caterpillars without harming beneficial insects. *B.t.* var. *kurstaki* (BTK) kills tomato hornworms. Follow label directions to spray a solution of BTK on plants when eggs begin to hatch or where young caterpillar pests are feeding. You can also sprinkle BTK granules into plant whorls.

PROBLEM: Peppers drop from plants while the peppers are green. Inside fruits, you find ⅛-inch-long worms.

CAUSE: Pepper weevils (*Anthonomus eugenii*). These pepper pests are ¼-inch-long, dark gray insects with large abdomens and long, pointed snouts. The adult weevils lay their eggs in pepper flowers and green fruits. When examining the fruits, you may find that the larvae have eaten them from the inside, leaving many dark cavities in the spongy inner tissues of the pepper fruits. Sometimes only a few plants will have weevils. Pepper weevils are most common in the South and Southwest.

WHAT TO DO:
• Pick and destroy infested and fallen fruits.
• Cut off and dispose of infested branches. Weevils are most numerous on fruits produced near the tops of pepper plants. Prune off top branches that show weevil damage and harvest the sound fruits from the side branches of plants.
• Compost garden debris. At the end of the season, pull up and compost dead plants, then mulch.
• Allow natural predators, such as fire ants, birds (especially meadowlarks), and wasps, to roam the garden.
• Rotate crops. Simply avoid planting peppers in the same spot two years in a row. Three-year rotations are ideal.

 Pepper Diseases

PROBLEM: Plants wilt on hot days but perk up if watered well. New growth is slow, and plants lack vigor.

CAUSE: Root-knot nematodes (*Meloidogyne* spp.). These microscopic soil-dwelling worms cause diseaselike symptoms. If you dig up an infested plant, you will see small, knotty-looking growths on its roots. These pests are most prevalent in warm climates where the ground seldom freezes in winter. If the problem is not severe and plants are given plenty of water, they may produce reasonably well, despite the presence of nematodes.

WHAT TO DO:
• Mulch peppers to keep the soil moist and to keep roots well supplied with water.
• Solarize the soil. Clear plastic sheeting placed over bare soil for three to four weeks uses the sun's energy to heat the soil enough to kill most nematodes in the top few inches of soil. After removing the plastic, plant crops without recultivating the soil.
• Add chitin-rich materials such as eggshells, crab shells, or packaged chitin products to the soil.
• Rotate plantings with marigolds (*Tagetes* spp.), which cannot host nematodes.

PROBLEM: The bottoms of immature pepper fruits develop dark brown or black spots ½ inch across and larger.

CAUSE: Blossom-end rot (soil calcium deficiency). This is a disorder that develops when the plants are temporarily unable to meet the demands for calcium made on them by the developing fruits. Blossom-end rot thrives in very wet or dry soil, and it can be brought on by rapid plant growth due to warm weather or the sudden availability of nitrogen in the soil.

WHAT TO DO:
• Mulch plants.
• Drench the soil the peppers grow in with seaweed solution weekly while fruits are forming.

PROBLEM: Seedlings suddenly fall over and rot. The stem at the soil line is bruised or shrinks to a dark thread.

CAUSE: Damping-off (*Pythium* spp. and *Rhizoctonia solani*). This disease is a common problem with young pepper seedlings. Damping-off is caused by several

species of soil-dwelling fungi, which attack the main stem and roots of seedlings, causing them to rot.

WHAT TO DO:
• Don't overwater. Keep the soil in which seedlings grow slightly dry. Bottom-water potted pepper seedlings, leaving the top ½ inch of soil slightly dry.
• Provide seedlings with bright light to encourage fast growth. Place the tops of the seedlings within 2 to 3 inches of fluorescent lights, and adjust the plants to maintain spacing as the seedlings grow.
• When planting seeds, start them in sterile potting medium, and use clean seed-starting containers.

PROBLEM: Mature pepper plants suddenly wilt. The base of the stem rots, and plants die within a few days.

CAUSE: Southern blight (*Sclerotium rolfsii*). This fungal disease is most common in warm climates. Southern blight often strikes one or two plants, while others in the pepper patch are unaffected. The spores of this fungi can live in soil for many years.

WHAT TO DO:
• Add compost to the bed before planting peppers.
• Rotate plants. Simply avoid planting peppers in the same plot two years in a row, or for longer periods, if possible.

PROBLEM: Purplish gray spots up to ¼ inch across are sunken on upper sides of leaves and raised on backs of leaves.

CAUSE: Bacterial spot (*Xanthomonas vesicatoria*). This bacterial disease travels on infected seeds or transplants and on splashing raindrops. Badly spotted leaves begin to look ragged after a while as the spots break open, and leaf edges curl up and turn yellow.

Meanwhile, pepper fruits develop small, circular, raised, brown, and scabby-textured spots. Peppers with bacterial spot often produce several peppers but are easily stressed by drought and hot weather. Spotted peppers are edible but may sunscald easily. The disease can persist in dead plant tissue for a year.

WHAT TO DO:
• Pull up and dispose of infected plants.
• Plant healthy seeds or seedlings.

PROBLEM: New leaves have crinkling with upward-curled edges. Plants grow slowly and produce few fruits.

CAUSE: Viruses. Viral diseases that infect peppers are numerous and include cucumber mosaic virus, tobacco mosaic virus, and several others. Feeding insects, including aphids, spread the disease to peppers. The leaves of infected plants sometimes become narrow and thickened, and they appear stringy rather than as broad and flat as they should. Plants with any of these symptoms produce fruits with skins marked by pale, concentric rings.

WHAT TO DO:
• Pull and dispose of severely affected pepper plants, but keep the plants that show only a slight bit of leaf puckering, since they may outgrow the disease.
• Plant resistant varieties, such as 'Ariane', 'Elisa', 'Galaxy', 'King Arthur', and 'Redwing'.

 Other Problems

PROBLEM: Peppers have soft, pale patches that gradually sink inward and become off-white or tan colored.

CAUSE: Sunscald. This type of fruit spotting happens when fruit is sunburned. Sunscald is more likely to appear on dark-colored peppers but can become a problem whenever the pepper fruits are not protected from full sun by a canopy of leaves.

WHAT TO DO:
• Shade pepper plants. Cover plants with shade cloth, or else plant fast-growing, light-filtering annual vines, such as morning glories, nearby.

PROBLEM: Pepper plants have good growing conditions, appear healthy, and flower, but they do not set fruit.

CAUSE: Hot weather or dry soil conditions. Heat stress and drought can cause peppers to drop their flowers or can cause pollination to fail so miserably that the plants produce no fruits. As days become shorter and cooler in late summer, fruit set on peppers usually improves dramatically.

WHAT TO DO:
• Water regularly when fruits are developing.
• Shade plants from the burning effects of full sun.
• Grow small-fruited pepper varieties, such as 'Ace', 'Banana', 'Cayenne', and 'Northstar', and the plants that produce the tiny, ornamental hot peppers.

OCCASIONAL PROBLEMS: Several of the pests that bother tomatoes can also become a problem for peppers because both of these plants are members of the same family (Family Solanaceae). The problems listed above are the most common ones for peppers. If you see problems you cannot identify, refer to the pests and diseases described in the "Tomato" entry on page 78.

Potato

(Solanum tuberosum)

 Potato Pests

PROBLEM: In late spring, you see brick red, soft grubs with black spots munching on leaf tips and flowers.

CAUSE: Colorado potato beetles (*Leptinotarsa decemlineata*). These beetles will find potatoes wherever they grow. Even a few potato beetles can create a big problem in the potato patch, because each female beetle can lay up to 500 bright yellow-orange eggs in clusters on the back sides of potato leaves. Both the yellow-and-black-striped beetles and their voracious larvae eat potato plants. Most of them munch on leaf tips and flower clusters, but these pests can appear anywhere on potato plants. The larvae eat constantly and become larger by the day, growing from $\frac{1}{16}$ inch to as long as $\frac{1}{2}$ inch.

WHAT TO DO:
• Handpick.
• Mulch with straw to deter this pest.
• Apply BTSD. *Bacillus thuringiensis* is an insect-stomach poison that kills caterpillars without harming beneficial insects. *B.t.* var *san diego* (BTSD) kills beetle grubs. Follow label directions to spray a solution of BTSD on the potato plants when you see the insect eggs begin to hatch or when young larvae are feeding. You can also sprinkle granulated BT products into plant leaf clusters.

COLORADO POTATO BEETLE ADULT

COLORADO POTATO BEETLE LARVA

POTATO STALK BORER ADULT

POTATO STALK BORER LARVA

PROBLEM: Small, circular holes appear in leaves. Some don't penetrate but just look like tan pinpricks.

CAUSE: Flea beetles (Family Chrysomelidae). Approach the plants quietly to keep from scaring the beetles away. You will see the $\frac{1}{10}$-inch-long bronze, brown, or black beetles on either side of the potato leaves. The holes that these pests chew in potato leaves do not cause major damage to the plants, but they may become entry points for diseases.

WHAT TO DO:
• Use floating row covers to exclude invading flea beetles. Cover the plants with these synthetic, spunbonded fabrics, and bury the edges of the row cover in the soil.

PROBLEM: The edges of leaves appear dry and have brown triangles at the tips. The leaf edges curl upward.

CAUSE: Potato leafhoppers (*Empoasca fabae*). These common potato pests usually feed in large groups. Examine the backs of your potato leaves and you will find ⅛-inch-long, green, wedge-shaped insects feeding on the tissues. As their name suggests, when disturbed, the leafhoppers hop away. Where these insects have been a problem before, start checking older potato leaves when the weather warms in spring. If the problem is caught and dealt with early, leafhoppers will not become numerous enough to cause the widespread damage to leaves that is called hopper burn.

WHAT TO DO:
• Use insecticidal soap.
• Apply horticultural oil. These commercial oil pesticides are mixed with water and sprayed on plants to smother all growth stages of most pests. Follow label directions for usage.

PROBLEM: Leaf clusters or whole branches wilt. The stem has a small cavity next to a dark, vertical streak.

CAUSES: Two similar pests, potato stalk borers (*Trichobaris trinotata*) and common stalk borers (*Papaipema nebris*), are to blame.

Both of these pests produce larvae that hollow out potato stems as they feed. Luckily, neither of them are widespread potato pests.

The ⅓-inch-long larvae of the potato stalk borers (⅕-inch-long gray beetles with long snouts) are yellowish white grubs with brown heads. Potato stalk borer larvae are most numerous where wild host plants—including jimsonweed (*Datura stramonium*), horse nettle (*Solanum carolinense*), and

ground cherries (*Physalis* spp.)—grow nearby.

You may also see the similar-looking larvae of common stalk borers feeding on your potato plants. These borers are the larvae of moths. The common stalk borers favor great ragweed (*Ambrosia trifida*) as a host plant.

WHAT TO DO:
• Prune off and dispose of infested stems.
• Clean up debris in fall.
• Control host weeds.
• Rotate plants. Simply avoid growing a crop in the same spot each year.

PROBLEM: Smooth-edged holes suddenly appear in leaves, but you can see no insects on them.

CAUSE: Slugs (Order Stylommatophora). Garden slugs are usually gray and look like snails without shells. They may be from ¼ to 4 inches long, and they produce a sticky slime wherever they go. Small slugs crawl up potato stems to feed after dark. By morning, the slugs are hiding in the soil, in mulch, or under plant debris.

WHAT TO DO:
• Handpick.
• Make beer traps from recycled cans sunk to the brim in soil, and fill the cans to the brim with yeasty beer. Create a roof over the trap with a piece of cardboard, wood or shingle, to keep out rain and to provide shade so the spot remains cool and moist. Attracted by the scent of beer, the slugs will fall into the traps and drown.
• Apply diatomaceous earth (DE) to the soil. This abrasive dust is made of fossilized shells called diatoms that penetrate the pests' skin as they crawl over DE. Wear a dust mask to avoid inhaling particles. Apply DE when plants are wet.

PROBLEM: Tunnels about ⅛ inch wide are on the outside or the inside of the potato tubers you harvest.

CAUSE: Wireworms (Family Elateridae). These pests are the larvae of slender click beetles. The adults are ⅓- to ¾-inch-long, brown or black beetles with grooved wings that make a clicking noise when they flip from their backs to their feet. The adults eat leaves and flowers but do little damage. However, their shiny brown, jointed, worm-like larvae with six legs do great damage as they eat potato roots. Wireworms feed primarily on grass roots. Problems are most serious when potatoes are grown in soil previously covered with grass.

WHAT TO DO:
• Grow potatoes in well-cultivated beds where grasses have not grown for at least three years.

 Potato Diseases

PROBLEM: Potato leaves have brown spots ranging in size from little specks to dime-sized spots with dark rings.

CAUSE: Early blight (*Alternaria solani*). This common fungal disease persists in potato tissue left behind in soil from year to year. The disease is disfiguring to the plants, but most of the spots caused by early blight are confined to older leaves close to the ground. The tubers harvested from infected plants, however, are safe to eat and taste fine, because the disease usually does not appear until the plants are ready to die back naturally.

WHAT TO DO:
• Plant disease-free seed potatoes.
• Mulch to keep contaminated soil from splashing on potatoes.
• Grow potatoes in full sun so that wet leaves dry rapidly.

PROBLEM: Older leaves and stems near the soil suddenly develop large, dark, puckery spots and white mold.

CAUSE: Late blight (*Phytophthora infestans*). This fungal disease usually overwinters on diseased potatoes and plant material left in garden soil. A period of cool, wet weather in late summer encourages this disease. Disease spores can blow on the wind or be carried by insects. Under ideal, wet conditions, the spots spread rapidly to new leaves and to nearby plants. To make matters worse, the late blight fungus mutates into new strains, so those potato varieties that were previously resistant to a particular strain become susceptible to new ones.

WHAT TO DO:
• Plant disease-free seed potatoes.
• Rotate plants. Beat late blight by growing disease-free potatoes in a different plot every year. Without a host (the potatoes), the fungus will die out. This is a good way to avoid infection, as well as to stop it.

PROBLEM: Potatoes have blemishes ranging from brown specks to scabby, corky areas and dry, sunken patches.

CAUSE: Scab (*Streptomyces scabies*). This fungal disease affects potato skins but not the flesh inside the tubers. It is safe to peel off the scabby patches and eat affected potatoes, but don't replant them, because the disease can survive from year to year in garden soil. The fungus that causes this disease is commonly found in soil, even where potatoes have never grown before.

WHAT TO DO:
• Plant disease-free seed potatoes.
• Amend the soil as needed with organic matter or sulfur to give it an acidic pH (from 5.5 to 6.7).
• Plant resistant varieties, including 'Butte' 'Norland', 'Red Gold', and 'Russian Banana'.

PROBLEM: Leaves are stunted and yellowing. Tubers are cracked and have a ring of decay inside.

CAUSE: Ring spot. This bacterial disease (*Clavibacter sepedonicum*) infects aboveground parts as well as tubers of potatoes. Tubers may rot in the ground or later during storage. The bacteria enter plants through wounds, often in tubers cut into seed pieces at planting time.

WHAT TO DO:
• Discard infected tubers.
• Plant certified disease-free seed potatoes.
• Disinfect tools with rubbing alcohol when working with diseased plants.

PROBLEM: New leaves are small with yellow or red tips. Some grow in tight bunches.

CAUSE: Aster yellows. This is a disease caused by a viruslike organism called a mycloplasma. Aster yellows spreads by entering feeding holes made by aster leafhoppers (*Macrosteles quadrilineatus*) and other leafhoppers.

WHAT TO DO:
• Wash leafhoppers off plants with a strong stream of water.
• Apply insecticidal soap as directed.
• Destroy infected leaves and roots.

 Other Problems

PROBLEM: No sprouts appear after you planted seed potatoes. When you dig up seed potatoes, they've rotted.

CAUSE: Wet, cold soil conditions. If the soil remains wet and cold for more than a week after planting, seed potatoes can rot.

WHAT TO DO:
• Plant whole seed potatoes.
• Allow cut potato pieces to dry for a day before planting them.

• Allow seed potatoes to turn green and sprout before you plant them.
• Plant seed potatoes when the soil temperature is above 45°F.

PROBLEM: Patches of potato skins, or one side of potatoes, are green. If eaten, the tubers taste bitter.

CAUSE: Exposure to sunlight. If potatoes are exposed to sunlight, they will become inedible. Potatoes turn green and produce a compound called solanine, a moderately toxic substance, in response to sun exposure.

WHAT TO DO:
• Mulch potatoes heavily.
• Store harvested potatoes in a dark place.

PROBLEM: Potato tubers have black or brown areas in the middle, sometimes with a hollow space.

CAUSE: High temperatures. This condition, which is sometimes called hollow heart, develops when a heat wave settles in while potato tubers are maturing. Storing harvested tubers at high temperatures can make the problem much worse.

WHAT TO DO:
• Plant seed potatoes early so that they are well developed before the hottest part of summer.
• Store harvested tubers in cool conditions (about 40°F).

OCCASIONAL PROBLEMS: Several of the pests that bother tomatoes and other vegetables can become a problem for potatoes. The problems listed above are the most common ones for potatoes. If you see a problem you cannot identify, refer to the following disease listed elsewhere in this book: Verticillium wilt (*Verticillium* spp.), listed under "Tomato" on page 78.

Radish

(Raphanus sativus)

 Radish Pests

PROBLEM: Small holes appear in radish leaves. Instead of holes, some leaves have tan, pinprick-sized spots.

CAUSE: Flea beetles (Family Chrysomelidae). These beetles are common radish pests. While inspecting the holes they make in your radish leaves, you will probably encounter ⅛-inch-long brown, bronze, or black beetles. They will jump away when you touch the radish leaves. Watch and you will see them return within a short time. In most climates, flea beetles appear just when radishes are starting to grow well in spring. If the radishes are almost mature when the flea beetles come, the plants will still produce a good crop of radish roots. But when flea beetles heavily damage the leaves of young plants, the roots will be smaller than usual. Flea beetles are often less numerous on radishes that are grown in the fall.

WHAT TO DO:
• Use floating row covers to exclude feeding insect pests. Cover the plants with these synthetic, spunbonded fabrics, and bury the edges of the row cover in the soil.
• Tolerate light damage.
• Apply beneficial nematodes (*Steinernema carpocapsae* and *Heterorhabditis heliothidis*). Mail-order suppliers ship live nematodes suspended in gels or sponges. Follow label instructions for application, and release nematodes when pest larvae are present.
• Time planting of radish seeds late enough in the season so they will mature after flea beetles are no longer a threat.

PROBLEM: Small, dark caterpillars, less than 1 inch long, eat leaves of radishes you planted for fall harvest.

CAUSE: Fall armyworms (*Spodoptera frugiperda*). Fall armyworms are the night-feeding caterpillar larvae of gray moths with a white dot on each wing. The adult moths can lay more than 500 eggs a week on lower plant leaves; so where you see a few larvae, there will likely be many more. Voracious fall armyworms can destroy young plants. These caterpillars are much more common some years than in others. You may even see them in spring.

WHAT TO DO:
• Handpick.
• Apply BT (*Bacillus thuringiensis*), an insect-

FLEA BEETLE

FALL ARMYWORM

stomach poison that kills caterpillars without harming beneficial insects. Follow label directions to spray a solution of BT on plants when eggs begin to hatch or where young pests are feeding. You can also sprinkle BT granules into plant whorls.

PROBLEM: Radish roots have holes and tunnels. Tunnels are lined with slime and contain small white maggots.

CAUSE: Cabbage maggots (*Delia radicum*). These maggots are less than ½ inch long. Cabbage maggots are the larvae of ¼-inch-long gray flies that look like houseflies. The flies prefer to lay their eggs around cabbage or broccoli; but if radishes are all that's available, the flies will make do with them.

WHAT TO DO:
• Weed regularly.
• Cultivate the soil shallowly.
• Apply beneficial nematodes (*Steinernema carpocapsae* and *Heterorhabditis heliothidis*). Mail-order suppliers ship live nematodes suspended in gels or sponges. Follow label instructions for application.
• Apply diatomaceous earth (DE) to the soil. This abrasive dust is made of fossilized shells called diatoms that penetrate the pests' skin as they crawl over DE.

 Radish Diseases

PROBLEM: The radish roots you harvest have brown, woody patches on their skin that feel rough to the touch.

CAUSE: Scab (*Streptomyces scabies*). The soil-dwelling fungus that causes this disease shows up often in soil with a magnesium deficiency and in soil that has a pH that deviates too far from a neutral 7.0. The flesh inside affected radishes has normal color, though there may be a toughening of tissues just under the patches.

WHAT TO DO:
• Raise soil pH close to 7.0 by adding lime or organic matter as needed.
• Rotate radishes with crops other than potatoes, which are also susceptible to scab.
• Test the soil. Provide magnesium as needed.

 Other Problems

PROBLEM: Your radish plants look healthy, but the roots that you harvest have large cracks in them.

CAUSE: Uneven soil moisture. Radish roots can crack when soil that has been dry or only slightly moist suddenly becomes saturated just as radish roots are expanding. Cracks can also develop after radishes plump up and are left unharvested for too long.

WHAT TO DO:
• Harvest radishes promptly as they ripen.
• Provide growing radishes with a steady supply of water so that the roots expand at a steady rate.

PROBLEM: The flavor of the radishes that you harvest is hot, but the plants look healthy and the roots look perfect.

CAUSES: Hot weather, stressful growing conditions, and beetles. Stressful growing conditions, such as heat waves, dry soil, or heavy flea beetle infestations, can make radish roots turn hot. Radishes left in the ground too long before harvesting can develop a hot taste.

WHAT TO DO:
• Use floating row covers to exclude feeding flea beetles. Cover the plants with these synthetic, spunbonded fabrics, and bury the edges of the row cover in the soil.
• Handpick beetles.
• Harvest promptly.
• Provide plenty of water as radishes are approaching maturity.
• Grow in the cool weather of spring or fall.

Rhubarb

(Rheum rhabarbarum)

 ## Rhubarb Pests

PROBLEM: Rhubarb plants fail to thrive; looking closely, you notice small holes in the stalks, crown, and roots.

CAUSE: Rhubarb curculios (*Lixus concavus*). The adults are approximately ½-inch-long, gray beetles with snouts. Beetles bore into the stalks of rhubarb and lay eggs in the stalks. The injuries result from the beetles feeding on rhubarb leaves and boring into the stems. The larvae feed on rhubarb but are not serious pests because they leave the plants to feed on curly dock, a weed.

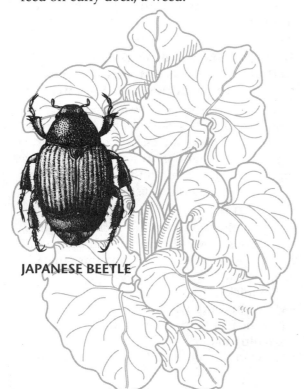

JAPANESE BEETLE

WHAT TO DO:
• Remove sunflowers, curly dock, and thistle plants from your garden, since the larvae also feed on these plants.

PROBLEM: Large holes with smooth edges suddenly appear in your rhubarb leaves.

CAUSE: Japanese beetles (*Popillia japonica*). These chunky, blue-green, ½-inch-long beetles have voracious appetites for rhubarb leaves.

WHAT TO DO:
• Handpick.
• Use floating row covers to exclude flying insects. Cover the plants with these synthetic, spunbonded fabrics, and bury the edges of the row cover in the soil.
• Place beetle-attracting pheromone traps to lure beetles *away* from your rhubarb plants.

 ## Rhubarb Diseases

PROBLEM: New stems are spindly, and their leaves are yellow. The stalks have brown, sunken spots at their bases.

CAUSE: Fusarium wilt, also called root rot (*Fusarium* spp.). This disease is caused by one or more fungi that live in soil and cause rhubarb roots to rot. The plants look increasingly feeble as summer progresses, with the stalks on each plant developing dark spots and turning yellow. Plant tissues damaged by feeding insects give root rot an easy entry into the plants. Root rot also can develop in soil that is poorly drained or too acidic.

WHAT TO DO:
• Raise soil alkalinity to pH 6.5 to 7.5 by adding lime to the soil.
• Destroy infected plants.
• Start disease-free plants in well-drained, raised beds. Use floating row covers to exclude insect pests that transmit diseases when they feed on plants. Cover the plants with these synthetic, spunbonded fabrics, and bury the edges of the row cover in the soil at the edges of the planting.

PROBLEM: Plants lose vigor. The leaves begin yellowing. The stalks collapse and can't be revived with water.

CAUSE: Verticillium wilt (*Verticillium* spp.). This a soilborne fungal disease that is most common in the country's midsection. The disease can build up to damaging levels in most parts of the country, but it rarely occurs in very hot climates. It lives in the soil for up to 15 years.

WHAT TO DO:
• Space rhubarb plants widely to allow for adequate air circulation.
• Set new rhubarb plants in a location where rhubarb has not previously grown.
• Grow plants in containers filled with sterilized soil.
• Pull up and dispose of infected plants.

PROBLEM: White, cottony strands appear at the base of stalks. Strands develop tiny tan beads; crowns rot.

CAUSE: Southern blight (*Sclerotium rolfsii*). This fungal disease is most common in warm climates and affects many vegetables and ornamentals. The fungi can live in soil for many years.

WHAT TO DO:
• Remove infected plants and 6 inches of surrounding soil.
• Add compost to the garden bed before planting healthy rhubarb plants.
• Avoid planting new plants in the same area where this blight has appeared.

PROBLEM: Sunken, water-soaked spots appear on the base of stalks. Leaves yellow and wilt. Plants collapse.

CAUSE: Phytophthora crown rot (*Phytophthora cactorum* and *P. parasitica*). This soilborne fungus is also called root rot, foot rot, or stem rot. It likes warm, waterlogged soils; and it spreads to healthy plants through rain or soil and on dirty tools, hands, and infected plants.

WHAT TO DO:
• Remove infected plants.
• Buy disease-free plants. Plant them in well-drained soil, such as raised beds; allow plenty of space for air circulation; and avoid overwatering.
• Spray crowns with bordeaux mixture or copper sulfate as a preventive measure if you have a warm, moist climate.

 Other Problems

PROBLEM: In past seasons your rhubarb plants were robust, but now the stalks look small and spindly.

CAUSES: Overcrowding and poor nutrition. As clumps of rhubarb expand over the course of several seasons, the roots become crowded and the competition for nutrition can cause the new stalks to become small and weak. Rhubarb is naturally a heavy feeder. It should have plenty of room to grow and should be planted in rich garden soil.

WHAT TO DO:
• Allow new plants to develop for several seasons before harvesting heavily. Sidedress rhubarb plants with compost or well-rotted manure each spring. Divide plants every five years to prevent overcrowding.

Rutabaga

(Brassica napus, Napobrassica group)

Rutabaga Pests

PROBLEM: Young plants collapse and die. Older plants grow slowly and wilt on hot days. Roots have brown tunnels.

CAUSE: Cabbage maggots (*Delia radicum*). These pests are the larvae of ¼-inch-long, tapering, gray flies. Cabbage maggots are occasional pests of rutabagas. They feed on mature plants but cause the most damage to young plants by feeding on their roots and the stem in the soil just below ground level. Usually only a few plants in a bed or row are affected, because cabbage maggots feed close to where they hatch and do not move from plant to plant. When you pull up a plant, you may see that the roots have brown grooves or tunnels in them. You may also find the tiny, white, ¼-inch-long maggots inside the tunnels.

WHAT TO DO:
• Destroy plant debris.
• Use floating row covers to exclude flying insects. Cover the plants with these synthetic, spunbonded fabrics, and bury the edges of the row cover in the soil. Encourage beneficial insects, like lady beetles and tiny wasps, by planting small-flowered nectar plants, including yarrow and dill.
• Apply beneficial nematodes (*Steinernema carpocapsae* and *Heterorhabditis heliothidis*), which you can purchase from mail-order suppliers. Live nematodes are shipped suspended in gels or sponges.
• Apply diatomaceous earth (DE) to the soil. This abrasive dust is made of fossilized shells called diatoms. The sharp shells penetrate the pests' skin as they crawl over DE.

FLEA BEETLE

APHID

PROBLEM: Tiny holes riddle the yellow-edged leaves of young rutabaga plants. You see small, dark, active beetles.

CAUSE: Flea beetles (Family Chrysomelidae). These ¹⁄₁₀-inch-long, bronze, brown, or black beetles are eager eaters of rutabaga leaves. They do not usually cause serious damage to the plants, but their feeding holes may become entry points for plant diseases.

WHAT TO DO:
• Spray plants with insecticidal soap.

• Gather beetles with a hand-held vacuum.
• Use floating row covers to protect against temperature fluctuations, animals, and feeding insects like flea beetles. Cover the plants with these synthetic, spunbonded fabrics, and bury the edges of the row cover in the soil.

PROBLEM: New leaves in centers of rutabaga plants are pale and curled. Tiny green insects are on them.

CAUSE: Aphids (Family Aphididae).These soft-bodied, pear-shaped, $\frac{1}{16}$- to $\frac{3}{8}$-inch-long insects damage leaves and stems by sucking plant juices. Their sticky secretions, called honeydew, can encourage the growth of mold; and they can transfer plant viruses as they feed. You can often see aphids on rutabaga leaves, but usually only a few. They only become a problem when they cluster together on the leaves and feed in large numbers.

WHAT TO DO:
• Snap off and dispose of leaves that host most of the aphids.
• Wash aphids off plants with a strong stream of water.
• Use insecticidal soap, applying a very dilute solution of it.
• Attract beneficial insects, like lady beetles and lacewings, by planting small-flowered nectar plants, including dill, Queen-Anne's-lace, and yarrow. Give the beneficials time to bring aphids under control.

 Rutabaga Diseases

PROBLEM: Leaves develop faint, powdery, white patches. New growth slows down, and badly affected leaves shrivel.

CAUSE: Powdery mildew (*Erysiphe polygoni*). This fungal disease sometimes infects rutabaga leaves but usually not until the plants are old enough to have developed a good root system.

WHAT TO DO:
• Tolerate light damage.
• If only a few leaves show mildew, snip them off to stop the spread of the disease.
• Rotate crops. Simply avoid growing the same crop in the same spot each year.
• Space plants widely to encourage air circulation.

 Other Problems

PROBLEM: The rutabaga roots that you harvest are unusually small and tough and have a bitter taste.

CAUSES: Hot weather and poor growing conditions. If a hot spell or a drought hits while rutabaga roots are growing and maturing, they can stop growing and take on a bitter taste. The best-tasting rutabagas are those that mature in cool weather and that go through at least one light frost just before harvesting.

WHAT TO DO:
• Time planting for late enough in the season that the rutabagas mature in cool autumn weather.

OCCASIONAL PROBLEMS: Several of the pests that bother cabbage and broccoli can become a problem for rutabagas because all three are members of the cabbage family (Family Cruciferae). The problems listed above are the most common ones for rutabagas. If you see problems you cannot identify, refer to the following pests and diseases listed elsewhere in this book: Imported cabbageworms (*Artogeia rapae*), listed under "Cabbage" on page 14. Clubroot (*Plasmodiophora brassicae*), listed under "Broccoli" on page 10.

Spinach

(Spinacia oleracea)

 Spinach Pests

PROBLEM: Spinach leaves have tan, meandering streaks in them but are not eaten all the way through.

CAUSE: Spinach leafminers (*Pegomya hyoscyami*). These pests are the larvae of $\frac{1}{10}$-inch-long, black or black-and-yellow flies. The flies lay small clusters of white eggs on leaf undersides, and the eggs hatch into tiny maggots. The pale green maggots feed inside spinach leaves but leave the outermost layer of leaf tissue intact.

WHAT TO DO:
• Use floating row covers to exclude feeding insects. Cover the plants with these synthetic, spunbonded fabrics, and bury the edges of the row cover in the soil.

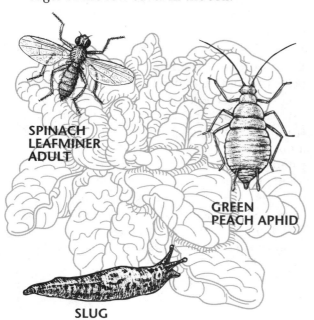

SPINACH LEAFMINER ADULT

GREEN PEACH APHID

SLUG

PROBLEM: New spinach leaves are small and pale. Small, light green insects cling to undersides of the leaves.

CAUSE: Green peach aphids (*Myzus persicae*). These soft-bodied, pear-shaped insects are $\frac{1}{16}$ to $\frac{3}{8}$ inch long. Aphids damage leaves and stems by sucking plant juices.

WHAT TO DO:
• Tolerate light damage.
• Use insecticidal soap, following label directions.

PROBLEM: Spinach leaves have holes in them up to $\frac{1}{2}$ inch across; although you look, you see no insects on the plants.

CAUSE: Slugs (Order Stylommatophora). Garden slugs are usually gray and look like snails without shells. They may be from $\frac{1}{4}$ inch to 4 inches long, and they leave a sticky slime on your fingers if you touch them. Slugs feed on spinach primarily at night.

WHAT TO DO:
• Handpick.
• Make beer traps from recycled cans sunk to the brim in soil and filled with yeasty beer.
• Apply diatomaceous earth (DE) to the soil. This abrasive dust is made of fossilized shells called diatoms that penetrate the pests' skin as they crawl over DE. Wear a dust mask to avoid inhaling particles, and apply DE when plants are wet with dew.

PROBLEM: Very small, pale specks and circular holes appear in the leaves of your spinach plants.

CAUSE: Spinach flea beetles (*Disonycha*

xanthomelas). These pests are ⅕-inch-long, greenish black beetles. Their larvae, which lurk on leaf undersides, are ⅕-inch-long, purplish gray, rather shapeless blobs covered with bumps and tiny black hairs. The larvae also eat spinach roots.

WHAT TO DO:
• Use floating row covers to exclude insect pests including spinach beetles. Cover the plants with these synthetic, spunbonded fabrics, and bury the edges in the soil.
• Make sticky traps. Flea beetles are attracted to white objects; so coat white cardboard or painted wooden boards with petroleum jelly or Tanglefoot (a commercial product for this purpose), and fasten them to stakes put near spinach plants. Replace traps when they become covered with insects.

Spinach Diseases

PROBLEM: Plants are stunted. Young leaves have yellow or tan edges and are narrow and wrinkled.

CAUSE: Spinach blight. This is the common name for the disease caused by the cucumber mosaic virus when it infects spinach plants. This common plant virus enters plants through the feeding holes of sap-sucking insect aphids in late spring. It spreads rapidly in hot weather. Once infected, the plants cannot recover. This virus can overwinter in perennial weeds.

WHAT TO DO:
• Plant resistant varieties, such as 'Melody', 'Vienna', and 'Winter Bloomsdale'.
• Pull out and destroy diseased plants.
• Control weeds.

PROBLEM: Yellowish patches appear on the top of spinach leaves. The backs have spots of purplish gray mold.

CAUSE: Blue mold (*Peronospora effusa*). This is the common name for downy mildew when it attacks spinach leaves. Cool, damp growing conditions encourage this fungal disease. Under such conditions, the patches of mold on leaves turn black, and the leaves collapse within a few days of showing the disease symptoms.

WHAT TO DO:
• Drench the soil with fermented compost tea.
• Plant resistant varieties, such as 'Melody', 'Olympia', 'Space', and 'Vienna'.
• Control weeds.
• Grow spinach in full sun.
• Rotate crops. Simply avoid growing a crop in the same spot each year.
• Space plants widely to encourage air circulation.
• Pick and destroy infected leaves.

Other Problems

PROBLEM: New leaves are small and pointed and light green. Then a long stalk suddenly shoots upward.

CAUSE: Bolting, which is the process a mature plant goes through when it flowers and sets seeds. Bolting is triggered when days become long in late spring and early summer, and it causes the flavor and texture of the leaves to decrease.

WHAT TO DO:
• Time planting of spinach in fall for early-spring harvests.
• Plant slow-bolting varieties, like 'Bloomsdale Longstanding'.
• Use succession planting. Start the same plant at two- or three-week intervals to stagger harvests.

Summer Squash

(*Cucurbita pepo* and varieties)

Summer Squash Pests

PROBLEM: During warm summer weather, adjoining leaves wilt on sunny days. The wilting steadily worsens.

CAUSE: Squash vine borers (*Melittia cucurbitae*). These caterpillars are the larvae of slender moths with wingspans of 1 to 1½ inches. The moths look almost like wasps, with olive brown front wings, clear hind wings, and a red abdomen with black rings. The adult moths lay very small eggs on the largest stems of summer squash. The eggs hatch into plump, white caterpillars called borers. The white borers are from ½ to 1 inch long and have dark heads. On the main stem, just below the joint where the wilted leaves are attached, you may see one or more small holes in the stem surrounded by sawdustlike frass (caterpillar excrement). Or the stem may show a large damaged patch that is rotted almost all the way through. Cut open the damaged portion of the stem, and you will find larvae feeding on the juicy tissues inside the squash stems. The larvae overwinter in the soil. No species of summer squash is truly resistant, though some gardeners have had luck with the long-vined, heirloom zucchinis known as 'Rampicante-tromboncino' and 'Zucchetta Rampicante'.

WHAT TO DO:
• Time the planting of squash early enough for it to mature and be strong enough to survive attacks.
• Use floating row covers to protect plants from feeding insects, animals, and temperature fluctuations. Cover the plants with these synthetic, spunbonded fabrics, and bury the edges of the row cover in the soil.

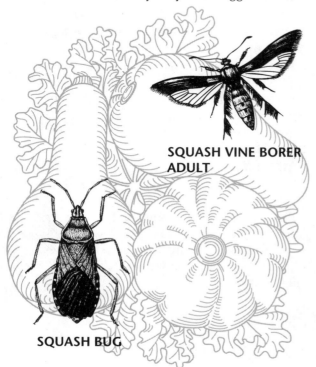

SQUASH VINE BORER ADULT

SQUASH BUG

PROBLEM: When plants bloom, small, ragged holes are chewed in the largest leaves by ½-inch-long, brown bugs.

CAUSE: Squash bugs (*Anasa tristis*). These are grayish brown bugs with orange markings, ½ to ¾ inch long, with flat backs shaped like elongated shields. Squash bugs like to hide under large squash leaves that lie close to the ground, or they may run into the shadows when you approach. They lay reddish brown, oval eggs, neatly arranged in evenly spaced clusters, on either side of squash leaves. The babies that hatch from the eggs are long-legged, gray, soft-bodied nymphs that tend to hang around together on the plants' leaves. Both adults and nymphs suck plant juices, but it takes a lot of them to seriously damage healthy squash plants. They tend to be most numerous in the middle of summer.

WHAT TO DO:
• Handpick.
• Knock bugs from squash leaves with a strong stream of water.
• Cover the plants with floating row covers to exclude insect pests. Bury the edges of the row cover in the soil.
• Do not mulch if you find these pests; the adults use organic mulches as shelter.

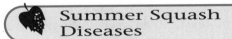

Summer Squash Diseases

PROBLEM: Soon after flowers shrivel and fruits begin growing, one end of fruits begins to shrink and turn black.

CAUSE: Choanephora wet rot, also called blossom blight (*Choanephora cucurbitarum*). The fungi that cause this disease are present in most gardens but do not cause problems unless weather conditions are just right—warm and wet for several days. At the same time the fruits begin to shrink and blacken, a cottony, gray mold topped with tiny black dots also forms on the affected parts of the squash. Problems often last only a short time, then disappear when dry weather returns.

WHAT TO DO:
• Tolerate light damage.

• Place squash plants far enough apart to promote air circulation.

PROBLEM: Strange changes are noticeable in the shape and texture of leaves or the appearance of the fruits.

CAUSE: Viruses. Several viral diseases can infect summer squash. These can spread among plants by feeding insects, such as aphids or cucumber beetles. Leaves may change their shape and become deeply cut, like skinny fingers on a hand. Or older leaves may turn yellow and curl up or may become dry and leathery, with a silvery cast. Young fruits may be covered with hard, raised warts or may have green streaks and puckers in them. New plant growth may be slow, small, and twisted.

WHAT TO DO:
• Remove diseased plants from the garden.
• Use floating row covers to protect plants from pests and temperature fluctuations. Cover the plants with the fabrics, and bury the edges of the row cover in the soil.

 ## Other Problems

PROBLEM: Squash plants look healthy and have a lot of flowers, but the plants are not producing fruits.

CAUSE: Male flowers. Summer squash plants produce both male and female flowers. The male flowers, which produce only pollen and no squash, open first. Female flowers, which appear a week or so after the male flowers start opening, are the fertile ones. You can easily tell male and female flowers apart. Female flowers have a bulge just under the base of the flower, usually shaped like the squash it will later become. Male flowers, by contrast, have only a slender stem below the flower base.

WHAT TO DO:
• Have patience. When both flowers open, start looking for fruit to develop.

Sweet Potato

(Ipomoea batatas)

 Sweet Potato Pests

PROBLEM: Long, narrow grooves appear along the length of leaves and vertically along stems in early summer.

CAUSE: Sweet potato flea beetles *(Chaetocnema confinis)*. The adult beetles eat leaves, and the affected leaves may turn brown and die. Look closely and you will see the 1/10-inch-long, bronze, brown, or black beetles on either side of the leaves, jumping about. Their thin, white, brown-headed larvae chew grooves in the tubers, which makes the tubers less than beautiful, though they are still edible.

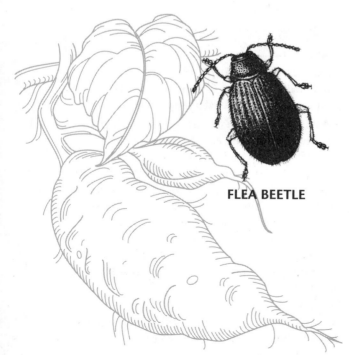

FLEA BEETLE

WHAT TO DO:
• Destroy weed hosts, such as bindweed and wild morning glory, that flea beetles also feed on.
• Use floating row covers to protect plants from feeding insects, animals, and temperature fluctuations. Cover the plants with these synthetic, spunbonded fabrics, and bury the edges of the row cover in the soil.
• Apply beneficial nematodes *(Steinernema carpocapsae* and *Heterorhabditis heliothidis)*. You can purchase these beneficials from mail-order suppliers. Live nematodes are shipped suspended in gels or sponges. Release nematodes when pest larvae are present.

PROBLEM: Sweet potato tubers are riddled with small, deep holes. White, 1/8-inch-long larvae may be in the holes.

CAUSE: Sweet potato weevils *(Cylas formicarius* var. *elegantulus)*. These insects are considered the worst pest of sweet potatoes. These beetles look like large black ants, though their heads are narrow and brown, with a long beaklike snout. In addition to the cosmetic damage they cause, their larvae also feed in roots, making them taste bitter. Quarantine laws usually keep these insects under control; but since they can live on wild morning glories, it's possible that some might find your sweet potato patch.

WHAT TO DO:
• Destroy affected plants.
• Keep morning glories out of the garden.
• Plant certified weevil-free slips.

Sweet Potato Diseases

PROBLEM: Leaves look pale and wilt. Older leaves turn yellow and fall, leaving puckered leaves at stem tips.

CAUSE: Fusarium wilt, also called root rot (*Fusarium oxysporum* f. *batatas*). This disease is caused by one or more fungi that live in soil and cause many of the plants' roots to rot. The disease also clogs sweet potato stems so that moisture and nutrients cannot reach the leaves. If you cut an affected stem and peel the skin from it, you will see a dark, discolored vein inside. This soilborne disease can persist for ten years, even when sweet potatoes are not grown.

WHAT TO DO:
• Destroy infected plants.
• Improve soil drainage.
• Plant resistant varieties, including 'Jewell'.

PROBLEM: Sweet potato tubers have hard, sunken spots on them that are dark brown, greenish black, or black.

CAUSE: Black rot (*Ceratocystis fimbriata*). Besides making sweet potatoes look bad, the fungal disease black rot causes them to lose their flavor and taste bitter. Over time the spots enlarge, and the discoloration spreads into the flesh beneath the spots, sometimes all the way to the center of the root. Sometimes sweet potatoes that look fine when you dig them develop these spots after they are stored. This fungal disease can persist in soil for years.

WHAT TO DO:
• Plant only certified disease-free slips.

PROBLEM: Plants grow slowly and wilt. Galls are on thin roots. Pits, corky patches, and cracks are on large roots.

CAUSE: Root-knot nematodes (*Meloidogyne* spp.). These microscopic worms that cause diseaselike symptoms live in the soil and are most common in sandy soils and warm climates, where the soil seldom freezes in winter. Root-knot nematodes are most active when temperatures are warm, which also happens to be the best condition for growing sweet potatoes. If you cut an infected sweet potato tuber into thin slices ⅛ inch thick, you may see very thin, brownish cavities that penetrate about ½ inch into the root. With the help of a magnifying glass, you can see the pearly white, wormy nematodes within these cavities.

WHAT TO DO:
• Solarize the soil. Clear plastic sheeting placed over bare soil for three to four weeks uses the sun's energy to heat the soil enough to kill most pests and weed seeds in the top few inches of soil. After removing the plastic, plant crops as usual.
• Incorporate chitinous soil amendments made from the shells of shellfish. As the shells break down, they create conditions that encourage beneficial soil organisms.
• Rotate crops. Simply avoid growing a crop in the same spot each year.

PROBLEM: Skins of tubers have rusty brown or blue-black circular spots and blotches.

CAUSE: Scurf (*Monilochaetes infuscans*). This fungal disease mars the beauty of sweet potato tubers but does not affect their flavor. Tubers with scurf often shrink and crack in storage, so eat them within two months after harvesting. Scurf can live in soil for more than two years and can be carried on slips.

WHAT TO DO:
• Rotate crops. Simply avoid growing a crop in the same spot each year.
• Buy certified disease-free slips, or grow your own from roots that show no signs of scurf.

Swiss Chard

(Beta vulgaris, Cicla group)

 Swiss Chard Pests

PROBLEM: Swiss chard leaves have tan, meandering trails on them, but the marks do not go all the way through.

CAUSE: Spinach leafminers (*Pegomya hyoscyami*). These pests are the larvae of $\frac{1}{10}$-inch-long, black or black-and-yellow flies. The flies lay small clusters of white eggs on backs of leaves, and the eggs hatch into tiny maggots. The pale green maggots feed inside swiss chard but leave the outermost layer of leaf tissue intact. After feeding inside the leaves for one to three weeks, the $\frac{1}{4}$-inch-long maggots drop to the soil and pupate into adults. While the miners are feeding, they can move from leaf to leaf but rarely move from one plant to another. The flies lay eggs around chard plants, and the larvae bore into the leaves to feed.

WHAT TO DO:
• Pick off and dispose of affected leaves.
• Use floating row covers to exclude feeding insects. Cover the plants with these synthetic, spunbonded fabrics, and bury the edges of the row cover in the soil.

PROBLEM: Leaves have small, dark spots in them, and the areas near the spots are curled and deformed.

CAUSE: Tarnished plant bugs (*Lygus lineolaris*). These pests are $\frac{1}{4}$-inch-long, oval insects. They are mostly brown, with yellow, black, and white markings. At the tail end, they have a bright triangle of yellow. When disturbed, they quickly run away and hide among Swiss chard leaves. You won't see eggs, because the adult beetles insert their eggs into the plant stems or leaves. These bugs suck sap from Swiss chard leaves.

WHAT TO DO:
• Handpick.
• Use floating row covers to exclude feeding insects. Cover the plants with these synthetic, spunbonded fabrics, and bury the edges of the row cover in the soil.

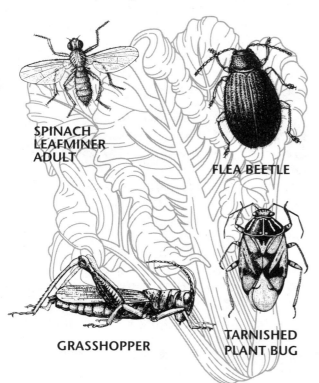

SPINACH LEAFMINER ADULT

FLEA BEETLE

GRASSHOPPER

TARNISHED PLANT BUG

PROBLEM: The leaves of your Swiss chard plants have many small holes in them, especially the outer leaves.

CAUSE: Flea beetles (Family Chrysomelidae). These beetles are common pests of leafy greens. If you approach the plants quietly, you may see a number of very small, greenish black beetles, less than ¼ inch long, feeding on the leaves. They hop away when disturbed. Their feeding seldom kills plants, but the holes they make in leaves may become entry points for diseases.

WHAT TO DO:
• Use insecticidal soap, following directions.
• Apply diatomaceous earth (DE) to the plants. This abrasive dust is made of fossilized shells called diatoms that penetrate the pests' skin as they crawl over DE. Wear a dust mask, and apply DE when plants are wet with dew.
• Grow trap crops. Watch your garden to see what plants the flea beetles favor. Plant some of these plants some distance from your Swiss chard to lure the beetles away. Pull up and destroy infested trap plants.
• Use floating row covers to exclude feeding insects. Cover the plants with these synthetic, spunbonded fabrics, and bury the edges of the row cover in the soil.

PROBLEM: Quite suddenly, in mid- and late summer, large holes appear in leaves, which can be eaten to the veins.

CAUSE: Grasshoppers (Order Orthoptera). Several common species of grasshoppers like to eat Swiss chard. Adults are brown, yellow, or green, 1- to 2-inch-long, winged insects with enlarged hind legs for jumping. The females lay eggs in burrows in the soil in late summer. The eggs overwinter and hatch into small grasshoppers the following spring.

WHAT TO DO:
• Handpick.
• Encourage grasshopper-eating natural enemies, such as birds, to visit the garden.
• Till the soil in autumn to expose eggs to fatal freezing temperatures.

• Attract beneficial insects by planting small-flowered nectar plants, including yarrow, dill, and Queen-Anne's-lace.
• Apply beneficial nematodes (*Steinernema carpocapsae* and *Heterorhabditis heliothidis*), which you can purchase from mail-order suppliers. Live nematodes are shipped suspended in gels or sponges.
• Use floating row covers to exclude feeding insects. Cover the plants with these synthetic, spunbonded fabrics, and bury the edges of the row cover in the soil.

 Swiss Chard Diseases

PROBLEM: Leaves develop small, circular spots with reddish purple edges. The middles of spots turn gray.

CAUSE: Cercospora leaf spot (*Cercospora beticola*). This fungal disease causes the center of the leaf spots it creates to drop out, leaving small holes in leaves. In hot humid weather, the spots may spread rapidly and weaken the plants so much that they die. The disease carries over from year to year in dead plant tissue.

WHAT TO DO:
• Pick off and dispose of spotted leaves.
• Rotate crops. Simply avoid growing a crop in the same spot each year.
• Space plants widely to encourage air circulation.

PROBLEM: You notice that the main stems on leaves are cracked open or that the ribs of inner leaves rotted.

CAUSE: Heart rot. This nutrient deficiency is caused by a shortage of boron in the soil.

WHAT TO DO:
• Amend the soil with compost.
• Drench soil around plants with seaweed solution twice weekly while the crop is growing.

Tomato

(Lycopersicon esculentum)

Tomato Pests

PROBLEM: The leaves of tomatoes display dozens or hundreds of little holes and small, bronze or black beetles.

CAUSE: Flea beetles (Family Chrysomelidae). Flea beetles frequently visit tomatoes but usually do not severely damage them. The very small, 1/10-inch-long, bronze, brown, or black beetles feed on either side of the leaves, but they quickly jump away when you approach the plants and they are disturbed. The beetles spread disease as they feed, moving between tomato plants or back and forth between potatoes and tomatoes. Flea beetle populations tend to decrease as the growing season progresses.

WHAT TO DO:
• Grow vegetable traps. Plant radishes, which are a favorite food of flea beetles, some distance from your tomatoes. When the radish plants are infested with these pests, pull them up and dispose of them.
• Use floating row covers to exclude feeding insects, such as flea beetles. Cover the plants with these synthetic, spunbonded fabrics, and bury the edges of the row cover in the soil.

PROBLEM: Anytime from early summer on, you notice some leaves missing from near the center of plants.

CAUSE: Tomato hornworms (*Manduca quinquemaculata*). These caterpillars are the larvae of the large hummingbird moth. The moths have fuzzy, orange abdomens with narrow wings and a wingspan of 4 to 5 inches. The moths scatter their eggs about tomato plants, and the larvae hatch into caterpillars that feed on tomato leaves.

A sign of trouble is a trail of dark green caterpillar excrement, called frass, that these pests leave behind them on your tomato leaves. This trail should lead you to fat, green caterpillars between 1 and 4 inches long, with eight diagonal white stripes on their sides. They also have a fleshy, black "horn" on their tail ends. When they're not eating

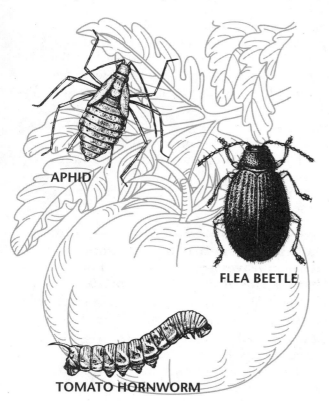

APHID

FLEA BEETLE

TOMATO HORNWORM

tomato leaves, you can often find these caterpillars clinging to plant stems.

Sometimes you may encounter tomato hornworms with a number of white cylinders attached to their backs. These are cocoons of braconid wasps, an important beneficial-insect predator in the garden. When you find these parasitized caterpillars, leave them in the garden so that the beneficial wasps can complete their life cycle.

WHAT TO DO:
• Handpick.
• Apply BTK. "BT" stands for *Bacillus thuringiensis*, an insect-stomach poison that kills caterpillars without harming beneficial insects. *B.t.* var. *kurstaki* (BTK) kills tomato hornworms.
• Attract beneficial insects, such as the braconid wasp, by planting small-flowered nectar plants, such as carrots, dill, and Queen-Anne's-lace.

PROBLEM: New leaves fold, and the tips bend over and wilt. Small, green, pear-shaped insects cling to leaves.

CAUSE: Aphids (Family Aphididae). These soft-bodied, pear-shaped insects, ranging in color from pale tan to light green to nearly black, are $\frac{1}{16}$ to $\frac{3}{8}$ inch long. Aphids damage leaves and stems by sucking plant juices. Their sticky secretions, called honeydew, can encourage the growth of mold and attract ants, which eat the honeydew. Aphids can transfer plant viruses as they feed.

WHAT TO DO:
• Wash aphids off plants with a strong stream of water.
• Use insecticidal soap, following label directions.
• Encourage beneficial insects, like lady beetles and lacewings, by planting small-flowered nectar plants, including yarrow, dill, and Queen-Anne's-lace; give the beneficials time to bring aphids under control.

PROBLEM: In early summer, 1-inch-long, slender, dark beetles swarm over tomato plants and eat the leaves.

CAUSE: Blister beetles (Family Meloidae). They are so named because their bodies contain an oil that can cause a blister if you touch a crushed beetle with your skin. The beetles have long abdomens with striped edges along their wing covers and a lighter-colored head that turns around. If you shake the tomato plant, many beetles drop to the ground and play dead, and then in a while they will begin crawling back up the plants. The adults lay their eggs in midsummer in grasshopper egg burrows, where blister beetle larvae eat grasshopper eggs. Adult beetles feed on plants for less than six weeks in summer.

WHAT TO DO:
• Handpick with gloved hands. Collect and dispose of beetles.
• Shake beetles from plants and gather with a hand-held vacuum.
• Use floating row covers to exclude feeding insects, such as blister beetles. Cover the plants with these synthetic, spunbonded fabrics, and bury the edges of the row cover in the soil.

PROBLEM: In mid- to late summer, in hot, dry weather, tomato leaves look pale and bleached despite watering.

CAUSE: Spider mites (Family Tetranychidae). These are very tiny pests, at only $\frac{1}{60}$ inch long. They can feed on a number of different plants, but they often pick tomatoes as a seasonal favorite. Spider mites feed by sucking juices from plant leaves, and they spin webbing that trails behind them as they move. The webbing helps to protect spider mite eggs and newly hatched young that are scattered about the leaves. You may see tiny pinpricks in the yellowing leaves, faint webbing on backs of leaves, and possibly a number of barely visible specks among the webs.

WHAT TO DO:
• Dislodge spider mites with a strong stream of water.
• Use insecticidal soap. Begin treatment early, at the pinprick stage. By the time the webs appear, it may be too late to save some plants. Spray both sides of leaves.

PROBLEM: Small, circular holes appear in tomato fruits, often at the top end near where the stems are attached.

CAUSE: Tomato fruitworms, also called corn earworms (*Helicoverpa zea*). This species is difficult to accurately identify because other caterpillars also make holes in tomato fruits.

Tomato fruitworms are the larvae of grayish brown moths. Adult moths lay over a thousand eggs, one at a time. These caterpillars may be light green, pink, brown, or nearly black. They always have yellow heads, dark legs, and lengthwise, light and dark strips running along their bodies. They often go from one fruit to another, leaving a shallow hole in each one. If you look inside the hole, you may find nothing there. As the tomato begins to ripen and the tissue softens, the worm hole often begins to rot.

WHAT TO DO:
• Handpick.
• Apply BTK. "BT" stands for *Bacillus thuringiensis*, an insect-stomach poison that kills caterpillars without harming beneficial insects. *B.t.* var. *kurstaki* (BTK) kills tomato fruitworms.

Tomato Diseases

PROBLEM: Plants wilt on hot days. New growth is slow, stems are short, leaves are small. Plants lack vigor.

CAUSE: Root-knot nematodes (*Meloidogyne* spp.). These pests, which are microscopic worms, live in the soil and parasitize plant roots. Normal tomato roots are thin and hairy looking and have no knobs or swellings on them. If you dig up a plant with root-knot nematodes, you will see knotty growths on the tomato plant roots. Root-knot nematodes are most common in warm-winter climates where the ground seldom freezes. If the problem is not severe and plants are given plenty of water, they may produce a reasonable crop of tomatos despite the nematodes.

WHAT TO DO:
• Plant resistant varieties with a capital N after the variety name.
• Solarize the soil. Clear plastic sheeting placed over bare soil for three to four weeks uses the sun's energy to heat the soil enough to kill most pests and weed seeds in the top few inches of soil. After removing the plastic, plant crops as usual.
• Rotate crops. Simply avoid growing tomatoes in the same spot each year.
• Add chitin to the soil. This soil additive is made from the shells of shellfish. Chitin provides nitrogen and potassium as it breaks down, creating conditions that encourage the beneficial soil organisms that attack soil nematodes.

PROBLEM: In mid- to late summer in cool climates, older leaves develop large, yellow patches that turn tan.

CAUSE: Verticillium wilt (*Verticillium* spp.). Verticillium wilt can build up to damaging levels in most parts of the country, but it rarely occurs in very hot climates. The fungal disease enters tomatoes through the roots and spreads upward through the plant. The affected parts of the leaves dry up, though sections of the leaves may remain green. Meanwhile, the tips of new growth wilt noticeably on hot days, and nearby green leaves may wilt slightly, with leaf tips curling upward. The old leaves eventually shrivel and drop as the disease spreads upward through the plant.

If you cut off a thick stem, the circle of tissue just inside the stem will be a dark, gray-green color. Once plants are infected, they cannot recover; but you can eat any tomatoes the plants manage to produce before they die.

WHAT TO DO:
• Pull up and dispose of infected plants.
• Plant resistant varieties that have a capital V after their variety name.
• Space plants widely to allow for adequate air circulation.
• Grow plants in containers filled with sterilized soil.

PROBLEM: Lower leaves turn buttery yellow and begin to droop. The yellowing spreads, and plants struggle.
CAUSE: Fusarium wilt, also called root rot *(Fusarium oxysporum* f. *lycopersici)*. This disease is caused by one or more fungi that live in soil and cause many of the plants' roots to rot. When the plants have loaded up with green fruits that are just beginning to ripen, the yellowing spreads upward through the plant. By the time the first fruits ripen, the plant is on the brink of death. You can eat tomatoes from infected plants.

WHAT TO DO:
• Destroy infected plants.
• Plant resistant varieties with a capital F after the variety name.

• Grow disease-free plants in well drained, raised beds in a new location or in containers of sterile soil mix.

PROBLEM: Just as plants begin to produce well, older leaves develop brown spots with concentric circles in them.
CAUSE: Early blight *(Alternaria solani)*. This fungal disease is the most common cause of leaf spots in tomatoes. The fungus spreads only when leaf surfaces are wet. It thrives on tomato varieties with curled leaves, because they are slow to dry off after rains. On plants where many leaves are affected, there are usually dark brown elliptical spots on stems, too. The older leaves shrivel to dark brown but remain attached to the stems. Frequently, all of the leaves on the lowest third of a plant will wither, while new growth shows no leaf spots at all. Healthy, vigorous plants continue to produce good crops after they are infected with this fungus.

WHAT TO DO:
• Mulch.
• Grow varieties suited to your climate.

PROBLEM: Whole tomato plants wilt. A plant may wilt slightly for a few days and then wilt badly and quickly die.
CAUSE: Bacterial wilt *(Pseudomonas solanacearum)*. This bacterial disease is also called southern bacterial wilt because it is most common in a broad band from Maryland to Texas. If you cut open the main stem, the middle of the stem will look brown and may show hollow cracks. Bacterial wilt can persist in soil for years and can be brought into a garden by infected tomato seedlings.

WHAT TO DO:
• Pick and destroy infected leaves.
• Amend the soil with organic compost or

sulfur, as needed, to make it acidic (from 5.5 to 6.7 pH).

• Space plants widely to encourage air circulation.

• Rotate crops. Simply avoid growing a crop in the same spot each year. Three-year rotations are recommended.

PROBLEM: During periods of cool, wet weather, tomato leaves develop large, greasy-looking, grayish brown patches.

CAUSE: Late blight (*Phytophthora infestans*). This disease is uncommon in tomatoes, but it can sometimes develop into local epidemics. Late blight is caused by the same fungus that causes similar symptoms in potatoes, and it can spread to tomatoes from infected potatoes. Around the edges of the infected leaf patches and underneath them on the opposite sides of the leaves, you can often also see patches of downy white mold.

WHAT TO DO:

• Promptly pull up and dispose of affected plants.

• Rotate plants. Simply avoid growing a crop in the same spot each year.

PROBLEM: Leaves have gray spots. The spots have dark gray margins, and the tissue between spots is yellow.

CAUSE: Septoria leaf spot. (*Septoria lycopersici*). This fungal disease affects only tomatoes. A related fungal disease, commonly called gray leaf spot, also makes small spots on tomato leaves, but the spots are more angular in shape.

WHAT TO DO:

• Clip off and dispose of affected leaves.

• Avoid wetting leaves when you water tomato plants.

PROBLEM: New leaves are stiff and crinkled, with an unusual mottled pattern in dark green, tan, and yellow.

CAUSE: Tobacco mosaic virus. This is one of the most widespread viral diseases that affects tomatoes. This virus spreads through the sap-sucking activities of insects feeding on tomato plants. It can also be spread by gardeners who smoke tobacco (which may host the virus) and then touch tomato plants. The disease slows down the new growth of tomatoes. If infected plants do produce tomatoes, they usually have brown marks on the skins and on tissue inside the fruits.

WHAT TO DO:

• Pull and dispose of severely affected tomato plants.

• Plant resistant varieties with a capital T after the variety name. Many resistant varieties are available.

PROBLEM: Tomatoes left to ripen on the vine develop soft spots that become sunken and wet. Fruits rot on the vine.

CAUSE: Anthracnose (*Colletotrichum* spp.). This fungal disease thrives in cool, rainy weather. It is spread by wind or rain. This is most likely to happen if tomatoes have first been damaged by insects or if they are allowed to touch the ground. The spots that develop on the fruits expand and increase in number until the fruit rots while still attached to the plant stem, without turning brown or black. Anthracnose carries over from season to season in soil or on infected seeds.

WHAT TO DO:

• Pick tomatoes promptly.

• Stake and mulch plants.

• Space plants for good air circulation.

• Compost plant debris.

• Plant healthy seeds.

Other Problems

PROBLEM: The bottoms of green tomato fruits have dark brown to black spots.

CAUSE: Blossom-end rot (soil calcium deficiency). This is a disorder that develops when the plants are temporarily unable to meet the calcium demands made on them by the developing fruits. Blossom-end rot occurs when plants grow in very wet or very dry soil.

It can also be brought on by rapid plant growth due to warm weather or the sudden availability of nitrogen in the soil. The spots that develop on the fruits may be less than ½ inch across, or so large that they cover the entire bottom of the fruits. Frequently all the fruits in a cluster have these spots. Fruit type is a factor, too. Small-fruited cherry tomatoes seldom have blossom-end rot problems, whereas the elongated, paste-type tomatoes often do. Most round slicing tomatoes fall somewhere in between.

WHAT TO DO:
• Mulch plants.
• Drench the soil they grow in with seaweed solution weekly while fruits are forming.
• Grow a variety of fruit types.

PROBLEM: Plants are huge and leafy and produce numerous yellow flowers, but the flowers shrivel or drop.

CAUSE: Hot weather. During flowering and fruit set, hot temperatures make it very difficult for the flowers to complete the pollination process. Indeterminate tomato varieties (those that set fruit all season) continue to flower for a long time, and eventually weather conditions will moderate enough to promote good fruit set.

WHAT TO DO:
• Have patience.
• Plant early in hot climates.

• Grow heat-resistant varieties, such as 'Heatwave', 'Solar Set', and most cherry-type tomatoes.

PROBLEM: Tomato fruits that have been developing normally suddenly crack open just as they begin to ripen.

CAUSE: Hot, rainy weather. Tomatoes expand so quickly in hot, rainy weather that their skin bursts. Some varieties resist cracking better than others, but all can develop this problem if very wet weather follows a prolonged dry spell. Cracked fruits can be eaten if harvested promptly. If you wait too long to pick them, fungi and insects will quickly move in.

WHAT TO DO:
• Mulch.
• Prune roots slightly with a shovel when a soaking rain is predicted.
• Plant several types of tomatoes.

OCCASIONAL PROBLEMS: Several of the pests that bother potatoes and peppers can become a problem for tomatoes because all are members of the same family (Family Solanaceae). The problems listed above are the most common ones for tomatoes. If you see problems you cannot identify, refer to the following pests and diseases listed elsewhere in this book: Slugs (Order Stylommatophora), listed under "Potato" on page 60. Colorado potato beetles (*Leptinotarsa decemlineata*), listed under "Potato." Cutworms (Family Noctuidae), listed under "Pepper" on page 56. Damping-off (caused by several species of fungi), listed under "Pepper." Southern blight (*Sclerotium rolfsii*), listed under "Pepper." Bacterial spot (*Xanthomonas vesicatoria*), listed under "Pepper." Sunscald, listed under "Pepper."

Turnip (*Brassica rapa*, Rapifera group)

Turnip Pests

PROBLEM: Young plants suddenly collapse, wilt, and die. Older plants grow slowly and may wilt on hot days.

CAUSE: Cabbage maggots (*Delia radicum*). These pests are the larvae of ¼-inch-long, gray flies that look like houseflies. When you pull up a plant, you may see that the roots have brown grooves or tunnels in them. You may also find the tiny, white, ¼-inch-long maggots inside the tunnels. Cabbage maggots are occasional pests of turnips. They feed on mature plants, but they cause the most damage to young plants by feeding on their roots and the stem in the soil just below ground level. Usually only a few plants in a bed or row are affected, because the maggots feed close to where they hatch and do not move from plant to plant.

WHAT TO DO:
• Destroy plant debris.
• Apply beneficial nematodes (*Steinernema carpocapsae* and *Heterorhabditis heliothidis*), which you can purchase from mail-order suppliers. Live nematodes are shipped suspended in gels or sponges.
• Apply diatomaceous earth (DE) to the soil. This abrasive dust is made of fossilized shells called diatoms that penetrate the pests' skin.
• Use floating row covers to exclude insect pests. Cover the plants with these synthetic, spunbonded fabrics, and bury the edges of the row cover in the soil.
• Attract beneficial insects, like lady beetles and tiny wasps, by planting small-flowered nectar plants, including yarrow and dill.

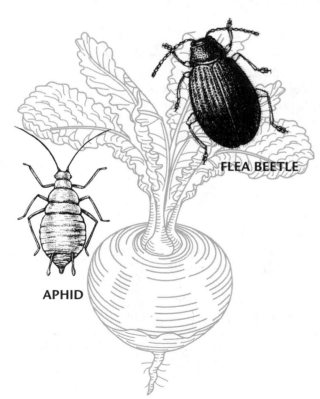

FLEA BEETLE

APHID

PROBLEM: Leaves of young plants have tiny holes with yellow edges. You see bronze, brown, or black beetles.

CAUSE: Flea beetles (Family Chrysomelidae). These beetles are eager eaters of turnip leaves, but they do not usually cause serious damage. The holes, however, may become entry points for diseases. The ¹/₁₀-inch-long, bronze, brown, or black beetles feed on either side of the leaves. Approach quietly to see them, because the little beetles jump away when they are disturbed.

WHAT TO DO:
• Gather beetles with a hand-held, rechargeable vacuum.
• Use insecticidal soap.
• Use floating row covers to exclude feeding insect pests. Cover the plants with these synthetic, spunbonded fabrics, and bury the edges of the row cover in the soil.

PROBLEM: New leaves of turnip plants are pale and curled. Small, pear-shaped insects cling to the leaves.

CAUSE: Aphids (Family Aphididae). These soft-bodied, green insects are $\frac{1}{16}$ to $\frac{3}{8}$ inch long. Aphids damage leaves and stems by sucking plant juices. Their sticky secretions, called honeydew, can encourage the growth of mold, and they can transfer plant viruses as they feed. You will usually see a few aphids on turnip leaves. They become a problem only when they cluster together on the leaves and feed in large numbers.

WHAT TO DO:
• Wash aphids off plants with a strong stream of water.
• Use insecticidal soap, following label directions.
• Snap off and dispose of leaves that host most of the aphids.
• Attract beneficial insects, like lady beetles and lacewings, by planting small-flowered nectar plants, including yarrow, dill, and Queen-Anne's-lace. Give the beneficials time to bring aphids under control.

 Turnip Diseases

PROBLEM: Leaves develop powdery, white patches and eventually shrivel and drop. New growth slows down.

CAUSE: Powdery mildew (*Erysiphe polygoni*). This fungal disease sometimes infects the leaves of turnips but usually not until the plants are old enough to have developed a good root system.

WHAT TO DO:
• Tolerate light damage.
• Remove infected leaves. If only a few leaves show mildew, snip them off to stop the spread of the disease.
• Space plants widely to encourage air circulation.
• Rotate crops. Simply avoid growing a crop in the same spot each year.

 Other Problems

PROBLEM: In spite of good growing conditions, the turnip roots you harvest are small, tough, and bitter.

CAUSE: Hot weather or poor growing conditions. If a hot spell or a drought hits while turnip roots are growing and maturing, they can take on a bitter taste. The best-tasting turnips are those that mature in cool weather and go through at least one light frost just before you harvest them.

WHAT TO DO:
• Time planting for late enough in the season that the turnips mature in cool autumn weather.

OCCASIONAL PROBLEMS: Several of the pests that bother cabbage and broccoli can become a problem for turnips because all three are members of the cabbage family (Family Cruciferae). The problems listed above are the most common ones for turnips. If you see problems that you cannot identify, refer to the following pests and diseases listed elsewhere in this book: Imported cabbageworms (*Artogeia rapae*), listed under "Cabbage" on page 14. Clubroot (*Plasmodiophora brassicae*), listed under "Broccoli" on page 10.

Watermelon

(*Citrullus lanatus*)

 ## Watermelon Pests

PROBLEM: Watermelon vines are healthy, but little chunks are missing from rinds of ripening melons.

CAUSE: Birds. These flying watermelon eaters thump the watermelons to see when they're ripe, just as gardeners do. As the melons get closer to perfection, the peck marks in the melons' skins will become deeper and deeper until the birds finally hit the sweet, juicy flesh.

SPOTTED CUCUMBER BEETLE

BIRD

WHAT TO DO:
• Cover watermelons with newspapers, or festoon them with fluttering metallic tape to scare birds away from your watermelon patch.

PROBLEM: Small, ragged-looking spots appear in leaves, and you see yellow beetles with black spots on their backs.

CAUSE: Spotted cucumber beetles (*Diabrotica undecimpunctata* var. *howardi*). Like striped cucumber beetles, spotted cucumber beetles can transmit bacterial wilt (*Pseudomonas solanacearum*) and other plant viruses as they feed.

WHAT TO DO:
• Handpick.
• Use floating row covers to exclude feeding insects, such as spotted cucumber beetles. Cover the plants with these synthetic, spun-bonded fabrics, and bury the edges of the row cover in the soil.
• Plant resistant varieties, such as 'Crimson Sweet' and 'Sweet Princess'.

 ## Watermelon Diseases

PROBLEM: Dark-colored spots up to ½ inch in diameter develop on leaf veins and stems.

CAUSE: Anthracnose (*Colletotrichum lagenarium*). The leaves of affected watermelon vines are usually free of spots; but the leaf veins on the backs of the lowest, oldest leaves darken, and the stems may darken. This fungal disease thrives in cool, rainy weather and is spread by wind or rain. The disease carries over from season to season in soil or on seeds.

WHAT TO DO:
• Space plants widely for good air circulation.
• Compost plant debris.
• Plant healthy seeds.
• If this disease has been a problem in past seasons, don't save seed from the potentially infected plants; instead, buy and plant fresh seed each season.

PROBLEM: Leaves begin to yellow and die. You find pale brown or gray spots on the leaves and stems.

CAUSE: Gummy stem blight (*Didymella bryoniae*). This is a fungal disease that can persist from year to year on plant debris left in the garden. It is also carried by infected seeds. As it progresses, some spots turn into streaks of gooey tissue. If the diseased vines produce fruits, fruits may have sunken, dark spots.

WHAT TO DO:
• Pull up and compost plant residue.
• Plant healthy seeds.
• Don't save seed if this disease has been a problem; instead, buy and plant fresh seed.
• Rotate crops. Simply avoid growing a crop in the same spot each year.

PROBLEM: Leaves develop small, brown spots; the area around the spots may yellow. Leaves wither and die.

CAUSE: Cercospora leaf spot (*Cercospora citrullina*) This fungal disease is common in warm climates and can spread quickly in warm, wet weather. It causes unsightly and falling leaves, but it will not kill plants.

WHAT TO DO:
• Pull up and compost plant debris.
• Rotate crops. Simply avoid planting a crop in the same spot two years in a row.

PROBLEM: The fruits of your watermelons begin to develop brown, sunken spots before you harvest them.

CAUSE: Watermelon fruit blotch. This disease is caused by bacteria that travel into the garden on infected seeds and in splashing water. If left unchecked, watermelon fruit blotch can wipe out an entire watermelon patch.

WHAT TO DO:
• Water the base of plants.
• Apply copper spray. Copper protects plants from a wide range of disease organisms. Complete coverage is important for the best protection. Use copper as a last resort, since it is a toxic irritant and persists indefinitely in soil. To avoid damaging watermelon leaves, mix copper spray to the lightest dilution, and apply when temperatures are 80°F or below.

 Other Problems

PROBLEM: When you cut a watermelon, some of the flesh is sweet and colorful, but some is pale and bland.

CAUSE: Uneven ripening. The small amount of vine damage that occurs during weeding is sometimes enough to set plant growth back and cause uneven ripening.

WHAT TO DO:
• Minimize working among melons while they are growing, to avoid damaging them.

OCCASIONAL PROBLEMS: Several of the pests and diseases that infect cucumbers and squash can become a problem for watermelons, for all of these plants are members of the same plant family (Family Cucurbitaceae). The problems listed above are the most common. If you see problems you cannot identify, refer to these entries: "Cucumber" on page 30, "Summer Squash" on page 72, and "Winter Squash and Pumpkin" on page 88.

Winter Squash and Pumpkin

(*Cucurbita maxima,* buttercup, hubbard), (*C. mixta,* cushaw), (*C. moschata,* butternut), and (*C. pepo* var. *pepo,* pumpkin)

 Winter Squash and Pumpkin Pests

PROBLEM: Seedlings show wilting and puckering of immature leaves. Plants are slow to develop true leaves.

CAUSE: Squash bugs (*Anasa tristis*). These ⅝-inch-long, brownish bugs have orange-speckled flat backs shaped like shields. They lay shiny eggs on the backs of leaves. The eggs start out yellow and turn to red before hatching into gray, powdery-looking nymphs. Both adults and nymphs suck plant juices from squash and pumpkin seedlings, either by attacking the stem or by feeding on the backs of the seedling leaves.

WHAT TO DO:
• Cover the plants with floating row covers to exclude insects. Bury the edges in the soil.
• Handpick.

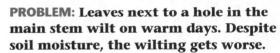

PROBLEM: Leaves next to a hole in the main stem wilt on warm days. Despite soil moisture, the wilting gets worse.

CAUSE: Squash vine borers (*Melittia cucurbitae*). These caterpillars are the larvae of slender moths with wingspans of 1 to 1½ inches. The moths look almost like wasps, with olive brown front wings, clear hind wings, and red-and-black ringed abdomen. The adults lay very small eggs on the largest stems of winter squash and pumpkins. The eggs hatch into plump, white caterpillars, from ½ to 1½ inches long, with dark heads and segmented bodies decorated with faint dark dots along their sides. These caterpillars, called borers, feed on the juicy tissues inside squash and pumpkin stems, then overwinter in the soil.

Winter squash varieties other than butternut types, and pumpkins other than the tan-skinned ones classified as *Cucurbita moschata,* may show the following symptoms:

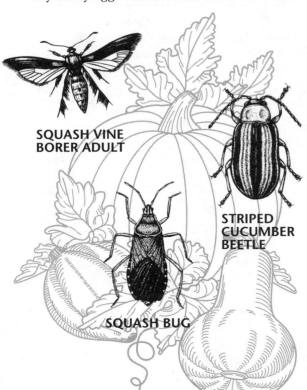

SQUASH VINE BORER ADULT

STRIPED CUCUMBER BEETLE

SQUASH BUG

A few adjoining leaves begin to wilt badly on warm days. Despite ample soil moisture, the wilting gets worse. On the main stem just below where the wilted leaves are attached, you may see one or several small holes in the stem, surrounded by sawdustlike frass (caterpillar excrement). Or, the stem may show a large damaged patch that appears to be rotted almost all the way through. Squash varieties that can develop roots where their stems touch the ground often continue to produce fruit after the main crown of the plant is infested with squash vine borers. Butternut squash has little juicy tissue, so it resists borers. Hubbard squash is extremely susceptible to squash vineborers. Buttercup, acorn, delicata, and spaghetti squashes fall somewhere in between.

WHAT TO DO:
• Wipe down stems with a damp cloth when you suspect eggs are laid.
• Inject damaged stems with beneficial nematodes (*Steinernema carpocapsae* and *Heterorhabditis heliothidis*), which you can purchase from mail-order suppliers. Live nematodes are shipped in gels or sponges.
• Use floating row covers to exclude feeding insects. Cover the plants with these synthetic, spunbonded fabrics, and bury the edges of the row cover in the soil.

PROBLEM: Small, ragged, chewed spots appear in plant leaves, and you see greenish yellow beetles.

CAUSE: Striped cucumber beetles (*Acalymma vittatum*). These ¼- to ⅓-inch-long, yellow or greenish yellow beetles with black stripes down their backs chew on leaves, stems, and roots. Unless the plants are young seedlings, you do not see extensive damage. Cucumber beetles can transmit the bacteria that causes the disease bacterial wilt (*Erwinia tracheiphila*).

WHAT TO DO:
• Handpick.
• Cover the plants with floating row covers to exclude feeding insects. Bury the edges of the row cover in the soil.

PROBLEM: Small, ragged, chewed spots appear in leaves; you see beetles with yellow with black spots.

CAUSE: Spotted cucumber beetles (*Diabrotica undecimpunctata* var. *howardi*). These ¼-inch-long, spotted beetles can transmit bacterial wilt disease (*Pseudomonas solanacearum*) (described under diseases) to butternut squash and some pumpkins. The culprits are white, ¾-inch-long, segmented caterpillars with brown patches on the first and last segments.

WHAT TO DO:
• Use floating row covers to exclude feeding insects. Cover the plants with these synthetic, spunbonded fabrics, and bury the edges of the row cover in the soil.

 **Winter Squash and Pumpkin Diseases**

PROBLEM: Part of a vine suddenly wilts. Wilting becomes severe. Eventually the plant dies.

CAUSE: Bacterial wilt (*Erwinia tracheiphila*). This bacterial disease is spread from plant to plant via feeding cucumber beetles. Once the bacterium gets inside a vine, it multiplies very rapidly no matter what you do. Pruning off wilted parts will have no impact on the disease. These symptoms may appear on buttercup squash and giant pumpkins but rarely on other types of winter squash.

WHAT TO DO:
• Use floating row covers to exclude feeding insects. Cover the plants with these synthetic, spunbonded fabrics, and bury the edges of the row cover in the soil.

PROBLEM: Leaves show white, powdery deposits on both sides. The substance cannot be rubbed off with your finger.

CAUSE: Powdery mildew (*Erysiphe cichoracearum; Sphaerotheca fuligenea*). This fungal disease is usually worse in late summer and tends to occur mostly on older leaves. Powdery mildew weakens plants but usually does not kill them. Unfortunately, infected plants often produce small fruits that lack flavor and do not keep well.

WHAT TO DO:
• Pull up and compost crop residue.

PROBLEM: Circular, discolored spots appear on pumpkin or winter squash fruits. Spots become sunken; flesh rots.

CAUSE: Black rot (*Didymella bryoniae*). This fungal disease affects almost all members of the cucurbit family, but it causes different symptoms on each vegetable. On winter squash and pumpkins, at first the spots are yellow, then brown, and finally black. The spots become deeper as the flesh beneath them darkens, softens, and rots. Pumpkins and winter squash that have black rot are not edible, because other microorganisms usually enter the diseased spots and cause the entire fruit to rot. The fungus that causes black rot can persist from year to year on seed and in dead plant tissues.

WHAT TO DO:
• Plant healthy seed.
• Rotate crops. Simply avoid growing a crop in the same spot each year.

 Other Problems

PROBLEM: Your winter squash or pumpkin plants have a lot of flowers but no fruit.

CAUSE: Male flowers. Squash and pumpkins have both male and female flowers. The male flowers begin opening first, but male flowers produce only pollen and no squash. Female flowers, which appear a week or so after the males start opening, are the fertile ones that develop fruit. You can tell them apart. Female flowers have a fuzzy bulge just under the base of the flower, usually shaped like the squash or pumpkin it will produce. Male flowers have only a slender stem below the base.

WHAT TO DO:
• Have patience. Wait for both male and female flowers to open, and then start looking for the fruits to develop.

PROBLEM: Large pumpkins are flat instead of round or globular, especially those that are lying on their sides.

CAUSE: A weight problem. Many large pumpkins flatten out as they ripen, especially varieties that produce giant fruits.

WHAT TO DO: Grow small-fruited varieties, such as 'Baby Bear', 'Jack Be Little', and 'Sugar Pie'. When thinning fruits, remove those that are lying on their sides.

OCCASIONAL PROBLEMS: Several of the pests and diseases that infect cucumber and melons can be a problem for winter squash and pumpkins because all are members of the same plant family (Family Cucurbitaceae). The problems listed above are the most common ones. If you see problems you cannot identify, refer to the following pests and diseases listed elsewhere in this book: Cutworms (Family Noctuidae), listed under "Cucumber" on page 30. Alternaria blight (*Alternaria cucumerina*), listed under "Melon" on page 46. Angular leaf spot (*Pseudomonas syringae* pv. *lachrymans*), listed under "Cucumber." Mosaic viruses, listed under "Melon."

Herbs

Basil...92
Bay 94
Bee Balm 95
Borage...96
Salad Burnet 97
Calendula, also called
 Pot Marigold...........................98
Caraway 100
Chervil..102
Coriander,
 also called Cilantro 103
Dill...104
Fennel 105
Lavender 106
Lemon Balm................................107
Lovage 108
Sweet Marjoram 109
Mint 110
Oregano......................................111
Parsley...112
Pennyroyal..................................114
Rosemary 115
Rue 118
Sage 119
French Tarragon 120
Thyme...121
Lemon Verbena..........................122

Basil

(Ocimum basilicum)

 Basil Pests

PROBLEM: In mid- to late summer you notice large holes in your basil leaves. All that's left of some are the leaf veins.

CAUSE: Grasshoppers (Order Orthoptera). Adults are brown, yellow, or green, 1- to 2-inch-long, winged insects with long, strong hind legs. Female grasshoppers lay eggs in clusters that look like small globs of rice. The eggs overwinter in burrows in the ground. In the spring, young grasshoppers hatch and begin to feed.

WHAT TO DO:
• Handpick.
• Remove and destroy egg clusters when you work the soil.

PROBLEM: Powdery-white, $\frac{1}{20}$-inch-long flying insects gather on leaf undersides. They fly away when disturbed.

CAUSE: Whiteflies (Family Aleyrodidae). Both the minute, translucent nymphs and the tiny, white, winged adults weaken plants by sucking plant juices. They are most numerous in late summer. They disappear after the first few frosts of autumn.

WHAT TO DO:
• Knock insects off plants with a strong spray of water.
• Use insecticidal soap, following label directions.
• Make yellow sticky traps. To make traps, coat yellow cardboard or painted boards with petroleum jelly or Tanglefoot (a commercial product made for this purpose) and fasten them to stakes near basil plants.
• Attract parasitic wasps and other beneficial insects by planting small-flowered nectar plants, including yarrow and dill.

PROBLEM: Large holes with smooth edges suddenly appear in your basil leaves.

CAUSE: Japanese beetles (*Popillia japonica*). These chunky, blue-green, ½-inch-long beetles, which are most active in midsummer, have voracious appetites for basil leaves.

WHAT TO DO:
• Handpick.
• Use floating rowcovers to exclude flying insects. Cover the plants with these synthetic, spunbonded fabrics, and bury the edges of the row cover in the soil.
• Place beetle-attracting pheromone traps where they will lure beetles *away* from your basil plants.
• Apply milky spore disease to lawn areas to kill Japanese beetle larvae.

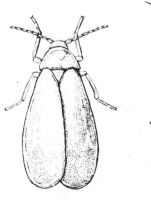 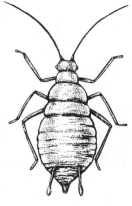

WHITEFLY   **APHID**

PROBLEM: You see a sticky, clear or black substance on basil plants and small, pear-shaped insects.

CAUSE: Aphids (Family Aphididae).These soft-bodied insects are ¹⁄₁₆ to ³⁄₈ inch long. Aphids damage plants by sucking plant juices. They leave behind sticky secretions called honeydew that create an ideal growing condition for mold. Aphids also transfer plant viruses as they feed.

WHAT TO DO:
• Snip off and dispose of infested leaves.
• Knock aphids off plants with a strong blast of water.
• Use insecticidal soap, following label directions.
• Attract beneficial insects, like lady beetles and lacewings, by planting small-flowered nectar plants, such as scabiosa, dill, and yarrow.

 Basil Diseases

PROBLEM: Your basil seeds sprouted, but soon after, many seedlings turned dark at the soil line, fell over, and died.

CAUSE: Damping-off. Several species of fungi cause this common seedling disease. Stem injuries are likely sites of infection; but because the fungi live in soil, roots are also vulnerable. Seedlings that germinate in the garden resist damping-off, and seedlings started indoors will develop resistance after they grow a few adult leaves.

WHAT TO DO:
• Use sterile seed-starting mix.
• Start seeds in clean containers.
• Improve air circulation around seedlings.
• Apply bottom heat to indoor seedlings. Use a heat mat made for this purpose, or set potted seedlings on top of the refrigerator.
• Direct-sow basil seeds in the garden only after the soil warms.

PROBLEM: You notice irregular yellow spots on basil leaves. The plants wilt suddenly. Watering does not help.

CAUSE: Fusarium wilt, also called root rot (*Fusarium* spp.). Several soil-dwelling fungi cause this disease. Fusarium wilt causes the roots of infected basil plants to rot.

WHAT TO DO:
• Remove and destroy infected plants.
• Rotate crops. Simply avoid growing basil in the same spot each year. Three-year rotations are recommended.

 Other Problems

PROBLEM: After setting healthy basil seedlings outside in spring, you notice that they don't put out new growth.

CAUSE: Cool temperatures or lack of sun. When the weather is unseasonably cool or cloudy, basil plants go into a temporary sulk.

WHAT TO DO:
• Set basil out after the last frost date, so that the soil and surrounding air have a chance to warm up before planting.
• Wait out bad weather. When the sun comes out, your basil will once again grow with vigor.
• Mulch only after the soil warms.

PROBLEM: Apparently healthy basil dies overnight. Surviving plants have limp, blackened leaves.

CAUSE: Frostbite. The thin leaves of basil plants are so tender that they die when exposed to the slightest touch of frost, and the entire plants are soon to follow.

WHAT TO DO:
• When frost threatens, cover plants with the synthetic, spunbonded fabrics called floating row covers, and bury the edges of the covering in the soil.

Bay

(Laurus nobilis)

Bay Pests

PROBLEM: In spite of good growing conditions, your bay plants fail to grow vigorously. You see ants on them.

CAUSE: Scale (Order Homoptera). These 1/10-inch-long insects look more like oval, waxy, tan, gray, or brown bumps than insects. Their shape and coloring make them blend in with the bark of the bay tree branches that they attach themselves to. Both the stationary adults and their similarly sized, fuzzy, mobile nymphs suck plant juices. Adult scale produce sticky honeydew that attracts ants and mildew.

WHAT TO DO:
• Scrape scale off branches with a plastic scouring pad.
• Attract beneficial insects, such as parasitic wasps, to your herb garden by growing small-flowered nectar plants, such as scabiosa, yarrow, dill, and Queen-Anne's-lace.

Bay Diseases

As long as they have basic, good growing conditions, including temperatures above freezing and well-drained soil, bay trees are usually disease-free.

Other Problems

PROBLEM: The ordinarily stiff, leathery leaves of your bay plants suddenly droop, and the sides of the leaves curl.

CAUSE: Drought stress. Bay plants need enough moisture to prevent them from wilting. Those grown in containers of soil are likely to dry out rapidly in hot, sunny sites and are especially susceptible to drought.

WHAT TO DO:
• Water generously until the plants recover. Then water regularly as needed to keep bay plants from wilting.

PROBLEM: Despite ideal growing conditions, the bay seeds you planted failed to germinate.

CAUSE: The seeds of bay plants are inherently difficult to germinate. For most gardeners, bay plants are almost impossible to start from seeds.

WHAT TO DO:
• Buy well-rooted, young plants.

BLACK SCALE

Bee Balm

(Monarda didyma; M. citriodora; M. fistulosa)

 Bee Balm Pests

PROBLEM: Large holes appear in bee balm leaves. Some young plants disappear overnight, yet you see no insects.

CAUSES: Slugs and snails (Order Stylommatophora). These common garden pests are related to clams and mussels. The gray or brown pests may be from ¼ inch to 4 inches long, and they leave slime trails everywhere they go. Slugs and snails eat plants from dusk to dawn, and they hide in dark places near the soil during the day.

WHAT TO DO:
• Make copper barriers. Edge plantings with a strip of copper, which hits these slimy pests with an electrical shock upon contact.
• Make beer traps from recycled cans sunk to the brim in soil and filled with yeasty beer.
• Destroy their egg clusters. Look under rocks or other hiding places for the pearly eggs, which are about ⅛ inch in diameter.
• Handpick. Two hours after dark, begin hunting for slugs and snails.

 Bee Balm Diseases

PROBLEM: Bee balm leaves are coated with a white or gray powdery substance that resists being scraped away.

CAUSE: Powdery mildew (*Erisphe* spp.). Bee balm is very susceptible to this disfiguring fungal disease, which thrives in cool, damp weather.

WHAT TO DO:
• Apply baking soda spray. Make a spray solution by dissolving 1 teaspoon baking soda in 1 quart warm water; add 1 teaspoon of liquid, biodegradable soap or insecticidal soap to make the solution stick to leaves when you spray.
• Space plants widely for better air circulation.
• If mildew attacks after bee balm blooms, cut the plants back hard, and they will grow a second crop of fresh, green leaves.

PROBLEM: Bee balm leaves and stems develop long, blisterlike, reddish orange spots that turn brown or black.

CAUSE: Rust (*Puccinia angustata* and *P. menthae*). Rust is a disfiguring disease caused by two or more fungi. The disease erupts in wet, humid weather.

WHAT TO DO: Nip off and destroy infected leaves. Clean up plant debris in winter. Space plants widely for maximum air circulation.

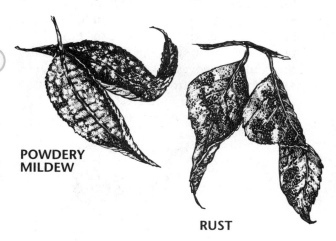

POWDERY MILDEW

RUST

Borage

(*Borago officinalis*)

 Borage Pests

PROBLEM: In mid- and late summer, you suddenly notice large holes in borage leaves. Veins are all that's left of some.

CAUSE: Grasshoppers (Order Orthoptera). Adults are brown, yellow, or green, 1- to 2-inch-long, winged insects with strong hind legs. The females lay egg clusters like small globs of rice in burrows in the soil, where they overwinter. In spring, the eggs hatch into small grasshoppers that begin feeding.

WHAT TO DO:
• Handpick.
• Attract birds with fresh water and nesting sites in shrubs and trees.
• Attract beneficial insects by planting small-flowered nectar plants, like yarrow and dill.
• Apply beneficial nematodes (*Steinernema carpocapsae* and *Heterorhabditis heliothidis*). Mail-order suppliers ship live nematodes suspended in gels or sponges. Follow label instructions for application, and release nematodes when pest larvae are present.
• Use floating row covers to exclude feeding insects, such as grasshoppers. Cover the plants with these synthetic, spunbonded fabrics, and bury edges of the cover in the soil.
• Remove and destroy egg clusters that you find when working in the soil.
• Till in autumn to expose eggs to frosts.

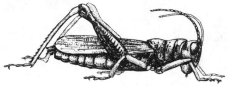

GRASSHOPPER

 Borage Diseases

Borage is an easy-to-grow herb. When planted in a sunny site with well-drained soil, borage is normally disease-free.

 Other Problems

PROBLEM: Your borage plants appeared healthy, but then suddenly turned yellow and died during rainy weather.

CAUSE: Poorly drained, damp soil. Like most herbs, borage thrives in a sunny spot with in-fertile, well-drained soil.

WHAT TO DO:
• Grow in well-drained, infertile soil.
• Grow borage in raised beds.

PROBLEM: Otherwise healthy-looking borage plants are failing to flower their first season in your garden.

CAUSE: Borage sometimes acts as a biennial plant by growing leaves during its first year and flowering during its second. Borage plants that grow a leafy rosette their first year but fail to flower are generally among the earliest ones to bloom the following year. These late-bloomers can beat newly planted borage by two weeks or more the second season.

WHAT TO DO:
• Have patience. You may have to wait until the second season for your borage to flower.
• Time the plantings. Plant a different plot of borage two years in a row, and repeat the annual plantings to ensure that you will have borage flowers every growing season.

Salad Burnet

(*Poterium sanguisorba*)

 Salad Burnet Pests

Salad burnet is an easy-to-grow herb. When it is grown in a site with well-drained soil and full sun, this herb is usually pest-free.

 Salad Burnet Diseases

PROBLEM: You notice that the leaves of your salad burnet plants have turned yellow, and the plants look unhealthy.

CAUSE: Fusarium wilt, also called root rot (*Fusarium* spp.). Several soil-dwelling fungi cause this potentially fatal disease. The roots of an infected salad burnet plant will rot. Root rot disease gains entry into plants through the damaged areas that feeding insects make in the stems and leaves. And the disease also can infect plants grown in poorly drained, soggy soil. If you dig up an infected plant and inspect its roots, you will find they have rotted and turned brown or black rather than the white of healthy roots. The outer coverings of the rotten roots will pull away easily.

WHAT TO DO:
• Destroy infected plants.
• Improve soil drainage. Add abundant organic matter, such as rotted hay or leaf mold, or add enough sand to increase soil drainage. Or grow salad burnet in raised beds filled with well-drained soil.
• Avoid overwatering.
• Start disease-free new plants in a different location.

 Other Problems

PROBLEM: Salad burnet leaves lose their characteristic cool, cucumber flavor and take on a bitter, spinach flavor.

CAUSE: Too much fertilizer. Like many herbs, salad burnet develops the best flavor when grown in infertile, well-drained soil.

WHAT TO DO:
• Allow the soil to dry out between waterings.
• Cut the plant back hard. Cutting salad burnet plants back to within a few inches of the soil and withholding fertilizer will cause them to produce succulent, flavorful leaves.
• Sow new seeds in less fertile soil, and avoid fertilizing the new plants with manure or other high-nitrogen fertilizers.

FUSARIUM WILT

Calendula

also called Pot Marigold (*Calendula officinalis*)

 Calendula Pests

PROBLEM: Leaves of young calendulas have smooth-edged holes. Some plants disappear overnight. You see no pests.

CAUSES: Slugs and snails (Order Stylommatophora). These common garden pests are related to, and look somewhat like, clams and mussels. They may be from ¼ inch to 4 inches long, and they leave slime trails everywhere they go. Slugs and snails are nocturnal, eating calendulas and many other plants from dusk to dawn. They begin climbing the stems of calendulas shortly after dusk. They climb down just before dawn and hide under up-turned pots, rocks, or mulch during the day.

WHAT TO DO:

• Remove potential hiding places, such as empty pots, rocks, and plant debris from the garden.

• Make copper barriers. Edge calendula plantings with a strip of copper, which will deliver an electrical shock to these slimy pests upon contact.

• Make beer traps from recycled cans sunk to the brim in soil and filled with yeasty beer. Attracted to the beer, slugs and snails will climb into the beer-filled containers and drown.

• Destroy their egg masses. Look under rocks, pots, or other hiding places for piles of pearly eggs about ⅛ inch in diameter.

• Handpick. Wait until at least two hours after dark for successful snail and slug hunting.

PROBLEM: White insects, ¹⁄₂₀ inch long, congregate on the undersides of calendula leaves. They fly when disturbed.

CAUSE: Whiteflies (Family Aleyrodidae). Both the similar-sized, translucent nymphs and tiny, white, winged adults weaken calendula plants by sucking plant juices from tender leaves and stems. You will see clouds of whiteflies rising from your plants most often in the late summer. Whiteflies usually disappear after the first few frosts of autumn.

WHAT TO DO:

• Knock whiteflies off calendulas with a strong spray of water.

• Use insecticidal soap, following label directions.

• Make yellow sticky traps by coating yellow cardboard or painted boards with petroleum jelly or Tanglefoot (a commercial product made for this purpose). Fasten the sticky traps to stakes near your calendula plants.

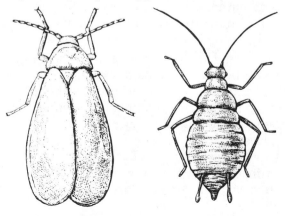

WHITEFLY   **APHID**

Replace the traps when they become coated with whiteflies.

• Attract parasitic wasps and other beneficial insects to the garden by planting small-flowered nectar plants, such as scabiosa, yarrow, and dill.

• Examine both sides of the leaves of calendula plants for pests before you buy them. These examinations will keep you from bringing whiteflies and other pests into your garden.

PROBLEM: **Calendula leaves and stems have sticky clear or black spots. There are small, pear-shaped insects on them.**

CAUSE: Aphids (Family Aphididae). These soft-bodied, $\frac{1}{16}$- to $\frac{3}{8}$-inch-long insects range in color from pale tan to light green to nearly black. Aphids damage plants by sucking plant juices. The sticky honeydew they secrete is a breeding ground for mold, and aphids can also transfer viruses to plants as they feed.

WHAT TO DO:

• Snip off and dispose of infested leaves.

• Knock aphids off calendula plants with a strong blast of water.

• Use insecticidal soap, following label directions.

• Attract beneficial insects, like lady beetles and lacewings, by planting small-flowered nectar plants, such as scabiosa, dill, and yarrow.

 Calendula Diseases

PROBLEM: **Leaves of calendula plants have a white or gray, powdery-looking coating that resists scraping off.**

CAUSE: Powdery mildew. This disfiguring air- and rain-borne fungal disease thrives in cool, damp weather. As this fungal disease progresses, the leaf area beneath the patches on the backs of the leaves dies and turns tan. If new leaves do emerge, they may be small and curled and may also turn yellow and wither.

WHAT TO DO:

• Apply baking soda spray. Make a solution by dissolving 1 teaspoon baking soda in 1 quart warm water. Add 1 teaspoon of liquid, biodegradable soap or insecticidal soap to make the spray solution stick to leaves. Spray both sides of the leaves with this solution to keep the disease from spreading.

• Space calendula plants widely for better air circulation.

• If mildew attacks after calendulas bloom, cut the plants back to within a few inches of the soil, and they will grow a second crop of fresh, green leaves.

• Rotate crops. Simply avoid growing the same crop in the same spot each year. Three-year rotations are recommended.

PROBLEM: **White spots surrounded by a red band mar leaves. The spots' centers fall out, leaving holes ringed in red.**

CAUSE: Cercospora leaf spot (*Cercospora calendulae*). This is an incurable fungal disease that spreads quickly once introduced to the garden. It is most active in warm summer weather. Cercospora leaf spot carries over from year to year in plant debris left in the garden.

WHAT TO DO:

• Pull and destroy infected plants immediately.

• Wash hands after handling infected plants and before touching other plants.

• Disinfect tools with rubbing alcohol.

• Plant healthy new calendula plants in a different place, where no calendulas have previously grown.

Caraway

(*Carum carvi*)

Caraway Pests

PROBLEM: Leaves are yellowing or wilting. The plants are stunted. Their roots are riddled with rust red tunnels.

CAUSE: Carrot rust fly larvae (*Psila rosae*). These pests are ⅓-inch-long maggots that burrow into caraway roots. After feeding for three or four weeks, they pupate and turn into metallic greenish black flies about ¼ inch long.

WHAT TO DO:

• Use floating row covers to prevent carrot rust flies from laying eggs in the crowns of the plants. Cover the plants with these synthetic, spunbonded fabrics in spring, and bury the edges of the row cover in the soil.

• Apply liquid seaweed to the soil at the base of caraway plants as a growth booster. With such help, established plants can usually shake off an attack.

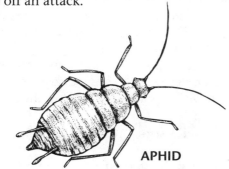

APHID

PARSLEYWORM

PROBLEM: Your caraway leaves suddenly develop ragged edges and many holes. You see green caterpillars on them.

CAUSE: Parsleyworms (*Papilio polyxenes*). These 1- to 2-inch-long caterpillars are the larvae of eastern black swallowtail butterflies. Hungry caterpillars can quickly strip a caraway plant of its foliage. But you may want to sacrifice a plant or two for the pleasure of watching the caterpillars grow and develop into chrysalises and then beautiful butterflies.

WHAT TO DO:

• Handpick.

• Plant extra caraway plants and other members of the Family Apiaceae to allow for depletion by the larvae of various swallowtail butterflies.

PROBLEM: In spring, you find leaves covered with sticky clear or black spots and small, pear-shaped insects.

CAUSE: Aphids (Family Aphididae). These soft-bodied, ¹⁄₁₆- to ⅜-inch-long insects range in color from pale tan to light green to nearly black. Aphids damage caraway plants by sucking juices from leaves and stems. The sticky honeydew that aphids secrete attracts ants and is a breeding ground for mold. Ants protect aphid eggs through winter and carry young aphids to caraway plants so they can feed. In return, ants consume the honeydew produced by aphids. Aphids can also spread viruses when they feed.

WHAT TO DO:

• Snip off and dispose of infested caraway leaves.

• Knock aphids and ants off caraway plants with a strong blast of water. Aim the water at the undersides, as well as the tops, of leaves.

• Pour boiling water into entry holes of anthills that are not adjacent to caraway plant roots.

• Use insecticidal soap, following label directions.

• Attract beneficial insects, like lady beetles and lacewings, by planting small-flowered nectar plants, such as scabiosa, dill, and yarrow.

 ## Caraway Diseases

PROBLEM: There is a white or gray, powdery coating on your caraway plant leaves that resists scraping off.

CAUSE: Powdery mildew (*Erysiphe* spp.). This disfiguring fungal disease is rarely fatal. It thrives in cool, damp weather. As this fungal disease progresses, the leaf area beneath the patches on the backs of the leaves dies and turns tan. If new leaves do emerge, they may be small and curled and may also turn yellow and wither.

WHAT TO DO:

• Apply baking soda spray. Make a spray solution by dissolving 1 teaspoon baking soda in 1 quart warm water. Add 1 teaspoon of liquid, biodegradable soap or insecticidal soap, to make a spraying solution that sticks to caraway leaves.

• Space plants widely for better air circulation.

PROBLEM: Plants wilt, often on one side, and don't revive with watering. Leaves are splotchy yellow or brown.

CAUSE: Verticillium wilt (*Verticillium* spp.). This fungal disease lives in the soil, and it can survive there for years. Infected plants may get off to a slow start in life. They have other unusual characteristics as well. Young plants may seem to grow normally for a while. Then their growth slows and the new leaves are smaller than they should be. Older leaves shrivel up and begin turning colors, including yellow and brown.

The disease is most common in the U.S. Midwest, but Verticillium wilt can build up to damaging levels in most parts of the country. Verticillum wilt is rare in climates with hot summers.

WHAT TO DO:

• Apply liquid fertilizer when symptoms appear. Caraway plants may recover from mild attacks if you give them several applications of fast-acting liquid fertilizer, following label directions.

• Plant a new crop of caraway in another location. Rotating plants on a three-year basis is recommended.

• Grow healthy caraway plants in containers of sterilized potting soil.

PROBLEM: Your caraway plants wilt and die. There are no other visual clues, such as yellowing or disfigured leaves.

CAUSE: Bacterial wilt (*Erwinia* spp.). Wilting not caused by dry soil or any other obvious cause is often a sign of bacterial wilt. The disease spreads from plant to plant, entering plants through the holes that feeding insects make in leaves and stems. When a plant becomes infected, the disease spreads rapidly no matter what you do.

WHAT TO DO:

• Pull and destroy infected plants.

• Use floating row covers to exclude feeding insects that spread disease. Cover the plants with these synthetic, spunbonded fabrics, and bury the edges of the row cover in the soil.

• Start a new crop of healthy caraway plants elsewhere in the garden. Rotating plants on a three-year basis is recommended.

Chervil

(Anthriscus cerefolium)

 Chervil Pests

PROBLEM: Sticky, clear or black spots and small, pear-shaped insects are on the stems and leaves of chervil plants.

CAUSE: Aphids (Family Aphididae). These soft-bodied, 1/16- to 3/8-inch-long insects range in color from pale tan to light green to nearly black. Aphids damage chervil plants by sucking plant juices from leaves and stems.

The sticky honeydew that aphids secrete is a breeding ground for mold and attracts ants. Aphids can transfer viruses to plants as they feed. Ants take care of aphids by protecting aphid eggs through winter and by carrying young aphids to plants so they can feed. In return, the ants consume the sticky, sweet honeydew produced by aphids. Aphids can also spread viruses when they feed.

WHAT TO DO:
• Snip off and dispose of infested leaves.
• Use insecticidal soap, following directions.
• Attract beneficial insects, like lady beetles and lacewings, by planting small-flowered nectar plants, such as dill and yarrow.
• If ants are protecting the aphids, banish the ants so that predatory insects can move in. Frequent sprays from a garden hose should do the trick. You can also pour boiling water into anthills that are far enough from plant roots to prevent the hot water from damaging the roots.

 Chervil Diseases

Chervil is an easy-to-grow herb. When given suitable growing conditions, including full sun and moist but well-drained soil, chervil is usually not troubled by diseases.

 Other Problems

PROBLEM: Apparently healthy chervil dies overnight. Surviving plants have limp, blackened leaves.

CAUSE: Frostbite. Chervil leaves are so tender that they die when exposed to frost.

WHAT TO DO:
• Protect chervil from frost with floating row covers. Cover the plants and bury the edges of the synthetic fabric in the soil.

• If chervil is exposed to a light frost, trim off damaged leaves. New leaves will grow until the ground freezes deep enough to kill the plants' roots.

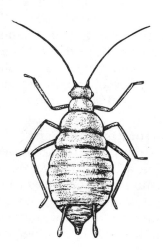

APHID

Coriander

also called Cilantro (*Coriandrum sativum*)

Coriander Pests

Coriander is an easy-to-grow herb that is usually pest-free.

Coriander Diseases

PROBLEM: **The leaves of your coriander are covered with a clinging, white or gray, powdery coating.**

CAUSES: Powdery mildew and downy mildew. These disfiguring fungal diseases thrive in cool, damp weather.

WHAT TO DO:

• Apply baking soda spray. Make a spray solution by dissolving 1 teaspoon baking soda in 1 quart warm water; add 1 teaspoon of liquid, biodegradable soap or insecticidal soap to make the spray solution stick to leaves.

• Space coriander plants widely for better air circulation.

• If the infestation is severe, cut the coriander plants back hard, and they will grow a second crop of fresh, green leaves. Note that by the time the leaves grow back and the plant blooms, the season may be too advanced for the renewed coriander plants to set seeds.

PROBLEM: **Plants wilt, often on one side, and watering doesn't help. Leaves turn splotchy yellow and then brown.**

CAUSE: Verticillium wilt (*Verticillium* spp.). This is a fungal disease that lives in the soil, and it can survive there for years.

WHAT TO DO:

• Apply liquid fertilizer when symptoms appear. Coriander plants may recover from mild attacks if you give them several applications of fast-acting, liquid fertilizer, following label directions.

• Plant a new crop of healthy plants in another location.

PROBLEM: **Coriander plants wilt and die. There are no other visual clues that they are ailing.**

CAUSE: Bacterial wilt. Wilting that isn't caused by dry soil or another obvious cause is often a sign of bacterial wilt. This disease spreads from plant to plant by entering holes that feeding insects make. When coriander plants are infected, the disease spreads rapidly no matter what you do.

WHAT TO DO:

• Use floating row covers to exclude insect pests. Cover the plants with these synthetic, spunbonded fabrics, and bury the edges in the soil.

• Pull and destroy infected plants.

• Start a new crop of coriander plants elsewhere in the garden.

POWDERY MILDEW   **DOWNY MILDEW**

Dill

(Anethum graveolens)

Dill Pests

PROBLEM: Your dill grows normally for a while, then new growth slows and new leaves appear pale and bleached.

CAUSE: Aphids (Family Aphididae). These pests are soft-bodied, wedge-shaped insects $\frac{1}{16}$ to $\frac{3}{8}$ inch long that range in color from pale tan to light green to nearly black. Aphids weaken plants by sucking juices. They also create entry points for diseases as they feed. Aphids usually congregate on tender new growth, and plants quickly become infested as aphids multiply. Aphids can spread diseases as they feed, and their sticky secretions, called honeydew, attract ants and mold.

WHAT TO DO:
• Cut off and dispose of leaves that host most of the aphids.
• Wash aphids off plants with a strong stream of water.
• Apply a weak solution of insecticidal soap.
• Attract beneficial insects, like lady beetles and lacewings, by planting small-flowered nectar plants, including yarrow, scabiosa, and Queen-Anne's-lace. Give the beneficials time to bring aphids under control.

PROBLEM: The lacy leaves of your dill plants are chewed. You see green caterpillars on them.

PARSLEYWORM

CAUSE: Parsleyworms (*Papilio polyxenes*). These caterpillars are the larvae of the big, beautiful, black and yellow swallowtail butterfly. The larvae feed on dill and other plants in the Family Apiaceae. Parsleyworms can quickly strip a dill plant of foliage, but you may want to sacrifice some dill for the pleasure of growing a crop of butterflies.

WHAT TO DO:
• Handpick.
• Plant extra dill plants and other members of the Family Apiaceae to feed butterfly larvae.

Dill Diseases

PROBLEM: Your dill plants are stunted-looking and grow slowly. Their leaves are yellowed and deformed.

CAUSE: Mosaic. Once viral diseases like mosaic invade dill plants, they interfere with the plants' genetic blueprint for growth. This virus is spread to dill plants by sap-sucking insects, such as leafhoppers and aphids. Once infected, there is no cure.

WHAT TO DO:
• Remove and dispose of infected dill plants.
• Wash your hands after handling infected plants and before touching tools.
• Use floating row covers to exclude feeding insects, which spread the disease. Cover the plants with these synthetic fabrics, and bury the edges of the row cover in the soil.
• Attract beneficial insects by planting small-flowered nectar plants, including yarrow and Queen-Anne's-lace.
• Use insecticidal soap; follow label directions.

Fennel

(Foeniculum vulgare)

Fennel Pests

PROBLEM: The new growth of your fennel slows down. The new leaves appear pale and bleached.

CAUSE: Aphids (Family Aphididae). These common garden pests are soft-bodied, wedge-shaped insects $1/16$ to $3/8$ inch long that range in color from pale tan to light green to nearly black. Aphids weaken fennel plants by sucking their juices. They also create entry points for diseases as they feed. Aphids usually congregate on tender new growth, and plants that host a few become heavily infested as aphids multiply. Their sticky secretions, called honeydew, attract ants and mold.

WHAT TO DO:
• Cut off and dispose of leaves that host most of the aphids.
• Wash aphids off plants with a strong stream of water.
• Apply a very dilute solution of insecticidal soap.
• Attract aphid-attacking beneficial insects, like lady beetles and lacewings, by planting small-flowered nectar plants, including yarrow, scabiosa, and Queen-Anne's-lace. Give the beneficials time to bring aphids under control.
• Pour boiling water into the entry holes of ant hills that are far enough from the roots of fennel to prevent damage to them.

PROBLEM: Fennel plants have leaves that are chewed at the edges. Some leaves have holes. Others are missing.

CAUSE: Parsleyworms (*Papilio polyxenes*). These 1- to 2-inch-long, green caterpillars are the larvae of beautiful eastern black swallowtail butterflies. The pleasure of watching their caterpillars grow and develop into chrysalises and then butterflies is usually worth sacrificing a few fennel leaves.

WHAT TO DO:
• Handpick.
• Plant extra fennel plants and other members of the Family Apiaceae to allow for depletion by the larvae of various swallowtail butterflies.

Fennel Diseases

Fennel is an easy-to-grow herb that is usually not bothered by diseases.

Other Problems

PROBLEM: Your fennel plants have poor seed production, or the plants produce no seeds at all.

CAUSE: The fennel has cross-pollinated with dill or coriander. Cross-pollination between fennel and its close relatives will reduce or eliminate a harvest of fennel seeds. If you don't intend to plant seeds or use them for culinary or craft purposes, cross-pollination is of no concern.

WHAT TO DO:
• Plant fennel far enough from related herbs, including dill and coriander, that the pollen won't be carried back and forth between plants by insects.

Lavender

(*Lavandula* spp.)

Lavender Pests

Lavender is an easy-to-grow herb that is usually pest-free.

Lavender Diseases

PROBLEM: The foliage of your lavender plants looks yellow or stunted. Their roots are disfigured with knotty galls.

CAUSE: Root-knot nematodes (*Meloidogyne* spp.). These soil-dwelling microscopic worms cause diseaselike symptoms. They thrive in mild and warm climates.

WHAT TO DO:
• Solarize the soil. Clear plastic sheeting placed over bare soil for three to four weeks uses the sun's energy to heat the soil enough to kill root-knot nematodes and most other pests and weed seeds in the top few inches of soil. After removing the plastic, plant the lavender.

PROBLEM: White spots surrounded by a red band appear on your lavender leaves. The center may fall out.

CAUSE: Cercospora leaf spot (*Cercospora* spp.). This disease spreads quickly. It is an untreatable fungal disease that can carry over from year to year in plant debris.

WHAT TO DO:
• Destroy infected plants immediately.
• Wash hands after handling infected plants and before touching other plants or tools.
• Disinfect tools with rubbing alcohol after working with infected plants.
• Avoid splashing water on the foliage when watering the plants.
• Start new lavender plants in a different place.

PROBLEM: You notice yellowing lavender leaves. Affected plants wilt suddenly, and watering does not help.

CAUSE: Fusarium wilt, also called root rot (*Fusarium* spp.). This serious disease is caused by several soil fungi. Fusarium wilt causes the roots of infected lavender plants to rot.

WHAT TO DO:
• Avoid overwatering.
• Avoid splashing water on foliage when watering the plants.
• Plant lavender in well-drained soil.
• Remove and destroy infected plants.
• Set new plants in a different location.

FUSARIUM WILT

Lemon Balm

(Melissa officinalis)

Lemon Balm Pests

Lemon balm is an easy-to-grow herb. When planted in a sunny site with well-drained soil, it is usually pest-free.

Lemon Balm Diseases

PROBLEM: The leaves of your lemon balm plants are covered with a white or gray, clinging, powdery coating.

CAUSES: Powdery mildew and downy mildew. These disfiguring fungal diseases thrive in cool, damp weather.

WHAT TO DO:

• Apply baking soda spray. Make a spray solution by dissolving 1 teaspoon baking soda in 1 quart warm water. Add 1 teaspoon of liquid, biodegradable soap or insecticidal soap to make the spray solution stick to the lemon balm leaves.

• Space lemon balm plants widely for optimum air circulation.

• You can cut severely affected plants back to within a few inches of the soil, and they will grow a second crop of fresh green leaves.

PROBLEM: You notice irregular yellow spots on leaves. Affected plants wilt suddenly. Watering does not help.

CAUSE: Fusarium wilt, also called root rot (*Fusarium* spp.). This disease is caused by several fungi that live in soil. It ruins the leaves and causes the roots of infected lemon balm plants to rot.

WHAT TO DO:

• Remove and destroy infected plants.

• Improve soil drainage.

• Don't overwater lemon balm.

• Rotate crops. Avoid siting new lemon balm plants where older ones are growing.

PROBLEM: Your lemon balm has unsightly powdery, orange, brown, black, or purple coatings on backs of leaves.

CAUSE: Rust (*Puccinia* spp.). This fungal disease causes trouble in wet, humid weather. Rust fungi are specialists, and various kinds attack only specific plants. The color of the powdery coating indicates which rust organism is at work. The disease overwinters in plant debris left in the garden.

WHAT TO DO:

• Nip off and destroy infected leaves.

• Clean up plant debris in winter.

POWDERY MILDEW

RUST

Lovage

(Levisticum officinale)

 Lovage Pests

PROBLEM: The leaves of some lovage plants show tan, meandering streaks that don't go all the way through.

CAUSE: Leafminers (Family Agromyzidae). These pests are the larvae of a ¹⁄₁₀-inch-long, black or black-and-yellow fly. The flies lay small clusters of tiny white eggs on leaf undersides. The eggs hatch into minute, pale green maggots. The maggots feed inside lovage leaves, leaving the outer layer of leaf tissue intact. The larvae emerge from eggs laid on the backs of lovage leaves by the adult flies. After mining and feeding for one to three weeks, larvae drop to the soil to pupate. Leafminers disfigure leaves, but the damage they do is rarely fatal to the plants they attack.

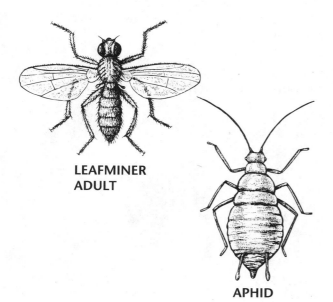

LEAFMINER ADULT

APHID

WHAT TO DO:
• Nip off and destroy infested leaves.
• Use floating row covers to exclude insects, such as the flies that lay leafminer eggs. Cover the plants with these synthetic, spun-bonded fabrics, and bury the edges of the row cover in the soil.

PROBLEM: In spring, lovage leaves have speckles that are sticky and clear or black and small, pear-shaped insects.

CAUSE: Aphids (Family Aphididae). These soft-bodied, ¹⁄₁₆- to ³⁄₈-inch-long insects range in color from pale tan to light green to nearly black. Aphids damage lovage plants by sucking the juices from their leaves and stems. The sticky honeydew that aphids secrete attracts ants and is a breeding ground for mold. Aphids can also transfer viruses to plants as they feed. Ants defend aphids against attacks by beneficial insects because the ants eat the honeydew secreted by aphids.

WHAT TO DO:
• Snip off and dispose of infested leaves.
• Knock aphids and ants off with water.
• Pour boiling water into anthills.
• Use insecticidal soap, following directions.
• Attract aphid-attacking beneficial insects, like lady beetles and lacewings, by planting small-flowered nectar plants, such as dill, fennel, and yarrow.

 Lovage Diseases

When grown in a sunny site in well-drained soil of average fertility, lovage is usually disease-free.

Sweet Marjoram

(Origanum majorana)

Marjoram Pests

PROBLEM: The leaves of marjoram plants are a bleached-out shade of green. Some are shrouded in cobwebs.

CAUSE: Spider mites (Family Tetranychidae). These minute, sap-sucking pests are ⅟₆₀ inch long and look like grains of red pepper. The first indication of infestation is the tiny, yellow pinprick holes in leaves that mites make as they suck plant juices. Dry growing conditions during the growing season can encourage infestations of mites.

WHAT TO DO:
• Nip off and destroy infested plant parts.
• Knock spider mites from marjoram plants with a strong stream of water.
• Use insecticidal soap, following directions.
• Attract beneficial insects with small-flowered nectar plants, like yarrow and dill.

Marjoram Diseases

This is an easy-to-grow annual. When grown in a sunny site in well-drained soil of average fertility, it is usually disease-free.

Other Problems

PROBLEM: Many seeds you sowed in the garden did not germinate. Plants that came up appear sparse and spindly.

CAUSES: Cold temperatures; sowing too thinly. Marjoram seeds require a soil temperature of about 70°F to germinate. And the plants look best when grown in clumps.

WHAT TO DO:
• Sow seeds indoors three or more weeks before the last frost date. Sow 20 seeds to a 4-inch pot of seed-starting mix covered with a dusting of sand. When the seedlings are about 4 inches tall, plant them outside when the soil temperature warms up to about 70°F.

PROBLEM: Apparently healthy marjoram dies overnight. Surviving plants have limp, blackened leaves.

CAUSE: Frostbite. Marjoram is a tender annual plant that dies in freezing temperatures.

WHAT TO DO:
• When frost threatens, cover marjoram with a bed sheet or floating row covers. Row covers are synthetic fabrics that protect plants from frost. Place the material over the plants, and bury the edges of it in the soil.

PROBLEM: Your container-grown marjoram grew well for three or four years but now grows slowly and looks sparse.

CAUSE: Short life span. While marjoram can be grown in containers and wintered over indoors, after three or four years the plants will naturally begin to die.

WHAT TO DO:
• Start new plants from cuttings taken in early summer.
• Sow seeds indoors three weeks or more before the last frost date.

Mint

(Mentha spp.)

 Mint Pests

PROBLEM: You notice brown-black, rounded spots on mint leaves. Affected leaves may drop from plants.

CAUSE: Four-lined plant bugs (*Poecilocapsus lineatus*). These ⅓-inch-long, yellowish green bugs have four black stripes on their wings.

WHAT TO DO:
• Handpick.
• Tolerate light damage.

PROBLEM: In early to midspring, your mint leaves show sticky clear or black speckles and small, pear-shaped insects.

CAUSE: Aphids (Family Aphididae). These soft-bodied, ¹⁄₁₆- to ⅜-inch-long insects range in color from pale tan to light green to nearly black. Aphids damage mint by sucking plant juices from leaves and stems. The sticky honeydew they secrete is a breeding ground for mold. Aphids can transfer viruses as they eat.

WHAT TO DO:
• Snip off and dispose of infested leaves.
• Knock aphids off plants with a strong blast of water.
• Use insecticidal soap. Follow directions.
• Attract beneficial insects, like lady beetles and lacewings, by planting small-flowered nectar plants, such as dill and yarrow.

PROBLEM: Some of your mint leaves are chewed at the edges. Others are peppered with sizable holes.

CAUSE: Caterpillars of gray hairstreak butterflies (*Strymon melinus*). These 1-inch-long, green, fuzzy caterpillars are the larvae of slate-gray butterflies with wingspans of 1 inch. Hairstreak butterflies have a vivid orange spot on each rear wing. The caterpillars eat mint leaves, and the gray hairstreak butterflies visit mint flowers for nectar. Since the butterflies are so beautiful, consider sharing some of your mint with them.

WHAT TO DO:
• Handpick.
• Grow extra mint plants to feed larvae.

 Mint Diseases

PROBLEM: Your mint plants have blistered, reddish orange spots on their stems or leaves that turn brown-black.

CAUSE: Rust (*Puccinia* spp.). This disfiguring disease is caused by several fungi. Rust erupts in wet, humid weather. It overwinters in plant debris left in the garden.

WHAT TO DO:
• Nip off and destroy infected leaves.
• Clean up plant debris in winter.

PROBLEM: Mint plants wilt, often on one side. They don't revive with watering.

CAUSE: Verticillium wilt (*Verticillium alboatrum* f. *menthae*). This fungal disease lives in the soil and survives there for years.

WHAT TO DO:
• Apply liquid fertilizer when symptoms appear to help them survive mild attacks.

• Plant a new crop of mint in another location. Three-year rotations are ideal.

Oregano

(Origanum heracleoticum)

 ## Oregano Pests

PROBLEM: The leaves of your oregano plants are stippled with yellowish dots. Some may be curled or have cobwebs.

CAUSE: Spider mites (Family Tetranychidae). These are 1/60-inch-long, spiderlike, sap-sucking pests that can kill oregano plants if allowed to breed. Spider mites are most problematic during periods of hot, dry weather. To check a plant for spider mites, shake a stem of leaves over a sheet of paper; the mites will drop to the paper and look like grains of pepper moving about.

WHAT TO DO:
• Nip off and destroy infested leaves.
• Use insecticidal soap, following directions.
• Knock spider mites from oregano plants with a strong stream of water.
• Attract beneficial insects by planting small-flowered nectar plants, like yarrow.

PROBLEM: The leaves of some of your oregano plants have tan, meandering streaks but are not eaten through.

CAUSE: Leafminers (Family Agromyzidae). These pests are the larvae of 1/10-inch-long, black or black-and-yellow flies. The flies lay tiny, white eggs on leaf undersides. The eggs hatch into minute maggots that feed inside leaves, leaving the outer layer of tissue. The damage leafminers do is unsightly but rarely fatal to plants.

WHAT TO DO:
• Nip off and destroy infested leaves.

• Use floating row covers to exclude feeding insects. Cover the plants with these synthetic, spunbonded fabrics, and bury the edges of the row cover in the soil.

PROBLEM: In early to midspring your oregano may have sticky clear or black spots and small, pear-shaped insects.

CAUSE: Aphids (Family Aphididae). These soft-bodied, 1/16- to 3/8-inch-long insects range in color from pale tan to light green to nearly black. Aphids damage oregano plants by sucking juices from leaves and stems.

WHAT TO DO:
• Snip off and dispose of infested leaves.
• Knock aphids off with a blast of water.
• Use insecticidal soap, following directions.
• Attract beneficial insects, like lacewings, by planting small-flowered nectar plants, like dill, yarrow, and Queen-Anne's-lace.

 ## Oregano Diseases

PROBLEM: The leaves of your oregano plants have irregular yellow spots. The plants wilt, and watering doesn't help.

CAUSE: Fusarium wilt, also called root rot (*Fusarium* spp.). This disease is caused by several fungi that live in soil. Fusarium wilt causes roots of infected plants to rot. The disease overwinters in plant debris.

WHAT TO DO:
• Remove and destroy infected plants.
• Rotate crops. Avoid siting new oregano plants where older ones are growing.

Parsley

(Petroselinum crispum)

 ## Parsley Pests

PROBLEM: You see a sticky clear or black substance and small, pear-shaped insects cluster on the leaves.

CAUSE: Aphids (Family Aphididae). These soft-bodied, 1/16- to 3/8-inch-long insects range in color from pale tan to light green to nearly black. Aphids damage parsley plants by sucking juices from the stems and leaves. Their sticky secretions, called honeydew, attract ants and encourage the growth of mold. Ants protect aphids from the attacks of beneficial insects because ants eat the honeydew that aphids secrete. Aphids can also transfer plant viruses as they feed.

WHAT TO DO:
• Snip off and dispose of infested leaves.
• Knock aphids and ants off plants with a strong blast of water.
• Pour boiling water into anthills that are far enough from plant roots that the hot water won't harm the roots.
• Use insecticidal soap, following directions.
• Attract beneficial insects, like lady beetles and lacewings, by planting small-flowered nectar plants, such as dill and yarrow.

PARSLEYWORM

PROBLEM: Parsley leaves are yellowing and wilting. The plants seem stunted. Roots have rust-colored tunnels.

CAUSE: Carrot rust fly larvae (*Psila rosae*). These pests are 1/3-inch-long maggots that burrow into parsley roots. After feeding for three or four weeks, the maggots pupate and become metallic, greenish black flies about 1/4 inch long.

WHAT TO DO:
• Apply liquid seaweed to the soil at the base of parsley plants. With the help of this growth booster, established parsley plants can usually shake off the attack.
• Use floating row covers to exclude flying insects. Cover the plants with these synthetic, spunbonded fabrics, and bury the edges of it in soil. Do this in the spring so that carrot rust flies can't lay eggs on the plants.

PROBLEM: Your parsley plants suddenly develop ragged edges and holes. You see green caterpillars on the plants.

CAUSE: Parsleyworms (*Papilio polyxenes*). These 1 to 2-inch-long caterpillars are the larvae of eastern black swallowtail butterflies. Hungry parsleyworms can quickly strip a parsley plant of its foliage. You should consider sacrificing a plant or two for the pleasure of watching the caterpillars grow and develop into chrysalises and then beautiful butterflies.

WHAT TO DO:
• Handpick.
• Grow extra parsley plants and other members of the Family Apiaceae to allow for de-

pletion by the larvae of various swallowtail butterflies.

PROBLEM: Some parsley leaves are greatly damaged. Some young plants vanish overnight. You see no insects.

CAUSES: Slugs and snails (Order Stylommatophora). These pests are related to clams and mussels. They may be from ¼ inch to 4 inches long, and they leave slime trails everywhere they go. Slugs and snails eat plants from dusk to dawn, and they hide in the shade of debris on the soil during the day.

WHAT TO DO:

• Make copper barriers. Edge plantings with a strip of copper, which hits these slimy pests with an electrical shock upon contact.
• Make beer traps from recycled cans sunk to the brim in soil and filled with yeasty beer. Attracted by the beer, slugs and snails will climb into the containers and drown.
• Destroy egg masses deposited under hiding places, such as rocks.
• Handpick. Start two hours after dark for the best slug and snail hunting.

 Parsley Diseases

PROBLEM: You notice irregular yellow spots on parsley leaves. The plants wilt suddenly, and watering will not help.

CAUSE: Fusarium wilt, also called root rot (*Fusarium oxysporum* f. *apii*). This disease is caused by several fungi that live in soil. It causes the roots of infected parsley plants to rot. Fusarium wilt spores overwinter on infected plant debris left in the garden.

WHAT TO DO:

• Remove and destroy infected plants.
• Rotate plantings. Simply avoid growing parsley in the same spot each year. Three-year rotations are ideal.

PROBLEM: Your parsley plants look yellow or stunted. When you dig them up, you see knotty galls on their roots.

CAUSE: Root-knot nematodes (*Meloidogyne* spp.). These are microscopic worms that cause diseaselike symptoms. They live in the soil and thrive in sandy soil and in warm climates. Root-knot nematodes become the greatest threat to parsley plants during the hot months of summer.

WHAT TO DO:

• Solarize the soil. Clear plastic sheeting placed over bare soil for three to four weeks uses the sun's energy to heat the soil enough to kill root-knot nematodes, other pests, and weed seeds living in the top few inches of soil. After you remove the plastic sheeting, plant parsley as you ordinarily would.
• Dig in compost. Parasitic fungi living in compost will work to control the nematodes in garden soil.

 Other Problems

PROBLEM: In spite of good growing conditions, parsley seeds fail to sprout.

CAUSE: Inherently slow germination. There is an old saying: Parsley seeds go to the devil and back before they sprout. In reality it can take as long as six weeks for them to germinate.

WHAT TO DO:

• Have patience. It is a good idea to start parsley seeds in pots indoors, in early spring, so that you aren't weeding a bare bed for a month and a half before the seedlings put in an appearance.
• Buy young plants instead of growing parsley from seed.

Pennyroyal

(Mentha pulegium; Hedeoma pulegioides)

Pennyroyal Pests

Pests prefer to pass by this strongly scented herb. In fact, fresh and dried pennyroyal plants are often used in closets, drawers, and other storage areas as insect repellants.

As long as pennyroyal has good growing conditions, it is virtually trouble-free and usually disease-free. Give pennyroyal plants a site that has full sun, well-drained, garden loam soil, and enough moisture to prevent the plants from wilting.

Other Problems

PROBLEM: The leaves of your previously healthy pennyroyal plants suddenly start wilting and falling off.

CAUSES: Drought stress; root shock. Leaf loss during the growing season is most likely caused by inadequate moisture. Container plants are especially sensitive to drought.

Root shock from transplanting will also cause leaves to drop, because transplant shock prevents the plants from taking up enough water.

WHAT TO DO:
• Water the plants lightly for several regular waterings, then water them generously.
• Cut a severely affected plant back to new growth, water it generously, fertilize it with a quick-acting liquid fertilizer (such as fish emulsion), and watch for signs of recovery.
• When you transplant pennyroyal, keep as much soil around its roots as possible.

PROBLEM: Pennyroyal plants that grew well all summer in the garden died out during the winter.

CAUSE: Poor drainage. Even pennyroyal that has grown well in the same spot for several years can be done in by an unusually wet winter. Plants grown in clay soils or other slow-to-drain soils are especially vulnerable.

WHAT TO DO:
• Start new pennyroyal plants in a raised bed.
• Improve soil drainage by incorporating sand.
• Lighten the soil by incorporating a wheelbarrow of compost, aged manure, leaf mold, or other organic material.
• Plant European pennyroyal (*M. pulegium*). It may die during an unusually cold, wet winter, but the plants grow so fast that you can still enjoy them as an annual no matter what USDA Hardiness Zone you live in.

PROBLEM: Whether fall- or spring-sown, your seeds have a disappointingly small percentage of germination.

CAUSE: Winter freeze damage or naturally poor germination. In cold-winter climates, pennyroyal seeds sown in fall may not survive the winter to sprout the following spring. But even so, pennyroyal has an unpredictable germination rate.

WHAT TO DO:
• In cold-winter regions, sow pennyroyal seed in spring.
• In all regions, sow the seed thickly to ensure enough germination for a reasonably good crop of plants.

Rosemary

(Rosmarinus officinalis)

 Rosemary Pests

PROBLEM: You see a sticky clear or black substance and small, pear-shaped insects on your rosemary leaves.

CAUSE: Aphids (Family Aphididae). These soft-bodied, 1/16- to 3/8-inch-long insects range in color from pale tan to light green to nearly black. Aphids damage rosemary plants by sucking juices from the stems and leaves. Their sticky secretions, called honeydew, attract ants and encourage the growth of mold. Ants protect aphids from the attacks of beneficial insects because ants eat the honeydew that aphids secrete. Aphids can also transfer plant viruses as they feed.

WHAT TO DO:
• Snip off and dispose of infested leaves.
• Knock aphids and ants off plants with a strong blast of water.

• Pour boiling water into anthills that are far enough from rosemary plant roots that the hot water won't harm the roots.
• Use insecticidal soap, following label directions.
• Attract beneficial insects, like lady beetles and lacewings, by planting small-flowered nectar plants, such as scabiosa, dill, and yarrow.

PROBLEM: Your rosemary leaves are a bleached-out shade of green and are shrouded in fine cobwebs.

CAUSE: Spider mites (Family Tetranychidae). These 1/60-inch-long, sap-sucking pests look like grains of red pepper sprinkled over your rosemary plants. Spider mites weaken the plants by sucking juices from rosemary leaves. They spin webs that trail behind them as they move. The webs protect spider mite eggs and newly hatched young that are scattered about the leaves. The first signs of spider mites are the tiny pinprick holes in the yellowing leaves, faint webbing on leaf backs, or possibly a number of barely visible specks among the webs. Dry or dusty conditions encourage infestations of spider mites, which can kill plants if allowed to breed.

WHAT TO DO:
• Nip off and destroy infested leaves.
• Knock spider mites from rosemary with a strong stream of water. Begin treatment early, at the pinprick stage; by the time the webs appear, it may be too late to save some plants.
• Attract beneficial insects by planting

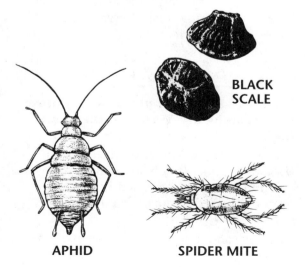

BLACK SCALE

APHID   SPIDER MITE

small-flowered nectar plants, including yarrow and Queen-Anne's-lace.
• Use insecticidal soap, following label directions.

PROBLEM: Your rosemary plants fail to grow vigorously, and you may see ants on their leaves and stems.

CAUSE: Black scale (*Saissetia oleae*). These 1/10-inch-long insects look like oval, waxy bumps that blend in with the bark of your rosemary branches. The stationary adults and their similarly sized, mobile nymphs both suck plant juices. Adult scale produce sticky honeydew that attracts ants and creates ideal growing conditions for mold.

WHAT TO DO:
• Scrape scale off branches with a plastic scouring pad.
• Attract parasitic wasps and other beneficial insects by growing small-flowered nectar plants, such as scabiosa, yarrow, and dill.

PROBLEM: White, cottony tufts on rosemary stems are accompanied by sticky honeydew and black mold.

CAUSE: Mealybugs (Family Pseudococcidae). Beneath the protective white fluff that covers these pests lurk 1/10-inch-long, yellowish mealybugs. These pests damage plants by sucking juices from leaves and tender stems. Mealybugs can overwinter outdoors in warm climates, but they lay cottony masses of eggs that overwinter in all climates.

WHAT TO DO:
• Knock mealybugs off plants with a strong spray of water.
• Use insecticidal soap, following label directions.
• Dab individual mealybugs with a cotton ball dipped in rubbing alcohol.
• Attract beneficial insects, like predatory

lacewings or mealybug destroyers (*Cryptolaemus montrouzieri*), by planting small-flowered nectar plants, like yarrow, dill, and scabiosa.

PROBLEM: Powdery-white, 1/20-inch-long flying insects gather on rosemary leaves and fly away when disturbed.

CAUSE: Whiteflies (Family Aleyrodidae). Both the minute translucent nymphs of this pest and the white adult flies are sucking insects that weaken plants as they feed. You will most often see small cloudlike groups of the tiny, white flies rising from your rosemary plants in late summer. Whiteflies disappear outdoors after the first few frosts, but you'll bring them indoors with your plants if you overwinter the plants inside.

WHAT TO DO:
• Knock whiteflies off rosemary with a strong spray of water.
• Use insecticidal soap, following label directions. Make yellow sticky traps. Coat yellow cardboard or painted boards with petroleum jelly or Tanglefoot (a commercial product made for this purpose), and fasten them to stakes placed near rosemary plants.
• Attract parasitic wasps and other beneficial insects by planting small-flowered nectar plants, such as yarrow and dill.

 Rosemary Diseases

PROBLEM: Rosemary plants may yellow or wilt suddenly. Watering the plants does not revive them.

CAUSE: Fusarium wilt, also called root rot (*Fusarium* spp.). This disease, caused by several fungi that live in the soil, causes the roots of infected rosemary plants to rot.

WHAT TO DO:
• Remove and destroy infected plants.

• Rotate plantings. Simply avoid growing rosemary in the same spot each year.

PROBLEM: Leaves and flowers show small yellow, brown, or orange blotches that develop fuzzy, gray mold.

CAUSE: Gray mold (*Botrytis* spp.). Also known as Botrytis, the fungi that cause gray mold are carried throughout the garden on dead and dying plants. The disease is present in the soil, but it seldom causes problems unless the weather is very damp.

WHAT TO DO:
• Clip off and dispose of diseased plant parts. As with all herbs, cutting back stimulates vigorous new growth, so don't hesitate to cut rosemary plants back if you see signs of gray mold.
• Mulch to keep mud from splashing on rosemary leaves.

 Other Problems

PROBLEM: The leaves of your rosemary plants curl and the stems droop, especially at the tips.

CAUSE: Drought stress. Rosemary, like many herbs, grows best in infertile, well-drained soil. It is easy for such soil to become too dry to supply adequate moisture to the plants. Rosemary grown in pots is especially vulnerable to drought-induced wilting.

WHAT TO DO:
• Water rosemary plants generously to revive them. Then water the plants regularly, giving them enough water to keep them from wilting.

PROBLEM: Your rosemary grew well all summer and into fall, but it suddenly wilted and died over two or three days.

CAUSE: Frostbite. Rosemary can be grown outdoors all year in climates that rarely freeze. In cold climates, they must be treated as tender plants or annuals.

WHAT TO DO:
• When autumn temperatures drop into the 40s, lift and pot up rosemary plants; then winter them indoors.

PROBLEM: Despite good growing conditions, the rosemary seeds you plant fail to germinate.

CAUSE: Inherently poor germination. Rosemary seeds are very difficult to germinate. And it takes as long as three years for a bush to grow enough to allow harvesting. Seed-grown rosemary plants are not as vigorous as those started from cuttings. The seed-grown plants may always have weak stems and pale leaves.

WHAT TO DO:
• Buy young plants started from cuttings.
• Take cuttings of your own plants if you want to propagate them.

PROBLEM: Your container-grown rosemary plants wilt and grow slowly.

CAUSES: Compacted roots; root rot; drought-damaged roots. Because rosemary is a woody shrub, it requires a large pot to accommodate its extensive root system. But because the plants are susceptible to root rot, the soil mix they grow in must have good drainage and retain enough water to prevent drought-stressing the plants.

WHAT TO DO:
• Pot rosemary plants in a commercial "cactus" mix.
• Allow the soil to dry between waterings, but do not allow it to remain dry for more than a day.
• Mist the foliage daily if plants grow in hot, sunny sites.

Rue

(Ruta graveolens)

Rue Pests

PROBLEM: White, ¹⁄₂₀-inch-long flying insects gather on undersides of rue leaves. The insects fly away when disturbed.

CAUSE: Whiteflies (Family Aleyrodidae). Both the minute, translucent nymphs and the tiny, white adult whiteflies are sucking insects that weaken rue plants when they feed. You will most often see clouds of these tiny, white flies rising from your rue plants in late summer. Whiteflies usually disappear after the first few frosts of autumn.

WHAT TO DO:
• Knock whiteflies from rue plants with a strong spray of water.
• Use insecticidal soap, following label directions.
• Make sticky traps. Coat yellow cardboard or painted boards with petroleum jelly or Tanglefoot (a commercial product made for this purpose), and fasten them to stakes near rue plants.
• Attract parasitic wasps and other beneficial insects by planting small-flowered nectar plants, such as yarrow and dill.

WHITEFLY　　　**PARSLEYWORM**

PROBLEM: The leaves of rue suddenly have ragged edges and many holes. You see green caterpillars on the plants.

CAUSE: Parsleyworms (*Papilio polyxenes*). These 1- to 2-inch-long caterpillars are the larvae of eastern black swallowtail butterflies. Hungry parsleyworms can quickly strip a rue plant of most of its foliage. Consider sacrificing some rue leaves for the pleasure of watching parsleyworms develop into chrysalises and then turn into beautiful butterflies.

WHAT TO DO:
• Handpick.
• Plant extra rue plants so that there is enough for you and the butterflies.

Rue Diseases

Rue plants are relatively care-free plants. When given a sunny location and well-drained, soil they are usually disease-free.

Other Problems

PROBLEM: After touching parts of a rue plant, you develop painful blisters on your skin.

CAUSE: Many people have a reaction to oils in the stems and foliage of rue plants. These oils can cause painful blistering and contact dermatitis when they come into contact with bare skin.

WHAT TO DO:
• Avoid brushing against rue plants with your bare skin.
• Wear long sleeves and gloves when you prune rue plants or weed around them.

Sage

(Salvia officinalis)

Sage Pests

PROBLEM: The leaves of sage are peppered with yellow dots. Some curl under or have fine spiderwebs.

CAUSE: Spider mites (Family Tetranychidae). These 1/60-inch-long, sap-sucking pests look like grains of red pepper sprinkled over your sage plants. Dry or dusty conditions encourage infestations of spider mites, which can kill plants if allowed to breed.

WHAT TO DO:
• Nip off and destroy infested leaves.
• Hit mites with a strong stream of water.
• Attract beneficial insects by planting small-flowered nectar plants, including yarrow and Queen-Anne's-lace.
• Use insecticidal soap, following directions.

PROBLEM: Large holes appear in sage leaves from day to day, but you never see insects on the plants.

CAUSES: Slugs and snails (Order Stylommatophora). These pests are related to clams and mussels. They may be from 1/4 inch to 4 inches long, and they leave slime trails everywhere they go. Slugs and snails eat sage and other plants from dusk to dawn, and they hide in garden debris during the day.

WHAT TO DO:
• Edging plants with copper hits these slimy pests with an electrical shock on contact.

SLUG

• Make beer traps from recycled cans sunk to the brim in soil and filled with yeasty beer.
• Destroy their egg clusters.
• Handpick slugs and snails after dark.

Sage Diseases

PROBLEM: You notice irregular, yellow spots on sage leaves. Affected plants wilt suddenly. Watering does help.

CAUSE: Fusarium wilt, also called root rot (*Fusarium* spp.). This disease is caused by several fungi that live in the soil. It causes the roots of infected sage plants to rot.

WHAT TO DO:
• Remove and destroy infected plants.
• Rotate plantings. Avoid siting new sage plants where older ones are growing.

PROBLEM: Sage plants appear healthy, with no yellowing leaves or other signs of trouble, but the plants wilt and die.

CAUSE: Bacterial wilt. Wilting that isn't due to dry soil or other obvious causes is often a sign of bacterial wilt. This disease is usually spread from plant to plant through feeding holes made by insects. When a plant is infected, the disease spreads rapidly no matter what you do.

WHAT TO DO:
• Pull and destroy infected plants.
• Use floating row covers to exclude feeding insects that can spread disease. Cover the plants with these synthetic, spunbonded fabrics, and bury the edges of the row cover in the soil.
• Start healthy new sage plants elsewhere.

French Tarragon

(*Artemisia dracunculus* var. *sativa*)

Tarragon Pests

PROBLEM: The leaves of your tarragon plants are chewed at the edges or have holes in them.

CAUSES: Oregon swallowtail larvae; western black swallowtail larvae (*Papilio* spp.). These 1- to 2-inch-long butterfly caterpillars prefer to eat Russian tarragon (*A. d.* var. *sativa*).

WHAT TO DO:
• Handpick.
• Plant extras for the butterflies.

Tarragon Diseases

PROBLEM: Irregular yellow spots are on tarragon leaves. Affected plants wilt suddenly. Watering does not help.

CAUSE: Fusarium wilt, also called root rot (*Fusarium* spp.). This disease is caused by several fungi that live in soil.

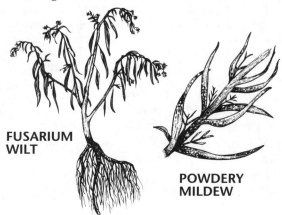

FUSARIUM WILT

POWDERY MILDEW

WHAT TO DO:
• Remove and destroy infected plants.
• Start new plants in a different location.

PROBLEM: Tarragon leaves are covered with a clinging, white or gray powdery coating that resists being scraped off.

CAUSES: Powdery mildew (*Erysiphe cichoracearum*); downy mildew (*Peronospora* spp.). These disfiguring fungal diseases enter plants through injuries, and they thrive in cool, damp weather.

WHAT TO DO:
• Apply baking soda spray. Make a spray solution by dissolving 1 teaspoon baking soda in 1 quart warm water; add 1 teaspoon of liquid, biodegradable soap or insecticidal soap.
• Space plants widely for good air circulation.
• Cut tarragon plants back to a few inches.

Other Problems

PROBLEM: Your tarragon plants look healthy but lack their typical licorice flavor and aroma.

CAUSE: You planted the wrong variety. Russian tarragon (*A. d.* var. *sativa*), often sold as tarragon, lacks the licorice scent and flavor of French tarragon (*A. d.* var. *sativa*).

WHAT TO DO:
• Buy correctly labeled plants. Squeeze and sniff a leaf before buying it.

Thyme
(*Thymus* spp.)

 ## Thyme Pests

PROBLEM: Thyme leaves are a bleached-out shade of green. Some of them are shrouded in fine cobwebs.

CAUSE: Spider mites (Family Tetranychidae). These minute, sap-sucking pests are $\frac{1}{60}$ inch long, and they look like grains of red pepper. The first indication of spider-mite infestation is the tiny, yellow pinprick holes in leaves that they make as they suck plant juices. Dry growing conditions or a period of drought during the growing season can encourage infestations of spider mites.

WHAT TO DO:
• Nip off and destroy infested plant parts.
• Knock spider mites from thyme plants with a strong stream of water.
• Use insecticidal soap, following label directions.
• Attract beneficial insects by planting small-flowered nectar plants, including yarrow and Queen-Anne's-lace.

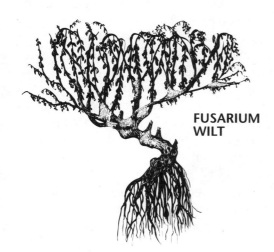

FUSARIUM WILT

 ## Thyme Diseases

PROBLEM: The leaves of your thyme plants are turning yellow and wilting. Watering does not revive them.

CAUSES: Fusarium wilt, also called root rot (*Fusarium* spp.); root rot (*Rhizoctonia solani*). These diseases are caused by several fungi that live in garden soil, and they make the roots of infected thyme plants rot. Thyme plants are susceptible to rot if water lingers too long in the soil around it, especially in winter.

WHAT TO DO:
• Remove and destroy infected plants.
• Plant healthy, new thyme plants in well-drained soil.
• If your soil is high in clay or otherwise slow to drain, add aged manure and compost to lighten the texture of soil.
• Grow thyme in a raised bed.

 ## Other Problems

PROBLEM: Many seeds you sowed in the garden did not germinate. Plants that came up appear sparse and spindly.

CAUSES: Cold temperatures; sowing too thinly. Thyme seeds require a soil temperature of about 70°F to germinate. And the plants look best when grown in clumps.

WHAT TO DO:
• Sow seeds indoors three weeks or more before the last frost date. Sow 20 seeds per 4-inch pot of seed-starting mix covered with a dusting of sand. When the seedlings are about 4 inches tall, plant them outside when the soil temperature warms up to about 70°F.

Lemon Verbena

(Aloysia triphylla)

 ## Lemon Verbena Pests

PROBLEM: Lemon verbena leaves are stippled with yellow. Some of them are curled under or covered in cobwebs.

CAUSE: Spider mites (Family Tetranychidae). These 1/60-inch-long, sap-sucking pests look like grains of red pepper sprinkled on the plants. Dry or dusty conditions encourage infestations of spider mites, which can kill plants if allowed to breed. The webs they spin on plant leaves protect their eggs and young mites.

WHAT TO DO:
• Knock spider mites off lemon verbena plants with a strong spray of water. Spray both sides of the leaves with water.
• Spray plants with insecticidal soap.
• Attract beneficial insects by growing small-flowered nectar plants, like yarrow, dill, and Queen-Anne's-lace.

 ## Lemon Verbena Diseases

Lemon verbena is not usually troubled by diseases.

SPIDER MITE

 ## Other Problems

PROBLEM: The leaves of your previously healthy lemon verbena plants suddenly start wilting and falling off.

CAUSE: Drought stress or root shock. If you notice leaf loss during the growing season, it is most likely because the plant is not getting the moisture it needs. Container plants are especially sensitive to drought. Root shock from transplanting prevents the lemon verbena from taking up enough water.

WHAT TO DO:
• Water the plants lightly for several regular waterings, then water them generously.
• Or, if plant has lost most of its leaves, cut it back to just above living buds on branches, water it generously, and fertilize it with a quick-acting liquid fertilizer, such as fish emulsion.
• When you transplant lemon verbena, keep as much soil around its roots as possible.

PROBLEM: In spite of good growing conditions, your lemon verbena plants produce spindly new growth.

CAUSE: Inadequate fertilizer. Lemon verbena is a heavy feeder. In a container, it rapidly depletes nutrient supplies in the limited amount of soil that its pot contains.

WHAT TO DO:
• Feed lemon verbena regularly with fish emulsion or other liquid fertilizer.
• Pinch back weak branches.

Fruits and Nuts

Almond 124

Apple...................................128

Apricot 132

Blackberry and Raspberry 136

Blueberry 142

Cherry 146

Citrus...................................150

Currant and Gooseberry 154

Grape 156

Hazelnut, also called Filbert ...162

Kiwi 164

Peach 166

Peanut..................................170

Pear 172

Pecan 174

Persimmon............................176

Plum 178

Strawberry 180

Walnut 184

Almond

(Prunus amygdalus)

Almond Pests

PROBLEM: There is insect excrement and webbing on the branches and leaves of almond trees. The nut meats disappear.

CAUSE: Navel orangeworms (*Amyelois transitella*). These pests are caterpillars, the reddish orange, ¾-inch-long larvae of gray moths. The moths have ¾-inch wingspans and dark, diagonal-striped wings. The navel orangeworms differ from oriental fruit moth larvae: Navel orangeworms have a pair of crescent-shaped marks on the second segment behind their heads. The destructive larvae enter almonds after the husks split open, and then they feed on the nut meats. As many as eight or nine larvae of various sizes can feed inside a single nut at the same time. The first and second generation of larvae breed in nuts that have fallen to the ground. Later generations lay eggs in the hulls of newly formed or ripening nuts. There are several overlapping generations each year. The nuts you collected from affected trees and stored may become infested with cocoons and silky webbing. Navel orangeworms are most serious as pests of tree fruit and nuts, including almonds, in the Southwest.

WHAT TO DO:
• Harvest nuts when the husks split open; store them in sealed containers when dry.
• Remove old nuts from the trees and from the ground after harvest.
• Attract beneficial insects and spider populations to your orchard by planting small-flowered nectar plants, including yarrow, dill, and Queen-Anne's-lace, and cover crops, such as *Vicia dasycarpa* 'Lana', in the orchard.
• Apply BT. "BT" stands for *Bacillus thuringiensis*, an insect-stomach poison that kills caterpillar and worm pests without harming beneficial insects. It's important to buy the correct strain. Follow directions and apply when pests are active.

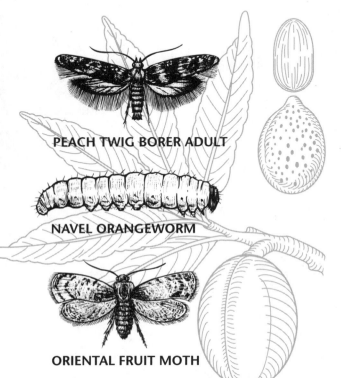

PEACH TWIG BORER ADULT

NAVEL ORANGEWORM

ORIENTAL FRUIT MOTH

PROBLEM: The tips of branches die back several inches. If you split affected twigs, you will see white or pink larvae.

CAUSE: Oriental fruit moth larvae (*Grapho-*

litha molesta). These worms are the larvae of dark gray moths. The moths have dark brown wings and ½-inch wingspans. Oriental fruit moth larvae are white or pink caterpillars with brown heads. The ⅝-inch-long larvae bore into tree branches early in the season and bore into both green and ripening nuts later in the season. On rare occasions, the nut meats of affected trees are eaten by the larvae. The larvae overwinter in cocoons on trees and weeds.

WHAT TO DO:
• Tolerate light damage.
• Place pheromone lures nearby. These commercial lures have a strip of cardboard coated with female insect scents. Male oriental fruit moths attracted to the scent fall into attached collection bags or become confused and unable to find a mate.
• Apply BT. "BT" stands for *Bacillus thuringiensis*, an insect-stomach poison that kills caterpillar and worm pests without harming beneficial insects. Follow directions and apply BT when pests are active.

PROBLEM: Young shoots of almond trees wilt and die back several inches in spring. Nuts may have scarring.

CAUSE: Peach twig borers (*Anarsia lineatella*). These pests are the larvae of tiny gray moths with ⅓-inch wingspans. Young larvae are light brown or cream-colored caterpillars with black heads. Older borers, which can grow up to ½ inch long, are a dark, reddish brown with white bands between the segments of their bodies. (These larvae differ from oriental fruit moth larvae, which are pinkish white caterpillars with brown heads.) Peach twig borers overwinter on branches and twigs as well as under loose bark, or in the crevices of tree-branch crotches. The larvae emerge in spring and bore into tree twigs and leaf buds. There are one to four

generations of peach twig borers each season. Generations that emerge later in the season feed on almond nuts.

WHAT TO DO:
• Tolerate small amounts of damage.
• Find borer entry holes in tree branches, and cut off the wilted branches just below the borers' holes.
• Destroy the infested prunings.
• Attract beneficial insects, including parasitic wasps and predaceous mites, by planting small-flowered nectar plants, including dill, yarrow, and Queen-Anne's-lace.
• Apply BT. "BT" stands for *Bacillus thuringiensis*, an insect-stomach poison that kills caterpillar and worm pests without harming beneficial insects. You can purchase BT from mail-order sources for beneficial insects. It's important to buy the correct strain. Follow directions and apply when pests are active.

PROBLEM: The leaves of your almond trees have yellow stippling, and webs may appear on leaf undersides.

CAUSE: Spider mites (Family Tetranychidae). These ¹⁄₆₀-inch-long pests look like grains of red pepper. Spider mites feed by sucking sap from the undersides of almond-tree leaves. Mite populations and the damage they do increase quickly during dry, hot, dusty summers. There are numerous generations each growing season. Severe infestations can defoliate trees. The mites overwinter on old leaves and infested branches.

WHAT TO DO:
• Attract beneficial insects, like predator mites, lacewings, and ladybird beetles, by planting small-flowered nectar plants, including yarrow, dill, scabiosa, and Queen-Anne's-lace, in the orchard. You can also purchase predator mites for release from mail-order sources for beneficial insects. The

mail-order firms will help you determine how many to buy and when to release them.
• Apply dormant oil, which will reduce the overwintering stages of mites by smothering them. Mix these commercial oil pesticides with water, and spray plants to smother all growth stages of most pests. Follow label directions for usage. In general, dormant plants tolerate the heaviest application of these commercial spray products.

PROBLEM: White, oval insects with ridges on their backs cling to branches and leaves of almond trees.

CAUSE: Cottonycushion scale (*Icerya purchasi*). These insects feed on the sap of tender, new almond tree branches and leaves. The insects overwinter on their host plants. Scale can weaken and kill a young tree if left untreated for several seasons.

WHAT TO DO:
• Spray trees with dormant oil before they bloom in spring. This horticultural oil coats leaves and stems, smothering pests and disease pathogens.
• Attract lady beetles and other beneficial insects by planting small-flowered nectar plants, including yarrow and dill.

PROBLEM: The bark of your almond trees is peppered with small, round holes and shallow tunnels.

CAUSE: Shothole borers, also called fruittree bark borers (*Scolytus rugulosus*). These pests are the larvae of $\frac{1}{10}$-inch-long, dark brown or black beetles with red wing tips. The adult beetles drill small, round holes in the bark so that they can tunnel and feed in the inner bark. After feeding under the bark, the beetles emerge and scoop out shallow, open-faced tunnels to lay their eggs in. When the eggs hatch, the $\frac{1}{8}$-inch-long white grubs with

brown heads also tunnel into the inner layer of bark to feed. There are up to three broods per season, and the adults overwinter under the bark.

WHAT TO DO:
• Paint lower trunk and low-hanging branches with whitewash when beetles lay eggs.

 ## Almond Diseases

PROBLEM: There are smelly, gummy cankers or watery lesions on the trunks and branches of your almond trees.

CAUSE: Bacterial blight (*Pseudomonas syringae* pv. *mors-prunorum*). This disease can cause flowers to drop and nut husks to develop blackened, sunken lesions. It can also cause leaves to wilt and drop early. The disease enters through injured tissues. Infection spreads rapidly in rainy spring weather.

WHAT TO DO:
• Prune and destroy infected branches.
• Prune weak branches.
• Spray with bordeaux mix in the fall as the leaves are dropping. Bordeaux mix is a combination of copper sulfate and hydrated lime in powdered form to use as a fungicide with insecticidal properties. Apply it as a dust or mixed with water for spraying. Follow label directions carefully because bordeaux mix can injure plant foliage.
• Plant windbreaks to prevent wind damage.

PROBLEM: Blossoms wither and develop gray mold. Cankers at the base of infected flowers cause twig dieback.

CAUSE: Brown rot, also called blossom blight (*Monilinia* spp.). This fungal disease overwinters in infected twigs and fruit left on trees. In the spring, almond flowers are susceptible to infection from the time buds open until the petals fall. Rain is necessary for the infection to develop. Brown, sticky droplets may form on the twigs, and almond hulls can also become infected from the time they split open until they dry. Circular brown spots develop on infected almond hulls. The spots spread rapidly and cause the hulls to rot.

WHAT TO DO:
• Destroy infected branches and old fruit.
• Apply bordeaux mix when the flower buds swell and when petals fall if these happen during rainy weather. Bordeaux mix is a combination of copper sulfate and hydrated lime. Apply it as a dust or mixed with water for spraying. Follow label directions carefully.
• Choose resistant cultivars, such as 'Nonpareil', 'Peerless', 'Price', 'Solano', and 'Texas'.

PROBLEM: Gray or white, feltlike patches form on leaves and nut hulls. The leaves may turn brittle and die.

CAUSE: Powdery mildew (*Podosphaera* spp.). This fungal disease overwinters in twigs or buds. Infections occur when the humidity is greater than 90 percent and the temperature is between 50° and 77°F. Powdery mildew may reduce yields, but it does not threaten the life of the tree.

WHAT TO DO:
• Space plants far enough apart for good air circulation.
• Spray with sulfur every seven to ten days in the spring. Do not apply sulfur if temperatures exceed 80°F, or you will burn the foliage.

PROBLEM: Small purple spots develop on the leaves and fruit. The centers of the leaf spots turn brown and crumble.

CAUSE: Shothole disease (*Coryneum carpophilum*). This fungal disease, along with others that cause similar symptoms, overwinters in the infected twigs and buds of almond trees. Disease spores travel in splashing rain or irrigation water. The disease requires 24

hours of contact with wet foliage in order to cause infections. Young, infected leaves may defoliate. Infected nuts become covered with gummy deposits and may fall from the trees.

WHAT TO DO:
• Prune and destroy the shiny, varnished-looking infected buds and twigs.
• Spray with bordeaux mix after leaves fall in early autumn and before the fall rains begin. Apply the spray again at the pink–flower bud stage in the spring. Bordeaux mix is a combination of copper sulfate and hydrated lime in powdered form to use as a fungicide with insecticidal properties. Apply it as a dust or mixed with water for spraying. Follow label directions carefully when spraying foliage with bordeaux because the mix can injure plant foliage.

 Other Problems

PROBLEM: During the winter months you notice chewed buds and shoots. The tree bark also looks gnawed.

CAUSE: Rodents. Ground squirrels, field mice, and rabbits damage almond trees by chewing the bark at the base of the trees and any tender twigs and buds they can reach. Usually more than one rodent is at work. Their combined efforts are very damaging. If rodents gnaw a ring around the base of a tree, it can die.

WHAT TO DO:
• Wrap the base of the tree with a commercial tree guard product or fine-meshed wire, such as hardware cloth.
• Make hair repellents. Hair in mesh bags or old stockings placed near the damaged areas is an effective repellent. You can collect human hair from barbers and add hair from your pets, too. Renew every few weeks.
• Put apple- and peanut butter–baited traps at the base of trees.

Apple

(*Malus pumila* and other species)

 Apple Pests

PROBLEM: Some apples are dimpled outside and have brown tunnels inside. Infested apples soften and turn brown.

CAUSE: Apple maggot flies (*Rhagoletis pomonella*). These pests are flies that are slightly smaller than houseflies. They have black bodies with white stripes on their abdomen and dark bands resembling a "w" across their wings. The female flies lay their eggs in apples. The larvae are small, white maggots that tunnel through the fruit for 14 to 30 days. Then the maggots leave the fruit and overwinter in the soil.

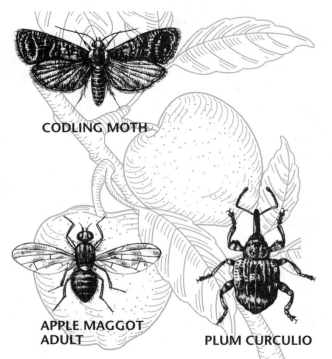

CODLING MOTH

APPLE MAGGOT ADULT

PLUM CURCULIO

WHAT TO DO:
• Make red sticky ball traps. Hang red spheres coated with Tanglefoot (a commercial tacky product) in apple trees to attract and trap female flies. Hang sticky balls at eye level, 2 to 3 feet from branch tips. Keep the foliage and real apples away from the sticky traps so that the traps are visible. Hang two traps in each dwarf tree and four to six traps in full-sized trees. Wipe dead insects off sticky traps and recoat them as needed.
• Pick up and remove fallen apples.
• Remove wild crabapples and hawthorns, which can be carriers, from within 300 feet of your orchard.

PROBLEM: Insect frass (excrement) is on the bottoms of some apples. Inside affected fruits, tunnels lead to the cores.

CAUSE: Codling moth larvae (*Cydia pomonella*). The adults are gray moths with ¾-inch wingspans. They have brown lines on their forewings and fringed back wings. Codling moth larvae are 1-inch-long, pink worms with brown heads. Female moths lay their eggs on apple leaves or developing fruit approximately a month after the tree blooms. When the larvae hatch, they feed on the fruit surface and then tunnel into the fruit. The pests overwinter in the soil.

WHAT TO DO:
• Wrap corrugated cardboard bands around tree trunks to discourage migrating soil pests in spring.
• Remove damaged fruits.
• Release beneficial insects, such as tricho-

gramma wasps, using careful timing. You can purchase live trichogramma wasps from mail-order suppliers. Follow label instructions for application, and release the beneficials when pest larvae are present. You can help tricho-gramma wasps provide better control by planting pollen and nectar food sources, such as dill, Queen-Anne's-lace, and black-eyed Susans.

PROBLEM: Developing apples have winding scars and insect excrement on skins, and they drop before maturing.

CAUSE: European apple sawflies (*Hoplocampa testudinea*). The adults are ⅕-inch-long, dark flies with yellowish legs. The pest larvae of these flies are brown worms with black heads. Adults emerge in spring right before bloom, and they lay their eggs in the developing fruit from the time the trees begin to bloom through petal fall.

WHAT TO DO:
• Make white sticky boards. The egg-bearing female European apple sawflies infest the white apple blossoms, so white sticky boards make effective traps. Coat white cardboard or painted wooden boards with Tanglefoot (a commercial product for this purpose). Hang the sticky traps when the flower buds are just beginning to show pink. Place them head-high from 1 to 3 feet from foliage, with the white side facing outward. Clean off and re-coat the boards as needed to keep them from becoming covered with insects. Discard traps two weeks after the bloom period ends.

PROBLEM: Crescent-shaped scars stunt and deform fruits. Infested fruits drop from trees early in the growing season.

CAUSE: Plum curculios (*Conotrachelus nenuphar*). These are the worst apple pests in the eastern United States. The ⅕-inch-long adults are dark brown beetles with curved, thick beaks. They cut holes in apple skin and lay their eggs under the skin. The nymphs are ⅓-inch-long, white grubs. The grubs tunnel through the fruit, causing it to drop before ripening. The adults eat ripening fruit and overwinter in leaf litter under the apple trees.

WHAT TO DO:
• Tolerate minor damage.
• Collect and destroy affected fruit.
• As the flower petals begin to fall, lay a sheet underneath the tree, and jar the limbs with a padded stick. Collect the beetles that drop to the sheet.,Do this daily for two weeks after petal fall.

PROBLEM: Some leaves on your apple trees have yellow stippling. Some are turning bronze and dropping early.

CAUSES: European red mites (*Panonychus ulmi*) and two-spotted spider mites (*Tetranychus urticae*). These mites are pin-point-sized, yellowish green pests with a dark spot on each side of their abdomen. European red mites damage apple leaves by sucking juices from leaf undersides. They increase quickly and cause the most damage—which can provoke defoliation—in hot, dry summers. They overwinter in crevices in tree branches.

WHAT TO DO:
• Attract beneficial insects, such as lady beetles, lacewings, and predaceous mites, by planting pollen and nectar food sources, including dill, Queen-Anne's-lace, and black-eyed Susans.
• Apply dormant oil, which will reduce the overwintering stages of mites by smothering them. Horticultural oils, such as dormant oil, coat leaves and branches and smother insects and disease pathogens. Dormant plants tolerate the heaviest application of these commercial spray products. Do not apply dormant

oil during cold weather (below 35°F) or within 24 four hours of such a cold spell.

PROBLEM: The leaves of your apple trees wilt and turn brown. There may be soggy, sunken spots on the bark.

CAUSE: Flathead borers (*Chrysobothris* spp.). These tunneling pests are the larvae of ½-inch-long, brown, shiny beetles. The yellowish, 1¼-inch-long grubs are named for a flat spot just behind their heads. These pests burrow into the bark and feed until they are fully grown. Then they burrow deeply into the trunk of the tree to overwinter as grubs. Strong, mature trees can withstand an attack, but flathead borers can kill seedlings. In the spring, adult beetles lay eggs on the tree bark.

WHAT TO DO:

• Wrap tree trunks with tree-wrap paper just after trees bloom in the spring to keep beetles from laying eggs on the bark.

• Irrigate and fertilize trees as needed to keep them growing vigorously.

 Apple Diseases

PROBLEM: Olive-drab spots appear on the undersides of leaves. Dark brown, velvety or corky spots disfigure fruits.

CAUSE: Apple scab (*Venturia inaequalis*). This fungal disease overwinters on fallen leaves. In spring, warm temperatures and rain promote the release of spores that infect new foliage and fruits. Scab is evident about ten days after infection.

WHAT TO DO:

• Compost old leaves in the fall.

• Prune for good air circulation.

• Plant scab-resistant cultivars, such as 'Freedom', 'Liberty', 'Pristine', 'Redfree', and 'William's Pride'.

• Spray with copper solution before bloom, and spray with sulfur or bordeaux mix every seven to ten days until temperatures reach 80°F. Bordeaux mix is a combination of copper sulfate and hydrated lime in powdered form to use as a fungicide with insecticidal properties. Apply it as a dust or mixed with water for spraying. Follow label directions carefully because bordeaux mix can injure plant foliage. Do not use sulfur within 30 days of spraying dormant oil.

PROBLEM: In midsummer yellow-orange spots appear on leaves. Deformed apples have concentric orange rings.

CAUSE: Cedar apple rust (*Gymnosporangium juniperi-virginianae*). This fungal disease needs two hosts to complete its life cycle: apple trees and certain juniper species, most notably the eastern red cedar (*Juniperus virginiana*). The fungus overwinters as a gall on the junipers; and in the spring the galls form orange horn-shaped growths and discharge spores that infect nearby apple trees. In severe infections, cedar apple rust can cause apple trees to defoliate early in the season. In July and August, spores travel from the apple tree back to the cedar.

WHAT TO DO:

• Remove eastern red cedars within ½ mile of your orchard.

• Remove galls from cedars in winter.

• Apply sulfur spray to prevent infections. Spray every seven to ten days from the time they begin flowering until temperatures reach 80°F.

• Plant resistant varieties, such as 'Macfree', 'Nova Easygro', and 'Priscilla'.

PROBLEM: In spring branch tips wilt, blacken, and bend. Dark, sunken cankers form on branches.

CAUSE: Fire blight (*Erwinia amylovora*). Fire blight is a serious bacterial disease. The cankers caused by the disease can kill branches and entire trees. In moist, warm spring weather, fire blight bacterium surfaces in drops of ooze from these cankers. The disease-laden droplets travel in the wind, rain, and insects to apple blossoms. Shoots and entire trees can turn black and wilt in less than a week. Outbreaks tend to be cyclical. You may not notice symptoms in your orchard for years until a "blight year" occurs when weather conditions are optimum.

WHAT TO DO:
• Prune infected branches 8 to 10 inches below the damage.
• If fire blight was present during the last growing season, apply copper spray before flowers appear. Copper spray reduces populations of blight bacteria.
• Plant resistant varieties, such as 'Freedom', 'Jonafree', 'Liberty', 'Macfree', and 'Nova Easygro'.
• Avoid overfertilizing and heavy pruning, which stimulate soft, susceptible growth.

PROBLEM: Gray or white, feltlike patches form on leaves and fruit of apple trees. Leaves turn brittle and die.

CAUSE: Powdery mildew (*Podosphaera* spp.). Infections occur when the humidity is greater than 90 percent and the temperature is between 50° and 77°F. Powdery mildew may reduce yields on susceptible cultivars, but it does not threaten the life of apple trees. This fungal disease overwinters in twigs or buds.

WHAT TO DO:
• Spray with sulfur every seven to ten days from the end of the flowering period until temperatures reach 80°F.

• Plant resistant cultivars, such as 'Freedom', 'Redfree', and 'Sir Prize'.

 Other Problems

PROBLEM: Some of the ripe apples on your trees have large holes hollowed out of them.

CAUSE: Birds. Birds love to eat apples. They peck at the ripening fruits, making holes and in time eating as much as half the apple. The damaged fruit can rot and become inedible.

WHAT TO DO:
• Make scarecrows. Aluminum pie plates, scare tape, and aluminum foil will deter birds as long as a breeze creates movement to frighten them.
• Cover apple trees with bird netting. Tie the netting to the trunk of the tree to keep it in place.
• Harvest apples when they ripen.

PROBLEM: Branches with many ripening apples on them break off and drop to the ground.

CAUSE: Too much weight for the branch to bear. Young trees with weak branches are likely to lose those branches when they are weighted down by ripening fruits. The branches of apple trees that produce large apples are also sometimes not strong enough to carry the weight of many ripening apples.

WHAT TO DO:
• Prune off the remnants of broken branches.
• Prop up branches that look as if they are sagging and about to break.
• During the dormant season, prune out weak branches.
• Thin developing fruits to distribute the weight of developing fruit evenly.

Apricot *(Prunus armeniaca)*

 Apricot Pests

PROBLEM: Trees stop growing and look unhealthy. Gummy masses mixed with sawdust are at the base of the trunks.

CAUSE: Borers (*Synanthedon* spp.). Borers are caterpillars and beetle grubs that tunnel into stems and fruits. Several species of these pests produce larvae that feed on the inner bark of apricot trees. They can girdle and kill young trees and seriously weaken older ones, making the trees the target of disease and other pests.

WHAT TO DO:
• Kill the larvae by inserting a wire into their tunnels.
• Dig the borers out of their tunnels with a pocket knife and destroy them.
• Inject beneficial nematodes into the borer's holes. You can purchase beneficial nematodes (*Steinernema carpocapsae* and *Heterorhabditis heliothidis*) from mail-order suppliers. Live nematodes are shipped suspended in gels or sponges. Follow label instructions for application, and apply while larvae are active.
• Attract natural predators, including ants, spiders, and birds.
• Attract beneficial insects, such as lacewing larvae, by planting small-flowered nectar plants, including dill, Queen-Anne's-lace, yarrow, and black-eyed Susans.

PROBLEM: Apricots have developed gummy globs on their fuzzy skins. Pink larvae are tunneling inside fruits.

CAUSE: Oriental fruit moth larvae (*Grapholitha molesta*). These worms are the larvae of dark gray moths with dark brown wings and wingspans of about ½ inch. The pests are white or pink caterpillars with brown heads. The ⅝-inch-long larvae bore into apricot tree branches early in the season and bore into both green and ripening fruits later in the season. When you cut the apricots open, you will see pink larvae tunneling inside. Larvae also tunnel into branch tips, causing the trees to take on an unusual, bushy appearance.

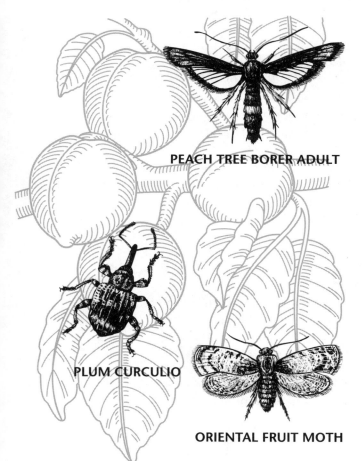

PEACH TREE BORER ADULT

PLUM CURCULIO

ORIENTAL FRUIT MOTH

The larvae overwinter in cocoons on trees and in surrounding plants.

WHAT TO DO:
• Tolerate light damage.
• Set out pheromone lures. These commercial lures have a strip of cardboard coated with female insect scents. Male pests attracted to the scent fall into attached collection bags or become confused and unable to find a mate.
• Monitor the populations in traps and spray with BT every two weeks from May through September. "BT" stands for *Bacillus thuringiensis*, an insect-stomach poison that kills caterpillar and worm pests without harming beneficial insects. It's important to buy the correct strain. Follow directions and apply when pests are active.
• Release trichogramma wasps. You can purchase these and other live beneficial insects from mail-order suppliers. Follow label instructions for application, and release beneficials when pest larvae are present. You can help trichogramma wasps provide better control by planting pollen and nectar food sources for them, including dill, Queen-Anne's-lace, and black-eyed Susans.
• Dispose of fallen fruits.
• Cultivate the ground under apricot trees before they flower in spring to expose larvae that have overwintered in the soil.

PROBLEM: Crescent-shaped scars are on the skins of young apricots. Marked fruits are stunted and deformed.

CAUSE: Plum curculios (*Conotrachelus nenuphar*). These are the worst apricot pests in the eastern half of the United States. The ⅕-inch-long adults are dark brown beetles with curved, thick beaks. The female beetles eat ripening fruit. They also cut crescent-shaped holes in apricot skins and lay eggs under the flaps of skin. The nymphs are ⅓-inch-long white grubs that tunnel through

the fruit as they feed, causing it to drop before ripening. The pests overwinter in leaf litter under the trees.

WHAT TO DO:
• Tolerate minor damage.
• Collect and dispose of the beetles for two weeks after petals fall. Lay a sheet underneath the tree, and jar the limbs with a padded stick until the beetles drop to the sheet.
• Collect and destroy infested fruit.

PROBLEM: Apricot tree branches have clusters of tiny gray-brown bumps. Leaves yellow; some branches die back.

CAUSE: San Jose scale (*Quadraspidiotus perniciosus*). These insects feed on the sap of apricot tree bark, leaves, and fruit. The fully grown females are the size of a pinhead. They are rounded gray-brown bumps with a dull yellow hump. Male scale are slightly smaller and have an oval shape with a raised bump near the larger end of the oval. The insects overwinter in a partly grown stage and begin to mature in the spring. Extremely cold weather greatly reduces populations. San Jose scale can weaken and kill a young tree in two or three years. Fruits that have red spots are telltale signs of the scale.

WHAT TO DO:
• Spray dormant oil on trees before bloom. This horticultural oil coats leaves and stems, smothering pests and disease pathogens.
• Attract beneficials, such as lady beetles and parasitic wasps, by planting small-flowered nectar plants, including yarrow, dill, and Queen-Anne's-lace.

PROBLEM: White, oval-shaped insects with ridges on their backs cling to branches and leaves of apricot trees.

CAUSE: Cottonycushion scale (*Icerya purchasi*). These insects feed on the sap of tender, new apricot tree branches and leaves. The insects overwinter on their host plants. Scale can weaken and kill a young tree if left untreated for several seasons.

WHAT TO DO:
• Spray trees with dormant oil before they bloom in spring. This horticultural oil coats leaves and stems, smothering pests and disease pathogens.
• Encourage beneficial insects, especially lady beetles, by planting small-flowered nectar plants, including yarrow, dill, and Queen-Anne's-lace, in the orchard.

PROBLEM: Leaves have thin, pale, winding trails or are rolled into tubes and tied together with webbing.

CAUSES: Obliquebanded leafrollers (*Choristoneura rosaceana*). These caterpillars are from ½ to ¾ inch long and can be pale green, brown, or yellow. The pests hatch from eggs laid by adult moths that are active only after dark. The moths are brown with three darker brown stripes on their front wings. Obliquebanded moths have wingspans of ¾ inch.

WHAT TO DO:
• Spray heavy infestations with the plant-derived insecticide pyrethrins or with *Bacillus thuringiensis* (BT). These products can be found in many garden centers and mail-order supply catalogs.
• Remove and destroy the folded leaves where the caterpillars hide.

 Apricot Diseases

PROBLEM: Fruits have small sunken spots or cracks. Leaves turn yellow and drop. Cankers are on branches.
CAUSE: Bacterial leaf spot (*Xanthomonas*

pruni). This disease is a serious problem in the Southeast, spreading in the spring from the liquid that oozes from the cankers. Bacterial leaf spot is most severe during rainy periods in spring. It also can weaken trees, making them prone to winter injury. This disease is very difficult to control.

WHAT TO DO:
• Spray infected trees with copper or bordeaux mix in the spring. Bordeaux mix is a combination of copper sulfate and hydrated lime in powdered form to use as a fungicide with insecticidal properties. Apply it as a dust or mixed with water for spraying. Follow label directions carefully because bordeaux mix can injure plant foliage.
• Rake up and remove leaves at the end of the growing season to reduce sites for wintering disease.
• Plant resistant varieties, such as 'Harcot' and 'Harlayne'.

PROBLEM: Gummy ooze is at the base of apricot blossoms. Small, rotting spots on fruits spread until entire fruits rot.
CAUSE: Brown rot. This serious disease of apricots is caused by several species of fungi. The fungi overwinter in infected twigs and in the dried (mummified) fruits left on trees in the fall. In the spring, apricot flowers become infected. Rain is necessary for infection to develop. The disease causes fruits to rot and dry (mummify).

WHAT TO DO:
• Spray with bordeaux mix when the flower buds swell and when petals fall if these happen during rainy weather. Apply it again before harvest as fruit changes color. Bordeaux mix is a combination of copper sulfate and hydrated lime in powdered form to use as a fungicide with insecticidal properties. Apply it as a dust or mixed with

water for spraying. Follow label directions carefully because bordeaux mix can injure plant foliage.
• Choose resistant cultivars, such as 'Harcot', 'Hargrand', and 'Harlayne'.
• Destroy infected branches and old fruit.

PROBLEM: Leaves have small, angular spots. The branches fail to leaf out properly, and they begin to die back.

CAUSE: Cankers. Several fungi and bacteria cause these disease symptoms. These diseases enter apricot trees through injured bark and leaves. Amber gum oozes from infected stems.

WHAT TO DO:
• Prune off and destroy wilted or dying branches several inches below the infection. Delay pruning until buds are open because early pruning can provide entry for cankers.
• Spray copper, which helps control bacterial canker when it first infects leaves.
• Plant resistant varieties, such as 'Harcot', 'Hargrand', 'Harlayne', and 'Harogen'.

PROBLEM: Limbs die back suddenly during the heat of summer. Oozing cankers develop on the branches.

CAUSE: Eutypa dieback (*Eutypa lata*). This fungal disease overwinters on diseased wood left on trees. Cankers can increase in size by 6 inches per year, and the fungus can spread from branches to trunks. Disease spores travel in rain and enter trees through wounds.

WHAT TO DO:
• Prune trees during dry summer weather.
• Remove and destroy infected branches at least 6 inches below discolored wood.

PROBLEM: Olive-drab spots appear on apricot leaves. Dark brown, velvety or corky spots disfigure the fruits.

CAUSE: Scab (*Cladosporium carpophilum*). This fungal disease overwinters on fallen leaves. In spring, warm temperatures and rain favor the release of spores. The disease can infect new foliage and fruits all through the growing season. Diseased apricots are often dwarfed, deformed, or cracked. Fruits are edible if peeled.

WHAT TO DO:
• Compost old leaves in the fall.
• Prune for good air circulation.
• Spray with copper solution before bloom.
• Spray with sulfur or bordeaux mix every seven to ten days until temperatures reach 80°F. Bordeaux mix is a combination of copper sulfate and hydrated lime in powdered form to use as a fungicide with insecticidal properties. Follow label directions carefully. Do not use sulfur within 30 days of spraying dormant oil.

PROBLEM: Leaves have small, round, purple spots. The centers of the spots turn brown and crumble.

CAUSE: Shothole disease (*Coryneum carpophilum*). This fungal disease is named for the "shothole" leaf spots it causes. The fruit of infected trees is scabby-looking. Shothole disease overwinters in the infected twigs and buds of apricot trees. The disease spores travel in splashing rain or irrigation water, and they require 24 hours of wetness to cause infections.

WHAT TO DO:
• Prune off and destroy the shiny, varnished-looking infected buds and twigs, blossoms, and fruits.
• Apply bordeaux mix after leaf fall and before the fall rains begin. Apply again at the pink–flower bud stage in the spring. Bordeaux mix is a combination of copper sulfate and hydrated lime in powdered form. Apply it as a dust or mixed with water for spraying. Follow label directions carefully.

Blackberry and Raspberry

(Rubus spp.)

Blackberry and Raspberry Pests

PROBLEM: New leaves fold, and the tips bend over and wilt. Small, pear-shaped, green insects cling to leaf backs.

CAUSE: Aphids (Family Aphididae). These soft-bodied, pear-shaped insects are from 1/16 to 3/8 inch long. Aphids range in color from pale tan to light green to nearly black. They damage leaves and stems of blackberry and raspberry plants (also called brambles) by sucking plant juices from them. Their sticky secretions, called honeydew, encourage mold growth and attract ants, which eat the sticky secretions. Aphids can also transfer plant viruses as they feed.

WHAT TO DO:
• Wash aphids off plants with a strong stream of water. Be sure to hit the backs of leaves as well as the tops when spraying.
• Use insecticidal soap, following label directions; be sure to spray the backs of leaves as well as the tops.
• Attract beneficial insects, like lady beetles and lacewings, by planting small-flowered nectar plants, including yarrow, dill, and Queen-Anne's-lace. Give the beneficials time to bring aphids under control.

PROBLEM: The leaves of your blackberry and raspberry plants are riddled with so many holes that they look lacy.

CAUSE: Japanese beetles (*Popillia japonica*). The ½-inch-long, metallic green beetles have bronze wings. These pests cluster together on foliage in midsummer to feed. Beetle grubs overwinter in the soil. In the late spring, larvae feed on plant roots before turning into leaf-eating beetles.

WHAT TO DO:
• Handpick Japanese beetles in early morning or evening, when cooler temperatures make them sluggish and easier to catch.

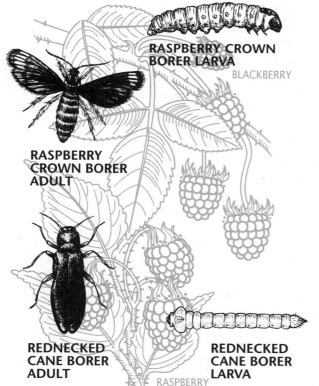

RASPBERRY CROWN BORER LARVA

BLACKBERRY

RASPBERRY CROWN BORER ADULT

REDNECKED CANE BORER ADULT

REDNECKED CANE BORER LARVA

RASPBERRY

• Apply beneficial nematodes (*Steinernema carpocapsae* and *Heterorhabditis heliothidis*) in late spring or late summer. The nematodes are shipped live from mail-order suppliers suspended in gels or sponges. Apply nematodes when larvae are still active in the soil.

• Apply milky disease spores to sod areas. This microbial insecticide, available under several trade names, is a combination of spores of *Bacillus popilliae* and *B. lentimorbus*. Grubs die after they eat the spores.

• Aerate your turf areas with spiked aerator sandals in late spring and early fall to kill grubs before they turn into beetles.

PROBLEM: Tips of canes wilt and die in early summer. Two rings of punctures about ½ to 1 inch apart appear in tips.

CAUSE: Raspberry cane borers (*Oberea bimaculata*). The raspberry cane borer is a slender black beetle about ½ inch long, with prominent antennae about as long as its body. The section behind its head is yellow-orange with two or three dark dots. In June, the adult female lays eggs in the tender new growth of the canes. The ¾-inch-long, white larvae feed within the canes for two years before emerging as adults.

WHAT TO DO:

• Use floating row covers to protect plants from flying insects, animals, and temperature fluctuations. Cover the plants with these synthetic, spunbonded fabrics, and bury the edges in the soil.

• Remove wilted branch tips several inches below the punctures when you notice the wilting.

• Remove and destroy older, weak canes.

PROBLEM: Your blackberry or raspberry plants wilt and lack vigor. When you grasp the canes, they break off easily.

CAUSE: Raspberry crown borers (*Pennisetia marginata*). The adults are 1-inch-long, clear-winged wasps that resemble yellow jackets. They emerge in midsummer and lay eggs on plant leaves. After hatching, the larvae crawl to the base of the canes, penetrate the bark, and overwinter there. The larvae are 1 inch long and are white with dark heads. They feed inside canes and crowns of plants for two growing seasons before maturing.

WHAT TO DO:

• Use floating row covers to protect plants from flying insects, animals, and temperature fluctuations. Cover the plants with these synthetic, spunbonded fabrics, and bury the edges in the soil.

• Keep your blackberry and raspberry plants irrigated and well maintained, because borers attack drought-weakened, overcrowded, and otherwise stressed plants.

• Dig out and destroy infested plants.

PROBLEM: The young leaves, buds, and blossoms of your plants look chewed. The fruits drop before they ripen.

CAUSE: Raspberry fruitworms (*Byturus unicolor*). Raspberry fruitworms are most prevalent in the northern United States and Canada. The adults are oval, light brown, ⅛-inch-long beetles. They eat young leaves, buds, and blossom clusters, causing reduced fruit set. The beetles emerge from the soil in early spring, feed, and then lay eggs. Their ¼-inch-long, light yellow larvae hatch and eat the developing berries. Upon maturity, the larvae burrow into the soil and transform into pupae that remain in the soil until the following spring.

WHAT TO DO:

• Collect and destroy worm-infested fruit daily before it drops to keep larvae from burrowing into the soil.

• In heavy infestations, spray pyrethrins just before blossoms open (around late April to early May) to kill adult beetles. Never spray during bloom, since you will kill bees and other pollinators. Pyrethrins are botanical insecticides derived from the dried flowerheads of the daisy *Chrysanthemum cinerariaefolium*. The active ingredient, pyrethrins, is a broad-spectrum nerve poison that kills chewing and sucking insects. Follow label instructions for mixing and applying. Since lime and soap products deactivate pyrethrins, avoid using them in combination with these products.

PROBLEM: Berries remain hard and sour. They never ripen properly, and only part of a berry may be affected.

CAUSE: Redberry mites (*Acalitus essigi*). Microscopic mites cause this condition. The mites overwinter in bud scale. In the spring the mites migrate to flowers and begin feeding on the developing fruit.

WHAT TO DO:
• Spray with bordeaux solution when new shoots are 1 inch long, and apply it again when the canes have developed an inch of new growth. Bordeaux mix is a combination of copper sulfate and hydrated lime to use as a fungicide with insecticidal properties.

PROBLEM: There are gall-like swellings on branches. The affected branches wilt and snap off easily at the swellings.

CAUSE: Rednecked cane borers (*Agrilus ruficollis*). These pests predominantly attack brambles grown in the eastern United States and Canada. The rednecked cane borer feeds on raspberries, blackberries, and dewberries. The adult beetle has a reddish section behind its head; the rest of the body is black. The adults are present from May to August. They feed on the foliage and lay eggs on the canes.

The white, ¾-inch-long larvae make spiral burrows just beneath the bark of canes, which causes the swellings. There is one generation each year.

WHAT TO DO:
• Cut out and remove infected canes from late fall to early spring.

PROBLEM: Foamy masses of bubbles appear on plant stems. The plants wilt and fail to grow well.

CAUSE: Meadow spittlebugs (*Philaenus spumarius*). These sap-sucking pests are the yellowish nymphs of insects called froghoppers. Spittlebugs live inside the piles of bubbles you see on your bramble plants. The adult froghoppers are ¼- to ½-inch long bugs with sharp spines on their back legs.

WHAT TO DO:
• Wipe off foam and nymphs with a paper towel.
• Use floating row covers to exclude feeding insects, including spittlebugs and froghoppers. Cover the plants with these synthetic, spunbonded fabrics, and bury the edges of the row cover in the soil.

PROBLEM: The canes of berry plants have small, white bumps. The plants grow poorly and seem unhealthy.

CAUSE: Rose scale (*Aulacaspis rosae*). Rose scale are white, ¹⁄₂₅-inch-long, stationary insects that feed on plant sap. Female scale are almost circular with an orange-yellow dot in the center of their backs. Male scale are smaller than the females and are long and narrow.

WHAT TO DO:
• Remove and burn infected canes.
• Apply dormant oil in the winter. This oil spray coats plants and smothers insect pests.
• Attract beneficial insects by growing small-

flowered nectar plants, such as dill, Queen-Anne's-lace, and black-eyed Susans.

PROBLEM: You see small, black-and-orange beetles congregating on your ripe blackberries and raspberries.

CAUSE: Sap beetles (*Glischrochilus quadrisignatus*). These pests are ¼-inch-long, black beetles with four orange spots on their backs. The adults feed on overripe berries. Nick-named "picnic beetles," sap beetles do little damage and are mostly an annoyance when you harvest your crop.

WHAT TO DO:
• Remove overripe, damaged, or diseased fruit regularly.

PROBLEM: Flower buds wilt and hang from the plant. Deformed fruits develop from remaining buds.

CAUSE: Strawberry bud weevils (*Anthonomus signatus*). The strawberry bud weevil is a ¹⁄₁₀-inch-long, brown, snouted beetle. The larvae are small, white, curved grubs. The adult weevils lay eggs in blossom buds, then clip or girdle the flower stems. The larvae complete their development in the buds.

WHAT TO DO:
• Handpick in early spring.
• Rake up and destroy plant debris, especially in the fall, to remove hiding places where pests may overwinter.

PROBLEM: Leaves are stippled in yellow, then turn yellow and bronze and drop early. There is fine webbing on leaves.

CAUSE: Two-spotted spider mites (*Tetranychus urticae*). Spider mites are pinpoint-sized pests that pierce plant cells to suck juices. Mites overwinter in leaves on the ground and in canes. Spider mites feed more and cause more damage during dry spells.

WHAT TO DO:
• Wash mites off foliage with a heavy stream of water.
• Use insecticidal soap, following label directions.
• Attract beneficial insects, such as predatory wasps and mites, by planting small-flowered nectar plants, including dill, fennel, and Queen-Anne's-lace. You can also purchase and release beneficials. A mail-order source for beneficial insects can advise you on what kinds to buy and when to release them.

Blackberry and Raspberry Diseases

PROBLEM: In spring, canes develop reddish purple spots and sunken lesions. Infected leaves have yellow-white spots.

CAUSE: Anthracnose (*Elsinoe veneta*). This fungal disease overwinters on infected canes and thrives in wet, rainy conditions above 60°F. The disease spore travels by wind, rain, and irrigation water.

WHAT TO DO:
• Remove and destroy infected canes.
• Spray susceptible varieties with bordeaux mix in spring. Bordeaux is a soluble mixture of sulfur and hydrated lime with disease-inhibiting effects.
• Plant certified disease-free plants. Several anthracnose-resistant blackberry varieties include 'Black Hawk', 'Black Satin', 'Dirksen Thornless', 'Jewel', 'Lowden', and 'Munger'.
• Plant in well-drained soil, and provide good air circulation.

PROBLEM: Canes break easily. Plants have brown, warty growths on crowns and roots and may stunt and die.

CAUSE: Bacterial crown gall (*Agrobacterium* spp.). Crown gall, a serious bacterial disease, travels through the soil in running water and is spread during cultivation. Galls develop in spring.

WHAT TO DO:
• Dig up infected plants and burn them.
• Inspect new stock for galls before planting.
• Soak the roots of new plants in a biological-control product containing the bacterium *Agrobacterium radiobacter,* which is available from mail-order sources for beneficial insects.
• Locate plants in an area with no history of the disease.

PROBLEM: Branches wilt and die in midsummer. The canes turn gray by the end of the growing season.

CAUSE: Cane blight (*Leptosphaeria coniothyrium*). This fungal disease spreads from plant to plant in wet weather in spring and in early summer. The infected branches wilt and die, and brown or purple spots develop on infected branches. The spores travel by wind or rain and enter plants through wounds. Plants weakened by the disease are susceptible to winter injury.

WHAT TO DO:
• Remove and destroy infected stems.
• Prune plants before growth starts in spring, pruning during dry weather so that wounds can heal before rain can spread the disease.

PROBLEM: Your berry plants look healthy; but the fruits are small, and they fall apart when you pick them.

CAUSE: Crumbly berry virus. The tomato ringspot virus causes the symptoms called crumbly berry virus disease in brambles. The disease is transmitted to blackberry and raspberry plants via feeding insects, such as dagger nematodes (*Xiphinema* spp.). Viral diseases develop slowly, so it may take several years for you to notice the symptoms.

WHAT TO DO:
• Dig up and destroy infected plants.
• Plant virus-free plants (sold as virus-indexed plants) at a new site.

PROBLEM: There is a gray, fuzzy mold covering your blackberry and raspberry fruits.

CAUSE: Gray mold (*Botrytis cinerea*). Also known as Botrytis, the fungus that causes this disease lives on dead and dying blackberry and raspberry plants and in the soil. These infections break out during the bloom period and spread in wet weather during the harvest period.

WHAT TO DO:
• Remove moldy and overripe fruit from the plants.
• Space plants widely to promote good air circulation.

PROBLEM: In the spring, leaves become mottled with yellow. The shoot tips of affected plants die back.

CAUSE: Mosaic. A number of viruses cause the symptoms called mosaic. Infected plants usually die several years after becoming infected. This disease is transmitted by sap-sucking insects, like aphids. It overwinters in the infected plants.

WHAT TO DO:
• Avoid planting new blackberry and raspberry plants near wild brambles or existing cultivated bramble plantings, which can be disease carriers.
• Keep plantings of red raspberries separate from black and purple raspberries.
• Plant resistant cultivars. Many raspberry varieties are unpalatable to aphids. They include 'Algonquin', 'Autumn Bliss', 'Canby', 'Chilcotin', 'Chilliwack', 'Haida', 'Killarney', 'Nootka', 'Nordic', 'Royalty', 'Skeena', and 'Tulameen'.

PROBLEM: New leaves and shoots have yellow spots and are spindly. Infected plants look bushy.

CAUSE: Orange rust (*Gymnoconia peckiana*). This fungal disease enters the plant through the leaves in early spring and moves through the canes, crowns, and roots. The disease overwinters in infected plants. There is no cure for infected plants.

WHAT TO DO:
• Remove and destroy infected plants before the spots develop.
• Plant rust-resistant blackberry cultivars, like 'Boysenberry', 'Cheyenne', 'Commanche', 'Eldorado', 'Evergreen', and 'Shawnee'.

PROBLEM: There is a white, powdery coating on fruit, leaves, and young canes. Infected leaves are deformed.

CAUSE: Powdery mildew (*Sphaerotheca macularisi; Phyllactinia corylea*). This fungal disease is most common late in the season when there is warm, humid weather without rainfall.

WHAT TO DO:
• Space plants widely for good air circulation.
• Spray with sulfur every seven to ten days in the spring. Do not apply sulfur if temperatures exceed 80°F, or you will burn the foliage.

PROBLEM: The planting looks uneven or patchy. Stunted plants die at fruiting time in their second season.

CAUSE: Root rot (*Phytophthora cinnamomi*). This soilborne fungus is most active in poorly drained soil. Infected plants are stunted and produce few berries. If you dig them up, you will find that they have black, rotting roots.

WHAT TO DO:
• Pull up and destroy infected plants.
• Plant brambles in well-drained soil.
• Grow healthy, new plants in raised beds.

PROBLEM: Leaves turn yellow, wilt, and drop. Canes get blue-black streaks and die. Fruits are small, tasteless, and dry.

CAUSE: Verticillium wilt, also called blue stem (*Verticillium albo-atrum*). Verticillium wilt is a soilborne fungal disease (it can live in the soil for up to 15 years) that enters the root system and causes a systemic infection. The disease is most pronounced in poorly drained soils and in cool, wet weather.

WHAT TO DO:
• Solarize the soil. Clear plastic sheeting placed over bare soil for three to four weeks uses the sun's energy to heat the soil enough to kill most pests and weed seeds in the top few inches of soil. After removing the plastic, plant crops as usual.
• Plant healthy, new blackberries and raspberries in a different location. Avoid planting them near susceptible plants like tomatoes; potatoes; eggplant; peppers; strawberries; stone fruit; and weeds, such as lamb's-quarters and red-root pigweed.

 Other Problems

PROBLEM: The fruits of your blackberry and raspberry plants are quickly disappearing!

CAUSE: Birds. These flying pests will often win the competition for who can harvest the most fruit, even before berries are ripened.

WHAT TO DO:
• Use bird netting or floating row covers to keep birds from picking your berries. Cover the planting with the material, and bury the edges in soil.
• Make scarecrows. Aluminum pie plates, scare tape, and aluminum foil tied near plantings will deter birds as long as a breeze creates movement.

Blueberry

(*Vaccinium* hybrids)

 Blueberry Pests

PROBLEM: Some berries look dimpled outside and have brown tunnels inside. Infested berries soften and turn brown.

CAUSE: Blueberry maggot flies (*Rhagoletis mendax*). These pests are flies that are slightly smaller than houseflies. They have black bodies with white stripes on their abdomen and dark bands resembling a "w" across their wings. The female flies lay their eggs in blueberries. The larvae are small, white maggots that tunnel through the fruit as they feed. Then the maggots leave the fruit and overwinter in the soil.

WHAT TO DO:
• Pick up and remove fallen fruits.

PROBLEM: Your blueberries are covered with frass (insect excrement) and silky cobwebs.

CAUSE: Cranberry fruitworms (*Acrobasis vaccinii*). Adults are gray, mottled moths with ¾-inch wingspans. They lay their eggs on developing fruit. Upon hatching, light green larvae enter the fruit, feed, and web several berries together. The larvae grow up to ⅞ inch long and will emerge from berries to overwinter in soil.

WHAT TO DO:
• Pick and destroy infested berries.
• Hoe the ground around blueberry bushes. Repeated shallow hoeing reduces larval population in the soil.

PROBLEM: Your blueberries are shriveled, prematurely blue, and webbed together.

CAUSE: Cherry fruitworms (*Grapholitha packardi*). These ⅜-inch-long, pink and red larvae feed inside several berries. The adults are mottled, dark gray moths with ⅓-inch wingspans. The pests overwinter in cavities in deadwood.

WHAT TO DO:
• Pick and destroy infested fruit.

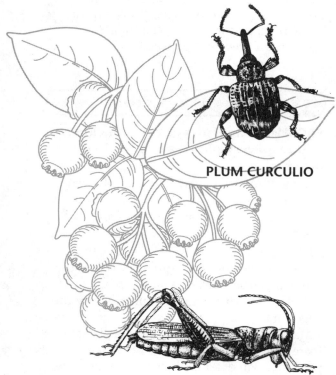

PLUM CURCULIO

GRASSHOPPER

• Spray with dormant oil when plants are dormant. Applying this commercial horticultural oil will smother overwintering cherry fruitworms.

PROBLEM: Suddenly, in mid- and late summer, large holes appear in blueberry leaves and in the fruits.

CAUSE: Grasshoppers (Order Orthoptera). Several common species of grasshoppers like to eat blueberry leaves. Adults are brown, yellow, or green, 1- to 2-inch-long, winged insects with enlarged hind legs for jumping. The females lay eggs in burrows in the soil in late summer. The eggs overwinter and hatch into small grasshoppers the following spring.

WHAT TO DO:
• Handpick.
• Offer nesting sites, water, and seeds to attract natural enemies, such as birds, which eat grasshoppers.
• Till the soil in autumn to expose eggs to fatal, freezing temperatures.
• Attract beneficial insects, like tiny wasps and predatory flies, by planting small-flowered nectar plants, including yarrow, dill, and Queen-Anne's-lace.
• Release beneficial nematodes (*Steinernema carpocapsae* and *Heterorhabditis heliothidis*), which you can purchase from mail-order suppliers. Live nematodes are shipped suspended in gels or sponges. Follow label instructions for application.
• Use floating row covers to exclude feeding insects. Cover the plants with these synthetic, spunbonded fabrics, and bury the edges of the row cover in the soil.

PROBLEM: Half-moon-shaped scars are noticeable on berries. Berries rot and drop prematurely.

CAUSE: Plum curculios (*Conotrachelus*

nenuphar). The adults are dark brown, ⅓-inch-long beetles with curved, thick beaks. These pests cut holes in the skins of blueberries and lay eggs in the berries. Their larvae are ⅓-inch-long, white grubs. The larvae tunnel through the fruit, causing it to rot and drop before ripening.

WHAT TO DO:
• Beginning at petal fall, place a light-colored tarp under the shrubs, and jar the limbs with a padded stick. The beetles will drop to the cloth. Collect and destroy them daily for two weeks.

PROBLEM: Your blueberry plants have reduced yield. There are clusters of circular bumps on branches and leaves.

CAUSE: Scale (Order Homoptera). These ⅒-inch-long insects look like oval, waxy bumps. Both the stationary adults and their similarly sized, fuzzy, mobile nymphs suck plant juices and produce sticky honeydew that encourages the growth of sooty mold.

WHAT TO DO:
• Attract beneficial insects, such as ladybird beetles and parasitic wasps, by planting small-flowered nectar plants, including dill, scabiosia, and yarrow.
• Prune and destroy diseased branches.
• Spray with dormant oil when plants are dormant. Applying this commercial horticultural oil will smother overwintering scale.

PROBLEM: Blueberry leaves are deformed, curled, and turning reddish green. Leaf tips turn dry and shriveled.

CAUSE: Thrips (*Frankliniella vaccinii*). These pests are tiny, ⅟₅₀- to ⅟₂₅-inch-long, brown insects with gray head and wings. When thrips feed in large numbers, they draw so much sap from plant leaves that the plants cannot grow.

WHAT TO DO:
• Use insecticidal soap, following label directions.
• Control weeds to allow light and air to reach blueberry plants.

PROBLEM: The buds and young leaves of your blueberry bushes are chewed and peppered with small holes.

CAUSES: Grape flea beetles (*Altica chalybea*) and steel blue flea beetles (*A. tarquata*). These tiny, ½-inch-long, shiny, metallic blue or green beetles chew holes in tender leaves and buds. Their black-spotted, yellowish larvae also eat tender foliage. The adults lay their eggs on the soil or in weeds to overwinter.

WHAT TO DO:
• Tolerate light damage.
• Remove weeds from the garden.
• Cultivate the soil in fall to expose the eggs to predators and freezing weather.

PROBLEM: There are holes in the leaves and fruits of your blueberry bushes. The damaged fruit may taste bad.

CAUSE: Negro bugs (*Corimelaena pulicaria*). These shiny, domed, ⅕-inch-long, beetle-like bugs congregate in groups to eat holes in leaves and berries. They produce several generations a year, and they overwinter in garden debris.

WHAT TO DO:
• Handpick.
• Collect the beetles with a hand-held vacuum.
• Put a drop cloth under the plant, and shake beetles onto it.
• Use insecticidal soap, following label directions.
• Remove and compost fallen leaves and other garden debris.

Blueberry Diseases

PROBLEM: Small, red lesions on stems develop into large, black, swollen cankers with deep cracks.

CAUSE: Botryosphaeria stem canker (*Botryosphaeria corticis*). This fungal disease invades the current season's growth. It develops over the next several years. The cankers grow in size and darken until entire stems are girdled by the black cankers.

WHAT TO DO:
• Plant resistant varieties. Check with your local extension agent on the best resistant varieties for your particular area, as there are different strains of this disease in various geographical areas. None of the resistant varieties are resistant to all forms. 'Bluechip', 'Croatan', 'Murphy', and 'O'Neal' are resistant to the predominant type of stem canker.

PROBLEM: In the summer, blueberry stems develop red spots, or cankers. The leaves wilt and turn reddish brown.

CAUSE: Fusicoccum canker (*Fusicoccum putrefaciens*). Infections occur during rainy periods throughout the growing season. As cankers enlarge, they develop a bull's-eye pattern. The disease can kill a few branches or an entire bush.

WHAT TO DO:
• Dispose of diseased stems.
• Plant resistant varieties, such as 'Concord' and 'Rancocas'.

PROBLEM: Your blueberry blossoms are water-soaked, brown, and covered with mold.

CAUSE: Gray mold/Botrytis blight (*Botrytis cinerea*). This fungal disease thrives in cool temperatures and high humidity. It begins with flowers but spreads to leaf and stem tissue. It overwinters in diseased and dead twigs and on plant debris.

WHAT TO DO:

• Do not overfertilize, because rapidly growing tips are most susceptible.

• Space plants widely and prune to encourage air circulation.

• Destroy infected plant parts.

PROBLEM: New shoots, leaves, and flowers wilt. They turn brown and powdery. Berries shrivel and drop.

CAUSE: Mummyberry (*Monilinia vaccinii-corymbosi*). This fungal disease overwinters on dried (mummified) fruit clinging to canes. In the spring, spores infect new growth. Cold, wet weather favors the disease, which travels from plant to plant in raindrops or irrigation water.

WHAT TO DO:

• Mulch to keep disease-carrying mud from splashing on plants.

• Plant resistant cultivars, such as 'Collins', 'Corville', 'Darrow', 'Dixie', and 'Rebel'.

• Dispose of plant debris.

PROBLEM: The leaves of blueberry branches turn yellow or red. Infected stems have brown, discolored tissue.

CAUSE: Stem blight (*Botryosphaeria dothidea*). This fungal disease usually occurs during May and June. It enters the plants through stem wounds. Infections in mature plants cause the loss of branches but not the entire plant.

WHAT TO DO:

• Prune off and dispose of diseased branches during the dormant period.

• Purchase healthy plants from a reputable nursery.

• Grow resistant varieties, such as 'Cape Fear', 'Murphy', and 'O'Neal'.

 Other Problems

PROBLEM: The blueberries from your bushes are quickly disappearing!

CAUSE: Birds will often win the competition for who can harvest the most fruit, even before berries fully ripen.

WHAT TO DO:

• Use bird netting or floating row covers to prevent birds from picking your berries. Cover the planting with the material, and bury the edges in soil.

• Make scarecrows. Aluminum pie plates, scare tape, and aluminum foil will deter birds as long as a breeze creates movement to frighten them.

PROBLEM: The leaves of your blueberry plants are turning yellow, but the leaf veins remain green.

CAUSE: Soil iron deficiency. Blueberries require acidic soil conditions ranging from 4.5 to 5.0 pH. More-alkaline conditions result in the unavailability of iron, resulting in nutrient deficiencies.

WHAT TO DO:

• Add sawdust or peat moss along with manure to the planting hole a year before planting.

• Mulch plants with rotted sawdust.

• Add sulfur as needed to acidify the soil.

Cherry

(Prunus spp.)

Cherry Pests

PROBLEM: Tree leaves are curled and twisted and are spotted with clear, sticky specks and sooty, black patches.

CAUSE: Black cherry aphids (*Myzus cerasi*). These ⅛-inch-long, soft-bodied, pear-shaped insects range in color from pale tan to light green to nearly black. In autumn the adult females lay shiny, black, oval eggs on buds or the bark of smaller branches. These eggs overwinter and then hatch in spring when buds open. Aphids damage tender young leaves and shoots by sucking plant juices. Honeydew, secreted by the aphids, covers the leaves and fruits, creating ideal conditions for the growth of sooty mold. The honeydew also attracts ants, which protect aphids from beneficial insects in order to eat the aphids' secretions. Aphid colonies establish rapidly, and several generations may occur per season. The damage causes young trees to die and reduces the crops from mature trees.

WHAT TO DO:
• Knock aphids off cherry trees with a strong spray of water. Be sure to spray the undersides of leaves as well as the tops.
• Use insecticidal soap, following label directions. Be sure to spray the undersides of leaves as well as the tops.
• Attract beneficial insects, such as parasitic wasps, by planting small-flowered nectar plants, including yarrow, scabiosa, and Queen-Anne's-lace.
• Apply dormant oil spray to cherry trees in winter. This horticultural oil coats tree tissues and smothers overwintering pests and disease pathogens.

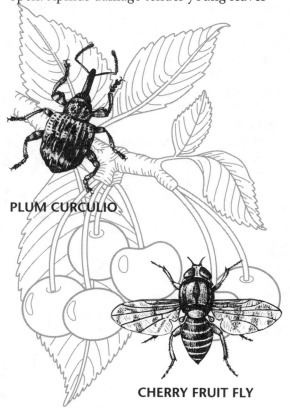

PLUM CURCULIO

CHERRY FRUIT FLY

PROBLEM: Your cherry trees have deformed, shrunken, maggot-infested fruits that drop before they ripen.

CAUSE: Cherry fruit flies (*Rhagoletis cingulata*). These flies are about half the size of houseflies but are otherwise similar looking. They have clear wings marked with dark bands. The adults emerge from the soil in the spring and lay their eggs in the fruits. The fruit-eating larvae are white maggots about ¼ inch long.

WHAT TO DO:
- Destroy infested fruit.
- Cultivate shallowly around trees to disrupt overwintering larvae.
- Make red sticky traps to catch the flies in late spring. Hang red spheres coated with Tanglefoot (a commercial tacky product) in the trees to attract and trap female flies. Hang sticky balls at eye level 2 to 3 feet from branch tips, and keep foliage and cherries away from them. Hang two traps per dwarf tree and four to six per full-sized tree. Clean off insect debris and recoat as needed.

PROBLEM: Cherries are deformed and have sunken spots. There is a sawdust-like material at the stem end of fruits.

CAUSE: Cherry fruitworms (*Grapholitha packardi*). The adults are mottled, gray moths with ⅜-inch wingspans. The fruitworm larvae are white with black heads and grow up to ⅜ inch long. Mature larvae hibernate in silk nests under bark and in broken branches. Moths begin emerging in May or early June and lay small, cream-colored eggs on developing fruits. About ten days later, the newly hatched larvae bore into the green cherries, feeding on the interior and depositing excrement (frass) at their tunnel entrances. If you cut open an infested cherry, you will see their tiny, brown trails in the flesh. Developing tart cherries have brown, sunken, rough areas. Infested fruits will become misshapen and rough-textured, with black areas.

WHAT TO DO:
- Destroy infested fruit to prevent the larvae from maturing.

PROBLEM: The young tips of cherry branches die back several inches. If you split affected twigs, you see larvae.

CAUSE: Oriental fruit moth larvae (*Grapholitha molesta*). These worms are the larvae of dark gray moths. The moths have dark brown wings and ½-inch wingspans. Oriental fruit moth larvae are white or pink caterpillars with brown heads. The ⅝-inch-long larvae bore into cherry tree branches early in the season and bore into both green and ripening nuts later in the season. The larvae overwinter in cocoons on trees and orchard weeds. On rare occasions, the nut meats of affected trees are eaten by the larvae.

WHAT TO DO:
- Tolerate light damage.
- Set out pheromone lures. Mating disruption using pheromone lures is effective in orchards of 5 acres and larger. These commercial lures have a strip of cardboard coated with female-insect scents. Male oriental fruit moths lured to the scent fall into attached collection bags or become confused and unable to find a mate.
- Apply BT. "BT" stands for *Bacillus thuringiensis,* an insect-stomach poison that kills caterpillar and worm pests without harming beneficial insects. Follow label directions, and apply BT when pests are active.

PROBLEM: The leaves of your cherry trees are skeletonized, and sluglike larvae are on the leaves.

CAUSE: Pear sawflies, also called pear slugs or cherry slugs (*Caliroa cerasi*). Adult sawflies are ⅕-inch-long, glossy, black-and-yellow flies with four wings. After the trees have completely leafed out in the spring, inspect the upper side of leaves for the olive green or orange, sluglike pests. Full-grown larvae are close to ½ inch long and have oversized heads. The first generation of these voracious, leaf-eating larvae completes development in less than a month and pupates in cocoons in the soil. A second, and more damaging, generation emerges in July or August.

WHAT TO DO:
• Handpick.
• Knock the larvae from foliage with a heavy stream of water. Be sure to spray the backs of leaves as well as the top surfaces.
• Use insecticidal soap, following label directions.
• Apply summer oil (also called superior or horticultural oil). Summer oil smothers all stages of most pests when you follow instructions for application.

PROBLEM: A half-moon-shaped scar is on fruits. Larvae tunneling into fruits cause them to rot and drop early.

CAUSE: Plum curculios (*Conotrachelus nenuphar*). The adults are dark brown, ⅕-inch-long beetles with curved, thick beaks. They cut holes in fruit skins and lay eggs under the skin. The fruit-eating nymphs are ⅓-inch-long white grubs. The grubs tunnel through the fruit, causing it to drop before ripening.

WHAT TO DO:
• When the flower petals begin to fall, place a light-colored tarp under cherry trees, and jar the limbs with a padded stick. The beetles will drop to the cloth. Collect and destroy them daily for two weeks.

PROBLEM: Fruits have red spots. The branches have small, gray bumps. Leaves are yellowing and dying back.

CAUSE: San Jose scale (*Quadraspidiotus perniciosus*). These insects feed on the sap of bark, leaves, and fruit. The fully grown females look like gray-brown, round bumps no bigger than a pinhead, with raised, dull yellow centers. Male scale are slightly smaller and have an oval shape with a raised dot near the

larger end of the oval. These insects overwinter in a partly grown stage and begin to feed and mature in the spring. There are two generations per year. A generation matures in five to seven weeks, depending on the weather. Infested trees will be weak and grow poorly. A heavy infestation can kill young trees in two or three years. Extremely cold weather reduces populations.

WHAT TO DO:
• Spray dormant oil in late winter or early spring. A solution of this horticultural oil smothers all growth stages of most pests. Follow label directions for usage.
• Attract beneficial insects, such as lady beetles and parasitic wasps, by growing small-flowered nectar plants, including yarrow, dill, and Queen-Anne's-lace.

 Cherry Diseases

PROBLEM: Flowers brown and decay. Fruits have tiny brown spots that enlarge and turn fuzzy in humid weather.

CAUSE: Brown rot (*Monilinia* spp.). This fungal disease is most serious in warm, humid climates, when temperatures are between 55° and 80°F. Under the right conditions, the disease can cause twigs to develop cankers and fruits to decay in less than two days. Cherries may drop early or remain on the tree as dried, shriveled fruits called mummies. Harvested cherries may rot in storage. The disease overwinters in twig cankers and in mummies that remain on the tree or on those that fall to the ground. In spring and summer, the wind and splashing rain or irrigation water spread the disease spores from infected plant parts and debris to opening blossoms and maturing fruit.

WHAT TO DO:
• Prune and destroy any twigs that have

gummy lesions on them.
• Apply sulfur sprays early in the season to control disease on blossoms, then again later in the season to protect fruit.
• Control insects such as plum curculios, which cause wounds in fruit that admit disease.
• In fall, gather and destroy mummified fruit, fallen leaves, and twigs.
• Prune trees to promote good air circulation.
• Plant resistant cultivars, such as 'Northstar' and 'Windsor'.

PROBLEM: Leaves get small, reddish purple spots. Spots brown, and centers drop out, producing a shothole effect.

CAUSE: Cherry leaf spot, also called shothole disease (*Coccomyces hiemalis*). This fungal disease primarily affects leaves, but it can attack shoots and fruits. The disease overwinters in infected, fallen leaves. From spring through fall, the fungus is spread by wind and splashing rain or irrigation water. In wet weather, pink to white masses appear in the center of spots on leaf undersides. Infected leaves turn yellow and can fall by mid-summer. After severe defoliation, fruits will fail to develop properly. The cherries will be small, light-colored, soft, and watery. Defoliated trees are susceptible to winter freeze injuries.

WHAT TO DO:
• Remove and destroy fallen leaves.
• Prune cherry trees to promote good air circulation.
• Grow resistant cultivars, such as 'Lambert', 'Meteor', and 'Northstar'.

PROBLEM: A white, powdery coating appears on leaves and cherries. Affected leaves are twisted or stunted.

CAUSE: Powdery mildew (*Podosphaera oxya-canthae*). This fungal disease is disfiguring and can also weaken infected trees. Infections can occur from spring through fall. Powdery mildew causes leaves to develop white, feltlike patches of fungus that spread rapidly, eventually covering the entire leaf. The infected leaves may fold upward, pucker and blister, and fall to the ground prematurely. Shoots may become stunted and twisted. Infected fruits, especially immature cherries, develop sunken spots. Powdery mildew travels on the wind, blowing from infected plants to new ones. Cool nights and warm days encourage the spread of this disease. The fungus overwinters in plant debris on the ground and in bark fissures or tree crotches.

WHAT TO DO:
• Remove and destroy infected leaves and fruits.
• Spray with bordeaux mix. Bordeaux is a combination of sulfur and hydrated lime with disease- and fungal-inhibiting effects.
• Choose resistant cultivars, such as 'Northstar'.
• Plant trees in well-drained soil.

 Other Problems

PROBLEM: The tree appears healthy, but amber-colored sap is oozing from one or more places along the trunk.

CAUSE: Gummosis. Cherry trees have a natural tendency to ooze sap. If the tree appears otherwise healthy, gummosis is not a threatening condition. Injured bark will ooze sap, and trees standing in wet soil for long periods of time will ooze sap.

WHAT TO DO:
• Do not overwater cherry trees. If the soil is saturated, do not water until it has dried.
• Prune as necessary to prevent branch breakage.

Citrus

(*Citrus* spp. and hybrids)

 Citrus Pests

PROBLEM: Fruits are speckled with small, round, reddish brown bumps. Some of the leaves are yellowing.

CAUSE: San Jose scale (*Quadraspidiotus perniciosus*). These immobile, yellowish brown, sapsucking insects attack the leaves and fruit rinds of citrus trees. They disfigure the skins of fruits, but the interiors are not damaged. These pests can cause leaves to yellow. In severe cases, trees can defoliate early. The sticky honeydew that the scale secrete can also attract ants, which eat the secretions, and sooty mold, which develops on the moist spots.

WHAT TO DO:
• Spray leaves with summer oil in late summer or early fall. This horticultural oil kills most insects and disease pathogens by coating leaves and fruit, smothering the pests.
• Attract beneficial insects, such as parasitic wasps and lady beetles, by growing small-flowered nectar plants, including yarrow, dill, and Queen-Anne's-lace. Supplement the local population of beneficials by releasing parasitic wasps (*Aphytis melinus*). You can order beneficial insects from mail-order sources. These firms will help you determine how many beneficials to buy and when to release them so that they will be most effective.

PROBLEM: Leaves of citrus trees are covered with pale yellow specks. There may be fine cobwebs on leaf undersides.

CAUSE: Citrus red mites (*Panonychus citri*). To the naked eye, these mites look like tiny moving dots. They pierce the cells on the leaf undersides and suck plant juices. Mites reproduce rapidly and have numerous generations each summer, especially during hot, dry summers. When feeding in masses, they can weaken plants.

WHAT TO DO:
• Spray summer oil on trees in early fall. Also called superior or horticultural oil, summer oil smothers all stages of most pests when you follow instructions for application.
• Keep orchards well irrigated. Trees that are not drought-stressed are less likely to be attacked by mites.
• Wash mites off leaves with a forceful stream of water to reduce their populations.

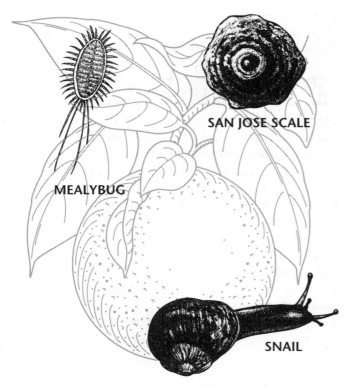

MEALYBUG

SAN JOSE SCALE

SNAIL

• Attract beneficial insects by planting small-flowered nectar plants, including yarrow, Queen-Anne's-lace, and scabiosa. If you observe serious mite damage, contact a mail-order source of beneficial insects to order beneficial mites.

PROBLEM: Leaves have bleached spots. The skin at the stem end of immature citrus fruits is scarred.

CAUSE: Citrus thrips (*Scirtophrips citri*). These pests are tiny, 1/50- to 1/25-inch-long, brown insects with gray heads and wings. When thrips feed in large numbers, they draw so much sap from plant leaves that the plants cannot grow.

Thrips rasp away the surface of young leaves and fruits with their mouthparts in order to lap up the oozing plant juices. The tiny insects hide in the folds of new leaves and around buds. The adults lay eggs in the leaves and stems of the trees in fall. After overwintering, the thrips emerge in spring and begin to feed on new growth. They continue to feed throughout the entire growing season. Infestations increase during periods of hot, dry weather.

WHAT TO DO:
• Use insecticidal soap, following label directions. Be sure to spray the crevices of flower buds and new leaves and both the undersides and top surfaces of older leaves.
• Control weeds, which provide a breeding ground and an alternate food source for thrips.
• Prune off and dispose of dead and damaged limbs, which can harbor overwintering pests, such as thrips.

PROBLEM: White, cottony bumps dot the leaves, stems, branches, and trunks of citrus trees. Leaves yellow and drop.

CAUSES: Citrus mealybugs (*Planococcus citri*) and cottonycushion scale (*Icerya purchasi*). Both of these pests look like small, fuzzy, white, immobile bumps.

These pests suck sap from tender parts of citrus trees and excrete a sticky honeydew. In severe cases, the leaves will yellow and drop early. Trees can become weakened and susceptible to diseases. The honeydew attracts ants and sooty mold. Ants protect these pests in order to feed on the honeydew that the pests secrete.

WHAT TO DO:
• Wash pests and honeydew off citrus trees with a strong stream of water.
• Use insecticidal soap, following label directions.
• Control ants by pouring boiling water into entry holes of anthills that are not adjacent to plant roots.
• Trap ants by putting sticky bands around the base of vines. Make your own easy-to-clean sticky preparation from equal parts petroleum jelly, mineral oil, and liquid dish soap.
• Place ant traps baited with boric acid in the ground around the vines.
• Apply dormant oil, following label directions. A solution of this commercial oil smothers all growth stages of most pests.
• Tolerate light infestations.

PROBLEM: There are holes chewed in the leaves and fruits of your citrus trees, but you can see no pests.

CAUSE: Snails (Order Stylommatophora). These relatives of clams and mussels enjoy eating the leaves and fruits of citrus trees. Snails are usually gray and have spiral-shaped shells. Snails may be from 1/4 to 4 inches long, and they leave a sticky slime everywhere they go. Snails crawl up into trees at night to feed, and they rest in plant debris on the ground during the day.

WHAT TO DO:

• Handpick. The best snail-hunting time begins two hours after sundown. Use a flashlight to find snails, and dispose of them by dropping them into a jar of soapy water.

• Wrap a copper band around the base of each tree to keep snails from climbing up the trunks of your citrus trees. The copper will zap these slimy creatures with an electrical shock upon contact.

 ## Citrus Diseases

PROBLEM: Tree trunks exude a thick, yellow, gummy substance. The bark gum forms dark, sunken cankers.

CAUSE: Brown rot gummosis (*Phytophthora* spp.). This soilborne fungal disease causes branches to wither and die as the disease progresses from sap oozing to the canker stage. The disease is most infectious during damp, rainy weather. The fungal spores of brown rot gummosis travel from the soil to tree trunks via splashing rain and irrigation water. Trees become infected when the spores contact injured bark.

WHAT TO DO:

• Scrape cankers away with a knife to reveal healthy wood.

• Allow the wound to dry and then spray it with a copper solution.

• Mulch to prevent the disease spores from splashing onto tree trunks.

• Avoid splashing water on tree trunks as you irrigate.

• Do not overwater citrus trees. Allow the soil to dry out between waterings.

• Prune the trees as necessary to prevent branch breakage.

PROBLEM: The fruits of your citrus trees have raised, rough-textured, light brown spots and streaks.

CAUSE: Citrus scab (*Elsinoe fawcetti*). This fungal disease can attack any type of citrus fruit but is most commonly seen on grapefruit. The disease spreads during damp, cool spring weather.

WHAT TO DO:

• Prune trees to open up the centers to circulating air.

• Site trees where fruits will dry out rapidly after rains.

• Space plants widely for air circulation.

PROBLEM: The backs of citrus leaves have brown, oily-feeling spots. Some fruits have shallow, pitted spots.

CAUSE: Greasy spot (*Mycosphaerella citri*). This fungal disease causes citrus trees to develop yellow-brown blisters on leaf backs. The disease spreads rapidly in the warm, rainy weather of early summer. Greasy spot overwinters in fallen leaves and other kinds of plant debris left in the orchard.

WHAT TO DO:

• Spray summer oil. Also called superior or horticultural oil, summer oil smothers all stages of most pests when you follow instructions for application.

• Spray bordeaux mix. Bordeaux is a wettable combination of copper sulfate and hydrated lime to use as a fungicide spray with insecticidal properties. Do not spray bordeaux mix if the temperature rises above 85°F, because it can damage foliage.

PROBLEM: Some fruits on your citrus trees have small, brown, sunken spots. Others have raised spots.

CAUSE: Melanose. The spores of this fungal disease travel from tree to tree in rain during the cool, damp weather of spring. The spots created by the spores take on the shape of rain spatters across fruits. The disfiguring disease does not penetrate the rinds of the fruits; they remain edible. Melanose overwinters in diseased and dead branches.

WHAT TO DO:
• Tolerate damage. Since the fruits remain edible, you can choose to ignore their disease-disfigured rinds.
• Spray with a solution of copper once at the time of fruit set.
• Prune and remove disease-harboring deadwood from trees.

 Other Problems

PROBLEM: The leaves of your citrus plants are yellowing and dropping during the growing season.

CAUSES: Poor growing conditions. Several cultural imbalances cause leaves to turn yellow and drop prematurely.

Overwatering can also cause leaves to turn yellow and fall.

Overfertilizing can cause citrus plants leaves to discolor or "burn" and drop.

A lack of nitrogen in the soil can cause leaves to yellow and drop.

A lack of iron in the soil can cause leaves to yellow around the veins, which remain green.

Small, container-grown citrus trees that have grown in the same pot for several years can become rootbound and use up all of the available nutrients, causing their leaves to yellow and drop.

WHAT TO DO:
• Water plants enough to prevent wilting, but allow the soil to dry out between waterings.
• Feed citrus plants with manure tea, fish emulsion, or other high-nitrogen organic fertilizer.
• Spray the foliage every two weeks with a solution of chelated iron to correct iron deficiency. Continue this until the leaves begin to turn green again. Then spray two or three more times during the growing season or as often as needed to keep leaves from yellowing.
• Root prune. Unpot and trim away the outermost one-third of roots and old soil. Then repot the root ball, adding fresh soil every two years.
• Water container-grown citrus plants twice a month with a half-strength solution of fish emulsion or compost tea.
• Grow citrus plants in well-drained soil rich in organic material such as compost or leaf mold.

PROBLEM: The rinds of some of your citrus fruits begin to split open as they ripen. The sizes of the openings vary.

CAUSE: Fruit splitting. This problem is caused by fluctuations in weather conditions or cultural conditions. The condition is brought on by abrupt changes in any or all of the following: humidity, temperature, soil moisture, and possibly fertilizing techniques. Although unsightly, damaged fruits are edible if the exposed parts are trimmed off.

WHAT TO DO:
• Keep the soil around your citrus trees evenly moist during dry spells.
• Do not vary fertilizer formulations or amounts of application while citrus fruits are growing.

Currant and Gooseberry

(Ribes nigrum; R. sativum) and *(R.* spp.)

 Currant and Gooseberry Pests

PROBLEM: Shrubs have blistered, reddened leaves. Small, pear-shaped insects cluster on leaf undersides.

CAUSE: Aphids (Family Aphididae). These soft-bodied, ¹⁄₁₆- to ³⁄₈-inch-long insects range in color from pale tan to light green to nearly black. These pests damage leaves and stems by sucking plant juices. Usually the damage is more cosmetic than truly serious.

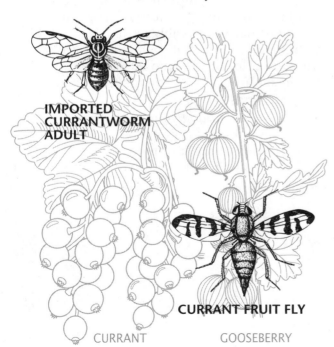

IMPORTED CURRANTWORM ADULT

CURRANT FRUIT FLY

CURRANT   GOOSEBERRY

WHAT TO DO:
• Attract beneficial insects, such as parasitic wasps, by planting small-flowered nectar plants, including yarrow and scabiosa.
• Spray with dormant oil in early spring. This smothers most pests. Follow label directions for usage.

PROBLEM: In spring, bushes develop yellowing leaves. Branches have small holes surrounded by sawdust.

CAUSE: Currant borers (*Synanthedon tipuliformis*). These wasplike, 1-inch-long moths lay eggs on branches in late May and early June. The ½-inch-long, yellow-white grubs hatch and burrow into branches. Infested branches become brittle and break easily. The borers overwinter in the branches.

WHAT TO DO:
• Prune and destroy infested branches.

PROBLEM: Fruits develop color and drop before they ripen. Affected berries have a dark spot ringed by a red halo.

CAUSE: Currant fruit flies (*Epochra canadensis*). Adults are ⅕ to ⅓ inch long and have yellow bodies with dark-banded wings. The ⅓- to ½-inch-long larvae eat currant and gooseberry fruits from the inside, causing them to drop early. After feeding, they exit the fruit and enter the soil to overwinter.

WHAT TO DO:
• Destroy infested berries.
• Spray summer oil. Also called superior or horticultural oil, summer oil smothers all stages of most pests.

PROBLEM: Foliage is stripped from shrubs. The damage begins in the center of the shrub and spreads outward.

CAUSE: Imported currantworms (*Nematus ribesii*). These are the larvae of ⅓-inch-long, black sawflies with yellow markings. The ⅘-inch-long, green larvae have black heads. Imported currantworms are voracious and can defoliate currant and gooseberry shrubs.

WHAT TO DO:
• Handpick.
• Spray pyrethrins into the center of the shrub. Pyrethrins are botanical insecticides derived from the dried flowerheads of the daisy *Chrysanthemum cinerariifolium*. The active ingredient, pyrethrins, are broad-spectrum nerve poisons that kill imported currantworms. Follow label instructions.

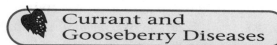

Currant and Gooseberry Diseases

PROBLEM: Powdery gray or white patches appear on new foliage and fruits. Affected leaves are stunted.

CAUSE: Powdery mildew (*Sphaerotheca* spp.; *Microsphaera grossulariae*; *Phyllactinia corylea*). This fungal disease, which is caused by several fungi, develops when there is high humidity and temperatures are 60° to 80°F. The disease overwinters in infected shoot tips; when conditions are optimum in spring, spores blow on the air to infect new foliage.

WHAT TO DO:
• Prune bushes for good air circulation.
• Spray with bordeaux mix when buds break in spring, again before bloom, and then again two or three weeks after bloom. Bordeaux is a combination of copper sulfate and hydrated lime to use as a fungicide and insecticide. Do not spray bordeaux mix if the temperature rises above 85°F.
• Apply washing soda spray. Mix 1 pound sodium carbonate (washing soda) with ¼ pound liquid soap and 5 gallons water, and spray plants when symptoms appear.
• Plant resistant gooseberry cultivars, like 'Captivator', 'Hinnonmakis Yellow', 'Invicta', 'Leepared', and 'Poorman'.

PROBLEM: Pale spots develop on the leaves, which eventually turn entirely yellow and drop early.

CAUSES: Septoria leaf spot (*Septoria* spp.) and anthracnose (*Pseudopeziza ribis*). These fungal diseases thrive in cool, rainy weather. Their spores travel via wind and splashing raindrops. The diseases overwinter on old leaves.

WHAT TO DO:
• Rake up and compost old leaves, which harbor overwintering diseases and pests.
• Spray with copper in early spring.

PROBLEM: Bright orange spots develop on the undersides of currant and gooseberry leaves.

CAUSE: White pine blister rust (*Cronartium ribicola*). This deadly fungal disease needs five-needled pine trees along with gooseberries or currants to complete its life cycle. Cultivated red and white currants are not very susceptible to white pine blister rust. A few states still ban home plantings of currants and gooseberries, so check with your local extension agent before planting these fruiting shrubs.

WHAT TO DO:
• Plant resistant types of currants, such as red and white currants.
• Do not grow five-needled pine trees.

Grape

(*Vitis* spp.)

Grape Pests

PROBLEM: Grape leaves have webbing on their undersides. They have yellow stippling, turn bronze, and drop early.

CAUSE: European red mites (*Panonychus ulmi*). To the naked eye, these mites look like tiny red moving dots on plant leaves. They pierce the cells on the leaf undersides and suck plant juices. European red mites reproduce rapidly and have numerous generations each summer, especially during hot, dry summers. Under these conditions, when they feed in large numbers, mites can weaken plants.

WHAT TO DO:
• Keep vineyards well irrigated. Mites are most attracted to drought-stressed plants.
• Wash leaves with a forceful stream of water. Be sure to hit the undersides of leaves as well as the top surfaces when spraying. It is possible to knock pests off leaves to reduce European red mite populations.
• Attract beneficial insects by planting small-flowered nectar plants, such as yarrow, Queen-Anne's-lace, and scabiosa. If you observe serious mite damage, contact a mail-order insectiary to order beneficial mites to release to supplement native populations.

PROBLEM: In early June, flower buds and young grapes are webbed together, and the affected grapes have red spots.

CAUSE: Grape berry moths (*Endopiza viteana*). These pests are small, mottled brown moths with ½-inch wingspans. Grape berry moths can be a serious problem in orchards east of the Rockies and in Canada.

The larvae are ⅜-inch-long, green or gray-green caterpillars with brown heads. Grape berry moth caterpillars eat grape flowers and the fruits. They spin webs around parts of the plant that they eat. By harvest time, the grapes have begun to rot and are infested with fruitflies.

The caterpillars overwinter in cocoons made from pieces of grape leaves. In spring the moths emerge and lay eggs on stems, flowers, and fruit. There are usually two generations per year. Damage is most severe in

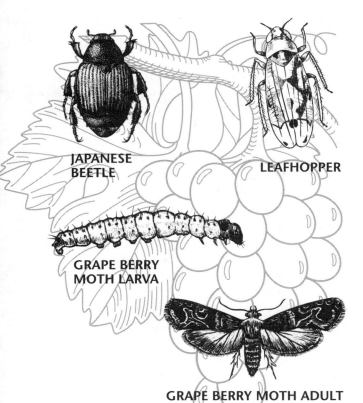

JAPANESE BEETLE

LEAFHOPPER

GRAPE BERRY MOTH LARVA

GRAPE BERRY MOTH ADULT

vineyards located near woods, where the caterpillars can overwinter in leaf litter.

WHAT TO DO:
• Destroy infested berries and leaf-covered cocoons.
• Apply BTK. "BT" stands for *Bacillus thuringiensis*, an insect-stomach poison that kills caterpillars without harming beneficial insects. *B.t.* var. *kurstaki* (BTK) kills the larvae of grape berry moths. BTK can be purchased from mail-order suppliers. Apply BTK when caterpillars are feeding.
• Disrupt mating by setting out pheromone lures. This is an effective control for vineyards larger than 3 acres. These commercial lures have a strip of cardboard coated with female insect scents. Male pests attracted to the scent fall into attached collection bags or become confused and are unable to find a mate.
• Gather and remove fallen leaves in autumn, or turn them into the soil.

PROBLEM: Newly developing buds have holes chewed in them, which destroys the emerging foliage and fruits.
CAUSE: Grape flea beetles (*Altica chalybea*). These pests are shiny, dark, metallic beetles about ³⁄₁₆ inch long, most often found near woodlots and fence rows. The adults emerge in spring and lay their eggs in cracks in the bark of grapevines. Emerging larvae are brown with black spots. The larvae feed for a month and then pupate in the soil for several weeks before emerging as adults.

WHAT TO DO:
• Handpick.
• Cultivate between rows. Cultivating the soil reduces the flea beetle larvae pupating in the soil by killing them and exposing them to hungry birds.
• Spray grape plants with summer oil (also called superior or horticultural oil). Summer

oil smothers all stages of most pests when you follow instructions for application.

PROBLEM: Grape leaves are speckled with sticky, clear or black spots and fuzzy, oval insects. Fruits break open.
CAUSE: Grape mealybugs (*Pseudococcus maritimus*). These pests are powdery, white, oval, wingless, ⅛-inch-long insects. These stationary insects suck plant sap and secrete a sticky substance, called honeydew. The honeydew encourages black, sooty mold and ants, which protect mealybugs from natural predators in order to eat the honeydew they produce. Mealybugs also attack grape clusters, causing grapes to crack.

Mealybugs suffer in high temperatures, and populations often drop in midsummer. Both adults and eggs overwinter under loose bark and emerge to feed on leaves and grapes at the start of the growing season.

WHAT TO DO:
• Attract beneficial insects by planting small-flowered nectar plants, such as yarrow, Queen-Anne's-lace, and scabiosa, in the vineyard.
• Remove loose vine bark in winter. This exposes overwintering mealybugs and their eggs to killing frost.
• Control ants. Trap ants by putting sticky bands around the base of vines; make your own easy-to-clean sticky preparation from equal parts petroleum jelly, mineral oil, and liquid dish soap. Smear this preparation onto cardboard strips and staple them to the main stem of the plant at the soil line. Replace the bands when they become coated with ants. Place ant traps baited with boric acid on the ground around the vines.
• Apply dormant oil to grapevines during winter. A solution of this commercial oil sprayed on plants smothers all growth stages of most pests and diseases. Follow label directions for usage.

PROBLEM: Small, green galls are on the undersides of grape leaves. Inside the galls are tiny, yellow insects and eggs.

CAUSE: Grape phylloxera (*Daktulosphaira vitifoliae*). These are tiny, aphidlike, sap-sucking pests $\frac{1}{30}$ to $\frac{1}{25}$ inch long. They vary in color from pale green, orange, and purple to brown, depending on what they eat.

There are both foliage- and root-eating forms of this soft-bodied insect. The root eaters do the most serious damage to grape plants. The leaf-eating grape phylloxera cause little damage, but they can indicate the presence of root eaters. In a serious infestation, grape plants become stunted and weakened and may die.

WHAT TO DO:
• Employ good cultural practices, such as adequate watering and fertilizing, to slow down plant decline.
• Plant resistant cultivars, such as the French cultivars.
• Grow native grapes, which are unaffected by this pest.

PROBLEM: Some of your grapevines are wilting. Some of them are wilted on only part of the vine.

CAUSE: Grape root borers (*Vitacea polistiformis*). These are the larvae of 1-inch-long, brown, clear-winged moths with orange-striped undersides. The moths emerge in July and August and lay eggs on grape leaves.

The larvae hatch and burrow into the soil, where they feed on the larger roots and crowns of grapevines for two years. Grape root borers reach about 1½ inches in length and are white with brown heads.

WHAT TO DO:
• Create a mulch barrier. Apply plastic sheeting as a mulch in the rows between grapevines before planting grapes to keep grape root borers from reaching the roots.
• Set out pheromone traps in late June. These commercial lures have a strip of cardboard coated with female insect scents. Male pests attracted to the scent fall into attached collection bags or become confused and are unable to find a mate.

Position traps around the vineyard perimeter at 35- to 50-foot intervals. Check and clean trap bottoms weekly. Trap each growing season to reduce pest populations.

PROBLEM: In summer, grape leaves have so many holes that they look lacy. You see beetles on the plants during the day.

CAUSE: Japanese beetles (*Popillia japonica*). Grape leaves are a preferred food of these ½-inch-long, metallic green beetles with bronze wings. The beetles overwinter under ground as grubs. In the spring the grubs feed on grass roots; they turn into the destructive beetles in early summer.

WHAT TO DO:
• Handpick.
• Apply grub-attacking parasitic nematodes to the sod surrounding your grape patch in late spring or late summer. You can purchase beneficial nematodes (*Steinernema carpocapsae* and *Heterorhabditis heliothidis*) from mail-order suppliers. Live nematodes are shipped suspended in gels or sponges. Follow label instructions for application.
• Apply milky disease spores to sod in spring. The microbial insecticide, available under several trade names, is a combination of spores of *Bacillus popilliae* and *B. lentimorbus*. Grubs become infected with milky disease and die after they eat the spores.
• Aerate turf with spiked sandals in late spring and early fall, when the larvae are close to the soil surface.

• Plant thick-leaved grape varieties. Vines with thin, smooth leaves, such as the French hybrids, are more often eaten by Japanese beetles than those with thick, coarse leaves, like the Concord grapes.

PROBLEM: Pale stippling mars leaf tops. Leaves are cup-shaped or turn yellow, then brown and drop to the ground.

CAUSE: Leafhoppers (Family Cicadellidae). Several common leafhopper species feed in vineyards. Leafhoppers suck plant juices from grape leaves and fruits. Leafhoppers are wedge-shaped, brown or green insects that are about $\frac{1}{10}$ inch long. They can be hard to see because leafhoppers hop away as you approach them.

The grapes from which they eat become covered with dark, sticky drops of insect excrement (frass). Grapevines can tolerate fairly large numbers of leafhoppers, and the damage seldom warrants control.

WHAT TO DO:
• Use insecticidal soap, following label directions. Be sure to spray both sides of the leaves when you apply insecticidal soap.
• Spray summer oil (also called superior or horticultural oil). Summer oil smothers all stages of most pests when you follow instructions for application. Apply summer oil to the first generation while leafhoppers are small.
• Attract beneficial insects. An important natural enemy of leafhoppers in California vineyards is the tiny parasitic wasp *Anagrus epos*. To attract such beneficials, plant small-flowered nectar plants, including dill, yarrow, and Queen-Anne's-lace.

PROBLEM: Leaves and flowers are skeletonized by insects, especially plants growing in sandy soil or grassy areas.

CAUSE: Rose chafers (*Macrodactylus subspinosus*). Often described as ungainly or clumsy, the ½-inch-long adult beetles are light brown with a black abdomen. Their larvae are small, curled, white grubs that feed on the roots of grape plants. Chafers and their grubs are not usually serious pests.

WHAT TO DO:
• Handpick.
• Cultivate shallowly between rows to reduce larval population. Cultivating will kill some grubs or expose them to hungry birds.

 Grape Diseases

PROBLEM: Grapes have brown spots that grow. Infected grapes shrivel into hard berries, called mummies.

CAUSE: Black rot (*Guignardia bidwellii*). This fungal disease overwinters on dried grapes left on the vine and in infected canes or shoots. Black rot is a serious disease of European grapes in the eastern United States. Spring rains and warm temperatures encourage the disease.

The most serious infections occur when the grapes are pea-sized and larger, leading to spoiled fruit throughout the growing season. The disease makes grape leaves develop reddish brown spots that enlarge and darken over time. The shoots and vines develop elongated, sunken, dark purple to black areas.

WHAT TO DO:
• Sterilize tools with rubbing alcohol and wash your hands after working with diseased plants.
• Remove and dispose of infected and dried raisins (fruit mummies) and infected vines.
• Prune vines to open the plants up for good air circulation.
• Spray bordeaux mix on the plants before they bloom, during flowering, and again

seven to ten days later. Bordeaux mix is a combination of copper sulfate and hydrated lime in powdered form to use as a fungicide with insecticidal properties. Apply it as a dust or mixed with water for spraying. Follow label directions carefully, since bordeaux mix can injure plant foliage.

PROBLEM: Ripening grape clusters on your vines are rotting and are covered with fuzzy, gray mold.

CAUSE: Botrytis bunch rot, also called gray mold (*Botrytis cinerea*). Any break in grape skins or an opening made by dying blossoms is an entry point for this fungal disease. The Botrytis bunch rot fungi are almost always present in the environment and can reproduce rapidly during rainy, humid conditions.

WHAT TO DO:
• Space plants widely and prune them for good air circulation.
• Plant resistant cultivars, such as 'Cabernet Franc', 'Cascade', 'Concord', 'Duchess', 'Ives', 'Niagara', and 'Vanessa'.

PROBLEM: Smooth swellings turn to rough, warty galls on vine roots, trunks, and vines.

CAUSE: Crown galls (*Agrobacterium tumefaciens*). These galls are caused by a bacterium that can survive in the soil without a host plant for several years. The bacterium enters grape stems through wounds and insect bites. Weakened plants grow poorly and may eventually die.

WHAT TO DO:
• Purchase plants from a reputable nursery, and examine them for signs of galls before you plant them.
• Prune off and destroy galls on plants.
• In fall, mound several inches of soil around the crowns of grape plants.

Insulating plant crowns with soil helps prevent winter injury.

PROBLEM: Yellow, circular spots mar upper leaf surfaces. A white, cottony growth is on the bottoms of the leaves.

CAUSE: Downy mildew (*Plasmopara viticola*). This common fungal disease thrives in cool, damp conditions. The disease causes fruit clusters to contain a mix of hard, reddish green berries and normal ones. Downy mildew overwinters in diseased tissue on plants and in plant debris left on the ground.

WHAT TO DO:
• Spray plants with copper or bordeaux mix just before and right after bloom, and spray a third application one week later. Bordeaux mix is a combination of copper sulfate and hydrated lime in powdered form to use as a fungicide with insecticidal properties. (Apply carefully because both copper and bordeaux mix may burn grape foliage.)
• Remove and destroy diseased leaves and shoots in the fall.
• Grow resistant cultivars, such as 'Baco Noir', 'Cascade', 'Cayuga White', 'Chancellor', 'Chelois', 'De Chaunac', 'Elvira', 'Ives', 'Vidal 256', and 'Vignoles'. Modern French hybrids are somewhat susceptible. Vinifera varieties are much more susceptible than Concord types.

PROBLEM: New shoots are stunted in spring. The leaves are small, yellow, and deformed.

CAUSE: Eutypa dieback (*Eutypa lata*). The symptoms of this fungal disease become apparent only after the fungus develops under deadwood for several years. Eutypa can kill branches and vines and move into the trunks of grapevines. To diagnose the disease, cut a cross section of an infected vine, and you will see a dark, wedge-shaped area of infected wood. Eutypa dieback overwinters in diseased branches left on plants.

WHAT TO DO:
• Prune plants back to healthy wood.
• Sterilize your pruning tools with rubbing alcohol and wash your hands between cuts to avoid spreading the disease.
• Remove and destroy diseased prunings.

PROBLEM: Reddish brown spots mar shoots and leaves. Grapes turn brown with black spots, rot, and shrivel.

CAUSE: Phomopsis cane spot, also called Phomopsis leaf spot or fruit rot (*Phomopsis viticola*). This fungal disease overwinters in the infected stems. Fruit and stem infections occur from bloom time until the grapes reach pea size. Infected grapes begin to rot at harvest time.

WHAT TO DO:
• Remove and destroy infected and dead vines.
• Sterilize your pruning tools with rubbing alcohol and wash your hands between cuts to avoid spreading the disease.
• Plant resistant cultivars, such as 'Aurora', 'Baco Noir', 'Cayuga White', 'Elvira', 'Merlot', 'Vanessa', 'Ventura', and 'Vidal 256'.

PROBLEM: The leaves of your previously healthy grapevines are yellowing along the edges and drying out.

CAUSE: Pierce's disease. This bacterial disease lives in grasses and weeds, and it is carried from the grasses and weeds to grapes by sap-sucking sharpshooter leafhoppers (Family Cicadellidae). There is no cure for the disease. It is a particular problem in mild climates that receive less than 700 hours of chilling temperatures in winter. This disease overwinters in infected branches left on plants and in garden debris and weeds.

WHAT TO DO:
• Wash leafhoppers off plants with a strong stream of water.
• Use insecticidal soap, following label directions. Be sure to spray the backs of leaves.
• Prune out and destroy infected plant parts.
• Sterilize your pruning tools with rubbing alcohol and wash your hands between cuts.
• Grow resistant grape plants, such as Muscadine grapes and the American cultivars 'Champanelle', 'Herbemont', and 'Lenoir'.
• Control weeds in the vineyard.

PROBLEM: The leaves of your grape plants have a white, powdery coating that resists scraping off.

CAUSE: Powdery mildew (*Uncinula necator*). This fungal disease can reduce vine growth, yield, quality, and winter hardiness. The fungus overwinters in bark crevices and in dormant buds. It thrives in humidity and temperatures between 68° and 77°F.

WHAT TO DO:
• Grow resistant cultivars, such as 'Canadice', 'Cayuga White', 'Chambourcin', 'Ives', 'Melody', and 'Steuben'.
• Spray plants with a fungicide solution of sulfur in the spring (but note that 'Concord' and other American cultivars are susceptible to sulfur-foliage burn).
• Apply summer oil spray. Highly refined, horticultural oil sprays, such as summer oil, also control powdery mildew. These sprays coat plants with a disease- and insect-smothering layer of oil.
• Water with compost tea.
• Spray plants with baking soda spray. Dissolve 1 teaspoon baking soda in 1 quart warm water; add 1 teaspoon liquid biodegradable soap or insecticidal soap to make it stick to leaves.

Hazelnut

also called Filbert (*Corylus* spp.)

 Hazelnut Pests

PROBLEM: New leaf growth is twisted and curled. Some leaves are covered with black, sooty mold.

CAUSE: Aphids (Family Aphididae). These soft-bodied, pear-shaped insects are 1/16 to 3/8 inch long. They range in color from pale tan to light green to nearly black. Aphids damage leaves and stems by sucking plant juices. The damage is usually more cosmetic than serious. The sticky honeydew that aphids

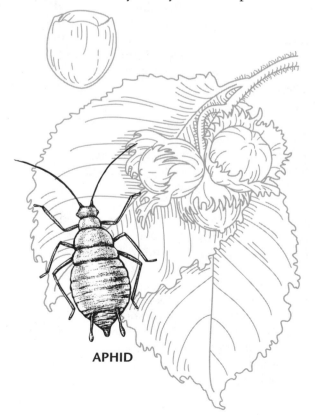

APHID

secrete attracts ants and mold. Ants protect aphids from natural predators, such as beneficial insects, in order to eat the honeydew that the aphids produce.

WHAT TO DO:
• Trap ants by putting sticky bands around the base of your trees. You can make sticky ant traps by spreading a sticky glue on cardboard bands and wrapping the bands around the base of your hazelnut trees. Make the sticky glue from equal parts petroleum jelly, mineral oil, and liquid dish soap; or use Tanglefoot, a commercial preparation made for this purpose. Replace the bands when they become covered with ants.
• Place ant traps baited with boric acid on the ground around the trees.
• Attract beneficial insects, such as parasitic wasps and lady beetles, by planting small-flowered nectar plants, including yarrow, scabiosa, and Queen-Anne's-lace, in the orchard.
• Apply dormant oil in early spring. Commercial oil sprays, such as this, coat tree branches and smother insect pests and diseases.

PROBLEM: The flower buds on your hazelnut trees are abnormally swollen. These buds are unable to produce nuts.

CAUSE: Filbert bud mites (*Phytocoptella avellanae*). You will need a hand lens to observe these tiny mites feeding in the flower buds of your hazelnut trees. The mites, which look like specks of moving pepper, crawl out of infested buds in May and infest healthy buds.

WHAT TO DO:
• Apply summer oil. This commercial horticultural oil coats tree foliage and buds, smothering insect pests and diseases.
• Plant resistant varieties, such as 'Barcelona', 'Cosford', 'Italian Red', and 'Purple Aveline'.

PROBLEM: Trees appear healthy, but some nut shells have holes in them. The kernels in the damaged shells are black.

CAUSE: Filbertworms, also called Catalina cherry moths (*Cydia latiferreana*). These pests are ½-inch-long, pale or dusky-toned moths with two copper-colored stripes near the tips of their forewings. Their larvae are ¾-inch-long, pink-tinted caterpillars. Filbertworms feed inside the nuts and then exit through holes in the shell. The larvae overwinter on plant debris on the soil.

WHAT TO DO:
• Collect fallen nuts. Dispose of discolored nuts and those with holes in them.
• Remove debris and leaves from the orchard to deprive filbertworms of their winter quarters.

 Hazelnut Diseases

PROBLEM: Twigs and branches are dying. More and more branches wither until the entire tree dies.

CAUSE: Eastern filbert blight (*Anisogramma anomala*). This fungal disease is carried throughout the eastern part of the United States by American hazelnut trees (*C. americana*). These native trees carry the disease but have enough resistance to survive infection. There is no cure for Eastern filbert blight.

WHAT TO DO:
• In areas with a history of the disease, grow the resistant, native hazelnut tree (*C. americana*) and its cultivars.

PROBLEM: Stems and branches develop open wounds, or cankers. Affected branches die back at the tips.

CAUSE: Hazelnut twig blight (*Apioporthe anomala*). This fungal disease overwinters in infected branches and fallen leaves. When the twigs become infected in midsummer, the purple or black spots turn into sunken cankers.

WHAT TO DO:
• Spray with sulfur when filbert trees have half their leaves open. Follow up with several sprays at two-week intervals throughout the growing season.

PROBLEM: A white, powdery coating covers hazelnut leaves. The undersides of some leaves are tinted red.

CAUSE: Powdery mildew (*Microsphaera alni; Phyllactivia corylea*). Dry weather and cool temperatures create favorable conditions for the development of powdery mildew. This common fungal disease overwinters on tree leaves. Powdery mildew does not require rain to develop. Warm temperatures and humid conditions lead to spore releases.

WHAT TO DO:
• Dust infected trees with sulfur.
• Prune trees to open up the interiors for maximum air circulation.

PROBLEM: Leaves develop small, reddish brown, water-soaked spots. Similar spots develop on branches.

CAUSE: Western filbert blight (*Xanthomonas corylina*). This bacterial disease of the Pacific Northwest overwinters on the infected leaves and branches of hazelnut trees.

WHAT TO DO:
• Prune off and dispose of infected branches.
• Protect hazelnut trees from damage caused by freezing and sunburn in winter.

Kiwi

(Actinidia spp.)

Kiwi Pests

PROBLEM: The leaves of previously thriving kiwis are suddenly eaten back to the leaf veins.

CAUSE: Japanese beetles (*Popillia japonica*). Kiwi leaves are a favorite food of Japanese beetles. Beginning in midsummer, the ½-inch-long, metallic green beetles with bronze wings cluster in groups to feed on kiwi foliage. Japanese beetle larvae are ¾-inch-long, gray-white grubs with brown heads. The grubs overwinter in the soil, and in late spring the larvae move closer to the surface of the soil, where they feed on grass roots.

WHAT TO DO:
• Handpick. In the cool of early morning or evening, when beetles are sluggish, pick them and knock them into a jar of soapy water.
• Apply group-attacking nematodes to the soil in late spring or late summer. These beneficials (*Steinernema carpocapsae* and *Heterorhabditis heliothidis*) are shipped live from mail-order suppliers, suspended in gels or sponges. Follow instructions and release nematodes when pest larvae are present.
• Apply milky disease spores to sod areas; milky disease will spread through the soil and kill larvae. Milky disease is a microbial insecticide that combines spores of *Bacillus popilliae* and *B. lentimorbus*. Grubs eat the spores, become infected with milky disease, and die.
• Aerate turf with spiked sandals in late spring and early fall to reduce grub populations.
• Cultivate the soil in late spring and early fall to expose grubs to hungry birds and freezing temperatures.

PROBLEM: The bark of your kiwi vines is spattered with small, oval bumps and spots of sticky clear or sooty substances.

CAUSE: Soft scale (Family Coccidae). These ⅒-inch-long, stationary insects blend in with the bark of the tree branches that they attack. Scale produce sticky secretions, called honeydew, that attract ants, which protect the scale from beneficial insects in order to eat the honeydew. And the moist honeydew provides an environment suitable for the development of mold.

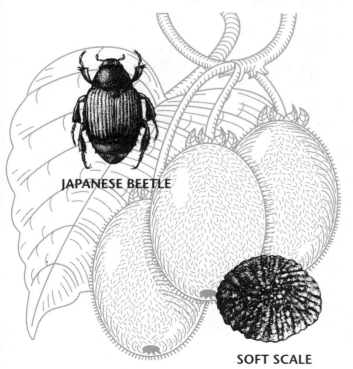

JAPANESE BEETLE

SOFT SCALE

WHAT TO DO:
• Attract beneficial insects, such as lady beetles, lacewings, and predaceous mites, by planting pollen and nectar plants, including dill, Queen-Anne's-lace, and black-eyed Susans.
• Spray dormant oil before vines leaf out to reduce populations. Do not apply dormant oil during cold weather (below 35°F) or within 24 hours of such a cold spell. This horticultural oil coats leaves and branches, smothering insects and disease pathogens.

 ## Kiwi Diseases

PROBLEM: Kiwi flowers are rotting and dying. Fruits that surviving flowers produce are growing fuzzy, gray mold.
CAUSE: Botrytis rot, also called storage rot (*Botrytis cinerea*). This fungal disease enters kiwi plants through holes in the skins of the fruits. Botrytis fungi are almost always present in the environment. The fungi reproduce rapidly in rainy, humid conditions, increasing the risk of infection during such conditions. Like many fungi, the spores of Botrytis rot overwinter in infected plant parts and plant debris left in the garden.
WHAT TO DO:
• Remove and destroy infected flowers and fruit.
• Space plants far enough apart to maintain good air circulation.

PROBLEM: The leaves of your kiwis are turning yellow. The base of the main stem and plant roots are rotting.
CAUSE: Crown rot (*Phytophthora* spp.). This fungal infection can enter a kiwi plant through bruised or broken stems and roots. Crown rot fungus thrives in damp and saturated soil. Roots that are deprived of oxygen by soggy soil are at risk of infection. The dis-ease, like many other fungal diseases, over-winters in the soil.
WHAT TO DO:
• Water kiwi roots without wetting the stems of the plant.
• Mulch around kiwi plants to prevent soil-borne disease spores from splashing onto stems and leaves during rain or while you're irrigating plants.
• Improve drainage or plant kiwis on a raised mound of soil.

 ## Other Problems

PROBLEM: Your kiwi vines are chewed and bedraggled-looking. The bark at the base of the vines is shredded.
CAUSE: Cat damage. Cats are as attracted to young kiwi vines as they are to catnip. Cats like to roll on the vines, chew the leaves, and scratch the stems of kiwi vines.
WHAT TO DO:
• Enclose young kiwi vines in homemade chicken-wire cages to protect them from playful cats.
• Plant a patch of catnip far enough away from your kiwi vines to entice cats away from them.

PROBLEM: Your kiwi vines appear healthy; they produce new leaves and stems but produce little or no fruit.
CAUSE: Frost damage. Kiwi plants are marginally hardy in cold-climate parts of the United States. In early spring the new shoots and flower buds are easily damaged by late frosts and cold winds. In fall, early frosts can also damage the plants and lingering fruits.
WHAT TO DO:
• Provide windbreaks. Plant kiwis where they are protected from winter wind. Do not plant them in low-lying areas or at the bottom of a hill, where cold air can pool in winter.

Peach

(Prunus persica)

Peach Pests

PROBLEM: Peach-tree twigs look unusually bushy. Some peaches have a gummy, black blotch and larvae inside.

CAUSES: Oriental fruit moths (*Grapholitha molesta*) and peach twig borers (*Anarsia lineatella*).

These two pests damage peach trees in similar ways. The larvae tunnel into the tips of rapidly growing twigs in early summer, causing the trees to put out unusual-looking, bushy growth. Peaches with a gummy, black blotch have larval damage. No other external damage is visible. But when you cut open an infested peach, you can see one of these caterpillars feeding on the fruit. The larvae of both oriental fruit moth and peach twig borers overwinter in the soil.

Oriental fruit moths are dark-gray moths with ½-inch wingspans. Only the larval stage of oriental fruit moths cause the damage to peach fruits. Oriental fruit moth larvae are ½-inch-long, white or pinkish caterpillars with brown heads.

Peach twig borers are small, reddish brown caterpillars. These pests are the larvae of tiny, gray moths that have a wingspan of ⅓ inch. Older peach twig borers, which can grow up to ½ inch long, are dark, reddish brown with white bands between each of the body segments.

WHAT TO DO:
• Remove peaches that fall to the ground. Cut away and dispose of the infested parts of the fruits, and dispose of those that are rotten.
• Cultivate the soil shallowly under trees before they flower to reduce larval populations that are overwintering in the soil.
• Apply BT. "BT" stands for *Bacillus thuringiensis*, an insect-stomach poison that kills caterpillars without harming beneficial insects. Follow directions and apply when pests are present. Spray with BT every two to three weeks from May through September. Javelin WG is a BT product that is effective against oriental fruit moths.
• Growers with 1-acre or larger orchards can effectively use pheromone mating disruption. These chemical sex lures reduce pest popula-

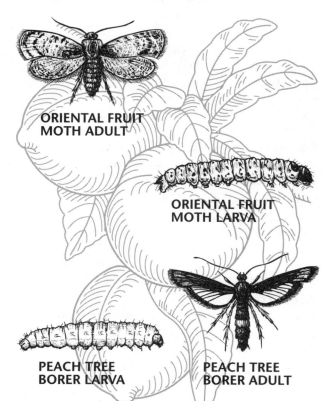

ORIENTAL FRUIT MOTH ADULT

ORIENTAL FRUIT MOTH LARVA

PEACH TREE BORER LARVA

PEACH TREE BORER ADULT

tions by confusing male moths, which are attracted to the lures and become unable to find a mate.

• Attract beneficial insects by growing small-flowered nectar plants, including scabiosa, yarrow, and dill, in the orchard.

Trichogramma minutum (an egg parasite) and *Macrocentrus ancylivorus* (a larval parasite) are beneficial insects that you can purchase from mail-order insectaries to help to control oriental fruit moth larvae and peach twig borers by parasitizing them. Release them when the larvae are active.

PROBLEM: There are globs of gum mixed with sawdust near holes on branches and at the base of your peach trees.

CAUSES: Peach tree borers (*Synanthedon exitiosa*) and lesser peach tree borers (*S. pictipes*). The adult stages of both pests are moths that have steel-blue bodies with an orange or yellow ring around their abdomen. The moths have clear hind wings, and their wingspans range from 1 to 1¼ inches. The 1-inch-long larvae of both are white with brown heads. The larvae bore holes in stems and tree trunks from early May to late June.

As they feed, the larvae can completely girdle and kill young trees. The damage can seriously weaken older trees, making them vulnerable to other pest and to disease problems. Either of these pests can have a lethal effect on peach trees.

WHAT TO DO:

• Kill the caterpillars by inserting a piece of wire into the hole to puncture the larvae, or dig the caterpillars out of the wood with a knife and destroy them.

• Inject a solution of beneficial nematodes (*Steinernema carpocapsae* and *Heterorhabditis heliothidis*) into the borer's hole. Mail-order suppliers ship the nematodes live, suspended in gels or sponges. Follow instructions for application; release when pests are present.

• Apply BT. "BT" stands for *Bacillus thuringiensis*, an insect stomach poison that kills caterpillar and worm pests without harming beneficial insects. BT is available from mail-order suppliers. Apply it when the caterpillars are present.

• Attract beneficial insects by planting small-flowered nectar plants, including dill, yarrow, and Queen-Anne's-lace.

• Allow ants, spiders, moles, birds, mice, and skunks to enter the garden, because they eat borers.

PROBLEM: Peaches have sunken, corky spots, and some fruits drop without ripening. New leaves are deformed.

CAUSE: Stink bugs (Family Pentatomidae). These ½-inch-long, gray or green bugs with flat, shield-shaped backs sink their mouth parts into peaches to suck plant juices. The resulting spots, which disfigure the fruits, are called "catfacing." Stink bugs feed on flower buds in spring and on fruits early and late in the growing season. Stink bugs overwinter in weeds.

WHAT TO DO:

• Handpick.

• Collect stink bugs with a hand-held vacuum.

• Tolerate light damage.

• Control weeds.

• In fall, clean up plant debris where these pests can overwinter.

PROBLEM: Some flowers drop without producing peaches. Some fruits have sunken, corky lesions and drop early.

CAUSE: Tarnished plant bugs (*Lygus lineolaris*). These pests are ¼-inch-long insects with brown, tan, or green markings. Tarnished plant bugs cause blossom injury and fruit drop. Insect feeding when the peach fruits are small results in sunken, corky lesions on them called "catfacing." Feeding at bloom time causes blossoms and developing fruits to drop.

WHAT TO DO:

• Make white sticky traps. Tarnished plant bugs are attracted to the color white, so coat white cardboard or painted wooden boards with petroleum jelly or Tanglefoot (a commercial product for this purpose), and fasten them to stakes 3 feet from the ground around your peach trees. Replace the traps when they become covered with insects.

• Do not mow around peach trees during flowering or early fruit development. Mowing at this time will drive tarnished plant bugs from the grass into your trees.

• Control weeds. Legumes, such as alfalfa, and other weeds harbor tarnished plant bugs.

 Peach Diseases

PROBLEM: Leaves have spots, some with open centers. They yellow and drop. Fruits exude gum.

CAUSE: Bacterial leaf spot (*Xanthomonas pruni*). This bacterial disease, which is most common east of the Rockies, is most severe during rainy periods in the spring. The disease weakens trees, making them prone to winter injury.

WHAT TO DO:

• Spray with a bordeaux mix when symptoms appear and again ten days later. Bordeaux is a combination of copper sulfate and hydrated lime to use as a fungicide with insecticidal properties.

• Plant resistant varieties, such as 'Belle of Georgia', 'Candor', 'Compact Red', 'Dixieland', 'Early Red Free', 'Harbrite', 'Loring', 'Madam', and 'Red Haven'.

PROBLEM: Brown spots form on flowers, gradually turning flowers completely brown. Fruits with spots rot.

CAUSE: Brown rot (*Monilinia* spp.). Brown rot fungus is a serious disease. It first appears in the spring and progresses until the whole flowers and fruits turn brown and rot. The infected fruit eventually shrinks and dries out, or mummifies. Twigs with infections have sunken brown cankers covered in gummy sap. Brown rot overwinters in mummified fruit and infected twigs. Insect-damaged fruit is susceptible to the disease.

WHAT TO DO:

• Remove and destroy infected and mummified fruits and twigs that are disfigured with patches of gummy sap.

• Prune trees to assure good air circulation.

• Apply sulfur spray twice: Spray once when blossoms begin to show pink and spray again before harvest, when the fruits begin to turn color.

PROBLEM: Some branches fail to leaf out in spring. Leaves wilt and die. Branches have sunken, gummy cankers.

CAUSE: Canker disease. This disease is caused by bacteria and other pathogens that enter peach trees through broken branches and otherwise-injured bark. The elliptical, sunken cankers that appear on diseased wood exude a sour-smelling gum.

WHAT TO DO:

• Prune off and remove wilted and dead branches below the site of infection. Delay pruning until buds are open because early pruning can provide entry points for the disease.

• Disinfect your pruning tools with rubbing alcohol and wash your hands after pruning diseased wood.

• Plant peach trees in well-drained soil.

• Paint tree trunks with white latex paint to reduce winter bark splitting.

PROBLEM: Young leaves pucker, turn reddish green, and fall. Fruits drop before ripening or have rough skin.

CAUSE: Peach leaf curl (*Taphrina deformans*). This fungal disease can cause entire trees to defoliate. Before the infected leaves fall from the tree, fungal spores are discharged and land on the bark. The spores remain viable over winter and in spring infect the new leaf buds.

WHAT TO DO:

• Spray seaweed solution once a month throughout the growing season as a foliar feed to strengthen the trees.

• Spray with bordeaux solution after leaves drop in the fall and again before buds swell in the spring. Bordeaux is a combination of copper sulfate and hydrated lime to use as a fungicide with insecticidal properties. Follow label directions carefully because bordeaux mix can injure foliage.

• Plant resistant varieties, including 'Mary Jane' and 'Q 1-8'.

PROBLEM: Olive or black spots appear on fruits and leaves six weeks after the trees bloom. Fruits become stunted.

CAUSE: Peach scab (*Cladosporium carpophilum*). This fungal infection thrives in warm, humid conditions, causing infected twigs to develop circular, yellow-brown blotches with bluish gray borders. Peach scab fungus overwinters on old leaves, fruit, and mulch.

WHAT TO DO:

• Rake up and remove fallen leaves, fruit, and mulch in the fall.

• Begin spraying a sulfur solution every 10 to 20 days, starting when flower buds show green and ending six weeks after the trees stop blooming.

PROBLEM: Small purple spots develop on the leaves and fruits. The centers of the leaf spots turn brown and crumble.

CAUSE: Shothole disease (*Coryneum carpophilum*). This fungal disease, along with others that cause similar symptoms, overwinters in the infected twigs and buds of peach trees. Disease spores travel via splashing rain or irrigation water, and they require 24-hour contact with wet foliage in order to cause infections. Young, infected leaves may defoliate. Infected fruits become covered with gummy deposits and may fall from the trees.

WHAT TO DO:

• Prune and destroy the shiny, varnished-looking, infected buds, twigs, blossoms, and fruits.

• Spray with bordeaux mix after leaves fall in early autumn and before the fall rains begin. Apply the spray again at the pink–flower bud stage in the spring. Bordeaux mix is a wettable combination of copper sulfate and hydrated lime. Follow label directions carefully because the mix can injure plant foliage.

 Other Problems

PROBLEM: The tree appears healthy, but amber-colored sap oozes from one or more places along the trunk.

CAUSE: Gummosis. Peach trees have a natural tendency to ooze sap. If the tree appears otherwise healthy, gummosis is not a threatening condition. But injured bark and trees that stand in wet soil for long periods of time can also ooze sap.

WHAT TO DO:

• Avoid overwatering peach trees. If the soil is saturated, do not water until it has dried.

• Prune as necessary to prevent branch breakage.

Peanut

(Arachis hypogaea)

 Peanut Pests

PROBLEM: Peanut leaves develop white, mottled spots. Some of the spotted leaves are also distorted and puckered.
CAUSE: Leafhoppers (Family Cicadellidae). Leafhoppers are ¼-inch-long, slender insects that move rapidly when disturbed. These pests have piercing mouth parts that they use to suck plant juices from the undersides of peanut leaves.

The saliva of leafhoppers is toxic to peanut plants: It causes the leaves that they feed on to become discolored and distorted.

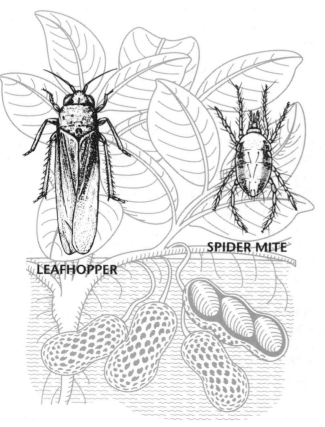

LEAFHOPPER

SPIDER MITE

WHAT TO DO:
• Tolerate light infestations.
• Use insecticidal soap, following label directions. Be sure to spray the backs of leaves, where insects often hide, as well as the tops.
• Attract beneficial insects, such as parasitic wasps and lady beetles, by growing small-flowered nectar plants, including dill, yarrow, and Queen-Anne's-lace.

PROBLEM: The leaves of your peanut plants have tiny yellow spots, and there is webbing under the leaves.
CAUSE: Spider mites (Family Tetranychidae). To the naked eye, spider mites look like tiny pinpoint-sized red dots, or grains of red pepper. Spider mites pierce the cells on the undersides of peanut leaves and suck the plant juices. Mites reproduce rapidly, and there are numerous generations each summer. Large populations of mites can be a serious threat to peanut plants during hot, dry summers.
WHAT TO DO:
• Knock mites off plants with a strong spray of water. Be sure to spray the backs of leaves, where insects often hide, as well as the tops.
• Water peanut plants regularly; mites are more likely to attack drought-stressed plants.
• Attract beneficial insects, such as parasitic wasps and lady beetles, by planting small-flowered nectar plants, including dill, yarrow, and Queen-Anne's-lace.

 Peanut Diseases

PROBLEM: Plants wilt in the midday sun. When you dig them up, you see hard, irregular swellings on the roots.

CAUSE: Root-knot nematodes (*Meloidogyne* spp.). These are microscopic, soil-dwelling organisms that cause diseaselike symptoms. They damage the root systems of peanuts, reducing their ability to absorb water and nutrients from the soil. Substances produced by the nematodes as they feed cause the formation of the root galls. Root-knot nematodes can be especially damaging to peanut plants grown in sandy soils. In warmer climates, nematodes are not killed by freezing soil.

WHAT TO DO:

• Remove and dispose of infected plants and the soil that contacts their roots.

• Rotate crops. Plan a rotational schedule that includes green manure crops, such as rye and Sudan grass. These plants stimulate the growth of beneficial soil fungi when the cover crops are turned under. Rotations of three years or longer are recommended.

• Solarize the soil. Clear plastic sheeting placed over bare soil for four weeks during the hottest part of the summer will heat the soil enough to kill most nematodes in the top few inches of soil. After removing the plastic, plant crops as usual.

PROBLEM: Leaves of your peanut plants develop brown or black spots with yellow edges, and then the leaves drop.

CAUSE: Peanut leaf spot (*Cercospora personata*). In severe cases, this fungal disease can cause entire plants to defoliate during the growing season. The disease overwinters on old peanut leaves left in the garden.

WHAT TO DO:

• Remove plant debris from the garden, especially in the fall.

• Dust infected peanut plants with sulfur every 10 to 14 days throughout the growing season.

• Rotate crops. Simply alternate peanut plants with other plants at least annually to protect them from soilborne pests and dis-

eases. Three- to five-year rotations are best.

• Plant resistant peanut varieties, such as 'Southern Runner'.

PROBLEM: A white, powdery coating covers leaves. Severely affected plants are stunted and produce small crops.

CAUSE: Powdery mildew (*Oidium arachidis*). This common fungal disease overwinters on plant debris left in the garden. Warm temperatures and humid conditions lead to spore releases. The disease does not require rain in order to develop.

WHAT TO DO:

• Dust the foliage of infected peanut plants with sulfur.

• Space plants widely for maximum air circulation.

 Other Problems

PROBLEM: Peanut plants grow and appear healthy, but they do not form nuts in time to harvest.

CAUSE: Inadequate growing conditions. Peanuts require loose, friable soil so that the peanut-forming "pegs" that grow from the plant's stem can burrow into the soil. Peanut plants also require a long growing season to form peanuts and to allow them to mature.

WHAT TO DO:

• Improve soil texture. Incorporate organic matter to clay or otherwise hard soil to loosen it.

• If you live in the North, choose short-season cultivars, such as the Spanish peanut types.

• Start plants early. By planting peanut plants in peat pots about six weeks before the frost-free date, you will get a proper head start on the season.

Pear

(*Pyrus* spp.)

 Pear Pests

PROBLEM: The leaves of your pear trees and the fruits have spots that are sticky and clear, or sooty and black.

CAUSE: Pear psyllids (*Cacopsylla pyricola*). The adults are ¹⁄₁₀-inch-long, yellow-brown, winged insects called jumping louses. The nymphs suck sap from pear leaves. Pear pyslla nymphs secrete a sticky honeydew that attracts ants and sooty, black fungus. You can wash the spots off fruits, but other diseases can enter trees through the insect-damaged tissues.

WHAT TO DO:
• Use insecticidal soap, following label directions, early in the season to reduce the population of pear psyllids.

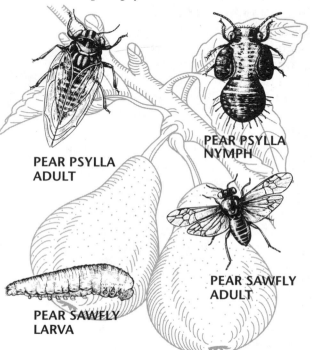

PEAR PSYLLA ADULT

PEAR PSYLLA NYMPH

PEAR SAWFLY LARVA

PEAR SAWFLY ADULT

• Prune and dispose of succulent water sprouts in midsummer to remove vulnerable, tender tissue.
• Spray dormant oil in early spring to kill many of the overwintering adults and eggs. This horticultural oil coats tree tissues and smothers pests and diseases.
• Attract beneficial insects, such as parasitic wasps and lady beetles, by planting flowering nectar crops, including Dutch white clover, yarrow, and dill.

PROBLEM: Some pear tree leaves are eaten all the way to the veins. You can see sluglike larvae on the leaves.

CAUSE: Pear sawflies, also called pear slugs (*Caliroa cerasi*). These pests are olive green to orange, sluglike, slimy larvae with oversized heads. Fully grown larvae are ½ inch long. Adults are ¹⁄₅-inch-long, glossy black-and-yellow flies with four wings. After feeding, the nymphs pupate in cocoons in the soil. The first generation attacks in spring, and a second, more damaging generation emerges in late July or August.

WHAT TO DO:
• Handpick.
• Knock larvae off foliage with a heavy stream of water.
• Use insecticidal soap, following directions.
• Apply summer oil spray. This horticultural oil coats leaves and stems, smothering insects and disease pathogens.

PROBLEM: Branches have clusters of tiny, gray-brown bumps. Leaves are yellowing, and some branches are dying.

CAUSE: San Jose scale (*Quadraspidiotus perniciosus*). These insects feed on the sap of pear tree bark, on the leaves, and also on the fruits. The fully grown females are the size of a pinhead. They are gray-brown bumps with dull, yellow humps. Male scale are slightly smaller and have an oval shape with a raised bump near the larger end of the oval. The insects overwinter in a partly grown stage and begin to mature in the spring. Extremely cold weather greatly reduces populations. San Jose scale can weaken and kill a young tree in two or three years.

WHAT TO DO:
• Spray dormant oil before trees flower in spring. This horticultural oil coats leaves and stems, smothering pests and disease pathogens.
• Attract beneficial insects, such as lady beetles and parasitic wasps, by planting small-flowered nectar plants, including yarrow, dill, and Queen-Anne's-lace.

 Pear Diseases

PROBLEM: In spring, the tips of some young branches wilt and turn black. The affected branches rapidly die.

CAUSE: Fire blight (*Erwinia amylovora*). This is a serious bacterial disease. In moist, warm, spring weather, fire blight bacterium surfaces in drops of ooze from cankers. These droplets travel by wind, rain, or insects to pear blossoms. Infected shoots and even whole trees can turn black and wilt in less than a week.

WHAT TO DO:
• Spray infected trees with the antibiotic spray solution streptomycin during bloom.
• Complete dormant pruning before buds swell in the spring.
• Do not fertilize. Fertilizing causes the plants to produce weak growth susceptible to fire blight.
• Grow resistant varieties, such as 'Harrow

Delight', 'Harvest Queen', 'Honeysweet', 'Kieffer', 'Magness', 'Orient', and 'Seckel'.
• If fire blight is a problem in your area, avoid growing susceptible types of pear trees. Asian pears except for 'Shinko' are susceptible, as are many European cultivars, such as 'Bartlett' and 'Bosc'.

PROBLEM: Some leaves have small, purple spots that yellow. They drop early. Fruits have red or black spots.

CAUSE: Pear leaf blight, also known as black fruit spot (*Fabraea maculata*). This disease overwinters in infected branches and fallen leaves. Infected fruit is misshapen and cracked. Twigs become infected in mid-summer, when the purple or black spots on stems turn into sunken cankers.

WHAT TO DO:
• Spray with sulfur when pear trees are half leafed out in spring. Continue spraying at two-week intervals throughout the growing season.
• Grow resistant cultivars, such as 'Maxine' and 'Moonglow'.

PROBLEM: Pear fruits have olive brown, corky-textured spots. The backs of some leaves have dark, velvety patches.

CAUSE: Pear scab (*Venturia pyrina*). This fungal disease overwinters on dead leaves and infected twigs left in the orchard. In the spring, warm temperatures and rainy periods promote the release of the disease spores, which infect developing fruits and tree leaves.

WHAT TO DO:
• Rake up and compost old leaves and dropped fruit in the fall.
• Spray with sulfur every seven to ten days before and after pear trees flower.
• Plant resistant cultivars, such as 'Arganche', 'Clapp's Favorite', and 'Orcas'.
• Do not grow susceptible cultivars, such as 'Anjou', 'Bosc', and 'Seckel'.

Pecan

(*Carya illinoinensis*)

 Pecan Pests

PROBLEM: The leaves of your pecan trees develop yellow spots, turn brown, and drop. Affected trees defoliate early.

CAUSE: Black pecan aphids (*Melanocallis caryaefoliae*). In early spring, overwintering eggs hatch into aphids that suck sap from buds and leaves. Black pecan aphid nymphs turn from yellow to light green and finally to olive green. The ⅛-inch-long adult aphids are black with small white marks.

WHAT TO DO:
• Attract beneficial insects, such as lady beetles, lacewings, and parasitic wasps, by planting small-flowered nectar plants, including crimson clover and hairy vetch.
• Late in the season, order beneficial lacewings from mail-order sources. The insectaries will help you determine how many to order and when to release them.

PROBLEM: When you open pecan nuts that drop early, you see that they are infested with insect larvae.

CAUSE: Hickory shuckworms (*Cydia caryae*). The cream-colored, ⅜-inch-long hickory shuckworm larvae bore into nut interiors before the shells harden. Shuckworm larvae overwinter in the outer covering of pecan nuts. The adults are ⅜-inch-long, brown or dark gray moths with ½-inch wingspans.

WHAT TO DO:
• Pick up and dispose of infested nuts to keep this pest from overwintering and infecting future crops.

PROBLEM: Pecan nuts are infested with larvae and shrouded in silken threads. Infested nuts drop prematurely.

CAUSE: Pecan nut casebearers (*Acrobasis nuxvorella*). These pests cause the most damage in May and early June. The ½-inch-long, olive gray to reddish green larvae leave their silky cocoons in early spring and bore into the stem end of pecan nuts. A

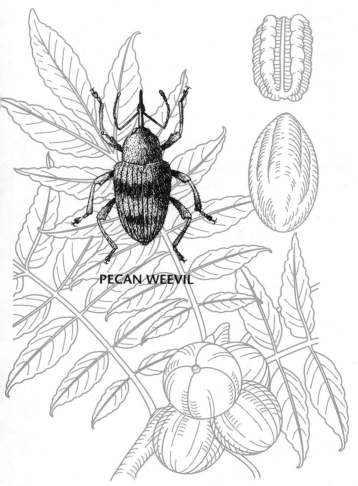

PECAN WEEVIL

single larva can destroy all the nuts in a cluster. The adult, dark gray moths with ¾-inch wingspans appear in late June and early July.

WHAT TO DO:
• Pick up and destroy infested nuts to keep this pest from overwintering in the orchard and infecting future crops.
• Attract beneficial insects, such as parasitic wasps and lady beetles, by planting small-flowered nectar plants, including dill and yarrow. To supplement native beneficial insects, contact a mail-order source for *Trichogramma minutum*, a small parasitic wasp. Release the wasps at a rate of 5,000 for each tree.

PROBLEM: Pecans are eaten from inside the shell while they are still on the trees, leaving hollow shells.

CAUSE: Pecan weevils (*Curculio caryae*). Pecan weevils cause serious crop losses in southeastern states. The adults are ¼- to ½-inch-long, gray beetles with long snouts. The adults emerge from July through October. Most emerge after periods of heavy rainfall. The adults feed on developing nuts and then lay eggs. The ⅜- to 9⁄16-inch-long, creamy white larvae have red-brown heads. Larvae burrow into nuts and destroy the kernels.

WHAT TO DO:
• Collect and destroy weevils. To do this, place sheets or plastic tarps under pecan trees in early August. Shake the limbs with padded poles; the adult weevils will drop onto the sheets. Collect weevils weekly until they are gone.

 Pecan Diseases

PROBLEM: Leaves have yellow spots that turn brown or black. Leaf undersides have a white coating. Trees defoliate.

CAUSE: Pecan downy spot (*Mycosphaerella caryigena*). This fungal disease overwinters in dead pecan leaves. The spores germinate and infect new foliage in the spring. The fungus thrives when rising temperatures and spring rains create warm, humid conditions.

WHAT TO DO:
• Spray a bordeaux mixture when leaves are half opened and again when the tips of small nuts turn brown. Bordeaux mix is a wettable combination of copper sulfate and hydrated lime in powdered form to use as a fungicide with insecticidal properties. Follow label directions carefully, since bordeaux mix can injure plant foliage.
• Rake up and dispose of fallen leaves to keep the disease from overwintering.

PROBLEM: Olive brown spots on leaf undersides cause leaves to blacken and drop. Nuts with lesions drop early.

CAUSE: Pecan scab (*Cladosporium effusum*). This fungal disease thrives in humid areas. Damp weather for six to eight hours at a time is required for an infection. Infections begin in the spring and early summer, and they continue to spread if conditions are favorable. The disease overwinters on infected twigs and leaves.

WHAT TO DO:
• Clean up plant debris in autumn.
• Dispose of old leaf stems and dead leaves before the trees leaf out in spring.
• Spray bordeaux solution four times: after trees leaf out, again after flower pollination, in three to four weeks after the second spray, and again in late July or early August. Bordeaux mix is a wettable combination of copper sulfate and hydrated lime in powdered form to use as a fungicide with insecticidal properties. Follow label directions carefully, since bordeaux mix can injure plant foliage.

Persimmon

(*Diospyros* spp.)

Persimmon Pests

PROBLEM: Small branches and twigs of persimmon trees are neatly sliced from the trees. You find them on the ground.

CAUSE: Twig girdlers (*Oncideres cingulata*). These pests are hard-shelled, gray beetles with antennae longer than their bodies. They lay from three to eight eggs in individual twigs or branches up to several feet long. Then the beetles use their jaws to cut around and around the twig from the bark inward, until the branch drops to the ground. Their eggs hatch in the fall and overwinter in the fallen branches. In spring, the larvae tunnel through the branches toward the severed end, eating and growing up to 1 inch long as they travel. They emerge in fall as adult beetles. Twig girdlers can seriously injure young trees, and the wounds they make on all trees become entry places for diseases.

WHAT TO DO:
• Gather and destroy fallen branches in late fall.

PROBLEM: Branches have clusters of tiny gray-brown bumps. Leaves are turning yellow; branches die back.

CAUSE: San Jose scale (*Quadraspidiotus perniciosus*). These insects feed on the sap of persimmon tree bark, leaves, and fruit. The fully grown females are the size of a pinhead and are rounded gray-brown bumps with a dull yellow hump. Male scale are slightly smaller and have an oval shape with a raised bump near the larger end of the oval. The insects overwinter in a partly grown stage and begin to mature in the spring. Extremely cold weather greatly reduces populations. San Jose scale can weaken and kill a young tree in two or three years. Fruits that have red spots on them are infested with the scale.

WHAT TO DO:
• Spray dormant oil before bloom. This horticultural oil coats leaves and stems, smothering pests and disease pathogens.
• Attract beneficial insects, such as lady beetles and parasitic wasps, by planting small-flowered nectar plants, including yarrow, dill, and Queen-Anne's-lace.

SAN JOSE SCALE

Persimmon Diseases

PROBLEM: Persimmon fruits and leaves are covered with purplish brown or yellow spots.

CAUSE: Anthracnose (*Gloeosporium diospyri*). This fungal disease weakens persimmon trees and ruins their fruit.

WHAT TO DO:
• Plant resistant varieties, including 'Morris Burton' and 'Runkwitz'.
• If anthracnose infections are serious on susceptible cultivars, spray trees with bordeaux mix in late winter. Bordeaux mix is a wettable combination of copper sulfate and hydrated lime. Follow label directions carefully, since bordeaux mix can injure plant foliage.

PROBLEM: The leaves and stem tips of your persimmon trees turn reddish and then yellow, wilt, and die.

CAUSE: Wilt (*Cephalosporium diospyri*). In spring, temperatures between 70° and 75°F and high humidity enable fungal spores to germinate and enter persimmon trees through wounds.

WHAT TO DO:
• Dispose of diseased branches and shoots.
• Prune trees to open up the centers for adequate air circulation.
• Grow oriental persimmon varieties, which are less susceptible to the disease than native trees and their varieties.

 Other Problems

PROBLEM: Your persimmon trees appear to be healthy and grow normally, but fruits are falling before they ripen.

CAUSE: Fruit drop. Persimmons have a natural tendency to drop their fruit. Periods of high temperatures, drought, and wet soil can all cause persimmons to drop their fruits prematurely.

WHAT TO DO:
• Maintain consistently healthy growing conditions.
• Do not apply large amounts of fertilizer at a time or fertilize on an erratic schedule.
• Keep the soil moist, but do not overwater.
• Prune to remove weak growth.

PROBLEM: You notice brown or black spots forming on fruits in late summer. The leaves may also develop dark spots.

CAUSE: Sunburn. During periods of hot temperatures, water evaporates from fruit and foliage faster than it can be replenished by the roots of the persimmon trees. The fruit surfaces, and sometimes the leaves, will overheat and blacken where the sun hits them. Sunburn is most likely to happen to trees growing in dry soil, those exposed to hot wind, and those with limited growing space. Damaged fruits are unsightly but still edible.

WHAT TO DO:
• Water plants deeply during droughts.
• Water regularly to maintain soil moisture during the growing season.

PROBLEM: You notice bark splitting on trunks of your trees, particularly on the southwestern-facing sides.

CAUSE: Sunscald. In late winter, temperature fluctuation between sunny afternoons and nighttime cold will cause uneven expansion in the tree bark, which can lead to splitting.

WHAT TO DO:
• Paint the side of the tree facing southwest with water-based, white latex paint. The white paint will reflect the sun's rays and keep the tree trunk a more uniform temperature, so the bark will be less likely to split.

Plum

(Prunus spp.)

 Plum Pests

PROBLEM: The new leaves of your plum trees are twisted and curled. They have a clear, sticky coating.

CAUSE: Aphids (Family Aphididae). Colonies of these $\frac{1}{16}$- to $\frac{3}{8}$-inch-long, soft-bodied, pear-shaped insects suck sap from leaves and tender stems. Aphids secrete a sticky honeydew substance that attracts ants and sooty mold. Ants protect aphids in order to feed on the honeydew that the aphids secrete. Aphids also transfer diseases to plants as they feed.

WHAT TO DO:

• Use insecticidal soap, following label direc-

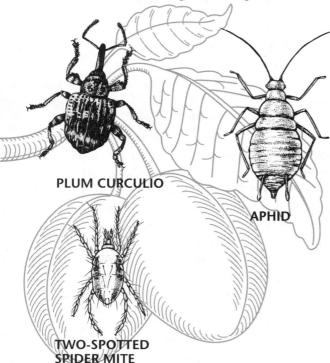

PLUM CURCULIO

APHID

TWO-SPOTTED SPIDER MITE

tions. Be sure to hit the backs of leaves, where aphids hide, as well as the tops when spraying.

• Pour boiling water into anthills that are far enough from the tree roots to prevent scalding them.

• Attract beneficial insects by planting nectar plants, including dill and Queen-Anne's-lace. Natural predators, such as lady beetles and syrphid fly larvae, will move in and effectively reduce aphid populations.

PROBLEM: The leaves of your plum trees have stippled, yellow spots. Severely affected leaves turn bronze and drop.

CAUSES: European red mites (*Panonychus ulmi*) and two-spotted spider mites (*Tetranychus urticae*). These tiny, pinpoint-sized creatures feed on the undersides of plum leaves. Mite populations flare up under hot, dry conditions. Under such conditions, they can last through the growing season, severely weakening trees. Weakened trees produce undersized fruits.

The adult European red mite is red with white spots on its back. Its tiny, red eggs overwinter in twig crevices.

Two-spotted mites overwinter under tree bark and in debris on the orchard floor. The adult two-spotted spider mites are yellowish green with a dark spot on each side of their abdomen.

WHAT TO DO:

• Attract beneficial insects by planting small-flowered nectar plants, including yarrow, scabiosa, and Queen-Anne's-lace. Excellent natural predators include predaceous mites;

the small, black ladybird beetle (*Stethorus punctum*); lacewings; and minute pirate bugs. You can also purchase predators from mail-order sources.

• Apply dormant oil spray. Do not apply dormant oil during cold weather (below 35°F) or within 24 hours of such a cold spell. Horticultural oils, such as dormant oil, coat leaves and branches and smother insects and disease pathogens.

PROBLEM: Crescent-shaped scars appear on some of the developing fruits on your plum trees.

CAUSE: Plum curculios (*Conotrachelus nenuphar*). The adults are dark brown, ⅕-inch-long beetles with curved, thick, beaklike mouth parts. These beetles eat ripening fruit. They then cut crescent-shaped holes in plum skin and lay eggs just beneath the skin. The nymphs are ⅓-inch-long white grubs. These larvae tunnel through the fruit, causing it to drop before ripening. The larvae overwinter in leaf litter under the trees.

WHAT TO DO:
• Tolerate minor damage.
• Collect and destroy affected fruit to keep the grubs from maturing.
• Lay a sheet underneath plum trees, and jar the limbs with a padded stick. Collect the beetles that drop to the sheet. Do this daily for two weeks after the flower petals fall in spring.

 Plum Diseases

PROBLEM: Dark-colored swellings that look like knots girdle and kill branches. Affected trees can be stunted.

CAUSE: Black knot (*Dibotryon morbosum*). Black knot is a fungal disease. The disease lives and reproduces in infected wood, which takes on knotlike shapes. Black knot is a serious plum-tree disease. The dark-colored, elongated swellings on tree limbs can eventually girdle and kill entire branches and severely stunt tree growth.

WHAT TO DO:
• Cut out all infected twigs and branches 4 to 6 inches below the knot in winter.
• Disinfect pruning tools in between cuts.
• Spray with bordeaux mix before buds break in early spring. Bordeaux is a wettable mixture of sulfur and hydrated lime with disease-inhibiting effects.
• Remove wild plum and cherry trees, which can be carriers of the disease.
• Plant resistant varieties, including Au-Producer', 'Au-Rosa', ''Bradshaw', 'Formosa', 'Milton', 'President', 'Santa Rosa', and 'Shiro'.

 Other Problems

PROBLEM: Your plum trees appear healthy and grow normally, but they produce disappointingly small fruits.

CAUSE: Trees are crowded. Unpruned trees can become overcrowded with branches and fruit, which causes the tree to produce many, small fruits. Some trees are heavy bearers and will produce many fruits even when they are pruned.

WHAT TO DO:
• Prune trees to open the centers to air.
• Remove crossing branches and those that are damaged or likely to break.
• When fruits form, thin them so that the remaining fruits will grow larger.
• On Japanese plum varieties, when the fruits are ½ to ¾ inch in diameter, remove enough fruits so that the remaining ones are 3 or 4 inches apart. Don't thin plums on European plum trees unless there is an exceptionally heavy crop.

Strawberry

(*Fragaria* spp.)

Strawberry Pests

PROBLEM: Plants look stunted. Leaf edges have half-moon-shaped notches. Roots and crowns are chewed.

CAUSE: Strawberry root weevils (*Otiorhynchus ovatus*). The black, ¼-inch-long adult weevils feed on strawberry leaves. The ⅜-inch-long, brown-headed, white larvae feed on the roots.

WHAT TO DO:

• Apply beneficial nematodes (*Steinernema carpocapsae* and *Heterorhabditis heliothidis*), which you can purchase from mail-order suppliers. Live nematodes are shipped suspended in gels or sponges. Following label instructions, apply beneficial nematodes to the soil in early May and again in August to reduce the larval populations.

PROBLEM: Your strawberry plants are wilted, but they have healthy roots. The crowns of affected plants are hollow.

CAUSE: Strawberry crown borers (*Tyloderma fragariae*). These are pests found in the eastern half of the United States. The adults are ³⁄₁₆-inch-long, dark-brown weevils that do not fly. They eat small holes in strawberry leaves and feed on the crowns of plants. The ⅕-inch-long, fat, white larvae bore into the crowns of plants, where they hollow out the crowns as they feed. There is one generation per year.

WHAT TO DO:

• Dig up and destroy infested plants.
• Locate new, disease-free strawberry plants 300 feet or more from your old patch.

PROBLEM: Leaves have green and yellow mottling. Some have fine webbing. Later, these leaves turn bronze.

CAUSE: Spider mites (Family Tetranychidae). These tiny, pinpoint-sized pests feed on strawberry leaves by sucking juices from the plant cells.

WHAT TO DO:

• Knock spider mites off plants with a strong stream of water.
• Irrigate plants during dry spells. Drought-stressed plants are more likely to be attacked by spider mites.

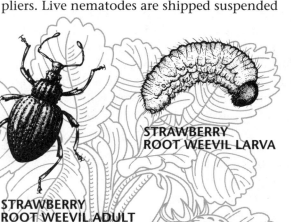

STRAWBERRY ROOT WEEVIL LARVA

STRAWBERRY ROOT WEEVIL ADULT

SPIDER MITE

• Use insecticidal soap, following label directions.

• Attract beneficial insects, such as lady beetles, lacewings, and predaceous mites, by planting pollen and nectar food resources, such as dill, Queen-Anne's-lace, and black-eyed Susans.

PROBLEM: Fruits are deformed, and some have a hard, green bump at the end.

CAUSE: Tarnished plant bugs (*Lygus lineolaris*). The tarnished plant bug is a ¼-inch-long, brown bug with black and yellow markings. The adults feed on strawberry blossoms and the developing fruits. Adults overwinter in plant debris left in the garden and begin feeding in early spring. There are numerous generations each year.

WHAT TO DO:
• Tolerate light damage.
• Use floating row covers to exclude feeding insects. Cover the plants with these synthetic, spunbonded fabrics, and bury the edges of the row cover in the soil.
• Attract beneficial insects, such as minute pirate bugs and parasitic wasps, by planting small-flowered nectar plants, including yarrow, dill, and Queen-Anne's-lace.
• Control weeds.
• Remove plant debris from the garden in fall.

PROBLEM: Stunted or distorted new leaves are spotted with shiny, sticky patches or black, sooty spots.

CAUSE: Aphids (Family Aphididae). Aphids are soft-bodied insects, ¹⁄₁₆ to ³⁄₈ inch long. They range in color from pale tan to light green to nearly black. Aphids suck plant juices from tender strawberry leaves and stems, and they can transfer plant viruses as they feed. The sticky substance aphids secrete, called honeydew, attracts ants, which defend the aphids from beneficial insects in order to eat the honeydew. And the damp honeydew encourages the growth of sooty mold.

WHAT TO DO:
• Knock aphids off plants with a strong spray of water.
• Wash the honeydew or sooty mold off plants with water.
• Spray infested plants with insecticidal soap.
• Attract beneficial insects, such as parasitic wasps and lady beetles, by planting small-flowered nectar plants. Purchase beneficial green lacewings and aphid midges from mail-order sources and release them to supplement natural populations.

 Strawberry Diseases

PROBLEM: The strawberry bed looks uneven or patchy. Stunted plants die at fruiting time in their second season.

CAUSE: Black root rot. Several soilborne fungi cause the symptoms called black root rot. The disease is most active in periods of cool weather and in poorly drained soil. Infected plants will be stunted and produce few berries and runners. If you dig the plants up, you will see that their roots are black and rotting.

WHAT TO DO:
• Pull up and destroy infected plants.
• Plant strawberries in well-drained soil.
• Grow healthy, new strawberry plants in raised beds.

PROBLEM: Blossoms spotted with gray mold turn brown and die. Fruits have a fuzzy, gray coating; some fruits rot.

CAUSE: Gray mold (*Botrytis cinerea*). This fungal disease is most apparent when berries touch the soil or rotten fruits. Moisture is necessary for the fungal spores to germinate and infect blossoms and fruit. The fungus can produce spores throughout the growing season. Strawberries can become spoiled and rotten almost overnight.

WHAT TO DO:
• Thin plants to avoid overcrowding, and mulch beds to keep fruit off the soil.
• Diligently remove rotten berries from the strawberry patch.

PROBLEM: Small, purple spots with tan centers and irregular purple blotches disfigure leaves. Plants defoliate.

CAUSE: Leaf spot. Several fungi can cause the symptoms known as leaf spot. The fungi overwinter on infected plants and plant debris left in the garden. In the spring, spores are released to infect new leaves. Warm, humid weather and rain create favorable conditions for the development of leaf spot.

WHAT TO DO:
• Plant resistant cultivars, such as 'Albritton', 'Blakemore', 'Earlibelle', 'Fairfax', and 'Midland'.
• Locate your strawberry patch in a sunny, well-drained site.
• Space plants widely for adequate air circulation.

PROBLEM: Some strawberries are tough and have a bitter taste. Infected berries have light lilac or darker purple spots.

CAUSE: Leather rot (*Phytophthora cactorum* and other species). These disease fungi live in the soil. This disease occurs when the berries touch the soil or are splashed with mud. On immature green fruits, the infected areas will be dark brown or green, instead of purple, and will be ringed in brown.

WHAT TO DO:
• Pick and dispose of infected strawberries.
• Mulch to keep fruit off the ground and to minimize rain splashing mud from the soil onto the fruit.

PROBLEM: Leaf surfaces are powdery white. Undersides of leaves are red. Fruits are stunted and don't ripen.

CAUSE: Powdery mildew (*Sphaerotheca macularis*). Powdery mildew is most often a foliar disease, but occasionally the disease causes fruits to rot. The fungal disease overwinters in living leaves. Dry weather and cool temperatures create favorable conditions for the development of powdery mildew.

WHAT TO DO:
• Plant resistant cultivars, such as 'Albritton', 'Catskill', 'Puget Beauty', 'Sparkle', 'Sunrise', and 'Surecrop'.
• Space plants widely for adequate air circulation.

PROBLEM: Spring leaves are small and gray. Last season's leaves are crisp and dry. Blooming stops; berries are small.

CAUSE: Red stele root rot (*Phytophthora fragariae*). This fungal disease is a serious problem for strawberry plants growing in heavy or poorly drained soil. It is most active in the rainy, cold days of early spring and late fall. The fungal spores of red stele root rot can survive in the soil for up to ten years, emerging when conditions are favorable. Infected plants die during the first dry period of the season. If the roots do survive, they are stunted. If you dig up an infected plant and cut across the root system, the interior of the root will be rusty red or brown. This disease is most problematic in the northern United States and southern Canada.

WHAT TO DO:
• Grow disease-resistant cultivars, such as 'Earliglow', 'Guardian', and 'Lester'.
• Grow strawberry plants in well-drained soil.
• Do not grow strawberry plants in contaminated soil for at least ten years after strawberries last grew there.

PROBLEM: Plants look stunted. Outer leaves turn reddish, then yellow, wilt, and die. The plants collapse.

CAUSE: Verticillium wilt (*Verticillium albo-atrum*). This common fungal disease can survive in the soil for up to 15 years. In spring, temperatures between 70° and 75°F combine with high humidity to enable the fungal spores to germinate and enter plants and their roots through wounds. Although outer leaves die, the new inner leaves remain upright. This symptom distinguishes Verticillium from other root diseases where all the leaves wilt at one time.

WHAT TO DO:

• Start healthy new plants where no strawberries or other susceptible plants grew. Susceptible plants include tomatoes, potatoes, peppers, eggplants, melons, okra, mint, blackberries and raspberries, garden mums, and roses.

• Plant resistant cultivars, such as 'Allstar', 'Blakemore', 'Catskill', 'Guardian', 'Robinson', 'Sunrise', and 'Surecrop'.

• Solarize the soil. Clear plastic sheeting placed over bare soil for four weeks during the hottest part of the summer uses the sun's energy to heat the soil. The heat produced is enough to kill most diseases, pests, and weed seeds in the top few inches of soil. After removing the plastic, plant crops as usual.

PROBLEM: Strawberry plants lose vigor and produce low yields. The leaves are a mottled yellow-green and are crinkled.

CAUSE: Viral diseases. Sap-sucking insects, such as aphids and leafhoppers, can transmit plant viruses by feeding on infected plants and then moving on to feed on healthy ones.

WHAT TO DO:

• Remove and destroy infected plants.

• Wait three years to plant strawberries in the same site where infected ones previously grew.

PROBLEM: Mature strawberry plants suddenly wilt. The base of the stems rot, and plants die within a few days.

CAUSE: Southern blight (*Sclerotium rolfsii*). This fungal disease is most common in warm climates, like that of the southern United States. Southern blight often strikes one or two plants, while others in the strawberry patch are unaffected. The fungi can live in soil for many years.

WHAT TO DO:

• Add compost to the bed before planting strawberry plants.

• Pull up and destroy infected plants.

• Disinfect tools with rubbing alcohol and clean hands after working with infected plants to keep from spreading the disease.

• Space plants widely when planting, or thin to encourage adequate air circulation.

• Rotate plants. Avoid planting strawberries in the same plot two years in a row, or for longer periods if possible.

 Other Problems

PROBLEM: You notice half-eaten berries. There are holes pecked in mature fruit, and some fruits have disappeared.

CAUSE: Birds. These intruders are notorious for helping themselves to your harvest. They peck at the ripening fruit, peppering it with holes. When it is sweet enough for them to eat, the birds will take entire fruits away.

WHAT TO DO:

• Use protective coverings, such as bird-netting and floating row covers, to keep birds from picking your strawberries. Cover the plants with the material, and bury the edges in the soil.

• Make scarecrows. Aluminum pie plates, scare tape, and aluminum foil will deter birds as long as a breeze creates movement to frighten them.

Walnut

(*Juglans* spp.)

Walnut Pests

PROBLEM: Heavy loss of nuts occurs during the June drop period. A small hole is in each shell of dropped nuts.

CAUSE: Black walnut curculios (*Conotrachelus retentus*). These nut-attacking pests are most problematic in the eastern part of the United States. The adults are ¼-inch-long, reddish brown weevils with snouts that are half the length of their bodies. They lay eggs in immature nuts. The larvae chew their way out of the nuts in June. The larvae drop and pupate in the soil, emerging as adults in late summer.

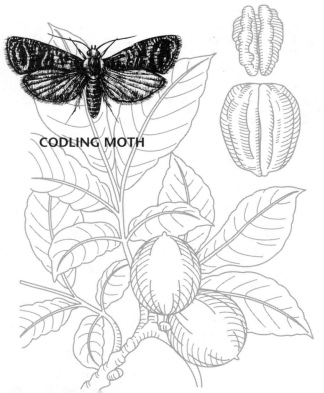

CODLING MOTH

WHAT TO DO:
• Gather up and dispose of infected nuts on a weekly basis during June and early July.

PROBLEM: Nuts have holes with brown insect excrement on their hulls. Infested green nuts dry up and drop.

CAUSE: Codling moths (*Cydia pomonella*). The adults are gray moths with ¾-inch wingspans. Codling moths have brown lines on their forewings and have fringed back wings. Codling moth adults emerge in the spring to mate and lay eggs on walnut foliage. The larvae are 1-inch-long, pink worms with brown heads. Larvae tunnel into nuts, feed, and then exit to pupate under loose bark or around the base of trees.

WHAT TO DO:
• Place corrugated-cardboard wraps around tree trunks to attract larvae looking for a place to pupate. Remove the wraps frequently, and destroy pupae that you find hiding under them.
• Set out pheromone traps in orchards of 3 acres or larger to disrupt mating. These commercial scent lures have a strip of cardboard coated with female insect scents. Male pests are lured to the scent and fall into attached collection bags or are confused by them and become unable to find a mate.
• Purchase and apply granulosis virus, a mail-order biocontrol product that infects and kills codling moth larvae.
• Release mail-order trichogramma wasps, small wasps that parasitize the egg stage of codling moths.

PROBLEM: Leaves of trees are curled, twisted, and spotted with clear, sticky specks and sooty, black patches.

CAUSE: Walnut aphids (*Chromaphis juglandicola*). These are ⅛-inch-long, soft-bodied, pear-shaped insects. In autumn, the adult females lay oval eggs on buds or the bark of smaller branches. These overwinter and then hatch in spring when buds open. Aphids damage young leaves by sucking plant juices. Honeydew, secreted by the aphids, covers the leaves and nuts, creating ideal conditions for sooty mold. Aphid colonies establish rapidly, and several generations may occur per season. The damage causes young trees to die and reduces the crops from mature trees.

WHAT TO DO:
• Knock aphids off walnut trees with a strong spray of water.
• Use insecticidal soap, following label directions. Be sure to hit the undersides of leaves, where aphids hide, as well as the tops when you spray.
• Attract beneficial insects, such as parasitic wasps, by planting small-flowered nectar plants, including yarrow, scabiosa, and Queen-Anne's-lace.
• Apply dormant oil spray in winter. This horticultural oil coats tree tissues and smothers most stages of walnut pests and diseases.

PROBLEM: Husks have black spots and are hard to remove at harvest. Nut shells are stained, but meats are fine.

CAUSES: Walnut husk flies (*Rhagoletis completa*) and walnut husk maggots (*R. suavis*). The adults of both species are flies slightly smaller than houseflies. Both are light brown flies with three dark bands on each clear wing. The larvae of both species are yellow-white maggots about ⅜ inch long. The maggots eat their way into the husks, feeding on them and turning them black and slimy.

The damaged husks stick to the nut shells, turning them black. The maggots do not penetrate the nut itself. After feeding on the husk, they tunnel out and drop to the ground to overwinter.

WHAT TO DO:
• Tolerate damage. The nut meats of infested walnuts will be discolored but will not be damaged or inedible.
• Dispose of infested husks. (To remove husks that stick to the shells, place the nuts in a damp burlap bag for a few days, and then remove husks.)
• Plant resistant varieties, such as 'Ashley', 'Hansen', and 'Placentia'.

PROBLEM: The leaves are being eaten and completely stripped from the branches of your walnut trees.

CAUSE: Walnut caterpillars (*Datana integerrima*). Walnut caterpillars are most common throughout eastern North America. When fully grown, the larvae are about 3 inches long and are black with long, gray hairs. The caterpillars cluster together in large groups to eat the walnut leaves.

WHAT TO DO:
• Handpick. Remove larvae from walnut tree leaves and destroy them.
• Apply BTK. "BT" stands for *Bacillus thuringiensis,* an insect-stomach poison that kills caterpillars without harming beneficial insects. *B.t.* var. *kurstaki* (BTK) kills the larvae of walnut caterpillars. Follow directions and apply when pests are active.

 Walnut Diseases

PROBLEM: The graft union has small holes and cracks. The tree has poor growth, becomes stunted, and dies.

CAUSE: Blackline virus. This viral disease can infect English walnut trees that are grafted to black walnut rootstock.

WHAT TO DO:
• There is no cure for blackline virus.
• Remove diseased trees to prevent remaining healthy ones from becoming infected with this virus.

PROBLEM: Early in summer, trees have dark brown or black spots on the leaves. The trees may defoliate.

CAUSE: Walnut anthracnose (*Gnomonia leptostyla*). This fungal disease attacks leaves in early summer, and severe attacks cause trees to defoliate early. It causes irregular brown or black spots to disfigure leaves. The disease fungi overwinter in fallen leaves.

WHAT TO DO:
• Gather up and destroy fallen leaves.
• Spray throughout the growing season with bordeaux mix. Apply the first spray when buds start to open, a second spray ten days later, and a third spray after leaves are fully developed. Bordeaux mix is a wettable combination of copper sulfate and hydrated lime. Follow label directions carefully, since bordeaux mix can injure plant foliage.

PROBLEM: Leaves turn yellow, and trees grow poorly for several years. Trunks may be discolored near the soil line.

CAUSE: Root rot. Several fungi, including *Armillaria mellea, Phymatotrichum omnivorum,* and *Cylindrocladium* sp., cause the symptoms called root rot in walnut trees. Prolonged water saturation of the soil favors the development of these fungi and the potentially fatal condition of root rot in walnuts.

WHAT TO DO:
• Pull away the soil to expose the crown and the top inch or so of the main roots in order to allow the roots to dry out during the growing season. Then cover the roots with soil again before winter.
• Do not overwater walnut trees. Allow the soil to dry out between waterings.
• Plant these trees in well-drained soil.

PROBLEM: Gray or white, feltlike patches form on leaves and nut hulls. The leaves may turn brittle and die.

CAUSE: Powdery mildew. This disease, caused by several fungi, overwinters in twigs or buds. Infections occur when the humidity is greater than 90 percent and the temperature is between 50° and 77°F. Powdery mildew may reduce yields, but it does not threaten the life of the tree.

WHAT TO DO:
• Space walnut trees far enough apart for good air circulation.
• Avoid wetting foliage when irrigating.
• Spray with sulfur in the spring every seven to ten days. Do not apply sulfur if temperatures exceed 80°F, or you will burn the foliage.
• Prune trees to open up the centers of the crown for adequate air circulation.

PROBLEM: Black spots are on nuts and foliage. Some nuts drop early. Others have blackened husks and kernels.

CAUSE: Walnut blight (*Xanthomonas juglandis*). This bacterial disease thrives in damp weather conditions. Walnut blight overwinters on leaf buds, twigs, and old nuts.

WHAT TO DO:
• Prune trees to provide good air circulation at the center of the tree.
• Avoid wetting foliage when irrigating.
• Spray with copper solution when 10 percent of the blossoms are open, spray again when 20 percent are open, and spray a third time after trees flower in spring.
• Grow resistant walnut varieties, like 'Reda' and 'Vina'.

Flowers

Ageratum 188
Sweet Alyssum 190
Anemones 192
Artemisias...............195
Asters.....................196
Astilbes 198
Baby's-Breath. 200
Bachelor's-Button 202
Begonias..................206
Black-Eyed Susans....210
Bleeding Hearts 212
Butterfly Weed.........214
Candytuft 215
Canna. 216
Cleome 217
Cockscomb..............218
Coleus.....................219
Columbines 220
Coral Bells 222
Coreopsis 224
Cosmos...................226
Crocuses 228
Daffodils.................229
Dahlias....................230
Daylilies 232
Delphiniums.............234
Dianthus..................236
Dusty Miller.............238
Flowering Tobacco...239
Forget-Me-Nots 241
Foxgloves 242
Hardy Geraniums.....244
Zonal Geraniums 246

Gladiolus 250
Hollyhock 252
Hostas......................254
Hyacinth 256
Impatiens 258
Irises 260
Lamb's-Ears 263
Larkspur 264
Lilies........................266
Lily-of-the-Valley 269
Lobelias 270
Lupines 272
Marigolds 274
Garden Mum 278
Nasturtiums 282
Pansy 284
Penstemons 288
Peonies 290
Petunia 294
Phlox 298
Poppies.....................300
Purple Coneflowers .302
Roses 304
Sedums.....................310
Snapdragon 312
Sunflowers 316
Sweet Peas 318
Tulips 320
Verbenas 322
Veronicas..................324
Violets......................326
Yarrows 327
Zinnias......................328

Ageratum

also called Flossflower and Mist Flower (*Ageratum houstonianum*)

Ageratum Pests

PROBLEM: Your previously healthy ageratums suddenly develop large holes in their leaves and flower buds.

CAUSE: Caterpillars. The two most common types have yellow heads, black legs, and stripes along their sides. The adult moths of both pests are night-flying moths. They have wingspans of 1 to 2 inches and have gray or brown wings with green lines.

Tobacco budworms (*Helicoverpa virescens*) are 1½-inch-long, rusty red or green-striped caterpillars. They are the larvae of small moths that have pale green wings with lighter stripes and wingspans of 1½ inches.

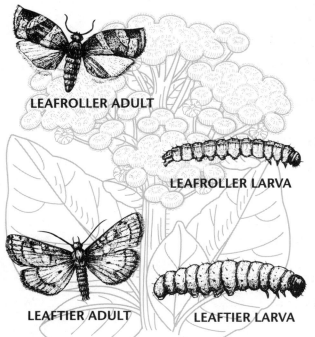

LEAFROLLER ADULT

LEAFROLLER LARVA

LEAFTIER ADULT

LEAFTIER LARVA

Corn earworms, also called tomato fruitworms (*Helicoverpa zea*) are 1- to 2-inch-long caterpillars that vary in color from yellow to green or from pink to brown.

WHAT TO DO:
• Handpick.
• Apply BTK. "BT" stands for *Bacillus thuringiensis,* an insect-stomach poison that kills caterpillars without harming beneficial insects. *B.t.* var. *kurstaki* (BTK) kills tobacco budworms and tomato hornworms. Follow label directions when spraying BTK.
• Spray with neem. This botanical pesticide repels and poisons insect pests but is harmless to beneficial insects. Follow directions.
• Attract beneficial insects, such as parasitic wasps, by growing pollen and nectar plants, including alyssum, yarrow, dill, and scabiosa.
• Avoid turning on outdoor lights at night in summer, because they attract moths.
• Cultivate the soil in fall and winter to kill pupae overwintering in the soil.

PROBLEM: Ageratum leaves are rolled into tubes and tied with webbing. Caterpillars in the tubes eat the leaves.

CAUSES: Leafrollers and leaftiers. Leafrollers, including the redbanded leafroller (*Argyrotaenia velutinana*) and the obliquebanded leafroller (*Choristoneura rosaceana*), along with leaftiers like the celery leaftier (*Udea rubigalis*), can damage ageratums. These caterpillars are from ½ to ¾ inch long. They can be pale green, brown, or yellow. The pests hatch from eggs laid by adult moths that are active only after dark. The adult redbanded moths have

¾-inch wingspans and red-striped, brown wings. Obliquebanded adults are brown moths with three darker brown stripes on their front wings. Obliquebanded moths have wingspans of ¾ inch. Celery leaftier moths have brown wings with dark, wavy lines on them and have wingspans of ¾ inch.

WHAT TO DO:
• Handpick.
• Pull off and dispose of the folded leaves.

PROBLEM: White or yellow specks disfigure the tops of ageratum leaves. Fine webs cover the leaf undersides.
CAUSE: Spider mites (Family Tetranychidae). These minute, $\frac{1}{60}$-inch-long pests suck sap from ageratum leaves and stems, especially in hot, dry spells.

WHAT TO DO:
• Knock spider mites off plants with a strong stream of water.
• Water plants well during dry spells.

PROBLEM: Plants look limp and pale. Some leaves have sticky, black mold. White insects fly up when disturbed.
CAUSE: Whiteflies (Family Aleyrodidae). These $\frac{1}{20}$-inch-long flying insects weaken ageratums by sucking sap from leaves and stems. Adults lay yellowish eggs no bigger than a pinpoint on the backs of leaves. Whiteflies disappear after the first frost.

WHAT TO DO:
• Knock insects off plants with a strong spray of water.
• Use insecticidal soap, following directions.
• Use soapy water traps. Put out yellow pans full of soapy water. The adults, attracted to the color, will land in the pans and drown.
• Water regularly; avoid nitrogen fertilizer, which promotes tender, edible growth.

 Ageratum Diseases

PROBLEM: Brown blotches develop on ageratum leaves. Fuzzy, gray mold appears on flowers, leaves, and stems.
CAUSE: Gray mold (*Botrytis* spp.). This fungal disease is a common problem on ageratums. Gray mold thrives in spring and in fall in cool temperatures and high humidity.

WHAT TO DO:
• Remove and destroy infected tissue.
• Mulch beds with compost.
• Space plants widely for air circulation.

PROBLEM: Plants rot at the base and die. Damp days cause threads of fungus to grow on the ground around them.
CAUSE: Southern blight, also called crown rot (*Sclerotium rolfsii*). This fungal disease thrives in warm climates. It appears first as a white, threadlike fungus at the base of plants. The threads ooze acidic fluid that eventually kills plants. Spores survive in the soil for years.

WHAT TO DO:
• Dig up and discard infected plants and soil 6 inches in all directions around the roots.
• Incorporate compost into the soil.

 Other Problems

PROBLEM: Leaves have crisp, dry edges. Some leaves turn brown and drop. Affected plants die in midsummer.
CAUSE: Drought stress. If plants dry out a few times they can recover. But a drought that lasts several days or weeks can kill ageratums.

WHAT TO DO:
• Water plants regularly during dry spells.
• Grow in light shade in southern zones.
• Add organic matter to the soil to increase its ability to retain moisture.
• Mulch to reduce evaporation from the soil.

Sweet Alyssum

(Lobularia maritima)

 Alyssum Pests

PROBLEM: Overnight, alyssum seedlings are cut off just above the soil. The plant tops are lying nearby on the soil.

CAUSE: Soil-dwelling cutworms (Family Noctuidae). These are the larvae of several night-flying moths, which have wingspans of 1½ inches. Their 1-to 2-inch-long, fat, gray or brown caterpillars attack seedlings in the spring. They feed at night and usually eat only through the stem of the plant, leaving the top lying on the soil to die. Cutworms usually attack plants less than two weeks old.

WHAT TO DO:
• Use cutworm collars to prevent crawling pests from reaching seedlings. To make collars, cut 2- to 3-inch-long sections from paper-towel tubes or tin cans. Place these short tubes over small seedlings as soon as they sprout.
• Apply BT granules. "BT" stands for *Bacillus thuringiensis,* a stomach poison that kills caterpillars without harming beneficials. Spread BT on the ground before planting.
• Cultivate garden beds in fall and spring to kill larvae that are overwintering in the soil.

 Alyssum Diseases

PROBLEM: New leaves are abnormally small, with yellow or red tips. Some appear deformed and clump together.

CAUSE: Aster yellows. A viruslike organism called a mycoplasma causes this disease. The disease enters plants through feeding holes made by aster leafhoppers (*Macrosteles quadrilineatus fascifrons*) and other leafhoppers.

WHAT TO DO:
• Remove and destroy infected plants.
• Wash leafhoppers off plants with a strong stream of water.
• Use insecticidal soap, following directions.

PROBLEM: Growth is stunted. Affected plants wilt, turn yellow, and slowly die. You see no pests or disease spots.

CAUSE: Southern root-knot nematodes (*Meloidogyne incognita* var. *incognita*). These

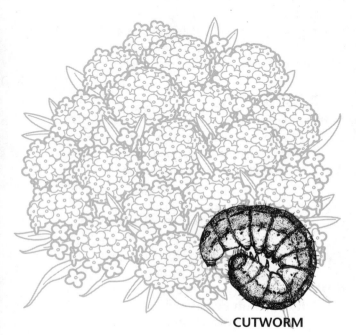

CUTWORM

pests are especially severe in warm areas with sandy or peaty soils. The nematodes are microscopic worms that live in the soil and attack alyssum roots, causing symptoms above ground that are similar to wilt diseases. If nematodes are present, the roots will have knots or swellings and excessive branching.

WHAT TO DO:
• Apply supplemental water and fertilizer. Turn under compost in garden beds and apply crab or shrimp wastes that contain chitin. Chitin, made from shellfish shells, provides nitrogen and potassium as it breaks down, creating conditions that encourage the beneficial soil organisms that attack nematodes.
• Solarize the soil. Clear plastic placed over bare soil for three to four weeks uses the sun's energy to heat the soil enough to kill pests and weed seeds in the top few inches of soil. Remove the plastic, and plant as usual.
• Starve nematodes by growing cover crops of resistant plants, such as rye or oats, or keep beds empty for a season to starve them.
• In regions where nematode problems are severe, grow flowers in containers, using sterile potting mix.

PROBLEM: Young alyssum seedlings suddenly turn dark at the soil line, fall over, and die.

CAUSE: Damping-off disease (*Rhizoctonia solani* and *Pythium ultimum*). This disease, caused by two fungi, is a common problem with seedlings. Several species of soil-dwelling fungi cause the disease. The fungi enter the stem and roots of seedlings, causing them to rot. The disease targets overcrowded or overwatered seedlings, those started indoors, or seeds started in heavy, poorly drained garden soil.

WHAT TO DO:
• Use a sterile seed-starting mix.
• Sow seeds, and then dust the surface of the seed tray with milled sphagnum moss, which repels the fungi.
• Provide indoor seedlings with bright light and good air circulation.
• When direct-seeding outdoors, choose well-drained locations that receive full sun, and amend the soil with compost.

PROBLEM: Alyssum plants turn yellow and wilt. White fungal strands may grow around lower leaves and stems.

CAUSES: Stem and root rot. Various soilborne fungi can cause these symptoms. These fungi thrive in wet, soggy soil. Rain splashes spore-laden mud onto plants. The fungi attack the stems and roots, causing them to rot.

WHAT TO DO:
• Remove and destroy infected plants.
• Allow soil to dry out between waterings.
• Mulch to prevent rain from splashing fungi-infected mud onto plants.
• Cultivate the soil with clean tools.
• Incorporate compost into the soil to improve drainage and to introduce beneficial soil organisms that fight disease fungi.
• Be sure plants receive full sunlight.
• Plant in raised beds and space plants 1 to 1½ feet apart to allow adequate air circulation so the soil can dry out between waterings.

 Other Problems

PROBLEM: Your alyssum plants are growing and appear healthy, but they flower sparsely.

CAUSE: Lack of sunlight. Like many flowering annuals, sweet alyssum needs six hours or more of full sun to bloom well.

WHAT TO DO:
• Grow in full sun for best flowering.

Anemones

(*Anemone* spp. and hybrids) and Japanese Anemones, also called Chinese Anemones (*Anemone* × *hybrida*; *A. hupehensis*)

Anemone Pests

PROBLEM: Swarms of narrow, black or striped beetles feed on anemone leaves and flowers and defoliate plants.

CAUSE: Black blister beetles (*Epicauta pennsylvanica*). These narrow, black beetles are ½ to ¾ inch long, with flexible wing covers. Blister beetles are named for their ability to raise a blisterlike welt on your bare skin if they come in contact with it.

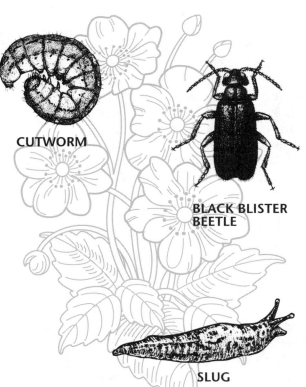

CUTWORM

BLACK BLISTER BEETLE

SLUG

These beetles attack anemone plants in late summer. Blister beetle larvae are predators of plant-eating insect pests, but the adults relish anemones. Blister beetles lay clusters of yellow eggs in the egg burrows of grasshoppers in the fall. When they hatch, the larvae eat the grasshopper eggs.

WHAT TO DO:
• Tolerate a light infestation. The cosmetic damage the adults cause is balanced by the numbers of grasshoppers that their larvae will destroy.
• Handpick. Wear gloves to protect hands, as blister beetles secrete a substance that can burn your skin.
• Vacuum beetles with a battery-run, hand-held vacuum.

PROBLEM: Young anemones are cut off at the soil line overnight. The tops of the plants are left lying on the soil.

CAUSE: Cutworms (Family Noctuidae). These pests are the larvae of several species of night-flying moths. Cutworms are gray or dull brown caterpillars, 1 to 2 inches long. They usually eat through the main stem of seedlings, leaving the top part of the plant lying on the soil. Cutworms feed at night and hide in soil or mulch during the day. Their attacks usually stop by the time seedlings are two weeks old.

WHAT TO DO:
• Handpick. Carefully dig around the base of damaged plants at night to lift and destroy soil-dwelling cutworms.

• Use cutworm collars. To make the collars, use shears to cut 2- to 3-inch sections of paper-towel tubes or tin cans. Place the collars over small seedlings as soon as they sprout.

• Apply BT granules. "BT" stands for *Bacillus thuringiensis,* an insect-stomach poison that kills caterpillars without harming beneficial insects. Spread BT on the ground before planting.

• Cultivate garden beds in fall and spring to kill some of the larvae that are overwintering in the soil and to expose others so that hungry birds can find them.

PROBLEM: Overnight, some pest reduces anemones to ragged leaves or flowers streaked with shiny slime trails.

CAUSES: Slugs and snails (Order Stylommatophora). These are ⅛- to 8-inch-long, soft-bodied, gray, tan, green, black, yellow, or spotted pests. They resemble their water-dwelling relatives—clams and mussels.

Snails have shells; slugs look like snails without shells. At night they climb up the stems of plants to eat large holes in foliage, stems, and flowers. In the morning they leave behind a trail of shiny slime as they climb down to hide under garden debris on the soil. Adults lay jellylike masses of clear eggs under garden debris.

WHAT TO DO:

• Handpick. The best time to begin hunting is two hours after dark.

• Make barriers that they can't climb over by sprinkling rings of wood ashes or crushed eggshells around flowerbeds or individual plants.

• Make copper barriers. Edge plantings with a strip of copper, which hits these slimy pests with an electrical shock upon contact.

• Make beer traps from recycled cans sunk to the brim in soil and filled with yeasty beer. Create a roof over the trap to provide shade so that the spot remains cool and moist. Attracted by the scent of beer, the slugs will fall into the traps and drown.

• Apply diatomaceous earth (DE). This abrasive dust is actually fossilized shells, called diatoms, that penetrate the pests' skin as they crawl over DE. Wear a dust mask to avoid inhaling particles. Apply DE when plants are wet.

• Remove mulch and garden debris, which provides hiding places and shelter for their eggs.

 Anemone Diseases

PROBLEM: New leaves are abnormally small, with yellow or red tips. Some appear deformed and clump together.

CAUSE: Aster yellows. A viruslike organism called a mycoplasma causes the disease. Aster yellows usually enters plants through feeding holes made in leaves and stems by aster leafhoppers (*Macrosteles quadrilineatus*) and other leafhoppers.

WHAT TO DO:

• Remove and destroy infected leaves and roots.

• Wash leafhoppers off plants with a strong stream of water. Be sure to hit the backs of leaves as well as the tops when spraying.

• Use insecticidal soap, following label directions, and be sure to spray both sides of the leaves when applying the soap.

PROBLEM: In summer, small yellow spots with powdery, orange spores in their centers form on yellowing leaves.

CAUSE: Rust (*Puccinia* spp.; *Tranzschelia* spp.). This fungal disease spreads quickly when its spores blow onto damp anemone leaves. The disease causes leaves to turn yellow, and it can stunt plant growth.

WHAT TO DO:

• Remove and dispose of infected leaves to keep the disease from spreading.

• Spray infected plants with sulfur.

• Avoid overhead watering, to keep from splashing spores on leaves.

• Water early in the day so plants will dry out before nightfall, since fungal diseases thrive in cool, damp conditions.

• Avoid touching infected plants and plants with wet leaves, to keep from spreading the disease.

• Sterilize garden tools with rubbing alcohol and wash your hands after working with infected plants to keep from spreading the disease from plant to plant as you work.

• Do not work among damp plants. Wait until the foliage dries, because disease spores are spread and activated when leaves are moist.

• Space or thin plants widely for good air circulation.

• Remove and compost garden debris to eliminate places where the disease can overwinter.

PROBLEM: Plants rot at the base and die. On damp days, threads of fungus grow on the ground around them.

CAUSE: Southern blight, also called crown rot (*Sclerotium rolfsii*). This fungal disease thrives in warm climates. The disease appears first as a white, threadlike fungus at the base of plants and then spreads outward across the soil. The threads ooze an acidic fluid that kills plant cells on contact, eventually killing entire plants. The spores survive in the soil for years.

WHAT TO DO:

• Dig up and destroy infected plants and soil 6 inches beyond the roots.

• Improve soil drainage by incorporating compost, which also contains disease-fighting beneficial organisms, into the soil.

 Other Problems

PROBLEM: Your anemones have dark green leaves and are growing just fine, but they will not bloom.

CAUSES: Lack of sunlight, plants are too young or too old, or the location you planted them in is too shady for anemones to bloom well. Immature plants will not bloom. Plants that have been in the ground for more than two years may be too crowded to grow properly and bloom.

WHAT TO DO:

• Be patient. Young plants may take a season to grow strong roots and bloom.

• Deadhead. Cut off old blooms as they fade.

• Move your plants. Grow anemones in partial shade, morning sun, or bright light.

• Divide older plants or take root cuttings to propagate new plants. Plant 2-inch-long root cuttings in sandy loam in early spring. Keep the soil evenly moist while seedlings grow roots.

• Take root cuttings in fall, plant them in a loose, sandy soil mix, and overwinter the cuttings in a greenhouse or cold frame.

PROBLEM: Your anemones grew well all summer and flowered, but the plants did not come back after the winter.

CAUSES: Wet soil and freezing temperatures. Soil that remains wet in winter can cause anemone roots to rot. If the winter temperatures are too cold, the anemones could suffer fatal frost damage. Anemones grow from USDA Hardiness Zone 6 (to −10°F) through Zone 8 (to 10°F), depending on the species.

WHAT TO DO:

• Grow Japanese anemones in well-drained but rich soil.

• Make sure water does not stand on the soil in winter.

• In the colder limits of their hardiness range, protect anemones in winter with a fluffy, organic mulch several inches thick.

• Take root cuttings in the fall. Plant the cuttings in sandy loam, and overwinter the cuttings in a greenhouse or cold frame.

Artemisias

(*Artemisia* spp.)

Artemisia Pests

PROBLEM: Artemisia leaves have sticky, clear or black spots. Colonies of small, soft-bodied insects huddle on leaves.

CAUSE: Aphids (Family Aphididae). These pests are wedge-shaped, 1/16- to 3/8-inch-long insects. Aphids range in color from pale tan to light green to nearly black. They suck sap and produce a sticky secretion called honeydew that attracts mold and ants, which protect aphids in order to eat the honeydew. Aphids can transfer plant viruses as they feed.

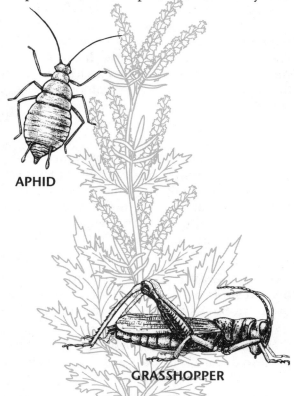

APHID

GRASSHOPPER

WHAT TO DO:
• Wash aphids off plants with water.
• Use insecticidal soap, following directions.
• Attract beneficial insects, such as parasitic wasps and lady beetles, by planting small-flowered nectar plants, like yarrow.
• Pour boiling water into anthills that are not adjacent to plant roots.

PROBLEM: Suddenly during the growing season, insects eat your artemisia leaves all the way to the leaf veins.

CAUSE: Grasshoppers (Order Orthoptera). Adults are brown, yellow, or green, 1- to 2-inch-long, winged insects with large hind legs for jumping. The females lay eggs in the soil in late summer, which hatch in spring.

WHAT TO DO:
• Handpick.
• Attract birds, which eat grasshoppers, by providing water and shrubby nesting places.
• Till the soil in autumn to expose eggs.

Artemisia Diseases

PROBLEM: Small, powdery, orange, rust, or brown spots of spores are on the undersides of leaves and on stems.

CAUSE: Rust (*Puccinia* spp.). This fungal disease thrives in damp weather. The spores spread quickly in wind and splashing water.

WHAT TO DO:
• Remove and dispose of infected leaves.
• Avoid overhead watering; water in morning.
• Space out or thin plants for air circulation.
• Remove and compost garden debris.

Asters

(*Aster* spp. and hybrids)

Aster Pests

PROBLEM: Aster leaves have sticky, clear or black spots. Colonies of small, soft-bodied insects huddle on leaves.

CAUSE: Aphids (Family Aphididae). These pests are wedge-shaped, $\frac{1}{16}$- to $\frac{3}{8}$-inch-long insects. Aphids range in color from pale tan to light green to nearly black. Aphids suck sap and produce a sticky secretion called honeydew that attracts mold and ants, which protect aphids from predators in order to eat the honeydew. Feeding aphids can transfer viruses.

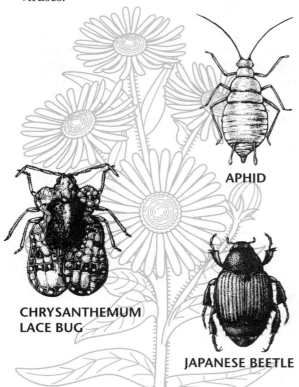

APHID

CHRYSANTHEMUM LACE BUG

JAPANESE BEETLE

WHAT TO DO:
• Wash aphids off plants with a strong stream of water.
• Use insecticidal soap, following directions.
• Snip off infested leaves.
• Attract beneficial insects, such as lady beetles, by planting small-flowered nectar plants, including yarrow and scabiosa.
• Pour boiling water into anthills.

PROBLEM: Leaves look bleached and have yellow or brown edges. Some leaves and stems are deformed.

CAUSE: Aster leafhoppers, also known as six-spotted leafhoppers (*Macrosteles quadrilineatus*). The $\frac{1}{8}$-inch-long adults are black with greenish yellow undersides and black-spotted heads. The adults infect plants with the disease aster yellows (a mycoplasma) as they suck sap from the undersides of leaves. Aster leafhoppers overwinter in weeds.

WHAT TO DO:
• Tolerate light damage.
• Attract parasitic flies, wasps, and other beneficials by planting nectar and pollen plants, including yarrow, alyssum, and scabiosa.
• Use insecticidal soap, following directions.
• Spray horticultural oil. This refined oil coats plant parts and smothers leafhoppers.

PROBLEM: Leaves have tiny, yellow or brown spots on tops and insect excrement on backs. Some are deformed.

CAUSE: Chrysanthemum lace bugs (*Corythucha marmorata*). These sap-sucking pests are $\frac{1}{8}$-inch-long bugs with lacy-looking, brown-striped wings. They have brown-speckled, creamy white bodies.

WHAT TO DO:
• Handpick.
• Spray with insecticidal soap or horticultural oil once every three days for two weeks. Horticultural oil smothers pests.
• Control host weeds, including goldenrod.

PROBLEM: Shiny green beetles are chewing aster leaves into a lacy pattern and devouring flowers and buds.

CAUSE: Japanese beetles (*Popillia japonica*). These ½-inch-long beetles eat plant leaves in midsummer. The beetles are most active during the day, and they prefer to feed on plants growing in full sun. Their grubs develop in the soil, where they eat grass roots in spring.

WHAT TO DO:
• Handpick.
• Spray with neem. This botanical pesticide is harmless to beneficial insects.
• Apply beneficial nematodes (*Steinernema carpocapsae* and *Heterorhabditis heliothidis*), which you can purchase from mail-order suppliers. Live nematodes are shipped suspended in gels or sponges. Follow instructions and release nematodes when pest larvae are present.
• Apply milky disease spores. The insecticide milky disease is a combination of spores of *Bacillus popilliae* and *B. lentimorbus*. The soil-dwelling grubs die after eating the spores.

 Aster Diseases

PROBLEM: The leaves of your asters have transparent, brown or black spots. The spots enlarge and run together.

CAUSE: Leaf spot, also called leaf blight. Several fungi cause this disease, which spreads rapidly from plant to plant in wet weather. The spores overwinter on plant debris.

WHAT TO DO:
• Cut off and destroy infected plant parts.
• Discard seriously infected plants and the soil their roots touch.
• Remove garden debris.
• Apply new mulch.
• Space plants widely for air circulation.
• Water only in the morning, and avoid splashing plants.
• Spray infected plants weekly with sulfur.

PROBLEM: A powdery, grayish white coating covers leaves, flowers, and stems. Affected plants do not die.

CAUSE: Powdery mildew (*Erysiphe cichoracearum*). This fungal disease travels on wind. It thrives in damp weather and in low-light conditions like shade, fog, and cloudy days.

WHAT TO DO:
• Cut off and destroy infected plant parts.
• Apply baking soda spray. Make a spray solution by dissolving 1 teaspoon baking soda in 1 quart warm water; add 1 teaspoon insecticidal soap to make the solution stick to leaves.
• Space plants widely for air circulation.
• Plant in full sun.
• Grow resistant varieties, including *Aster × frikartii* and 'Wood's Pink'.

PROBLEM: In summer, small yellow spots with powdery, orange spores form on leaves. Leaves turn yellow.

CAUSE: Rust. This fungal disease, caused by several pathogens, spreads quickly when its spores blow onto damp aster leaves.

WHAT TO DO:
• Remove and dispose of infected leaves.
• Spray infected plants with sulfur.
• Water in the morning.
• Space or thin plants for air circulation.
• Remove and compost garden debris.

Astilbes

(*Astilbe* spp. and hybrids)

Astilbe Pests

PROBLEM: Dark brown beetles eat leaf edges into scallops. The plants grow poorly.

CAUSE: Black vine weevils (*Otiorhynchus sulcatus*). Adults are ⅓-inch-long, dark brown weevils. Their ½-inch-long, white, grublike larvae have yellowish heads. Adults emerge in June, feed on leaves for two weeks, then lay eggs near the crowns of plants. When the eggs hatch, the larvae burrow into soil, where they feed on roots and overwinter.

WHAT TO DO:
• Handpick.

BLACK VINE WEEVIL

JAPANESE BEETLE

SLUG

• Collect weevils by spreading a cloth on the ground under plants (in the evening about an hour after dark when they come up to feed) and shaking astilbe branches over the cloth. Remove the weevils that fall onto it.

• Apply beneficial nematodes (*Steinernema carpocapsae* and *Heterorhabditis heliothidis*) in the spring; repeat treatment in late summer. You can purchase these from mail-order suppliers. Live nematodes are shipped suspended in gels or sponges. Release them according to instructions when pests are present.

PROBLEM: Shiny green beetles chew holes in astilbe leaves. They devour flowers, buds, and young leaves.

CAUSE: Japanese beetles (*Popillia japonica*). These ½-inch-long beetles eat plant leaves in midsummer. Japanese beetles are most active during the day. Their grubs develop in the soil, where they feed on grass roots in spring.

WHAT TO DO:
• Handpick.

• Spray with neem. This botanical pesticide repels and poisons insect pests but is harmless to beneficial insects.

• Apply beneficial nematodes (*Steinernema carpocapsae* and *Heterorhabditis heliothidis*), which you can order from mail-order suppliers. Live nematodes are shipped suspended in gels or sponges. Release the nematodes when pest larvae are present.

• Apply milky disease spores. The insecticide milky disease contains *Bacillus popilliae* and *B. lentimorbus*. Beetle grubs die after eating it.

PROBLEM: Overnight, unseen pests reduce astilbes to ragged leaves and flowers, streaked with shiny slime.

CAUSES: Slugs and snails (Order Stylommatophora). These ⅛- to 8-inch-long, soft-bodied, gray, tan, green, black, yellow, or spotted pests resemble clams and mussels. Snails have shells; slugs look like snails without shells. At night they climb up the stems of astilbes to feed. In the morning they hide under garden debris. Adults lay jellylike masses of clear eggs under garden debris.

WHAT TO DO:
• Handpick. Begin hunting after dark.
• Sprinkle rings of wood ashes or crushed eggshells around flowerbeds or plants.
• Make copper barriers. Edge plants with a strip of copper, which hits these slimy pests with an electrical shock upon contact.
• Make beer traps from recycled cans sunk to the brim in soil and filled with yeasty beer.
• Apply diatomaceous earth (DE) to plants. This abrasive dust, made of fossilized shells, called diatoms, penetrates the pests' skin.
• Remove mulch and garden debris.

PROBLEM: Stunted or distorted new leaves are spotted. Look for shiny, sticky, or black, sooty material.

CAUSE: Aphids (Family Aphididae). Aphids are soft-bodied insects, $\frac{1}{16}$ to $\frac{3}{8}$ inch long. They range in color from pale tan to light green to nearly black. Aphids suck plant juices and can transfer plant viruses as they feed. The sticky substance they secrete, called honeydew, attracts ants and sooty mold.

WHAT TO DO:
• Tolerate a light infestation.
• Hit aphids with a strong spray of water.
• Wash honeydew or mold off with water.
• Use insecticidal soap, following directions.
• Apply horticultural oil to smother pests.

• Attract beneficial insects, such as parasitic wasps and lady beetles, by planting nectar plants. Purchase beneficial green lacewings and aphid midges from mail-order sources and release them to supplement populations.

 Astilbe Diseases

PROBLEM: Astilbes turn yellow and wilt. Leaves turn brown, drop and don't respond to watering. Plants die.

CAUSE: Fusarium wilt (*Fusarium* sp.). This long-lived, soilborne fungal disease is common in warm, wet climates. Infected plants loose their roots. If you cut open the main stem at its base, you will see dark streaks caused by the disease.

WHAT TO DO:
• Remove and destroy infected plants plus the soil that their roots touch.
• Remove garden debris.
• Improve soil drainage.
• Solarize the soil. Clear plastic sheeting placed over bare soil for three to four weeks uses the sun's energy to heat the soil enough to kill pests and some soilborne diseases. After removing plastic, plant crops as usual.

PROBLEM: A powdery, grayish white coating covers leaves, flowers, and stems. Plants usually do not die.

CAUSE: Powdery mildew (*Erysiphe polygoni*). This fungal disease travels on wind and thrives in damp weather and low-light conditions, like shade, fog, and cloudy days.

WHAT TO DO:
• Cut off and destroy infected plant parts.
• Apply baking soda spray. Dissolve 1 teaspoon baking soda in 1 quart warm water; add 1 teaspoon insecticidal soap to make the solution stick to leaves.
• Space astilbes widely for air circulation.

Baby's-Breath

(Gypsophila paniculata)

Baby's-Breath Pests

PROBLEM: Leaves look bleached and have yellow or brown edges. Some leaves and stems are deformed or curled.

CAUSE: Aster leafhoppers, also known as six-spotted leafhoppers (*Macrosteles quadri-lineatus*). The ⅛-inch-long adults are black with greenish yellow undersides and black-spotted heads. The adults infect baby's-breath plants with the disease called aster yellows (caused by a mycoplasma) as they suck sap from the leaves. Aster leafhoppers overwinter in weeds.

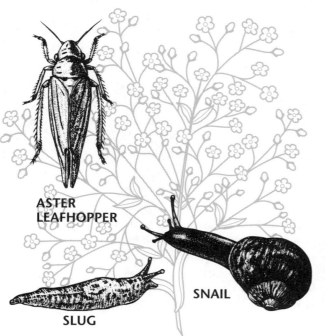

ASTER LEAFHOPPER

SNAIL

SLUG

WHAT TO DO:
- Tolerate light damage.
- Attract parasitic flies, wasps, lady beetles, lacewings, spiders, and other beneficials by planting nectar and pollen plants, including yarrow, alyssum, and scabiosa.
- Use insecticidal soap, following directions.
- Spray horticultural oil. This refined oil coats plant parts and smothers leafhoppers.

PROBLEM: Overnight, unseen pests chew baby's-breath into ragged remains of leaves and flowers covered with slime.

CAUSES: Slugs and snails (Order Stylom-matophora). These are ⅛- to 8-inch-long, soft-bodied, gray, tan, green, black, yellow, or spotted pests. They resemble their water-dwelling relatives—clams and mussels. Snails have shells; slugs look like snails without shells. At night they climb up the stems of plants to eat large holes in foliage, stems, and flowers. In the morning they leave behind a trail of shiny slime as they climb down to hide under garden debris. Adults lay jellylike masses of clear eggs under debris.

WHAT TO DO:
- Handpick. The best time to begin hunting is two hours after dark.
- Sprinkle rings of wood ashes or crushed eggshells around beds or individual plants.
- Make copper barriers. Edge plantings with a strip of copper, which hits these slimy pests with an electrical shock upon contact.
- Make beer traps from recycled cans sunk to

the brim in soil and filled with yeasty beer. Create a roof over the trap to provide shade so the spot remains cool and moist. Attracted by the scent, slugs will fall in and drown.
• Apply diatomaceous earth (DE) to plants when they are wet. This abrasive dust of fossilized shells, called diatoms, penetrates the pests' skins as they crawl over DE. Wear a dust mask to avoid inhaling particles.
• Remove mulch and garden debris.
• Attract pest-eating toads and frogs, or raise poultry in your garden.

 Baby's-Breath Diseases

PROBLEM: New leaves are abnormally small, with yellow or red tips. Some appear deformed and clump together.

CAUSE: Aster yellows. A viruslike organism called a mycoplasma causes the disease. Aster yellows usually enters baby's-breath plants through feeding holes made by aster leafhoppers (*Macrosteles quadrilineatus*) and other leafhoppers. Once infected, there is no cure.

WHAT TO DO:
• Remove and destroy infected plants.
• Wash leafhoppers off plants with a strong stream of water.
• Use insecticidal soap, following directions.

PROBLEM: Soft swellings called galls develop at the base of plants. Infected plants grow poorly, and some die.

CAUSE: Crown gall (*Erwinia herbicola* f. sp. *gypsophilae*). Bacterium causes these swellings, which can completely encircle the main stems of baby's-breath plants and can kill them.

WHAT TO DO:
• Remove and dispose of infected plants and the soil that their roots touch.
• Plant new plants in a different location.

• Solarize the soil. Clear plastic sheeting placed over bare soil for three to four weeks uses the sun's energy to heat the soil enough to kill most disease-carrying pests and some soilborne diseases in the top few inches of soil. After removing the plastic, plant crops as usual.

 Other Problems

PROBLEM: Baby's-breath plants grew well and flowered last season, but they did not come back after the winter.

CAUSE: Frost damage. Baby's-breath is marginally cold-hardy to USDA Hardiness Zone 5 (to –20°F).

WHAT TO DO:
• In Zone 5 and those zones that are colder, apply several inches of fluffy, protective mulch, such as straw, evergreen boughs, or salt hay, after the ground freezes.

PROBLEM: Some plants do not come up in spring. Others are stunted and turn yellow. Affected plants wilt and die.

CAUSE: Wet soil. Soil that remains waterlogged for several days or weeks, especially in winter, can cause plant crowns or roots to rot.

WHAT TO DO:
• Remove dying and dead plants.
• Allow soil to dry out between waterings.
• Pull mulch from plants to increase air circulation.
• Start healthy, new baby's-breath plants in well-drained soil.
• Solarize the soil. Clear plastic sheeting placed over bare soil for three to four weeks uses the sun's energy to heat the soil enough to kill soilborne pathogens, in the top few inches of soil, that enter damaged roots and cause them to rot. After removing the plastic, plant crops as usual.

Bachelor's-Button

also called Cornflower (*Centaurea cyanus*)

 Bachelor's-Button Pests

PROBLEM: Plants have pale, curled or puckered leaves. Small, pear-shaped insects huddle on leaves and stems.

CAUSE: Aphids (Family Aphididae). Aphids, including the leaf-curl plum aphid (*Brachycaudus helichrysi*), are $\frac{1}{16}$- to $\frac{3}{8}$-inch-long, soft-bodied insects. They range in color from pale tan to light green to nearly black. Aphids damage leaves and stems by sucking plant juices, and they can transmit plant diseases as they feed. Their sticky secretions, called honeydew, attract ants, which protect aphids from predators in order to eat the secretions. And the moist honeydew encourages the growth of sooty, black mold.

WHAT TO DO:
• Wash aphids off plants with a strong stream of water. Be sure to hit the backs of leaves, where aphids hide, as well as the upper surfaces when spraying.
• Use insecticidal soap, following label directions. Spray both sides of leaves with the soap to hit any aphids that are hiding.
• Attract beneficial insects, like lady beetles and lacewings, which prey on aphids, by planting small-flowered nectar plants, including yarrow, dill, and Queen-Anne's-lace. Give the beneficials time to bring the aphids under control.
• Pour boiling water into anthills that are not adjacent to plant roots.

PROBLEM: The leaves of your bachelor's-button plants are chewed and ragged. The plants may wilt and grow poorly.

CAUSE: Common stalk borers (*Papaipema nebris*). When young, these thin, $\frac{3}{4}$-inch-long, dark brown or purple caterpillars have white stripes. As they mature, they become solid brown or purple. Common stalk borers eat leaves and then tunnel through the main stems of ornamentals like bachelor's-buttons,

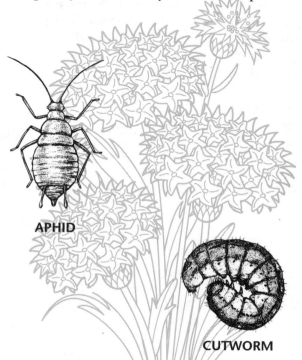

APHID

CUTWORM

eating from the bottom up. Other host plants include ragweed and corn. The eggs overwinter in weeds and in garden debris. The adults are gray or brown moths (Family Noctuidae) with white spots on their forewings and wingspreads of 1 inch.

WHAT TO DO:

• Pull out and dispose of dying plants.

• Slit the stem lengthwise, remove the borer, and tape the stem together with masking tape until it heals.

• Remove plant debris and weeds, such as ragweed, from the garden to remove overwintering sites.

PROBLEM: Overnight, bachelor's-button seedlings are cut off near the ground. You find severed tops next to the stems.

CAUSE: Cutworms (Family Noctuidae). These pests are the larvae of several species of night-flying moths with wingspans of 1½ inches. Cutworms are gray or dull brown caterpillars, 1 to 2 inches long. Cutworms eat their way through seedling stems at night. You will find the tops of the plants lying on the soil surface in the morning. These pests hide in the soil, near the plants they cut off, during the day. Cutworms eat tender, young seedlings, leaving those that are more than two weeks old.

WHAT TO DO:

• Handpick. Carefully dig around the base of damaged plants at night to lift and destroy soil-dwelling cutworms.

• Use cutworm collars to prevent cutworms and other crawling pests from reaching your seedlings. To make the collars, use shears to cut 2- to 3-inch-long sections from paper-towel tubes or aluminum cans. Place these short tubes over small seedlings when transplanting or as seedlings emerge from the soil. Or cut both ends from shallow cans, such as tuna cans, and place these "collars" over seedlings.

• Apply BT granules. "BT" stands for *Bacillus thuringiensis,* an insect-stomach poison that kills caterpillars without harming beneficial insects. Spread BT on the ground before planting.

• Cultivate garden beds in fall and spring to kill some of the larvae overwintering in the soil and to expose others to be eaten by birds.

PROBLEM: Leaves and stems are encrusted with small, round, brown bumps and have a sticky, clear coating.

CAUSE: Hemispherical scale (*Saissetia coffeae*). These ⅛-inch-diameter insects look like brown, waxy bumps. Both the stationary adults and their similar-sized, fuzzy, mobile nymphs suck plant juices. Adult scale produce sticky honeydew that attracts ants and sooty mildew.

WHAT TO DO:

• Scrape scale off branches with a plastic scouring pad.

• Attract parasitic wasps and other beneficials by growing small-flowered nectar plants, including scabiosa, yarrow, dill, and Queen-Anne's-lace.

PROBLEM: Leaves are rolled into tubes and covered in webbing. Caterpillars in the tubes are eating the leaves.

CAUSE: Omnivorous leaftiers (*Cnephasia longana*). These larval pests are ¼-inch-long, cream-colored caterpillars with white stripes. The pests hatch from eggs laid by adult moths that are active only after dark. The moths are tan with brown spots on the forewings and ½-inch wingspans.

WHAT TO DO:

• Handpick.

• Pull off and dispose of the folded leaves where the caterpillars hide.

• Apply BT. "BT" stands for *Bacillus thuringiensis,* an insect-stomach poison that kills caterpillars without harming beneficial insects. BT is most effective when applied while pests are young. Follow label directions to spray a solution of BT on plants as soon as eggs hatch or where you find young caterpillars feeding.

 ## Bachelor's-Button Diseases

PROBLEM: Plants are stunted, and their new leaves turn yellow. Flowers are dwarfed or do not appear.

CAUSE: Aster yellows. A viruslike organism called a mycoplasma causes this disease. It enters baby's-breath plants through holes made by aster leafhoppers (*Macrosteles quadrilineatus*). Once infected, there is no cure. Leafhoppers are wedge-shaped, brown or green, winged insects with triangular heads. They jump rapidly when disturbed.

WHAT TO DO:
• Remove and destroy infected plants to keep the disease from spreading.

• Wash leafhoppers off plants with a strong stream of water. Be sure to hit both sides of the leaves in order to find leafhoppers that may be hiding on the backs of leaves.

• Use insecticidal soap, following label directions. Hit both sides of leaves when you spray the soap solution.

• Attract beneficial insects by planting small-flowered nectar plants, like scabiosa, alyssum, and yarrow, to help control leafhoppers.

PROBLEM: Old leaves close to the ground or leaves at the tops of plants have black, tan, or white patches.

CAUSE: Downy mildew. Cool, damp weather encourages this disease, which is caused by several fungi. The tops of plants, where rain and dew accumulate, and bottom leaves that touch damp soil are most susceptible. If you look on the backs of the leaves opposite the discolored patches, you will see gray fuzz. Infected plants are unsightly but rarely die.

WHAT TO DO:
• Remove diseased growth when you see signs of infection.

• Space plants widely for adequate air circulation.

PROBLEM: Your bachelor's-button plants suddenly wilt and die, especially during rainy weather. Their roots rot.

CAUSE: Fusarium basal rot, also called root rot (*Fusarium oxysporum* f. *cepae*, and other forms). One or more fungi cause this disease. Newly infected plants appear to stop growing, and the leaves wilt slowly. Root rot can develop in poorly drained soil or where the soil is too acidic.

WHAT TO DO:
• Improve soil drainage.

• Space plants widely for adequate air circulation.

• Grow bachelor's-buttons in raised beds.

• Add lime as needed to neutralize acidic soil to provide optimal growing conditions.

PROBLEM: The leaves of your bachelor's-button plants have a white, powdery coating that resists rubbing off.

CAUSE: Powdery mildew (*Erysiphe cichoracearum*). This fungal disease is visible on leaf surfaces, but it is anchored in leaf tissues, making it hard to remove. The disease thrives in cool, damp weather.

WHAT TO DO:
• Pick and destroy infected leaves.

• Rotate crops. Simply avoid growing the same plants in the same spot each year.
• Water plants in the morning so that the leaves will dry before sundown.
• Space plants widely for good air circulation.

PROBLEM: Numerous small, brown or reddish spots appear first on lower leaves. The affected leaves may die.

CAUSE: Rust (*Puccinia* spp.). This fungal disease spreads quickly when its dusty-orange spores blow on the wind, splash in rain, or are carried by insects to damp bachelor's-button leaves.

WHAT TO DO:
• Remove and dispose of severely infected leaves and plants.
• Spray infected plants with sulfur.
• Water in the morning, and avoid splashing plants.
• Space or thin plants for good air circulation.
• Remove and compost garden debris.

PROBLEM: Plants rot at the base and die. On damp days, white threads of fungus grow on the ground around the plants.

CAUSE: Southern blight, also called crown rot (*Sclerotium rolfsii*). This fungal disease thrives in warm climates. The disease appears first as a white, threadlike fungus at the base of plants, and then it spreads outward across the soil. The threads ooze an acidic fluid that kills plant cells on contact, and it can eventually kill entire plants. The spores survive in the soil for years.

WHAT TO DO:
• Dig up and dispose of infected plants and soil 6 inches beyond their roots.
• Add compost to the soil to increase drainage and to introduce beneficial soil organisms.

• Space plants widely when planting for adequate air circulation.

PROBLEM: A cottony-textured mold forms on plant stems. The plants wilt, turn slimy, and feel wet to the touch.

CAUSE: Stem rot (*Sclerotinia sclerotiorum*). This fungal disease thrives in poorly drained soil and during warm, wet or humid weather.

WHAT TO DO:
• Cut off and dispose of infected stems.
• Dust infected plants with sulfur.

 Other Problems

PROBLEM: Leaves have crisp, dry edges. Some leaves turn brown and drop. Plants die in midsummer.

CAUSE: Drought stress. If bachelor's-button plants dry out a few times during the season, they can recover. But a drought of several days or weeks can kill roots and weaken and kill the plants.

WHAT TO DO:
• Water bachelor's-button plants regularly during hot, dry spells.
• Add organic matter, such as compost, to soil to increase its ability to retain moisture.
• Mulch to reduce water evaporation.

PROBLEM: In midsummer your bachelor's-button plants appear healthy, but they suddenly stop flowering.

CAUSE: Heat stress. Bachelor's-buttons grow and flower best in cool weather. As summer temperatures rise, the plants will stop flowering.

WHAT TO DO:
• Sow seeds twice a season to lengthen the flowering season. Sow seeds in early spring and again in midsummer.

Begonias

(Begonia spp.)

Begonia Pests

PROBLEM: Begonia leaves have scalloped bite marks along their edges. The plants grow poorly and wilt.

CAUSE: Black vine weevils (*Otiorhynchus sulcatus*). These ⅓-inch-long, oval, brownish black beetles chew the distinctive scallop marks into leaf edges when they feed at night. But it is their ½-inch-long, yellow-headed, white larvae that do the most damage. Adult beetles emerge in June and lay tiny, white eggs in the soil. The eggs hatch into the larvae that burrow into soil at the base of the plants, where they eat their roots.

WHAT TO DO:
• Collect adult weevils by spreading a cloth on the ground under the plant (in the evening about an hour after dark, when they come up to feed) and shaking the branches over the cloth. Collect and destroy the beetles that drop (they cannot fly).
• Apply beneficial nematodes (*Steinernema carpocapsae* and *Heterorhabditis heliothidis*). To kill the larvae, treat the soil with beneficial nematodes beginning in the spring; repeat in late summer. Water well before and after each treatment. These beneficials are shipped live from mail-order sources, suspended in gels or sponges. Release nematodes when pest larvae are present.

PROBLEM: Your begonias are not growing, and there are fuzzy, white bumps on their succulent leaf stems.

CAUSE: Mealybugs (Family Pseudococcidae). Mealybugs move slowly and are covered with white, cottony fuzz. These sap-sucking insects are about ¼ inch long when fully grown. They cause the most damage to begonias grown as houseplants indoors, where they are not stopped by predators or freezing temperatures.

WHAT TO DO:
• Knock mealybugs off garden plants with a strong stream of water.
• Use insecticidal soap, following label directions. Be sure to spray both sides of the leaves, because mealybugs may hide in crevices and on the backs of leaves.

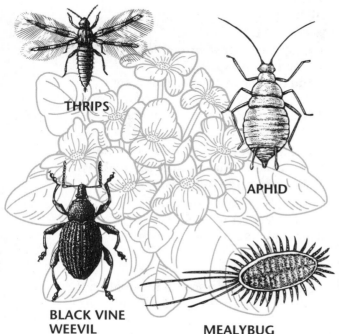

THRIPS

APHID

BLACK VINE WEEVIL

MEALYBUG

• Attract beneficial insects to the garden. If mealybugs appear on outdoor plants, they are usually controlled by native parasitic wasps, which you can attract by planting nectar plants, such as alyssum, yarrow, and Queen-Anne's-lace.

• Inspect plants carefully before buying them.

• On houseplants with a few mealybugs, dab the individual insects with a cotton ball dipped in rubbing alcohol.

PROBLEM: New leaves and shoots are distorted and coated with a shiny substance. Ants may gather on the leaves.

CAUSE: Melon aphids (*Aphis gossypii*). These pests are $1/16$- to $3/8$-inch-long, soft-bodied insects. Aphids range in color from pale tan to light green to nearly black. They damage leaves and stems by sucking plant juices. Aphids can transmit plant diseases as they feed, and their sticky secretions, called honeydew, attract ants, which protect aphids from predators in order to eat the honeydew. The moist honeydew also attracts sooty mold. This pest is found throughout the United States but is most harmful in the South and Southwest. In the North, serious outbreaks may occur during hot, dry summers that follow wet springs.

WHAT TO DO:

• Wash aphids off plants with a strong stream of water.

• Use insecticidal soap, following label directions. Be sure to spray both sides of the leaves because aphids often hide on the backs of leaves.

• Attract beneficial insects, like lady beetles and lacewings, by planting small-flowered nectar plants, including yarrow, dill, and Queen-Anne's-lace. You can also purchase beneficial "bug food" products from mail-order sources, or put out shallow pans of sugar-water to attract beneficials. Give the beneficials time to bring the aphids under control.

• Pour boiling water into entry holes of anthills that are not adjacent to plant roots to keep from scalding the roots of your begonias.

PROBLEM: Overnight, your begonias are reduced to ragged remains of leaves or flowers streaked with shiny slime.

CAUSES: Slugs and snails (Order Stylommatophora). These pests are $1/8$- to 8-inch-long, soft-bodied, gray, tan, green, black, yellow, or spotted insects. They resemble their water-dwelling relatives—clams and mussels. Snails have shells; slugs look like snails without shells. At night they climb up the stems of begonia plants to eat large holes in foliage, stems, and flowers. In the morning, they leave behind a trail of shiny slime as they climb down to hide under garden debris. Adults lay jellylike masses of clear eggs under garden debris. Damage is usually worst in spring, when plants are small, and also during rainy periods.

WHAT TO DO:

• Handpick. The best time to begin hunting is two hours after dark.

• Sprinkle rings of wood ashes or crushed eggshells around flowerbeds or individual plants.

• Make copper barriers. Edge plantings with a strip of copper, which hits these slimy pests with an electrical shock upon contact.

• Make beer traps from recycled cans sunk to the brim in soil and filled with yeasty beer. Create a roof over the trap to provide shade so the spot remains cool and moist. Attracted by the scent of beer, the slugs will fall into the traps and drown.

• Apply diatomaceous earth (DE) when plants are wet. This abrasive dust is made of fossilized shells, called diatoms, that penetrate the pests' skin as they crawl over DE. Wear a dust mask to avoid inhaling particles.
• Remove mulch and garden debris.

PROBLEM: Mature leaves have speckling or streaking. The growing tips or buds of plants may be distorted.

CAUSE: Thrips (Order Thysanoptera). These extremely tiny, narrow-bodied insects are only $\frac{1}{25}$ inch long. They like to hide deep inside the leaf shoots and flowers of begonias. Thrips are almost impossible to see on the plant without a magnifying glass. If you suspect a plant has thrips, try this test. Pick a damaged shoot or flower, and shake it over a clean sheet of white paper. If thrips are present, they will drop onto the paper; they will look like dark specks moving around on the paper.

WHAT TO DO:
• Knock thrips off plants with a strong stream of water.
• Use insecticidal soap, following label directions.
• Apply neem. This botanical pesticide repels and poisons insect pests but is harmless to beneficial insects.
• Attract beneficial insects by growing small-flowered nectar plants, like alyssum, scabiosa, and yarrow. Set out very shallow dishes of water for the beneficials. You can spray garden plants with commercial "bug food," which you can order from mail-order sources, or set out shallow pans of sugar-water to attract beneficials.
• Mulch plants to attract beneficial beetles.

PROBLEM: Clouds of tiny, white insects fly up when plants are disturbed. Leaves may be covered with mold.

CAUSE: Whiteflies (Family Aleyrodidae). These $\frac{1}{25}$-inch-long, flying insects weaken plants by sucking sap. Whiteflies can also transmit viruses from plant to plant as they feed. Whiteflies lay yellowish eggs the size of a pinpoint on the backs of leaves. The eggs hatch into $\frac{1}{20}$-inch-long, translucent nymphs. Both nymphs and adults weaken plants when they feed in large numbers. You are most likely to see them late in summer. Whiteflies usually disappear after the first frost.

WHAT TO DO:
• Use insecticidal soap, following label directions.
• Apply neem. This botanical pesticide repels and poisons insect pests but is harmless to beneficial insects.
• Attract beneficial insects by growing small-flowered nectar plants, like alyssum, scabiosa, and yarrow. You can spray garden plants with commercial "bug food," which you can order from mail-order sources, to attract beneficials. Set out very shallow dishes of water for the beneficials.
• Mulch plants to attract beneficial beetles.
• Spray summer oil. Horticultural oils, such as summer oil, coat plant leaves and branches, smothering insects and disease pathogens.

 Begonia Diseases

PROBLEM: There are small spots on the leaves of your begonias. The spots enlarge; the leaves turn yellow and drop.

CAUSE: Bacterial leaf spot (*Xanthomonas begoniae*) and other bacteria and fungi can cause leaf spots, yellowing, and defoliation of begonias. Leaf spot is most severe during rainy periods in the spring. The disease is spread by splashing rain and irrigation water. The spores of fungal leaf spots overwinter in garden debris.

WHAT TO DO:
- Cut off and dispose of damaged leaves.
- Remove seriously diseased plants.
- Water begonias early in the morning so that leaves will dry out before sunset.
- Avoid wetting leaves when watering.
- Allow the soil to dry between waterings.
- Plant begonias where they will receive morning sun.
- Space plants widely for adequate air circulation.
- Wash hands and tools after working with infected plants to keep from spreading the disease.

PROBLEM: Brown blotches are on the bottoms of leaves. The blotches spread to the tops. Leaves wither and drop.

CAUSE: Harmful nematodes. Spring dwarf nematodes (*Aphelenchoides fragariae*) and other species of nematode feed inside begonia leaves. Nematodes are microscopic worms that cause diseaselike symptoms in their hosts, including yellowing, distorted leaves and stunted growth. Spring dwarf nematodes are most common in cold-winter areas, where they overwinter in buds or bulbs.

WHAT TO DO:
- Remove and dispose of infected leaves to keep from spreading the disease.
- Dig up and dispose of severely infected plants.
- Remove and compost garden debris.
- Avoid splashing water on leaves when watering.

PROBLEM: The base and lower stems of some of your begonia plants are rotting.

CAUSE: Root rot. This fungal disease causes most of the roots to disappear, leaving little more than a few shriveled, darkened roots.

WHAT TO DO:
- Remove dying plants.
- Mulch with compost.
- Allow the soil to dry out between waterings.
- Space plants widely for adequate air circulation.
- Grow begonias in well-drained soil.

 Other Problems

PROBLEM: Your begonia plants grow tall and thin, turn a pale shade of green, and produce few flowers.

CAUSE: Lack of light. Although begonias grow best in light shade, heavily shaded locations will cause them to grow tall and spindly and stop flowering.

WHAT TO DO:
- Grow begonias in the garden in filtered shade or morning sun.
- Indoors, grow them on an east- or south-facing windowsill or a few inches below fluorescent lights.

PROBLEM: Some plants grow slowly, are stunted, and turn yellow. Affected plants wilt and die.

CAUSE: Wet soil. Soil that remains waterlogged for several days or weeks, especially in early spring, when the weather is chilly, can cause the crowns of begonia plants or the roots to rot.

WHAT TO DO:
- Remove dying and dead plants.
- Allow soil to dry out between waterings.
- Pull mulch from plants to increase air circulation around the crowns of the plants.

Black-Eyed Susans

(*Rudbeckia* spp.)

 Black-Eyed Susan Pests

PROBLEM: Leaves look bleached and have yellow or brown edges. Some leaves and stems are deformed.

CAUSE: Aster leafhoppers, also known as six-spotted leafhoppers (*Macrosteles quadrilineatus*). The $\frac{1}{8}$-inch-long adults are black with greenish yellow undersides and black-spotted heads. The adults infect black-eyed Susans with the disease aster yellows (caused by a mycoplasma) as they suck sap from the leaves. Aster leafhoppers overwinter in weeds.

ASTER LEAFHOPPER

WHAT TO DO:
• Tolerate light damage.
• Attract parasitic flies, wasps, lady beetles, lacewings, spiders, and other beneficials by planting small-flowered nectar plants, including yarrow, alyssum, and scabiosa.
• Use insecticidal soap, following label directions.
• Spray horticultural oil. This refined oil coats plant parts, and it smothers leafhoppers.

PROBLEM: New leaves and shoots are distorted and coated with a shiny substance. Leaves may have sooty spots.

CAUSE: Brown ambrosia aphids (*Dactynotus ambrosiae*). These $\frac{1}{16}$- to $\frac{3}{8}$-inch-long, soft-bodied insects damage leaves and stems by sucking plant juices. Their feeding causes buds and young growth to become stunted, curled, or distorted. Aphids can transmit plant diseases as they feed. Their sticky secretions, called honeydew, attract ants, which protect aphids from predators in order to eat the honeydew. The black spots that accompany honeydew are a fungus called sooty mold. Sooty mold is unattractive but harmless, except where there is enough of it on leaves to block the sun, limiting a plant's ability to manufacture food (photosynthesize). Serious outbreaks may occur during hot, dry summers following wet springs.

WHAT TO DO:
• Tolerate light damage.

• Wash aphids off plants with a strong stream of water.
• Use insecticidal soap, following directions.
• Attract beneficial insects, like lady beetles and lacewings, by planting small-flowered nectar plants, including yarrow, dill, and Queen-Anne's-lace. Purchase beneficial "bug food" products from mail-order sources, or put out shallow pans of sugar-water to attract beneficials. Purchase beneficial green lacewings and aphid midges from mail-order sources, and release them in your garden. Give the beneficials time to bring the aphids under control.
• Pour boiling water into entry holes of anthills that are not adjacent to plant roots.
• Reduce fertilizer applications, which promote the tender growth preferred by aphids.
• Grow these plants in full sun.

Black-Eyed Susan Diseases

PROBLEM: A powdery, grayish white coating covers leaves, flowers, and stems. Plants usually do not die.

CAUSE: Powdery mildew (*Erysiphe cichoracearum*). This fungal disease is unique in that it is more prevalent in semi-arid regions than in the high-rainfall regions where most fungal diseases thrive. Powdery mildew travels on wind. It thrives in stagnant air and low-light conditions, such as shade, fog, and cloudy weather.

WHAT TO DO:
• Cut off and destroy infected plant parts.
• Water with fermented compost tea every two to four weeks.
• Spray foliage with sulfur. Or spray with a 2 percent solution of light horticultural oil, which coats plants, suffocating pests.
• Apply baking soda spray. Dissolve 1 teaspoon of baking soda in 1 quart warm water;

add 1 teaspoon insecticidal soap to make the solution stick to leaves.
• Space plants widely or thin them for adequate air circulation.
• Plant black-eyed Susans in full sun.
• Water plants regularly.
• Grow mildew-resistant varieties, like *R. fulgida* var. *sullivantii* 'Goldsturm'.

PROBLEM: Numerous small, powdery, bright orange spots of spores are on the undersides of leaves and along stems.

CAUSE: Rust. Several fungi cause this disease. Rust spreads by wind and water and is most often seen in damp weather. As the disease progresses, yellow or dark areas appear on the tops of leaves. Infected plants grow slowly.

WHAT TO DO:
• Remove and dispose of infected leaves.
• Spray with sulfur.
• Avoid overhead watering, or water early in the day so the plants will dry quickly.
• Space or thin plants for adequate air circulation.

 ## Other Problems

PROBLEM: Plants are not growing well. They may attract an unusual number of pests or have repeated infections.

CAUSE: Poor growing conditions. Black-eyed Susans that grow in the shade or in wet, poorly drained soil will produce weak, succulent stems and leaves that are targeted by insects and many diseases.

WHAT TO DO:
• Move plants. If your black-eyed Susans are growing in the shade or soggy soil, lift them and replant them.
• Grow these and other rudbeckias in full sun and in well-drained garden soil of average fertility.

Bleeding Hearts

(*Dicentra* spp.)

 Bleeding Heart Pests

PROBLEM: The leaves and stems of your bleeding hearts are speckled with small bumps and sticky, clear spots.

CAUSE: Scale. These ⅛-inch-diameter insects, including the scaly looking latania scale (*Hemiberlesia lataniae*) and the sandy-textured, clamshell-shaped scale (*Palinaspis quohogiformis*), suck plant juices. Adult scale look like immobile bumps; they produce sticky honeydew that attracts ants and sooty mildew.

WHAT TO DO:
• Scrape scale off with a plastic scouring pad.
• Attract parasitic wasps and other beneficials by growing small-flowered nectar plants, including scabiosa, yarrow, dill, and Queen-Anne's-lace.

PROBLEM: Overnight, bleeding hearts are reduced to ragged remains of leaves and flowers streaked with shiny slime.

CAUSES: Slugs and snails (Order Stylommatophora). These ⅛- to 8-inch-long, soft-bodied, gray, tan, green, black, yellow, or spotted pests resemble clams and mussels. Snails have shells; slugs look like snails without shells. At night these pests climb up the stems of bleeding hearts to feed. In the morning they leave behind a trail of shiny slime as they climb down to hide under garden debris. Adults lay jellylike masses of clear eggs under mulch and garden debris.

WHAT TO DO:
• Handpick. The best time to begin hunting is two hours after dark.
• Remove mulch and garden debris.
• Sprinkle rings of wood ashes or crushed eggshells around flowerbeds or individual plants.
• Make copper barriers. Edge plants with a strip of copper, which hits these slimy pests with an electrical shock upon contact.
• Make beer traps from recycled cans sunk to the brim in soil and filled with yeasty beer. Attracted by the scent of beer, the slugs will

STEM ROT

SLUG

fall into the traps and drown.
• Apply diatomaceous earth (DE) to plants. This abrasive dust is made of fossilized shells, called diatoms, that penetrate the pests' skin as they crawl over DE.

Bleeding Heart Diseases

PROBLEM: Stems turn black at the base and may grow mold. Leaves yellow and wilt. Watering does not revive plants.

CAUSE: Stem rot (*Sclerotium* spp.). These fungal diseases attack bleeding heart plants that grow in soggy, poorly drained soil. Infected plants may collapse and eventually die.

WHAT TO DO:
• Remove and dispose of infected plants and the soil that their roots touch.
• Disinfect tools with rubbing alcohol after working with diseased plants to keep from spreading the disease to other plants.
• Keep mulch away from the base of plants.
• Allow soil to dry out between waterings.
• Improve soil drainage and moisture retention by adding organic matter.
• Space plants widely for air circulation.

Other Problems

PROBLEM: Bleeding hearts grew and flowered during the growing season, but don't come back after winter.

CAUSE: Mild, wet winters. Bleeding hearts are short-lived perennials in areas with soggy soil and mild, wet winters.

WHAT TO DO:
• Improve soil drainage. Incorporate organic material, such as compost, into the soil to increase drainage and moisture retention.
• In cold-winter climates, apply several inches of a fluffy mulch, such as straw or evergreen boughs, after the ground freezes in fall to insulate plants and keep them from heaving out of the ground.
• Plant bleeding hearts that are native to your area. In the mild-winter western coastal areas, plant the western bleeding heart (*D. formosa*). In the eastern part of the United States, plant fringed bleeding heart (*D. eximia*).

PROBLEM: After several seasons of growth and flowering, clumps of plants die out in the center.

CAUSE: Overcrowding. Like many perennials, bleeding hearts reproduce. The young plants come up around the perimeter of the original plant in ever-expanding rings. After about five years, the plants at the center of each clump can become nutrient-starved.

WHAT TO DO:
• Divide bleeding hearts every five years. Replant 6-inch-diameter groups of young plants taken from the outer edges of the clump. Discard the center of the clump.

PROBLEM: Leaves of previously healthy plants yellow. Plants die back after blooming. Transplants turn yellow.

CAUSES: Summer dieback and transplant shock. Common bleeding heart (*D. spectabilis*) will ordinarily die back (go dormant) during the heat of summer. Bleeding hearts do not transplant well, and the leaves may bleach out afterward.

WHAT TO DO:
• Allow plants to die back naturally.
• Cut plants back to the ground after the foliage turns yellow, and mark their location with a stake so that you do not damage the roots when cultivating the bed.
• Tolerate dormancy.
• When transplanting a bleeding heart, try to keep the roots and surrounding soil intact to minimize transplant shock.

Butterfly Weed

(Asclepias tuberosa)

Butterfly Weed Pests

PROBLEM: There are light tan, winding trails on leaves of butterfly weed. The marks do not turn into holes.

CAUSE: Serpentine leafminers (*Liriomyza lorassicae*). These pests are the minute, pale green larvae of an ⅛-inch-long black or black-and-yellow fly. The larvae tunnel between the upper and lower surfaces of leaves, eating as they go. Leafminers overwinter in fallen leaves.

WHAT TO DO:
• Pick and destroy affected leaves.
• Locate the large end of a trail and press that area to kill the larva inside each tunnel.
• Clean up and destroy all fallen leaves.
• Treat soil with beneficial nematodes.

PROBLEM: The leaves of your butterfly weed plants have holes in them. You see striped caterpillars on the leaves.

CAUSE: Monarch butterfly larvae (*Danaus plexippus*). Butterfly weed is a favorite food of the caterpillar larvae of the beautiful monarch butterflies. These 1- to 2-inch-long, colorful caterpillars have black, yellow, and greenish white stripes the length of their bodies.

WHAT TO DO:
• Handpick.
• Tolerate the damage.
• Grow extra butterfly weed plants so that there is enough for the caterpillars.

Butterfly Weed Diseases

PROBLEM: Numerous small, powdery, bright orange spots are on the undersides of leaves and along the stems.

CAUSE: Rust. This is a disease that is caused by several fungi. It thrives in damp weather and spreads in wind and splashing water. As the disease progresses, infected plants grow slowly.

WHAT TO DO:
• Remove and dispose of infected leaves.
• Spray with sulfur.
• Water early in the day.
• Space plants widely for air circulation.
• Add compost to soil to improve drainage.

LEAFMINER ADULT

Candytuft

(Iberis sempervirens)

Candytuft Pests

PROBLEM: Some candytuft leaves have squiggly, tan lines in them. Other leaves have holes chewed in them.

CAUSE: Diamondback moths (*Plutella xylostella*). These are gray or brown moths with white-spotted wings and ¾-inch wingspans. Their yellow-green, ⅓-inch-long caterpillars mine the leaves when they are small; and as they grow larger, they eat the leaves.

WHAT TO DO:
• Handpick.
• Apply BT. "BT" stands for *Bacillus thuringiensis,* an insect-stomach poison that kills caterpillars without harming beneficial insects.

EXCEPT FOR THE DIAMONDBACK MOTHS, CANDYTUFT IS NOT TROUBLED BY MOST COMMON INSECT PESTS.

Candytuft Diseases

PROBLEM: A powdery, grayish white coating covers leaves, flowers, and stems. Plants usually do not die.

CAUSE: Powdery mildew (*Erysiphe polygoni*). This fungal disease is more prevalent in semi-arid regions than in those with high rainfall. Powdery mildew spores travel on the wind. It thrives in shade, fog, and cloudy weather.

WHAT TO DO:
• Cut off and destroy infected plant parts.
• Apply baking soda spray. Dissolve 1 teaspoon baking soda in 1 quart warm water; add 1 teaspoon insecticidal soap to make the solution stick to leaves.
• Water plants regularly.
• Space plants widely for air circulation.
• Grow candytuft in full sun.

Other Problems

PROBLEM: Some plants suffered over winter, have yellowing leaves, and are growing poorly. Some plants died.

CAUSES: Soil is too alkaline; lack of water; winter freeze damage. Candytuft prefers well-drained, moisture-retentive, slightly acid soil. And it may not survive long, frigid winters.

WHAT TO DO:
• Add organic matter such as compost, leaf mold, and peat moss to acidify the soil.
• Water candytuft during droughts.
• In cold winters, layer several inches of loose mulch, such as evergreen boughs or straw, around plants to protect them.

Canna

(Canna × generalis)

Canna Pests

PROBLEM: There are holes in your canna leaves and flowers. You find iridescent, greenish bronze beetles on the plants.

CAUSE: Japanese beetles *(Popillia japonica)*. These shiny, ½-inch-long beetles emerge in midsummer. The fat, ½-inch-long, white grubs develop in the soil over the winter.

WHAT TO DO:
• Handpick.
• Use insecticidal soap, following directions.
• Apply milky disease spores. This disease combines spores of *Bacillus popilliae* and *B. lentimorbus*. Grubs eat the spores and die.

PROBLEM: Canna leaves are ragged and turning brown. Some leaves are rolled and tied together with strands of silk.

JAPANESE BEETLE

LARGER CANNA LEAFROLLER ADULT

SPOTTED CUCUMBER BEETLE

LARGER CANNA LEAFROLLER LARVA

CAUSES: Larger and lesser canna leafrollers (*Calpodes ethlius* and *Geshna cannalis*). The larger canna leafrollers are green, 2-inch-long caterpillars with orange heads. The lesser canna leafrollers are yellow-green, 1-inch-long caterpillars. The larger canna leafrollers are the larvae of brown-and-white skipper butterflies. The lesser canna leafrollers are the larvae of brown moths. Both overwinter in garden debris.

WHAT TO DO:
• Handpick.
• Remove garden debris.

PROBLEM: The leaves and flowers of your cannas are eaten by greenish yellow beetles with black spots.

CAUSE: Spotted cucumber beetles (*Diabrotica undecimpunctata* var. *howardi*). These beetles are about ¼ inch long.

WHAT TO DO:
• Handpick.
• Plant cucumbers to lure beetles away.
• Apply beneficial nematodes (*Steinernema carpocapsae* and *Heterorhabditis heliothidis*), which you can purchase by mail-order.

Canna Diseases

PROBLEM: Leaves have water-soaked streaks and spots that make them look striped. Flower buds blacken and die.

CAUSE: Canna bud rot (*Xanthomonas cannae*). This bacterial disease overwinters in roots.

WHAT TO DO:
• Destroy infected roots.
• Grow cannas in well-drained soil.

Cleome

(Cleome hasslerana)

 Cleome Pests

PROBLEM: New leaves are small and pale. Very small, light green insects cling to the undersides of the leaves.

CAUSE: Green peach aphids (*Myzus persicae*). Green peach aphids are 1/16- to 3/8-inch-long, soft-bodied, pear-shaped insects. They suck plant juices and can transmit plant diseases as they feed. Their sticky secretions, called honeydew, attract ants, which protect aphids from predators in order to eat the secretions, and encourage the growth of sooty mold. Outbreaks occur in hot, dry summers.

**GREEN PEACH
APHID**

WHAT TO DO:
• Tolerate light damage.
• Wash aphids off plants with a strong stream of water.
• Use insecticidal soap, following directions.
• Attract beneficial insects, like lady beetles and lacewings, by planting small-flowered nectar plants, including yarrow, dill, and Queen-Anne's-lace. Purchase beneficial "bug food" products from mail-order sources, or put out shallow pans of sugar-water to attract beneficials. Purchase beneficial green lacewings and aphid midges from mail-order sources, and release them in your garden. Give the beneficials time to bring the aphids under control.
• Pour boiling water into entry holes of anthills that are not adjacent to plant roots.
• Reduce fertilizer applications to limit tender, new growth, which is preferred by aphids.
• Grow cleomes in full sun to prevent susceptible, weak growth.

 Cleome Diseases

PROBLEM: The leaves of your cleome plants develop pale spots during rainy growing seasons.

CAUSE: Leaf spot (*Cercospora* spp., *Heterosporium hybridum*). This fungal disease spreads by wind and rain and is most active in warm weather. Leaf spot spores spread via splashing rain and irrigation water. The spores overwinter in garden debris.

WHAT TO DO:
• Pick off and dispose of infected leaves.
• Mulch with compost.

Cockscomb

(Celosia cristata)

 ## Cockscomb Pests

PROBLEM: The leaves of your cockscomb plants are stippled with small, yellow spots. Some have fine webs on them.

CAUSE: Spider mites (Family Tetranychidae). These pinpoint-sized, spiderlike pests pierce plant leaves and suck nutrients. The mites feed more during dry spells. They overwinter in leaves on the ground and in plant crevices.

WHAT TO DO:
• Dislodge spider mites with a strong stream of water.
• Use insecticidal soap, following directions. Begin treatment at the pinprick stage.

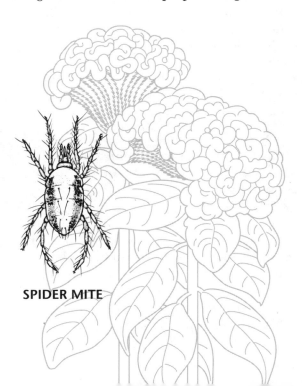

SPIDER MITE

 ## Cockscomb Diseases

PROBLEM: The leaves of your cockscomb plants develop pale spots during rainy growing seasons.

CAUSE: Leaf spot (*Cercospora celosiae*, *Phyllosticta* sp., and *Alternaria* sp.). Several fungi cause this disease, which travels in wind and rain. It thrives in warm weather. The spores overwinter in garden debris.

WHAT TO DO:
• Pick off and dispose of infected leaves.
• Mulch with compost.

PROBLEM: Growth is stunted. Plants wilt, turn yellow, and slowly die even though no pests or spots are visible.

CAUSE: Southern root-knot nematodes (*Meloidogyne incognita* var. *incognita*). These microscopic worms live in the soil. They attack plant roots, causing diseaselike symptoms. They are especially troublesome in sandy soils and warm-winter climates. If nematodes are present, the roots will have small or large knots or swellings.

WHAT TO DO:
• Provide plenty of water and fertilizer.
• Dig compost into garden beds.
• Apply crab or shrimp wastes that contain chitin, which stimulates growth of microorganisms that attack nematodes.
• Solarize the soil. Clear plastic sheeting placed over bare soil for three to four weeks uses the sun's energy to heat the soil enough to kill most pests and weed seeds in the top few inches of soil.

Coleus

(Coleus × hybridus)

Coleus Pests

PROBLEM: Leaves are deformed and shiny or are covered with black mold. You see cottony insects and ants.

CAUSE: Mealybugs (Family Pseudococcidae). Their powdery, white coating makes these ¼-inch-long pests look like specks of cotton. Mealybugs suck plant juices. The shiny honeydew they excrete attracts black mold.

WHAT TO DO:
• Knock mealybugs off plants with a strong stream of water.
• Use insecticidal soap, following directions.
• Attract native parasitic wasps and other beneficials by planting small-flowered nectar plants, including alyssum and yarrow.

PROBLEM: Clouds of tiny, white flies scatter when leaves are disturbed. White specks are on leaf undersides.

CAUSE: Whiteflies (Family Aleyrodidae). These tiny (¹⁄₂₅-inch-long), white, winged insects suck sap. They can also transmit viruses as they feed. Whiteflies disappear after frost.

WHAT TO DO:
• Use insecticidal soap, following directions.
• Spray neem. This botanical pesticide is harmless to beneficial insects.
• Attract beneficial insect predators by planting small-flowered nectar plants, including alyssum, scabiosa, and yarrow.
• Spray summer oil. Horticultural oils, such as summer oil, smother insects and disease pathogens.

Coleus Diseases

PROBLEM: Growth is stunted. Plants wilt, turn yellow, and slowly die. You see no pests or spots on the plants.

CAUSE: Southern root-knot nematodes (*Meloidogyne incognita* var. *incognita*). Nematodes are actually microscopic worms that live in the soil and attack plant roots, causing the roots to have knots or swellings and the plant tops to wither and die.

WHAT TO DO:
• Provide supplementary water and fertilizer.
• Turn under compost in garden beds.
• Apply crab or shrimp wastes that contain chitin. Chitin creates conditions that encourage beneficial soil organisms.
• Solarize the soil. Clear plastic sheeting placed over bare soil for three to four weeks uses the sun's energy to heat the soil enough to kill most pests and weed seeds in the top few inches of soil.

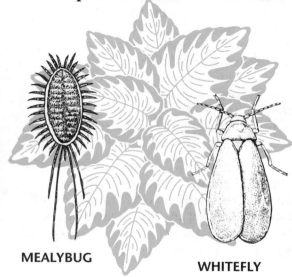

MEALYBUG

WHITEFLY

Columbines

(*Aquilegia* spp. and hybrids)

Columbine Pests

PROBLEM: Clusters of small, pear-shaped insects are on columbine leaves, buds, or stems. Growth may be stunted.

CAUSE: Aphids (Family Aphididae). Adult aphids are soft-bodied insects, $1/16$ to $3/8$ inch long. They range in color from pale tan to light green to nearly black. Aphids damage plants by sucking sap, and they can transfer diseases as they feed. Their sticky secretions, called honeydew, attract sooty mold and ants, which protect aphids from predators in order to eat the honeydew.

WHAT TO DO:
• Tolerate light damage.
• Wash aphids off plants with a strong stream of water.
• Use insecticidal soap, following label directions. Be sure to hit the backs of leaves, where aphids hide, when spraying.
• Attract beneficial insects, like lady beetles and lacewings, by planting small-flowered nectar plants, including yarrow, dill, and Queen-Anne's-lace. Purchase beneficial "bug food" products from mail-order sources, or put out shallow pans of sugar-water to attract beneficials. Purchase beneficial green lacewings and aphid midges from mail-order sources, and release them in your garden. Give the beneficials time to bring the aphids under control.
• Pour boiling water into entry holes of anthills that are not adjacent to plant roots.
• Reduce fertilizer applications, which promote the tender, new growth that is is preferred by aphids.
• Grow columbines in full sun to prevent susceptible, weak growth.

PROBLEM: Plants suddenly collapse. Stems break; leaves wilt. Small, round holes appear on the stems or crowns.

CAUSES: Columbine borers (*Papaipema purpurifascia*). These are the $1\frac{1}{2}$-inch-long, salmon-

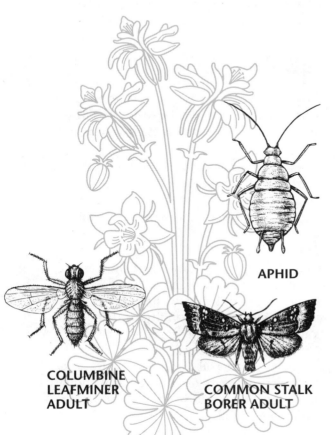

APHID

COLUMBINE
LEAFMINER
ADULT

COMMON STALK
BORER ADULT

colored caterpillar larvae of reddish brown moths with 1-inch wingspans. The caterpillars eat the stems and fleshy roots of columbines.

Common stalk borers (*P. nebris*). These borers are ¾- to 1½-inch-long, brown caterpillars with purple stripes the length of their bodies. These pests burrow through plant stems. The adults are white-spotted, grayish brown moths with 1-inch wingspans.

WHAT TO DO:
• Cut off and dispose of infested stems.
• Scrape the surface of the soil in spring to kill the eggs.
• Spray BT before the borers have entered the stems. "BT" stands for *Bacillus thuringiensis,* an insect-stomach poison that kills caterpillars without harming beneficial insects.

PROBLEM: Light tan, winding trails disfigure some of the leaves on your columbines.

CAUSE: Columbine leafminers (*Phytomyza* spp.). These pests are the minute, pale green larvae of tiny flies. The larvae tunnel and feed between the upper and lower surfaces of leaves. They overwinter in garden debris.

WHAT TO DO:
• Pick and destroy infested leaves.
• Clean up and destroy all fallen leaves under plants, especially in the fall, to remove overwintering leafminers.
• Apply beneficial nematodes (*Steinernema carpocapsae* and *Heterorhabditis heliothidis*), which are shipped live from mail-order suppliers.

 Columbine Diseases

PROBLEM: Leaves have purple-rimmed spots. Some develop yellow-green halos around them and gray or white centers.

CAUSE: Leaf spot. This disease is caused by various fungi, including *Ascochyta aquilegiae, Cercospora aquilegiae, Septoria aquilegiae,* and *Haplobasidium pavoninum.* The disease thrives in wet or humid weather and on moist leaf surfaces. Leaf spot spores travel in splashing rain and irrigation water. The spores overwinter in garden debris.

WHAT TO DO:
• Cut off and dispose of diseased leaves and severely infected plants.
• Clean up plant debris.
• Wash hands and tools after handling plants and debris.
• Space plants widely for ample sunshine and good air circulation.

 Other Problems

PROBLEM: Your columbines are growing poorly. They attract a large number of pests or have repeated infections.

CAUSES: Environmental stress. Columbines need excellent drainage and prefer cool, moist soil. Stressed plants can fall prey to insects and diseases or may go dormant during periods of summer heat.

WHAT TO DO:
• Add compost to the soil to improve drainage and moisture retention.
• Grow columbines in partial shade except in cool climates, where they can take full sun.

PROBLEM: Columbines were healthy and bloomed well for several seasons, but now grow slowly and have few flowers.

CAUSE: Columbines are naturally short-lived perennials.

WHAT TO DO:
• Allow plants to self-sow.
• Replace old ones with new plants after a few years.

Coral Bells

(*Heuchera sanguinea* and other species and hybrids)

 Coral Bells Pests

PROBLEM: Some leaves turn yellow and drop. Sticky, white, woolly specks and black mold are on leaves and leaf nodes.

CAUSE: Mealybugs (Family Pseudococcidae). Their powdery, white coating makes these ¼-inch-long pests look more like little specks of cotton than insects. Mealybugs suck plant juices and cause leaves to wither and turn yellow. The shiny honeydew they excrete becomes visible on leaves and may develop black mold.

WHAT TO DO:
• Knock mealybugs off plants with a strong stream of water.
• Use insecticidal soap, following label directions. Make sure you spray the backs of the leaves, where pests sometimes hide.
• Attract native parasitic wasps and other beneficials by planting nectar plants, including alyssum, yarrow, and Queen-Anne's-lace.
• Purchase beneficials, such as mealybug destroyers (*Cryptolaemus montrouzieri*) or parasitic wasps, from mail-order suppliers, and release them in the garden.

PROBLEM: Some leaf edges are chewed. The crowns of affected plants are eaten or turn black. Some plants die.

CAUSE: Strawberry root weevils (*Otiorhynchus ovatus*). The black, ¼-inch-long weevil adults feed on the leaves and crowns of coral bell plants. The brown-headed, ⅜-inch-long, white larvae feed on their roots. The larvae overwinter in garden debris on the soil.

WHAT TO DO:
• Handpick. Look for adult weevils after dark.
• Cut off and dispose of infested plant parts.
• Completely remove and destroy heavily infested plants along with surrounding soil.
• Apply beneficial nematodes (*Steinernema carpocapsae* and *Heterorhabditis heliothidis*) beginning in midspring. Treat again in late summer. Mail-order suppliers ship live nematodes suspended in gels or sponges.

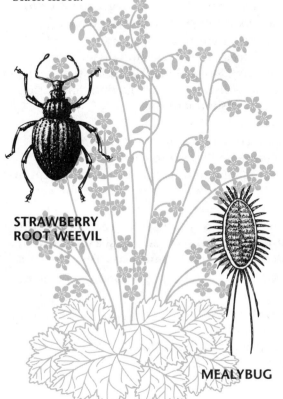

STRAWBERRY ROOT WEEVIL

MEALYBUG

Coral Bells Diseases

PROBLEM: There are purplish, yellow, brown, or black spots of various sizes on the leaves of your coral bell plants.

CAUSE: Leaf spot. This disease is caused by various fungi. The disease thrives in wet or humid weather and on moist leaf surfaces. Leaf spot travels in splashing rain and irrigation water. The spores overwinter in garden debris.

WHAT TO DO:
• Tolerate light damage.
• Cut off and dispose of diseased leaves and severely infected plants.
• Clean up plant debris.
• Wash hands and tools after handling plants and debris.
• Space plants widely for ample sunshine and good air circulation.

PROBLEM: A powdery, grayish white coating covers leaves, flowers, and stems. Plants usually do not die.

CAUSE: Powdery mildew. This disease, caused by several kinds of fungi, is more prevalent in semi-arid regions than in those with high rainfall. Powdery mildew spores travel on wind. The disease thrives in mild temperatures and in the low light of shade, fog, and cloudy days.

WHAT TO DO:
• Cut off and destroy infected plant parts.
• Apply baking soda spray. Dissolve 1 teaspoon baking soda in 1 quart warm water; add 1 teaspoon insecticidal soap to make the solution stick to leaves.
• Water plants regularly during droughts.
• Space plants widely for good air circulation.
• In warm climates, plant coral bells in partial shade. In mild areas, such as along a coast, plant them in full sun.

PROBLEM: Numerous small, powdery, bright orange spots are on the undersides of leaves and along the stems.

CAUSE: Rust (*Puccinia keucherae*). This is a disease that is caused by several fungi. Rust spreads in wind and rain, and it thrives in damp weather. As the disease progresses, pale yellow or dark areas appear on the top surfaces of the leaves. Infected plants grow slowly.

WHAT TO DO:
• Remove and dispose of infected leaves.
• Spray with sulfur.
• Water early in the day so plants will dry quickly.
• Space plants widely for air circulation.
• Grow coral bells in well-drained soil. Add compost to soil to improve drainage.

PROBLEM: The bases of stems are dark and discolored. Stems die from the base upward. Plants can collapse and die.

CAUSE: Stem rot (*Sclerotinia sclerotiorum*). This soilborne fungal disease is encouraged by poor soil drainage and wet or very humid, warm weather. Coral bells are native to rocky cliffs and mountain slopes, and they need good drainage to grow properly.

WHAT TO DO:
• Cut off and dispose of infected stems.
• Dust infected plants with sulfur.
• Improve soil drainage by incorporating organic matter, such as compost or leaf mold.
• Disinfect tools after using them with rubbing alcohol or 10 percent bleach solution.
• Avoid overwatering.
• Pull mulch or debris away from base of plants to increase air circulation.
• Plant in well-drained soil or raised beds.
• Space plants widely for air circulation.

Coreopsis

(*Coreopsis* spp. and hybrids)

Coreopsis Pests

PROBLEM: Your coreopsis plants have distorted growth, especially at the stem tips. Flowers may also be deformed.

CAUSE: Aphids (Family Aphididae). Adults are soft-bodied insects, $\frac{1}{16}$ to $\frac{3}{8}$ inch long. They range in color from pale tan to light green to nearly black. Aphids damage plants by sucking sap. They can also transmit diseases as they feed. The sticky honeydew that aphids excrete attracts sooty, black mold and ants, which protect aphids from predators in order to eat the honeydew.

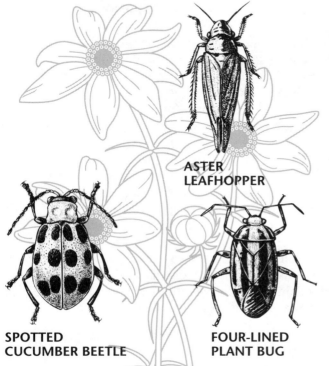

ASTER LEAFHOPPER

SPOTTED CUCUMBER BEETLE

FOUR-LINED PLANT BUG

WHAT TO DO:
• Tolerate light damage.
• Wash aphids off plants with a strong stream of water.
• Use insecticidal soap, following label directions.
• Attract beneficial insects, like lady beetles and lacewings, by planting small-flowered nectar plants, including yarrow, dill, and Queen-Anne's-lace.
• Pour boiling water into anthills that are not adjacent to plant roots.

PROBLEM: Coreopsis leaves look bleached and have yellow or brown edges. Some are deformed or curled.

CAUSE: Aster leafhoppers, also known as six-spotted leafhoppers (*Macrosteles quadrilineatus*). The wedge-shaped, $\frac{1}{8}$-inch-long adults are black with greenish yellow undersides and black-spotted heads. The adults infect coreopsis plants with the disease called aster yellows (a mycoplasma) as they suck sap from the leaves. Aster leafhoppers overwinter in weeds.

WHAT TO DO:
• Tolerate light damage.
• Attract parasitic flies, wasps, lady beetles, and other beneficials by planting small-flowered nectar plants, including yarrow, alyssum, and scabiosa.
• Use insecticidal soap, following label directions.
• Spray horticultural oil. This refined oil coats plant parts and smothers leafhoppers.

PROBLEM: Leaves and flowers are distorted. Stem tips wilt. Yellow, tan, or brown spots are on leaves and flowers.

CAUSE: Four-lined plant bugs (*Poecilocapsus lineatus*). These sap-sucking pests are ⅓-inch-long, yellowish green bugs with four black stripes on their wings. In May or June, their eggs hatch into bright red nymphs with a black dot on their chests. Their feeding ends in midsummer. The eggs overwinter in garden debris.

WHAT TO DO:
• Handpick.
• Use insecticidal soap, following label directions. Spray the soap on undersides of leaves every third day for two weeks until pests disappear.
• Clean up garden debris in spring and fall.

PROBLEM: Greenish yellow beetles with black spots are eating the leaves and flowers of your coreopsis.

CAUSE: Spotted cucumber beetles (*Diabrotica undecimpunctata* var. *howardi*). These beetles are about ¼ inch long. As their name suggests, they are fond of cucumber plants. But they also feed on coreopsis, and they can spread diseases as they go from plant to plant. Their larvae may also eat coreopsis roots. Spotted cucumber beetle larvae are white, ½-inch-long grubs with brown heads and brown patches on their body segments.

WHAT TO DO:
• Handpick.
• Plant cucumbers to lure the beetles away.
• Apply beneficial nematodes (*Steinernema carpocapsae* and *Heterorhabditis heliothidis*), which you can purchase from mail-order suppliers. Live nematodes are shipped suspended in gels or sponges.
• Apply milky disease spores. This disease combines spores of *Bacillus popilliae* and *B. lentimorbus*. Grubs eat the spores and die.

 Coreopsis Diseases

PROBLEM: Stunted, yellowing plants have spindly stems. Flowers may be deformed and turn yellow-green.

CAUSE: Aster yellows. This disease is caused by a viruslike organism called a mycoplasma. The disease is spread via feeding aster leafhoppers (*Macrosteles quadrilineatus*). These winged, wedge-shaped insects have triangular heads. The brown or green insects jump when disturbed.

WHAT TO DO:
• Remove and destroy infected plants.
• Wash leafhoppers off plants with a strong stream of water.
• Use insecticidal soap, following directions.
• Attract beneficial insects by planting small-flowered nectar plants, including scabiosa, alyssum, and yarrow.

PROBLEM: A powdery, grayish white coating covers leaves, flowers, and stems. Plants usually do not die.

CAUSE: Powdery mildew (*Erysiphe cichoracearum*). This fungal disease is more prevalent in semi-arid regions than in those with high rainfall. Powdery mildew spores travel on the wind. The disease thrives in mild temperatures and low-light situations, such as shade, fog, and cloudy days.

WHAT TO DO:
• Cut off and destroy infected plant parts.
• Apply baking soda spray. Dissolve 1 teaspoon baking soda in 1 quart warm water; add 1 teaspoon insecticidal soap to make the solution stick to leaves.
• Water plants regularly during droughts.
• Space plants widely for air circulation.

Cosmos

(*Cosmos* spp.)

 Cosmos Pests

PROBLEM: Your cosmos plants have distorted growth, especially at the stem tips. Their flowers may be deformed.

CAUSE: Aphids (Family Aphididae). Adults are soft-bodied insects, $\frac{1}{16}$ to $\frac{3}{8}$ inch long. They range in color from pale tan to light green to nearly black. Aphids damage plants by sucking sap, and they can also transmit diseases as they feed. The sticky honeydew they excrete attracts sooty, black mold and ants, which protect aphids from predators in order to eat the honeydew.

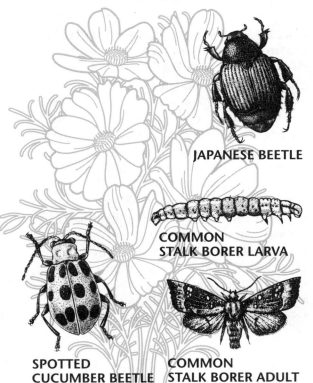

JAPANESE BEETLE

COMMON
STALK BORER LARVA

SPOTTED
CUCUMBER BEETLE

COMMON
STALK BORER ADULT

WHAT TO DO:
- Tolerate light damage.
- Wash aphids off plants with a strong stream of water.
- Use insecticidal soap, following directions.
- Attract beneficial insects, like lady beetles and lacewings, by planting small-flowered nectar plants, including yarrow, dill, and Queen-Anne's-lace. Purchase beneficial "bug food" products from mail-order sources, or put out shallow pans of sugar-water to attract beneficials. Purchase beneficial green lacewings and aphid midges from mail-order sources, and release them in your garden. Give the beneficials time to bring the aphids under control.
- Pour boiling water into entry holes of anthills that are not adjacent to plant roots.
- Reduce fertilizer applications, because tender, new growth is preferred by aphids.
- Grow in full sun to prevent weak growth.

PROBLEM: The stems of your cosmos plants break, and the leaves wilt. You can see small holes in the stems.

CAUSES: European corn borers and common stalk borers. Both of these pests burrow through plant stems during the growing season, eating as they go. They overwinter in plant debris in the garden.

European corn borers (*Ostrinia nubilalis*) are 1-inch-long, gray or beige, segmented caterpillars with brown dots on each segment. The adults are pale beige, night-flying moths with 1-inch wingspans. The females have zigzag wing patterns. The males have darker gray wings. The moths lay masses of overlapping white or tan eggs on the leaf backs of young plants in early summer.

Common stalk borers (*Papaipema nebris*) are ¾- to 1½-inch-long, brown caterpillars with purple stripes the length of their bodies. The adults are white-spotted, grayish brown moths with 1-inch wingspans.

WHAT TO DO:
• Cut off and dispose of infested stems.
• Scrape the soil in spring to kill eggs.
• Spray BT before the borers have entered the stems. "BT" stands for *Bacillus thuringiensis*, an insect-stomach poison that kills caterpillars without harming beneficial insects.

PROBLEM: Iridescent, greenish bronze beetles are eating holes in the leaves and flowers of your cosmos.

CAUSE: Japanese beetles (*Popillia japonica*). These shiny, ½-inch-long beetles are found in the eastern United States and are moving westward. The adults emerge in midsummer and feed on plants growing in full sun. They are especially fond of flowers. Their fat, white, ½-inch-long grubs develop in the soil over winter and eat grass roots in spring.

WHAT TO DO:
• Handpick.
• Use insecticidal soap, following directions.
• Apply milky disease spores (*Bacillus popilliae* and *B. lentimorbus*). Grubs eat these and die.

PROBLEM: Greenish yellow beetles with black spots are eating the leaves and flowers of your cosmos plants.

CAUSE: Spotted cucumber beetles (*Diabrotica undecimpunctata* var. *howardi*). These beetles are about ¼ inch long. As their name suggests, they are especially fond of cucumber plants. Unfortunately, they also feed on cosmos, and they can spread viral diseases as they go from plant to plant.

WHAT TO DO:
• Handpick.
• Plant cucumbers to lure the beetles away.
• Apply beneficial nematodes (*Steinernema carpocapsae* and *Heterorhabditis heliothidis*), which you can purchase live from mail-order suppliers.

 Cosmos Diseases

PROBLEM: Stunted, yellowing plants have spindly stems. Flowers may be deformed and turn yellow-green.

CAUSE: Aster yellows. This disease is caused by a viruslike organism called a mycoplasma. The disease enters plants through feeding holes made by aster leafhoppers (*Macrosteles quadrilineatus*). Once infected, there is no cure. These winged, wedge-shaped, brown or green insects have triangular heads. Leafhoppers jump rapidly when disturbed.

WHAT TO DO:
• Remove and destroy infected plants.
• Wash leafhoppers off plants with a strong stream of water.
• Use insecticidal soap, following directions.
• Attract parasitic wasps and other beneficials by planting small-flowered nectar plants, including alyssum and yarrow.

 Other Problems

PROBLEM: Although they appear healthy and bloom normally, your cosmos plants keep falling over.

CAUSE: Weak-stemmed plants. Cosmos are thin-stemmed plants that sometimes blow over or are knocked down by heavy rains.

WHAT TO DO:
• Stake plants.
• Pinch out the tips of young plants.
• Grow in sun. Water and fertilize sparingly.

Crocuses

(*Crocus* spp.)

 Crocus Pests

PROBLEM: In spring some crocus plants fail to appear. The flower buds of those that do come up suddenly disappear.

CAUSES: Animals and birds. Squirrels, mice, voles, deer, and even birds eat crocus leaves and flowers. Rodents dig up and eat the bulbs.

WHAT TO DO:
• In spring, spray emerging plants with egg-based repellent or hot-pepper spray. To make egg spray, beat 18 eggs; add to a bucket containing 5 gallons of water. To make pepper spray, liquefy ½ cup hot peppers and ½ cup water in a blender. Strain and spray.

SQUIRREL

BIRD

MOUSE

• When planting crocuses in the fall, put several handfuls of sharp, crushed rock around groups of corms, or enclose them in pieces of chicken wire to deter burrowing rodents.

PROBLEM: Some crocuses do not sprout. Some do, but their leaves yellow and die early. Some corms rot in storage.

CAUSE: Bulb mites (*Rhizoglyphus echinopus*). These pests are minute, white mites from $\frac{1}{25}$ to $\frac{1}{50}$ inch long. These mites can infest rotting corms or burrow into healthy ones. The mites carry diseases that cause infested corms growing in the ground as well as those in storage to rot.

WHAT TO DO:
• Dispose of rotting or soft corms.
• Attract predaceous mites and other beneficials by planting small-flowered nectar plants, including alyssum and scabiosa.

 Crocus Diseases

PROBLEM: Plants yellow and die early. Stored corms have sunken, reddish spots that spread into brown areas.

CAUSE: Dry rot (*Stromatinia gladioli*). This soilborne fungal disease causes corms to decay, both in storage and in the ground. The decay moves upward from the bulb, causing leaves also to die. Corms planted in cold, wet soil are most susceptible. The disease can survive for ten years or more in the soil.

WHAT TO DO:
• Destroy infected and lightweight corms.
• Plant crocuses in well-drained soils. Air-dry corms right after digging, before storing.

Daffodils *(Narcissus* spp.)

Daffodil Pests

PROBLEM: Daffodils produce few flowers. Their bulbs have soft necks and small holes or shiny, white offsets.

CAUSE: Narcissus bulb flies *(Merodon equestris).* These flies look like yellow-and-brown bumblebees. They lay eggs at the base of daffodil leaves. Larvae bore into bulbs to feed.

WHAT TO DO:
• Pull off yellowing foliage.
• When digging, discard infested bulbs.

Daffodil Diseases

PROBLEM: The leaf stems are swollen and leaf blades are stunted. Affected daffodil plants usually fail to flower.

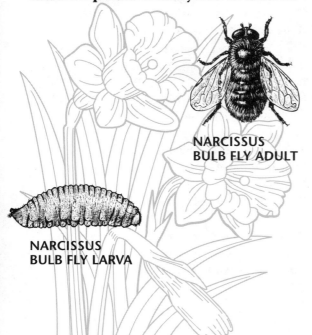

NARCISSUS BULB FLY ADULT

NARCISSUS BULB FLY LARVA

CAUSE: Stem nematodes *(Ditylenchus dipsaci).* These minute, soil-dwelling worms burrow into roots and bulbs. They stunt plants and can transmit diseases as they feed.

WHAT TO DO:
• Dig up and destroy infested plants.
• Solarize the soil. Clear plastic sheeting placed over bare soil for three to four weeks uses the sun's energy to heat the soil enough to kill most pests in the top few inches of soil.
• Incorporate compost into the soil.

PROBLEM: Daffodils fail to sprout in spring. Stored bulbs have a white band at the base, brown streaks, and are soft.

CAUSE: Basal rot *(Fusarium oxysporum* f. *narcissi).* This soilborne fungus stunts plants and causes stored bulbs to turn brown and rot.

WHAT TO DO:
• Plant daffodils in well-drained soil.
• In warm climates, plant in summer shade.
• Solarize the soil. Clear plastic sheeting placed over bare soil for four weeks uses the sun's energy to kill diseases in the top inches.

PROBLEM: Your daffodils have pale streaks in the leaves or flowers. Leaves may wilt and fall over too soon.

CAUSES: Narcissus mosaic; narcissus flower streak; narcissus white streak; narcissus yellow stripe. These viral diseases are transmitted by sap-sucking insects.

WHAT TO DO:
• Dig bulbs and replant only the largest.
• Knock disease-carrying insects off plants with a strong spray of water.
• Use insecticidal soap; follow directions.

Dahlias

(Dahlia hybrids)

Dahlia Pests

PROBLEM: The leaves of your dahlias wilt, and their leaf stems break. You can see small holes in the affected stems.

CAUSES: European corn borers and common stalk borers. These pests burrow through plant stems, eating as they go. They overwinter in plant debris left in the garden.

European corn borers (*Ostrinia nubilalis*). These caterpillars are 1-inch-long, gray or beige, with brown dots on each segment. The adults are pale beige, night-flying moths with 1-inch wingspans. The females have zigzag wing patterns. The males have darker gray wings. The moths lay masses of overlapping white or tan eggs on the leaf backs of young plants in early summer.

Common stalk borers (*Papaipema nebris*) are ¾- to 1½-inch-long, brown caterpillars with purple stripes the length of their bodies. The adults are white-spotted, grayish brown moths with 1-inch wingspans.

WHAT TO DO:
• Cut off and dispose of infested stems.
• Kill borers by inserting a wire or injecting beneficial nematodes into their holes.
• Spray BT before the borers have entered the stems. "BT" stands for *Bacillus thuringiensis,* an insect-stomach poison that kills caterpillars without harming beneficial insects.
• Remove weeds and garden debris in fall.

PROBLEM: Seedlings or older plants and flowers are partially eaten. Long, reddish brown insects are on plants.

CAUSE: European earwigs (*Forficula auricularia*). These pests are ⅘ inch long, and they have large pincers on their rear ends. Earwigs feed at night and hide in flowers or under debris during the day.

WHAT TO DO:
• Trap earwigs by placing pieces of garden hose or paper-towel tubes on the soil under plants at night. Empty earwigs from the tubes into a pail of soapy water in the morning.

PROBLEM: Iridescent, greenish bronze beetles are eating holes in the leaves and flowers of your dahlias.

CAUSE: Japanese beetles (*Popillia japonica*). These shiny, ½-inch-long beetles emerge in

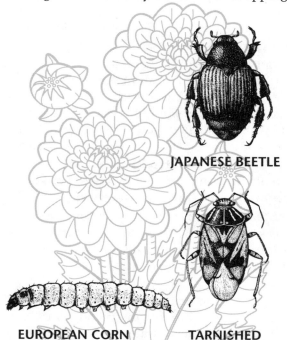

JAPANESE BEETLE

EUROPEAN CORN BORER

TARNISHED PLANT BUG

midsummer. They are most active during the day, and they prefer to feed on plants growing in full sun. Their grubs develop in soil, where they damage grass roots in lawns.

WHAT TO DO:
• Handpick.
• Use insecticidal soap, following directions.
• Apply milky disease spores. This disease combines spores of *Bacillus popilliae* and *B. lentimorbus*. Grubs eat the spores and die.

PROBLEM: New dahlia shoots and buds have small, dark spots in them. Leaves and flowers are damaged or deformed.

CAUSE: Tarnished plant bugs (*Lygus lineolaris*). These fast-moving, mottled, green or brown, ¼-inch-long bugs have a yellow triangle on each side of their bodies near their back ends. The yellow-green nymphs have five black dots on their bodies. Tarnished plant bugs are very active in early spring and may increase during the summer. When they feed, they inject toxic saliva into plants, causing leaves and flowers to become deformed. Branch tips may blacken and die. Adults overwinter in fallen leaves and garden debris and emerge in early spring to feed before laying eggs.

WHAT TO DO:
• Handpick.
• Use insecticidal soap, following directions.
• Control weeds and garden debris.

 Dahlia Diseases

PROBLEM: Growth is stunted. Dahlia plants wilt, turn yellow, and slowly die. No pests or disease spots are visible.

CAUSE: Harmful nematodes (Phylum Nematoda). Several species of minute, soil-dwelling nematodes, including root-knot nematodes (*Meloidogyne* sp.), attack dahlias. The tiny worms burrow into roots, causing knotlike swellings as they feed. They secrete chemicals that cause root cells to enlarge.

WHAT TO DO:
• Water and fertilize weak plants.
• Turn under compost in garden beds, and apply crab or shrimp wastes, which contain chitin. Chitin creates favorable conditions for beneficial organisms that attack nematodes.
• Solarize the soil. Clear plastic sheeting placed over bare soil for three to four weeks uses the sun's energy to heat the soil enough to kill most pests and weed seeds in the top few inches of soil.

PROBLEM: A powdery, grayish white coating covers leaves, flowers, and stems, but plants usually do not die.

CAUSE: Powdery mildew (*Erysiphe cichoracearum; E. polygoni; Uncinula* sp.). This fungal disease travels on the wind. It thrives in mild temperatures and the low light of shade, fog, and cloudy days.

WHAT TO DO:
• Cut off and destroy infected plant parts.
• Apply baking soda spray. Dissolve 1 teaspoon baking soda in 1 quart warm water; add 1 teaspoon insecticidal soap to make it stick to leaves.
• Water plants regularly during droughts.
• Space plants widely for good air circulation.

PROBLEM: White, tan, or bronze spots appear on leaf undersides. The spots soon turn into a silvery glaze.

CAUSE: Pollution damage. When sunlight reacts with smog, the air pollutant peroxyacyl nitrate damages leaves on dahlias that are grown in polluted, urban areas. Affected plants are unsightly and grow slowly.

WHAT TO DO:
• Remove damaged leaves.
• Replace severely affected plants.

Daylilies

(Hemerocallis spp. and hybrids)

 Daylily Pests

PROBLEM: Clusters of small, pear-shaped insects are on leaves, buds, or stems. Young growth may be stunted.

CAUSE: Aphids (Family Aphididae). Adults are soft-bodied, pear-shaped insects, $\frac{1}{16}$ to $\frac{3}{8}$ inch long. They range in color from pale tan to light green to nearly black. Aphids damage daylily plants and flowers by sucking sap, and they can transmit diseases as they feed. The sticky honeydew that aphids excrete attracts black mold and ants, which protect aphids from predators in order to eat the honeydew.

WHAT TO DO:
- Tolerate light damage.
- Wash aphids off plants with a strong stream of water.
- Use insecticidal soap, following directions.
- Attract beneficial insects, like lady beetles and lacewings, by planting small-flowered nectar plants, including yarrow and dill.
- Pour boiling water into anthills that are not adjacent to plant roots.

PROBLEM: The leaves of your daylilies are stippled with small, yellow spots. Some leaves have fine webs on them.

CAUSE: Spider mites (Family Tetranychidae). These pinpoint-sized, spiderlike pests pierce plant leaves to suck nutrients. Mites feed more during dry spells. Their webs protect eggs and young. Spider mites overwinter in leaves on the ground and in plant crevices.

WHAT TO DO:
- Dislodge spider mites with a blast of water.
- Use insecticidal soap, following label directions. Begin treatment early, at the pinprick stage. By the time the webs appear, it may be too late to save some plants.

PROBLEM: Leaves and flowers have silvery streaks or speckling. They may turn brown and develop black specks.

CAUSE: Thrips (Order Thysanoptera). These extremely tiny, narrow-bodied insects are only $\frac{1}{25}$ inch long. They like to hide deep inside the leaf shoots and flowers of daylilies. Thrips are almost impossible to see on the plant without a magnifying glass. If you suspect a plant has thrips, pick a damaged

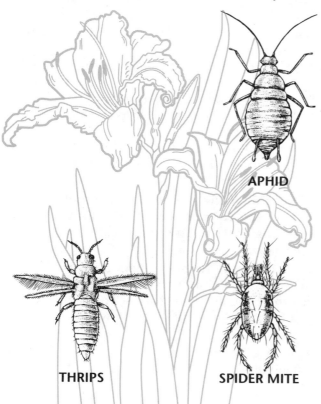

APHID

THRIPS

SPIDER MITE

flower and shake it over a clean sheet of white paper. Thrips will drop onto the paper and look like dark, moving specks.

WHAT TO DO:
• Knock thrips off plants with a strong stream of water.
• Make sticky blue cards to trap thrips. Coat blue cardboard or painted wooden boards with petroleum jelly or Tanglefoot (a commercial product for this purpose), and fasten them to stakes near plants.
• Use insecticidal soap, following directions.
• Apply neem. This botanical pesticide repels and poisons insect pests but is harmless to beneficial insects.

 Daylily Diseases

PROBLEM: The leaves and flowers of some daylilies turn mushy, rot, and begin to smell rotten.

CAUSE: Bacterial soft rot (*Erwinia* spp.). This bacterial disease thrives in wet weather and heavy, poorly drained soils. Once a plant is infected, the disease multiplies very rapidly. Pruning off wilted parts has no impact.

WHAT TO DO:
• Remove and dispose of infected plants.
• Disinfect your tools with rubbing alcohol or 10 percent bleach solution after working with infected plants.
• Raise beds to improve drainage.
• Remove mulch and debris from around remaining daylilies to increase air circulation.

PROBLEM: Growth is stunted. Daylily plants wilt, turn yellow, and slowly die, but no pests or disease spots are visible.

CAUSE: Root-knot nematodes (*Meloidogyne* spp.). These microscopic worms, which cause diseaselike symptoms, burrow into daylily roots, causing knotlike swellings as they feed. They secrete chemicals that cause the root

cells to enlarge into knots the size of marbles.

WHAT TO DO:
• Provide weakened plants with supplemental water and fertilizer.
• Turn under compost in garden beds and apply crab or shrimp wastes that contain chitin. Chitin creates conditions that encourage beneficial soil organisms.
• Solarize the soil. Clear plastic sheeting placed over bare soil for three to four weeks uses the sun's energy to heat the soil enough to kill most pests and weed seeds in the top few inches of soil.

 Other Problems

PROBLEM: Your daylilies appear healthy; they have lush, green foliage but very few flowers.

CAUSE: Too much shade or fertilizer. Daylilies need at least six hours of sunlight a day. High-nitrogen fertilizer causes them to grow leaves at the expense of flowers.

WHAT TO DO:
• Move your daylilies into a sunny site.
• Decrease fertilizer.

PROBLEM: The tips, or sometimes entire leaves, of your daylilies turn brown and papery.

CAUSES: Natural aging process; drought stress. It is typical of some species of daylilies to develop brown tips or brown leaves as they go dormant after flowering. A dry spell of a week or more during the growing season can throw them into early dormancy.

WHAT TO DO:
• Pull out dead leaves.
• Mulch plants.
• Provide additional water during droughts.
• Ask your local nursery to recommend varieties that are not prone to tip dieback.

Delphiniums

(*Delphinium elatum* and other species and hybrids)

 Delphinium Pests

PROBLEM: Overnight, your delphinium seedlings are cut off near the ground. Severed plants lie next to the stems.

CAUSE: Cutworms (Family Noctuidae). These pests are the larvae of several species of night-flying moths with wingspans of 1½ inches. Cutworms are gray or dull brown caterpillars, 1 to 2 inches long. They eat through new seedling stems at night and hide in the soil during the day.

WHAT TO DO:
• Handpick. Dig around the base of damaged plants at night, lift, and destroy cutworms.
• Make cutworm collars. Use tin shears to cut 2- to 3-inch-long sections from paper-towel tubes or tin cans; place these short tubes over seedlings.
• Apply BT granules. "BT" stands for *Bacillus thuringiensis,* an insect-stomach poison that kills caterpillars without harming beneficials.

PROBLEM: Plants are stunted and deformed. Buds and flowers turn black. Leaves curl and may have dark streaks.

CAUSE: Cyclamen mites (*Phytonemus pallidus*). These minute, $\frac{1}{100}$-inch-long, translucent or pale green, eight-legged mites travel on wind and on tools and gardeners' hands. They flourish in cool weather and overwinter at the bases of plants.

WHAT TO DO:
• Dig up and destroy infested plants.
• Wash hands and tools with soapy water.

PROBLEM: Leaves wilt. Stems fall over and break. Sawdustlike frass (insect excrement) is near holes in the stems.

CAUSE: Common stalk borers (*Papaipema nebris*). Borer caterpillars feed on new leaves and flower buds. Then they bore into the stems. Common stalk borers are ¾- to 1½-inch-long, brown caterpillars with purple stripes. The adults are white-spotted, grayish brown moths with 1-inch wingspans. They overwinter in debris.

LEAFMINER ADULT

CUTWORM

COMMON STALK BORER ADULT

SLUG

COMMON STALK BORER LARVA

WHAT TO DO:
• Cut off and dispose of infested stems.
• Insert a wire or inject BT into stem holes. "BT" is *Bacillus thuringiensis,* an insect-stomach poison that kills only caterpillars.
• Remove weeds and garden debris in fall.

PROBLEM: Light-colored blotches or winding trails disfigure the leaves of some of your delphinium plants.

CAUSE: Larkspur leafminers (*Phytomyza* spp.). They are minute larvae of tiny flies. The larvae tunnel and feed between upper and lower leaf surfaces and overwinter in debris.

WHAT TO DO:
• Pick and destroy infested and fallen leaves.
• Apply beneficial nematodes (*Steinernema carpocapsae* and *Heterorhabditis heliothidis*), which you can buy from mail-order suppliers. Live nematodes are shipped in gels or sponges.

PROBLEM: The leaves and flowers of some delphiniums are riddled with holes. Others are ragged and slimy.

CAUSES: Slugs and snails (Order Stylommatophora). These pests are ⅛- to 8-inch-long, gray, tan, green, black, yellow, or spotted pests that are related to clams and mussels. Snails have shells; slugs look like snails without shells. At night these pests climb up stems to feed. Adults lay jellylike masses of clear eggs under garden debris.

WHAT TO DO:
• Handpick. Start two hours after dark.
• Remove debris and mulch.
• Sprinkle rings of wood ashes or crushed eggshells around plants.
• Make beer traps from recycled cans sunk to the brim in soil and filled with yeasty beer. Attracted to the scent of beer, the slugs will fall into the traps and drown.

 Delphinium Diseases

PROBLEM: Stunted, yellowing plants have spindly stems. Flowers may be deformed and turn yellow.

CAUSE: Aster yellows. This disease is caused by a viruslike organism called a mycoplasma. It is spread by wedge-shaped insects called aster leafhoppers (*Macrosteles quadrilineatus*).

WHAT TO DO:
• Remove and destroy infected plants.
• Wash pests off with a stream of water.
• Use insecticidal soap, following directions.
• Attract beneficial insects by planting small-flowered nectar plants, like scabiosa and dill.

PROBLEM: Black, tarlike spots are on your delphinium leaves. The spots may merge and develop into holes.

CAUSE: Bacterial black spot (*Pseudomonas syringae* pv. *delphinii*). This disease thrives in cool, damp weather and enters plants through leaf pores. It overwinters on debris.

WHAT TO DO:
• Remove and dispose of infected plants.
• Do not work around wet plants.
• Spray with copper sulfate.

PROBLEM: Delphinium stems turn black at the base. Leaves turn yellow and mushy. Affected parts rot.

CAUSE: Black leg, also called crown rot (*Erwinia carotovora* subsp. *atroseptica*). This bacterial disease thrives in warm, wet weather and poorly drained soils. It multiplies rapidly and is carried by infected seeds.

WHAT TO DO:
• Remove and dispose of infected plants.
• Spray with bordeaux mix, a wettable combination of copper sulfate and hydrated lime.
• Remove mulch and debris.
• Allow soil to dry out between waterings.

Dianthus *(Dianthus* spp.)

Dianthus Pests

PROBLEM: Overnight, dianthus seedlings are cut off near the ground. You find the severed plants next to the stems.

CAUSE: Cutworms (Family Noctuidae). These pests are the larvae of several species of night-flying moths with wingspans of 1½ inches. Cutworms are gray or dull brown caterpillars, 1 to 2 inches long. Cutworms eat their way through seedling stems at night and hide in soil during the day.

WHAT TO DO:
• Handpick. Dig around the base of damaged plants at night, and lift and destroy cutworms.
• Use cutworm collars. Use tin shears to cut 2- to 3-inch-long sections of paper-towel tubes or tin cans; place tubes over seedlings.
• Apply BT granules. "BT" stands for *Bacillus thuringiensis,* an insect-stomach poison that kills caterpillars without harming beneficials.

PROBLEM: Leaves appear pale green and stippled because of tiny yellow or white spots. Fine webbing may be present.

CAUSE: Spider mites (Family Tetranychidae). These pinpoint-sized, spiderlike pests pierce plant leaves to suck nutrients. The mites feed more during dry spells. Their cobwebs protect eggs and hatchlings. Spider mites overwinter in leaves on the ground and in plant crevices.

WHAT TO DO:
• Dislodge spider mites with a strong stream of water.
• Use insecticidal soap, following label directions. Begin treatment early, at the pinprick stage. By the time the webs appear, it may be too late to save some plants.

CUTWORM

SPIDER MITE

Dianthus Diseases

PROBLEM: Leaves have purple-rimmed spots. Spots merge; leaves yellow, blacken, and die. Affected plants die.

CAUSE: Alternaria leaf spot, also called carnation collar blight (*Alternaria dianthi*). Plants infected with this fungal disease rot at ground level and at leaf nodes. The leaves may be covered with black fungus, become distorted, and die at the tip. The spores are spread in splashing rain or irrigation water.

WHAT TO DO:
• Remove and destroy infected plant parts and debris.
• Avoid overhead watering.
• Mulch to prevent splashing spores on plants.

PROBLEM: Dianthus plants wilt when soil is moist in warm weather. They do not recover after you water them.

CAUSE: Bacterial wilt or Fusarium wilt. Bacterial wilt (*Pseudomonas caryophylli*) and the fungal disease Fusarium wilt (*Fusarium oxysporum* f. *dianthi*) are soilborne diseases that thrive in warm weather. They enter plants through wounds. Wilts interfere with the flow of water and nutrients, causing wilting and death.

WHAT TO DO:
• Remove and destroy the infected plant, the surrounding soil, and the surface debris.
• Solarize the soil. Clear plastic sheeting placed over bare soil for three to four weeks uses the sun's energy to heat the soil enough to kill most pests, which can carry diseases, and some soilborne diseases in the top few inches of soil.

PROBLEM: Powdery brown spots are on undersides of leaves and on stems. Leaf surfaces have yellow or dark spots.

CAUSE: Rust (*Puccinia arenariae* and *Uromyces dianthi*). The spores of this fungal disease travel on wind and in water. It thrives in damp weather. Infected plants grow slowly.

WHAT TO DO:
• Remove and dispose of infected leaves.
• Water early in the day.
• Space plants widely for air circulation.
• Spray with sulfur.

PROBLEM: Dianthus leaves turn pale and wilt. Lower leaves rot. Stems are slimy and rotten, with dry, corky cores.

CAUSE: Stem rot (*Rhizoctonia solani*). This fungal disease flourishes in warm, wet weather or in wet soil.

WHAT TO DO:
• Remove and discard infected plants.
• If only a portion of the plant is affected, remove that part.
• Allow the soil to dry out between waterings.
• Remove mulch.
• Plant in well-drained soil or raised beds.

PROBLEM: Leaves have mottling, rings, or streaks. Flowers are streaked or blotched. Lower leaves turn yellow.

CAUSES: Viruses. Beet curly top, carnation latent disease, carnation mottle virus, carnation streak virus, and carnation ringspot virus are all incurable diseases that can distort, stunt, and eventually kill dianthus plants. Yellowing of lower leaves signals a severe infection. Sucking insects like aphids and leafhoppers spread the disease.

WHAT TO DO:
• Remove and destroy infected plants.
• Use insecticidal soap, following label directions.

 Other Problems

PROBLEM: Previously healthy, blooming dianthus plants suddenly stop growing or die during hot weather.

CAUSES: Heat and humidity stress. Cottage pinks (*Dianthus plumarius*) do not do well in areas that have humid summers. Varieties are sensitive to varying degrees.

WHAT TO DO:
• In hot-summer areas, grow dianthus as annuals. Plant in fall for spring bloom.

Dusty Miller

(Centaurea spp.)

Dusty Miller Pests

The pungently scented, fuzzy silver leaves of dusty miller are unattractive to pests, making this a nearly care-free garden plant.

Dusty Miller Diseases

PROBLEM: Plants wilt; leaves yellow; stems near the soil may rot and have a white, threadlike fungus.

CAUSES: Root and stem rot. Fungal diseases, such as *Rhizoctonia solani* and *Pythium ultimum,* sometimes called damping-off, cause stems to rot at soil level. Pythium root rot (*P.* spp.) causes roots to disappear, leaving little more than a few shriveled, dark roots. These diseases thrive in heavy, poorly drained soils.

WHAT TO DO:
• Destroy infected plants.
• Allow soil to dry out between waterings.
• Incorporate compost into soil to improve drainage and introduce beneficial organisms.

PROBLEM: Powdery, brown spots are on undersides of leaves and on stems. Leaf surfaces get yellow or dark spots.

CAUSE: Rust (*Puccinia cyani* and *P. irrequiseta*). This fungal disease travels on wind and in water, and it thrives in damp weather. Infected plants grow slowly.

WHAT TO DO:
• Remove and dispose of infected leaves.
• Water early in the day.
• Space plants widely for air circulation.
• Spray with sulfur.

PROBLEM: Plants rot at the base and die. On damp days, threads of fungus form on the ground around the plants.

CAUSE: Southern blight or crown rot (*Sclerotium rolfsii*). This fungal disease thrives in warm climates. The disease appears first as a white, threadlike fungus at the base of the plants and then spreads outward across the soil. The threads ooze an acidic fluid that kills plant cells on contact. The spores survive in the soil for years.

WHAT TO DO:
• Dig up infected plants and soil 6 inches beyond the roots, and discard.
• Add compost to the soil.
• Space plants widely for good air circulation.

DUSTY MILLER IS NOT TROUBLED BY MOST COMMON INSECT PESTS

Flowering Tobacco

(Nicotiana alata)

 Flowering Tobacco Pests

PROBLEM: Overnight, seedlings are cut off near the ground. You find the severed plants next to the stem.

CAUSE: Cutworms (Family Noctuidae). These are the larvae of several species of night-flying moths with wingspans of 1½ inches. Cutworms are gray or dull brown caterpillars, 1 to 2 inches long. They eat through seedling stems at night and hide in soil during the day.

WHAT TO DO:

• Handpick. Dig around the base of damaged plants at night, and lift and destroy cutworms.

• Use cutworm collars. Use tin shears to cut 2- to 3-inch-long sections of paper-towel tubes or tin cans; place tubes over seedlings.

• Apply BT granules. "BT" stands for *Bacillus thuringiensis,* an insect-stomach poison that kills caterpillars without harming beneficial insects.

PROBLEM: Your flowering tobacco plants are defoliated. Fat, yellowish beetles with black stripes are on plants.

CAUSE: Colorado potato beetles (*Leptinotarsa decemlineata*). Both the ½-inch-long, yellow-and-black-striped beetles and their larvae eat leaves, stems, and flowers. The fat, ¹⁄₁₆-inch to ½-inch-long, yellow larvae have black dots along their sides. The adults overwinter in garden debris and lay eggs on leaf backs in spring.

WHAT TO DO:

• Destroy eggs.

• Spray nymphs with BTSD. *Bacillus thuringiensis* is an insect-stomach poison that kills caterpillars without harming beneficial insects. *B.t.* var. *san diego* (BTSD) kills beetle grubs.

• Remove debris in fall and cultivate beds so overwintering beetles will be exposed to freezing temperatures

---

PROBLEM: Leaves have small holes in them. Some holes are so small they don't go all the way through the leaves.

CAUSE: Potato flea beetles (*Epitrix cucumeris*). These ¹⁄₁₆-inch-long, shiny black beetles are

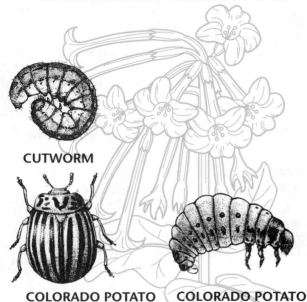

CUTWORM

COLORADO POTATO BEETLE ADULT

COLORADO POTATO BEETLE LARVA

most damaging to seedlings in early spring.

WHAT TO DO:

• Use insecticidal soap, following label directions.

• Make sticky traps. Coat pieces of white cardboard with petroleum jelly, and fasten them to stakes put near plants.

 ## Flowering Tobacco Diseases

PROBLEM: Old leaves close to the ground, or leaves at the tops of plants, have black, tan, or white patches.

CAUSE: Downy mildew (*Peronospora tabacina*). Cool, damp weather encourages this disease. The tops of the plants, where rain and dew accumulate, and the bottom leaves that touch damp soil are where you will see the most damage. If you look on the backs of the leaves opposite the discolored patches, you will see gray fuzz. The disease makes plants unsightly but is rarely fatal.

WHAT TO DO:

• Remove diseased growth when you see signs of infection.

• Space plants widely for adequate air circulation.

PROBLEM: Leaves have purple-rimmed spots. Spots merge; leaves yellow, blacken, and die. Affected plants die.

CAUSE: Leaf spot (*Alternaria longipes*). This fungal disease causes leaves to become covered with black fungus, become distorted, and die at the tip. The spores are spread in splashing rain or irrigation water.

WHAT TO DO:

• Remove and destroy infected plant parts and debris.

• Avoid overhead watering.

• Mulch to prevent splashing spores on plants.

PROBLEM: A powdery, grayish white coating covers leaves, flowers, and stems. Plants usually do not die.

CAUSE: Powdery mildew (*Oidium* sp.). This fungal disease travels on the wind. It thrives in mild temperatures and low light, such as shade, fog, and cloudy days.

WHAT TO DO:

• Cut off and destroy seriously infected plant parts.

• Apply baking soda spray. Dissolve 1 teaspoon baking soda in 1 quart warm water; add 1 teaspoon insecticidal soap to make the solution stick to leaves.

• Water plants regularly during droughts.

• Space plants widely for good air circulation.

PROBLEM: Your flowering tobacco plants wilt and die. When you dig them up, you see that the roots are rotten.

CAUSE: Root rot (*Phymatotrichum omnivorum*). Often the first symptom of this soil-borne fungal disease is that plants appear to stop growing, and the leaves wilt slowly.

WHAT TO DO:

• Improve soil drainage.

• Space plants widely for adequate air circulation.

• Grow flowering tobacco in raised beds.

PROBLEM: New leaves are stiff and crinkled, with an unusual, mottled pattern in dark green, tan, and yellow.

CAUSE: Tobacco mosaic virus. This is a viral disease spread by sap-sucking insects. It can also be spread by gardeners who smoke tobacco (which may host the virus) and then touch flowering tobacco plants. Tobacco mosaic virus slows down the new growth of the plants.

WHAT TO DO:

• Pull and dispose of severely affected plants.

Forget-Me-Nots

(*Myosotis* spp.)

 Forget-Me-Not Pests

PROBLEM: Leaves, buds, and flowers are curled and spotted. Clusters of tiny, pear-shaped insects are on leaves.

CAUSES: Green peach aphids (*Myzus persicae*) and leafcurl plum aphids (*Brachycaudus helichrysi*). Adults are soft-bodied, sap-sucking insects, ¹⁄₁₆ to ³⁄₈ inch long, that are usually green, gray or tan.

WHAT TO DO:
• Wash aphids off with a stream of water.
• Use insecticidal soap, following directions.

PROBLEM: Leaves have small holes in them. Some holes are so small they don't go all the way through the leaves.

CAUSE: Potato flea beetles (*Epitrix cucumeris*). These ¹⁄₁₆-inch-long, shiny black beetles are most damaging in early spring.

WHAT TO DO:
• Use insecticidal soap, following directions.
• Make sticky traps. Coat pieces of white cardboard with petroleum jelly, and fasten them to stakes near the plants.

 Forget-Me-Not Diseases

PROBLEM: Stems and flowers rot, especially during periods of damp, cloudy weather.

CAUSE: Botrytis blight, also called gray mold (*Botrytis cinerea*). This fungal disease travels on wind and thrives in cool, moist weather.

WHAT TO DO:
• Remove and destroy diseased plant parts.
• Space plants widely for air circulation.

PROBLEM: During summer, your forget-me-not plants wilt, turn brown, and appear scalded.

CAUSE: Crown rot (*Sclerotinia sclerotiorum*). This soilborne fungal disease is encouraged by poor soil drainage and wet or very humid, warm weather. It enters plants at the soil line.

WHAT TO DO:
• Discard infected plants and adjacent soil.
• Improve soil drainage.

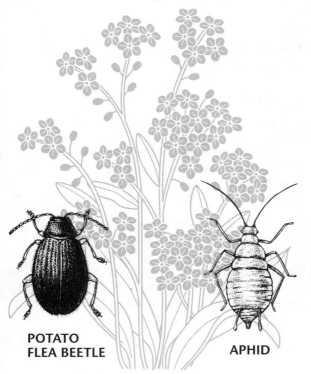

POTATO FLEA BEETLE

APHID

Foxgloves

(*Digitalis purpurea* and other species)

Foxglove Pests

PROBLEM: Leaves and flowers have silvery streaks or specks. They brown and show specks of insect excrement (frass).

CAUSE: Thrips (Order Thysanoptera). These extremely tiny, narrow-bodied insects are only 1/25 inch long. They like to hide deep inside leaf shoots and flowers. Thrips are almost impossible to see on the plant without a magnifying glass. If you suspect a plant has thrips, pick a young shoot or damaged flower and shake it over a clean sheet of white paper; if thrips are present, they will drop onto the paper and will look like dark, moving specks.

WHAT TO DO:

• Pick off and destroy infested plant parts.

• Knock thrips off plants with a strong stream of water.

• Make blue sticky cards. Coat blue cardboard or painted wooden boards with petroleum jelly or Tanglefoot (a commercial product for this purpose), and fasten them to stakes near plants.

• Use insecticidal soap, following label directions.

• Apply neem. This botanical pesticide repels and poisons insect pests but is harmless to beneficial insects.

• Mulch to keep the soil moist.

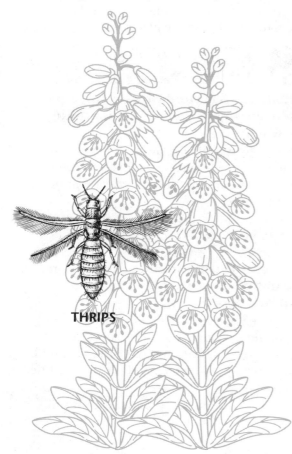

THRIPS

Foxglove Diseases

PROBLEM: Small, irregular-shaped, light brown to purple-brown spots are on leaves. Leaves yellow, shrivel, and drop.

CAUSE: Foxglove anthracnose (*Colletotrichum fuscum*). This fungal disease occurs only on foxgloves. It thrives in warm, moist conditions and is spread by splashing water and contact with tools or gardeners' hands. Seedlings are most susceptible and, if infected, will die. In severe cases, mature plants may die. Foxglove anthracnose overwinters in garden debris.

WHAT TO DO:
- Remove and destroy infected leaves.
- Dispose of debris, especially in the fall to deplete overwintering places for spores.
- Avoid overhead watering.
- Allow the soil to dry out between waterings.

PROBLEM: Plants wilt, often on one side. Watering does not revive them. The leaves have yellow and brown blotches.

CAUSE: Verticillium wilt (*Verticillium alboatrum*). This disease is caused by fungi that live in the soil. Verticillium wilt can survive in the soil for years.

WHAT TO DO:
- Apply liquid fertilizer as soon as symptoms appear. Plants may recover from mild attacks if you give them several applications of fast-acting, liquid fertilizer, following directions.
- Plant new, healthy foxglove plants in a different location.

PROBLEM: Plants turn yellow and wilt. Leaves brown and drop. Plants do not respond to watering and die.

CAUSE: Fusarium wilt (*Fusarium* sp.). This long-lived, soilborne fungal disease is common in warm, wet climates. Infected plants lose their roots. If you cut open the main stem at its base, you will see dark streaks caused by the disease.

WHAT TO DO:
- Remove and destroy infected plants plus the soil that their roots touch.
- Remove garden debris.
- Improve soil drainage.
- Solarize. Clear plastic sheeting placed over bare soil for three to four weeks before planting, early in the season, uses the sun's energy to heat the soil enough to kill most diseases in the top few inches of soil. After removing the plastic, plant foxgloves as usual.

 Other Problems

PROBLEM: They grow well but don't bloom the first season. Or after blooming the second season, they die.

CAUSE: Life cycle changes. Most foxgloves are biennials. This means that the plants grow roots and foliage during their first season, and then they bloom, set seed, and die during their second season.

WHAT TO DO:
- Let some of your foxgloves go to seed each season, as foxgloves will reseed readily and new plants can replace those that die out naturally.
- Plant some of the less common, perennial species, such as small yellow foxglove (*D. lutea*) or strawberry foxglove (*D.* × *mertonensis*).

PROBLEM: Leaves have crisp, dry edges. Some turn brown and drop. Affected plants wilt or die in midsummer.

CAUSE: Drought stress. If foxglove plants dry out a few times during the season, they can recover. But a drought that lasts as long as several days or weeks can permanently weaken and kill the plants.

WHAT TO DO:
- Water plants regularly during hot, dry spells.
- Add organic matter, such as compost, to the soil to increase its ability to retain moisture.
- Mulch to reduce water evaporation from the soil.
- Plant foxgloves in partial to full shade, especially in hot-summer climates, to reduce wilting and soil moisture loss.

Hardy Geraniums

also called Cranesbills (*Geranium* spp.)

Hardy Geranium Pests

PROBLEM: Leaves and flowers are distorted. Leaves that have clear, sticky or moldy patches turn brown and die.

CAUSE: Aphids (Family Aphididae). Adults are $\frac{1}{16}$- to $\frac{3}{8}$-inch-long, soft-bodied insects that range in color from pale tan to light green to nearly black. These little, pear-shaped insects damage plants by sucking plant juices. They can spread diseases as they feed. The sticky honeydew that aphids secrete attracts ants and encourages sooty mold.

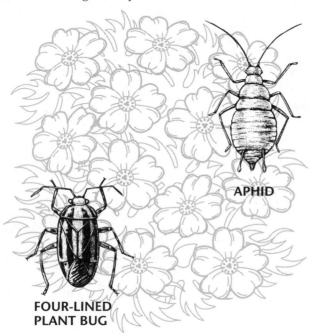

FOUR-LINED PLANT BUG

APHID

WHAT TO DO:
• Tolerate a light infestation.
• Knock aphids off with a strong water spray.
• Wash honeydew or mold off with water.
• Use insecticidal soap, following directions.
• Spray with horticultural oils. These commercial oils smother most pests.
• Attract lady beetles, and other beneficial insects by planting small-flowered nectar plants, such as alyssum and scabiosa.
• Purchase beneficial green lacewings and aphid midges from mail-order sources.

PROBLEM: Leaves and flowers are distorted or dwarfed. They develop yellow, tan, or brown spots in early summer.

CAUSE: Four-lined plant bugs (*Poecilocapsus lineatus*). These sap-sucking pests are $\frac{1}{3}$-inch-long, yellowish green bugs with four black stripes on each wing. In May or June, their eggs hatch into bright red nymphs with a black dot on their chests. Their feeding ends in midsummer. Eggs overwinter in debris.

WHAT TO DO:
• Handpick.
• Spray insecticidal soap on undersides of leaves every third day until pests disappear.
• Clean up garden debris in spring and fall.

PROBLEM: The stems of your hardy geraniums are damaged. They may begin to rot. New stem shoots turn yellow.

CAUSE: Wireworms (Family Elateridae). These

pests are the larvae of slender click beetles. The adults are ⅓- to ¾-inch-long, brown or black beetles with grooved wings. The beetles make a clicking noise when they flip from their backs to their feet. Their shiny brown, jointed, six-legged larvae live underground and can eat hardy geranium roots. The adults eat leaves but do little damage.

WHAT TO DO:
• Trap wireworms by burying pieces of carrots or potatoes. The wireworms will bore into the vegetables. Dig up the vegetables every two or three days, and destroy wireworms you find.
• Apply beneficial nematodes (*Steinernema carpocapsae* and *Heterorhabditis heliothidis*); order these live from mail-order suppliers.
• Grow in well-cultivated beds where grasses have not grown for at least three years.

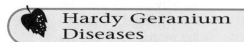

Hardy Geranium Diseases

PROBLEM: There are small spots on geranium leaves. The spots enlarge, and the leaves turn yellow and drop.

CAUSE: Bacterial leaf spot (*Xanthomonas geranii* and *Pseudomonas erodii*). This fungal disease causes leaf spots, followed by yellowing leaves and defoliation. Leaf spot is most severe during rainy periods in the spring. The disease is spread in splashing rain and irrigation water. Leaf spot spores overwinter in garden debris.

WHAT TO DO:
• Cut off and dispose of damaged leaves.
• Remove seriously diseased plants.
• Water plants early in the morning.
• Avoid wetting leaves when watering.
• Allow the soil to dry between waterings.
• Grow hardy geraniums in morning sun.
• Space plants widely for adequate air circulation.
• Wash tools after touching diseased plants.

PROBLEM: The leaves of your hardy geraniums have a white, powdery coating that resists rubbing off.

CAUSE: Powdery mildew (*Erysiphe polygoni* and *Sphaerotheca macularis*). This fungal disease is visible on leaf surfaces; but it is anchored in leaf tissues, making it hard to remove. The disease thrives in cool, damp weather.

WHAT TO DO:
• Pick and destroy infected leaves.
• Water plants in the morning.
• Space plants widely for air circulation.

PROBLEM: Small yellow spots with powdery, orange spores in their centers form on leaves. Leaves yellow.

CAUSE: Rust (*Puccinia* spp. and *Uromyces geranii*). This fungal disease thrives in damp weather. Rust spreads quickly when its spores blow onto damp geranium leaves.

WHAT TO DO:
• Remove and dispose of infected leaves.
• Spray with sulfur.
• Water in the morning; don't splash plants.
• Space or thin plants widely for circulation.
• Remove and compost garden debris.

PROBLEM: Leaves near the ground or leaves at the tops of plants have black, tan, or white patches.

CAUSE: Downy mildew (*Plasmopara geranii*). Cool, damp weather encourages this disease. Most damaged are the top leaves, where rain and dew accumulate, and the bottom leaves, which touch damp soil. If you look on the backs of the leaves opposite the discolored patches, you will see gray fuzz. The disease makes plants unsightly but is rarely fatal.

WHAT TO DO:
• Remove diseased growth when you see signs of infection.
• Space plants widely for air circulation.

Zonal Geraniums

(*Pelargonium* spp. and hybrids)

Geranium Pests

PROBLEM: Leaves are rolled into tubes and tied with webbing. Caterpillars inside the rolls are eating the leaves.

CAUSES: Leafrollers and leaftiers. Leafrollers, including the redbanded leafroller (*Argyrotaenia velutinana*) and the obliquebanded leafroller (*Choristoneura rosaceana*), along with leaftiers, like the celery leaftier (*Udea rubigalis*), can damage geraniums. These caterpillars devour geranium leaves. The similar-looking caterpillars are from ½ to ¾ inch long and can be pale green, brown, or yellow. The pests hatch from eggs laid by adult moths that are active only after dark.

The adult redbanded moths have ¾-inch wingspans and red-striped, brown wings.

Obliquebanded adults are brown moths with three darker brown stripes on their front wings and have wingspans of ¾ inch.

Celery leaftier moths have brown wings with dark, wavy lines and wingspans of ¾ inch.

WHAT TO DO:
• Handpick.
• Remove and destroy the folded leaves where the caterpillars hide.

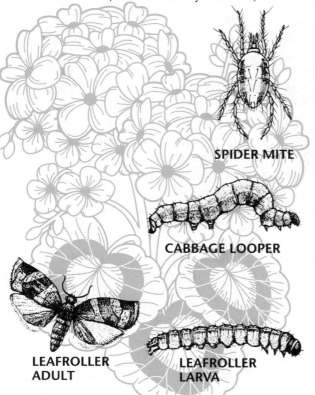

SPIDER MITE

CABBAGE LOOPER

LEAFROLLER ADULT

LEAFROLLER LARVA

PROBLEM: Leaves and flowers are distorted and have clear, sticky or black, moldy patches. Leaves brown and die.

CAUSES: Geranium aphids (*Arcythosiphon pelargonii*) or green peach aphids (*Myzus persicae*). These similar looking pests are ¹⁄₁₆- to ³⁄₈-inch-long, soft-bodied insects. These pear-shaped insects suck plant juices and can transfer viruses as they feed. The sticky substance that aphids secrete, called honeydew, attracts ants and sooty mold.

WHAT TO DO:
• Tolerate a light infestation.
• Knock aphids off plants with a strong spray of water.

• Wash the honeydew or sooty mold off plants with water.

• Use insecticidal soap, following label directions. Be sure to hit the undersides of leaves when spraying, because this is a favorite hiding place for many pests.

• Spray with horticultural oils. These commercial oils coat plant parts and smother all growth stages of most pests.

• Attract parasitic wasps, lady beetles, and other beneficials by planting small-flowered nectar plants, including alyssum and scabiosa.

• Purchase beneficial green lacewings and aphid midges from mail-order sources, and release them to supplement natural populations.

PROBLEM: The leaves of your geraniums have scalloped, chewed edges or holes chewed in the leaves and flowers.

CAUSES: Several species of caterpillars. The tobacco budworm (*Helicoverpa virescens*) and several loopers, including the wide-ranging cabbage looper (*Trichoplusia ni*), are caterpillars that commonly feed on geraniums.

Tobacco budworms are 1½-inch-long, rusty red, or green-striped caterpillars. They are the larvae of small moths with pale green wings with lighter stripes and wingspans of 1½ inches.

Cabbage loopers are the larvae of gray moths with wing markings that make them look like tree bark. The loopers are light green with white stripes on their sides. They raise the center of their bodies up to form a loop.

Plume moth caterpillars are the larvae of small, tan moths with 1-inch wingspans. The ½-inch-long caterpillars are red or yellow-green. At the end of the growing season, these larvae overwinter in the soil.

WHAT TO DO:

• Handpick.

• Spray a solution of BT on plants where young pests are feeding. "BT" stands for *Bacillus thuringiensis*, an insect-stomach poison that kills caterpillars without harming beneficial insects. *B.t.* var. *kurstaki* (BTK) kills budworms, loopers, and other caterpillars.

• Attract parasitic wasps, lady beetles, and other beneficials by growing small-flowered nectar plants, including alyssum, yarrow, dill, and scabiosa.

• Cultivate the soil in fall and winter to kill overwintering pupae.

PROBLEM: Leaves appear stippled and faded. Webbing is visible on the leaves. Plants grow slowly and may be stunted.

CAUSE: Spider mites (Family Tetranychidae). These minute, $\frac{1}{60}$-inch-long pests suck sap from geraniums, especially during hot, dry spells.

WHAT TO DO:

• Knock spider mites off plants with a strong stream of water.

• Water geranium plants well during dry spells.

• Attract predatory wasps and flies and other beneficials by planting small-flowered nectar plants, including yarrow, dill, and Queen-Anne's-lace.

• Attract mite-eating hummingbirds by growing plants with red, trumpet-shaped flowers, like trumpet vine (*Campsis radicans*), wild columbine (*Aquilegia canadensis*), and cardinal flower (*Lobelia cardinalis*).

PROBLEM: Tiny white insects fly up as plants are disturbed. Leaves have black, sooty mold. Plants grow poorly.

CAUSE: Whiteflies (Family Aleyrodidae). These pests are tiny, $\frac{1}{25}$-inch-long, flying white insects. Both the $\frac{1}{20}$-inch-long, translucent nymphs and adult flies are sucking insects that weaken plants when they feed in large numbers. They can transmit diseases as they feed. You are most likely to see them in late summer; whiteflies usually disappear after the first frost.

WHAT TO DO:
• Use insecticidal soap, following label directions.
• Spray with neem, being sure to spray undersides of leaves. Neem is a botanical pesticide that repels and poisons insect pests, but neem is harmless to beneficial insects.
• Spray with summer oil, being sure to spray undersides of leaves. This horticultural oil coats plant parts and smothers pests.
• Water plants well during dry spells.
• Attract predatory wasps and flies and other beneficials by planting small-flowered nectar plants, including yarrow, dill, and Queen-Anne's-lace.
• Make yellow sticky traps. Coat yellow cardboard or painted wooden boards with petroleum jelly or Tanglefoot (a commercial product for this purpose), and then fasten them to stakes near plants.

PROBLEM: Leaves of geraniums are withered and sticky. Fuzzy, white bumps are on stems. Ants crawl over them.

CAUSE: Mealybugs (Family Pseudococcidae). These sap-sucking insects are about $\frac{1}{4}$ inch long when full grown. As they feed, they excrete sticky "honeydew" that attracts ants.

WHAT TO DO:
• Knock mealybugs off geraniums with a strong stream of water.
• Use insecticidal soap, following label directions.
• Attract native parasitic wasps and other beneficial insects by planting small-flowered nectar plants, such as scabiosa and alyssum.

PROBLEM: Holes are chewed in geranium leaves and flowers. The raggedy remains are streaked with slime trails.

CAUSES: Slugs and snails (Order Stylommatophora). These $\frac{1}{8}$- to 8-inch-long, soft-bodied, gray, tan, green, black, yellow, or spotted pests resemble clams and mussels. Snails have shells; slugs look like snails without shells. At night these pests climb the stems of geraniums to feed. During the day they sleep under soil debris. Adults lay jellylike masses of clear eggs under garden debris.

WHAT TO DO:
• Handpick. The best time to begin hunting is two hours after dark.
• Remove mulch and garden debris.
• Create barriers by sprinkling rings of wood ashes or crushed eggshells around plants.
• Make beer traps by filling cans with beer and sinking them to the brim in soil. The pests will be attracted to the smell, fall in, and drown.

 Geranium Diseases

PROBLEM: Growth is stunted. Geraniums wilt, yellow, and die. But you can see no pests or disease spots.

CAUSE: Southern root-knot nematodes (*Meloidogyne incognita* var. *incognita*). These soil-dwelling microscopic worms attack geranium plant roots and cause diseaselike symptoms above ground. They are especially troublesome in sandy soils and in warm-winter climates. Infested roots have knots or swellings.

WHAT TO DO:
• Provide plenty of water and fertilizer.
• Dig compost into garden beds to introduce nematode-fighting beneficial soil organisms.
• Amend soil with crab or shrimp wastes that contain chitin, which stimulates growth of microorganisms that attack nematodes.
• Solarize the soil. Clear plastic sheeting placed over bare soil for three to four weeks uses the sun's energy to heat the soil enough

to kill most pests and weed seeds in the top few inches of soil.

PROBLEM: The leaves of geraniums develop brown or black spots with yellow edges. Leaves drop, and stems rot.

CAUSES: Cercospora leaf spot (*Cercospora brunkii*); alternaria leaf spot (*Alternaria* sp.); bacterial leaf spot (*Xanthomonas pelargonii*). These diseases, which produce similar symptoms, develop during warm, moist weather. They spread from plant to plant on splashing water drops or garden tools and unwashed hands. The diseases overwinter on plant debris left in the garden.

WHAT TO DO:
• Cut off and destroy infected plant parts.
• Discard seriously infected plants along with the soil that their roots touch.
• Remove garden debris.
• Apply new mulch.
• Space plants widely for good air circulation.
• Water plants in the morning, and avoid splashing water on the foliage.

PROBLEM: Geranium stems and flowers rot and develop gray mold, especially in damp, cloudy weather.

CAUSE: Botrytis blight, also called gray mold (*Botrytis cinerea*). This fungal disease travels on wind. It thrives in cool, moist weather.

WHAT TO DO:
• Remove and destroy diseased plant parts.
• Allow the soil to dry between waterings.
• Space plants widely for good air circulation.

PROBLEM: Small, yellow spots form on leaf surfaces. Powdery, orange spores form on undersides. Leaves yellow.

CAUSE: Pelargonium rust (*Puccinia pelargonii-zonalis*). This fungal disease spreads quickly when its spores blow onto damp leaves. The

disease can stunt plant growth.

WHAT TO DO:
• Remove and destroy badly infected leaves or plants.
• Spray infected plants with sulfur.
• Avoid overhead watering.
• Water early in the day so plants will dry out before nightfall.
• Space or thin plants for good air circulation.
• Remove and compost garden debris.

PROBLEM: Mottling, streaking, or abnormally colored patterns mar leaves. Leaves curl, and plants are stunted.

CAUSES: Viral diseases, including pelargonium leaf curl, cucumber mosaic, and beet curly top. Viral diseases can be transmitted by aphids, leafhoppers, and other sucking insects. The diseases enter geraniums through holes made by insect pests. Once infected, there is no cure.

WHAT TO DO:
• Destroy infected plants.
• Inspect container plants for visible signs of viruses before purchasing them.
• Water and fertilize plants as needed to keep them healthy.

 Other Problems

PROBLEM: Your geraniums are pale green, are spindly, and are not producing very many flowers.

CAUSES: Lack of light; too much fertilizer. Geraniums grow best in full sun and in well-drained soil of average to lean fertility.

WHAT TO DO:
• Move plants to a sunnier location, and cut plants back by one-third.
• Allow the soil to dry between waterings.
• Allow potted geraniums to become slightly potbound before replanting.

Gladiolus (Gladiolus spp.)

Gladiolus Pests

PROBLEM: Leaves turn silvery, then brown. Flowers are deformed and spotted. Stored corms darken.

CAUSE: Gladiolus thrips (*Thrips simplex*). These sap-sucking insects are only $\frac{1}{16}$ inch long, and they are very slender. They like to hide deep inside flowers. In cold climates their eggs or larvae cling to corms at digging time, and they overwinter on stored corms, and in the ground in warm climates.

WHAT TO DO:
• Knock thrips off with a stream of water.
• Apply diatomaceous earth (DE). This abra-

sive dust is made from fossilized shells, called diatoms, which penetrate the pests' skins.
• Discard infested corms.
• Disinfect corms before storing them, by soaking the corms in water heated to 120°F for 20 to 30 minutes. Dry the corms. Then dust them with DE before storing them.
• Rotate plantings in warm climates.

PROBLEM: Gladiolus leaves have spots of sticky, clear or black substances. Small, soft-bodied insects huddle on leaves.

CAUSE: Aphids (Family Aphididae). These pests are wedge-shaped, $\frac{1}{16}$- to $\frac{3}{8}$-inch-long insects. Aphids range in color from pale tan to light green to nearly black. Aphids suck sap and produce a sticky secretion called honeydew. Honeydew attracts ants, which protect aphids from predators in order to eat their secretions, and also encourages mold. Aphids can transfer viruses as they feed.

WHAT TO DO:
• Wash aphids off with a stream of water.
• Snip off infested leaves.
• Use insecticidal soap, following directions.
• Attract beneficial insects, such as parasitic wasps and lady beetles, by planting small-flowered nectar plants, including yarrow, alyssum, and scabiosa.
• Pour boiling water into entry holes of anthills that are not adjacent to plant roots.

PROBLEM: The leaves of your gladiolus plants are chewed until they look ragged.

CAUSES: Borers, such as common stalk borers and European corn borers. Borers tunnel through the main stems, from the bottom up.

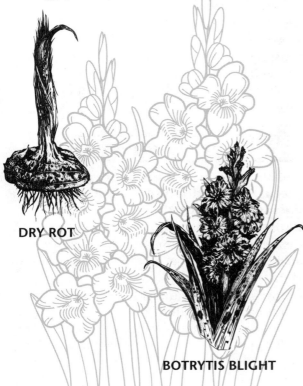

DRY ROT

BOTRYTIS BLIGHT

Common stalk borers (*Papaipema nebris*), when young, are thin, ¾-inch-long, dark brown or purple caterpillars with white stripes. As they mature, the caterpillars become solid brown or purple. The adults are gray or brown moths with white spots on their forewings and wingspans of 1 inch. The eggs overwinter in weeds and garden debris.

European corn borers (*Ostrinia nubilalis*) are 1-inch-long, gray or beige, segmented caterpillars with brown dots on each segment. The adults are pale beige, night-flying moths with 1-inch wingspans. The females have zigzag wing patterns. The males have darker gray wings. The moths lay masses of overlapping white or tan eggs on the leaf backs of young glads plants in early summer.

WHAT TO DO:
• Pull out and dispose of dying plants.
• Remove plant debris and weeds.

PROBLEM: Some glads do not sprout. Some sprout, but their leaves yellow and die early. Corms may rot in storage.

CAUSE: Bulb mites (*Rhizoglyphus echinopus*). These pests are minute, white mites from ⅟₂₅ to ⅟₅₀ inch long. Bulb mites infest rotting corms, or they burrow into healthy ones, causing corms in the ground as well as those in storage to turn brown and rot.

WHAT TO DO:
• Dispose of soft corms.
• Attract beneficials with small-flowered nectar plants, like alyssum and scabiosa.

PROBLEM: The new shoots and new buds have small dark spots. Affected leaves are damaged, or flowers are deformed.

CAUSE: Tarnished plant bugs (*Lygus lineolaris*). These fast-moving, mottled, green or brown bugs are about ¼ inch long. They have a yellow triangle on each side of their body near their back end. The nymphs are yellow-green, and they have five black dots on their bodies. Tarnished plant bugs are very active in early spring, and their population may increase during summer. When they feed, the bugs inject toxic saliva into plants that causes leaves and flowers to become deformed. Adults overwinter in fallen leaves and in garden debris. They emerge in spring.

WHAT TO DO:
• Handpick.
• Use insecticidal soap, following directions.
• Control weeds, and remove garden debris.

 Gladiolus Diseases

PROBLEM: Plants turn yellow, and they die prematurely. Stored corms have reddish spots with sunken centers.

CAUSE: Dry rot (*Stromatinia gladioli*). This soilborne fungal disease causes corms to decay, both in storage and in the ground. Decay moves upward from the bulb, causing leaves to die. Corms planted in cold, wet soil are most susceptible. The disease can survive for ten years or more in the soil.

WHAT TO DO:
• Destroy infected and lightweight corms.
• Plant glads in well-drained soil.
• Air-dry corms after digging, before storing.

PROBLEM: Flowers, leaves, and stalks become spotted. The affected plants look blighted. The corms may rot.

CAUSE: Botrytis blight (*Botrytis gladiolorum*). This fungal disease thrives in spring and in fall, during periods of cool temperatures and high humidity; it also thrives in moderate, moist climates such as the Pacific Northwest.

WHAT TO DO:
• Destroy infected flowers and stems.
• Mulch beds with compost.

Hollyhock

(*Alcea rosea*)

Hollyhock Pests

PROBLEM: Blossoms and buds have brown edges or streaks. Buds do not open properly. Leaves are silvery.

CAUSE: Thrips. Hollyhock thrips (*Liriothrips varicornis*) and gladiolus thrips (*Taeniothrips simplex*) feed on hollyhock flowers. These similar-looking, black or brown, sap-sucking insects are only ¹⁄₁₆ inch long, and they are very slender. They like to hide and feed deep inside flowers and stem crevices. Thrips are more active during dry spells in the growing season. In warm-winter climates, they survive in the soil over winter.

WHAT TO DO:
• Knock thrips off plants with a blast of water.
• Water plants regularly during dry spells.
• Mulch plants.
• Attract parasitic wasps, lady beetles, and other beneficial insects by planting small-flowered nectar plants, including alyssum and scabiosa.
• Purchase green lacewings and beneficial nematodes (*Steinernema carpocapsae* and *Heterorhabditis heliothidis*) from mail-order sources. Release them to supplement natural populations.
• In warm climates, do not plant hollyhocks in beds where thrips were present last season.

PROBLEM: Leaves are chewed between veins. Flowers are completely devoured. You see green-and-copper beetles.

CAUSE: Japanese beetles (*Popillia japonica*). These shiny, ½-inch-long beetles are found throughout the eastern United States, and they are moving westward. Japanese beetles love to eat hollyhock leaves and flowers. They emerge in midsummer, and they can do great damage, focusing their feeding on hollyhocks growing in full sun. Their fat, ½-inch-long, white grubs develop in the soil over winter. In spring, they eat grass roots.

WHAT TO DO:
• Handpick.
• Collect beetles with a hand-held vacuum.

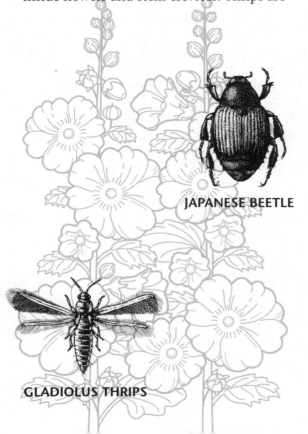

JAPANESE BEETLE

GLADIOLUS THRIPS

• Put a drop cloth under the plant, and shake beetles onto it.
• Use insecticidal soap, following directions.
• Apply milky disease spores to the soil. Milky disease combines spores of *Bacillus popilliae* and *B. lentimorbus*. Grubs eat the spores and die.
• Plant in dappled or half-day shade.

PROBLEM: Leaves are pale green and stippled with tiny yellow or white spots. Fine webbing may be on leaves.

CAUSE: Two-spotted spider mites (*Tetranychus urticae*). These pinpoint-sized, red, spiderlike pests pierce plant leaves in order to suck nutrients. Mites overwinter in leaves on the ground and also in plant crevices. Spider mites feed more during dry spells and more in enclosed areas with stagnant air. The cobwebs protect mite eggs and larvae.

WHAT TO DO:
• Dislodge spider mites with a strong stream of water.
• Use insecticidal soap, following label directions. Begin treatment at the pinprick stage. By the time the webs appear, it may be too late to save some plants.
• Water plants regularly during dry spells.
• Space plants widely for adequate air circulation.

 Hollyhock Diseases

PROBLEM: Purple, yellow, brown, or black spots are on hollyhock leaves. Spots are various shapes and sizes.

CAUSE: Leaf spot. This disease is caused by several fungi and bacteria. Leaf spot thrives in moist or humid weather, and it is most severe during rainy periods in the spring. The disease is spread in splashing rain and irrigation water. The spores of fungal leaf spots overwinter in garden debris.

WHAT TO DO:
• Tolerate light damage.
• Cut off and dispose of damaged leaves.
• Remove seriously diseased plants.
• Water hollyhocks early in the morning so that leaves will dry out before sunset.
• Avoid wetting leaves when watering.
• Allow the soil to dry between waterings.
• Grow them in morning sun.
• Space plants widely for air circulation.
• Wash tools after touching infected plants.

PROBLEM: Small, yellow or orange spots are on stems and on undersides of leaves. Pale areas are on leaf tops.

CAUSE: Rust (*Puccinia* spp. and *Endophyllum tuberculatum*). Spores blow on the wind and travel in splashing water. Rust thrives in damp air. Hollyhocks are very susceptible.

WHAT TO DO:
• Remove and destroy infected leaves.
• Spray infected plants with sulfur.
• Avoid overhead watering.
• Space or thin plants for air circulation.
• Remove the related weed, *Malva neglecta*, since it is a host for rust.

PROBLEM: Plants wilt; watering does not revive them. Strands of fungus form on soil. Plants die over three days.

CAUSE: Texas root rot, also called cotton root rot (*Phymatotrichum omnivorum*). This fungal disease is most common in heavy, alkaline soils. It occurs primarily during summer and early fall in southern states.

WHAT TO DO:
• Remove and destroy diseased plants.
• Add compost to improve the soil.
• Grow hollyhocks as annuals.
• In the South, plant hollyhocks in the fall and remove the plants in early summer.

Hostas

(*Hosta* spp. and hybrids)

Hosta Pests

PROBLEM: Overnight, your hostas are reduced to ragged remains of leaves or flowers streaked with shiny slime.

CAUSES: Slugs and snails (Order Stylommatophora). These pests are ⅛- to 8-inch-long, soft-bodied, gray, tan, green, black, yellow, or spotted insects. They resemble their water-dwelling relatives—clams and mussels. Snails have shells; slugs look like snails without shells. Hostas are one of their favorite foods. At night these slimy pests climb the stems to eat large holes in leaves, stems, and flowers. In the morning they leave behind a trail of shiny slime as they climb down to hide under garden debris. Adults lay masses of clear eggs under garden debris. Damage is usually worst in spring, when plants are small, and damage is also severe during rainy periods.

WHAT TO DO:
• Handpick. The best time to begin hunting is two hours after dark.
• Make barriers by sprinkling rings of wood ashes or crushed eggshells around plants.
• Edge plantings with a strip of copper, which hits these slimy pests with an electrical shock upon contact.
• Make beer traps from recycled cans sunk to the brim in soil and filled with yeasty beer. Attracted by the scent of beer, slugs and snails will fall into the traps and drown.
• Apply diatomaceous earth (DE). This abrasive dust is made of fossilized shells, called diatoms, which penetrate the pests' skin as they crawl over DE. Wear a dust mask to avoid inhaling particles. Apply DE to plants when they are wet.
• Remove mulch and garden debris.

PROBLEM: The leaves and stems of your hostas are speckled with small bumps, and they also have sticky, clear spots.

CAUSE: Florida wax scale (*Ceroplastes floridensis*). These pests are mostly seen in the southern and central states. The ³⁄₁₆-inch-long dark red or brown insects are covered with a white, waxy coating that makes them look solid pink or else pink with darker spots. The

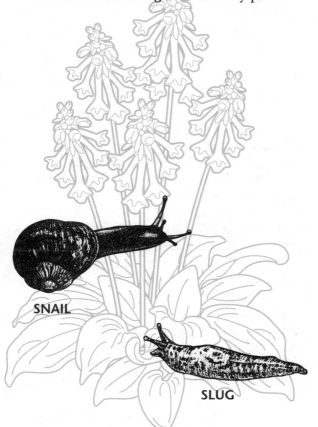

SNAIL

SLUG

adults cover their red eggs with their bodies. Both the tiny, wiggling larvae and the stationary adults damage hostas by sucking plant juices. Adult scale produce sticky honeydew that attracts ants and sooty mildew.

WHAT TO DO:
• Scrape scale off with a plastic scouring pad.
• Attract parasitic wasps and other beneficial insects by growing small-flowered nectar plants, such as scabiosa, yarrow, dill, and Queen-Anne's-lace.
• Pour boiling water into anthills that are not next to plant roots.

 Hosta Diseases

PROBLEM: Leaves turn yellow and plants wilt. Additional watering doesn't help. Fungal strands form at the plant's base.

CAUSES: Crown rot (*Botrytis cinerea* and *Sclerotium rolfsii*) or root rot (*Rhizoctonia solani*). These diseases are caused by soil-dwelling fungi. They are brought on by growing hostas in poorly drained soil, especially during long periods of warm, rainy weather.

WHAT TO DO:
• Remove and destroy diseased plant parts and seriously infected plants.
• Allow the soil to dry between waterings.
• Incorporate compost into the soil to improve drainage.
• Grow hostas in raised beds.
• Space or thin plants widely for circulation.

 Other Problems

PROBLEM: Hosta leaves are turning brown or bleached and dry. Plants may stop growing and have small leaves.

CAUSE: Too much sun. Hostas prefer partial or full shade in all but cool, cloudy climates, such as that of the Northwest. Exposure to full sun in most parts of the United States can bleach, burn, and dry out their leaves.

WHAT TO DO:
• Transplant hostas into a shadier site.
• Mulch plants.
• Water hostas often during dry spells.
• Match the plant to the site. Hosta varieties with variegated leaves can tolerate stronger sunlight than those with golden or blue-green leaves.

PROBLEM: Hostas wilt during the day, but usually recover the following morning. Leaves may be brown.

CAUSE: Lack of water. Hostas grow best in moist, well-drained garden soil. The plants may wilt and recover after short dry spells. But if they are exposed to a drought of several weeks, the plants may become stunted and eventually go dormant or die.

WHAT TO DO:
• Water often enough to keep the soil that hostas grow in evenly moist.
• Mulch to shade the soil and conserve water.
• Incorporate compost or other organic matter to increase moisture retention in the soil.
• Grow hosta varieties with waxy leaves, which are more drought-resistant than those with thin leaves.

PROBLEM: Hostas are growing slowly. Plants are very close together. Plants in the center of the clump may die.

CAUSE: Overcrowding. Young plants come up around the perimeter of the original plant in ever-expanding rings.

WHAT TO DO:
• Divide hostas every five years or when they begin to look overcrowded.
• Replant 6-inch-diameter groups of young plants from outer edges of each clump, and discard aging plants at the center of clumps.

Hyacinth

(Hyacinthus orientalis)

 Hyacinth Pests

PROBLEM: New shoots and young leaves are distorted. Clusters of small, soft insects are on stems and leaf backs.

CAUSE: Aphids (Family Aphididae). Aphids are soft-bodied, $\frac{1}{16}$- to $\frac{3}{8}$-inch-long insects that range in color from pale tan to light green to nearly black. Aphids suck plant juices, and they can transfer plant viruses as they feed. The sticky substance they secrete, called honeydew, attracts ants and encourages the growth of sooty mold. Ants protect aphids from predators in order to eat their honeydew.

WHAT TO DO:
• Tolerate a light infestation.
• Knock aphids off plants with a strong spray of water, and wash honeydew or sooty mold off plants with water.
• Use insecticidal soap, following directions.
• Spray horticultural oil on plants, which will smother all growth stages of most pests. Follow label directions for usage.
• Attract beneficials, such as parasitic wasps and lady beetles, by growing small-flowered nectar plants, like scabiosa and alyssum.

PROBLEM: Hyacinths develop slowly. Leaves yellow and flowers may not appear. Bulbs rot in soil or in storage.

CAUSE: Bulb mites (*Rhizoglyphus echinopus*). These pests are minute, spiderlike, white mites, from $\frac{1}{25}$ to $\frac{1}{50}$ inch long. Bulb mites infest rotting or healthy corms. They cause corms growing in the ground, as well as those in storage, to turn brown and then rot.

WHAT TO DO:
• Dispose of soft corms.
• Attract predaceous mites and other beneficial insects by planting small-flowered nectar plants, such as alyssum and scabiosa.

 Hyacinth Diseases

PROBLEM: Leaf stems are swollen. Leaf blades are stunted and streaked with yellow. Affected plants fail to flower.

CAUSE: Stem and bulb nematodes (*Ditylenchus dipsaci*). These minute, soil-

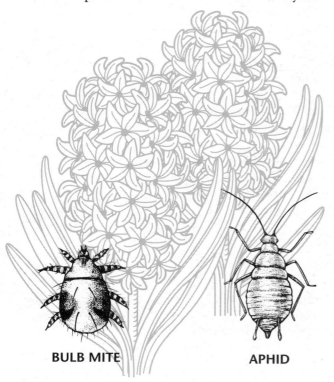

BULB MITE　　**APHID**

dwelling worms that cause diselike symptoms can burrow into bulbs at the base of the leaves. They travel through the soil to invade nearby bulbs. When the soil and foliage are dry, nematodes are less troublesome than under moist conditions. Nematodes travel in running water, and they can be carried on contaminated tools and dirty hands. Harmful nematodes overwinter in weeds.

WHAT TO DO:
• Dig up and destroy infested plants.
• Solarize the soil by placing clear plastic sheeting over bare soil for three to four weeks. The sun's energy will heat the soil enough to kill most pests and weed seeds.
• Work compost into beds before planting.

PROBLEM: Plants grow normally for a while, then leafstalks develop discolored spots that rot. They fail to flower.

CAUSE: Bacterial soft rot (*Erwinia carotovora*). Soilborne bacteria cause soft rot in hyacinths. As the disease progresses, the leaves turn prematurely yellow or light green. The plants wilt on warm days, and they are unable to flower. Eventually they die.

WHAT TO DO:
• Remove and destroy diseased plants.
• Allow the soil to dry out between waterings.
• Incorporate organic matter into the soil.
• Compost garden debris.
• Buy bulbs that show no signs of shriveling, softness, or rotting.
• Space plants widely for air circulation.

PROBLEM: Hyacinth leaves and flowers rot. The affected plant parts may develop gray mold or small black specks.

CAUSE: Botrytis blight, also called gray mold (*Botrytis hyacinthi* and *B.* sp.). This soilborne fungal disease appears often in cool, wet weather. Spores travel on the wind or water.

WHAT TO DO:
• Remove and destroy infected plant parts, and remove severely infected plants.
• Avoid overhead watering.
• Allow the soil to dry out between waterings.
• Clean up plant debris.
• Incorporate compost, or other organic matter, to improve soil drainage.
• Space plants widely for good air circulation.

PROBLEM: Pale streaks are in leaves or flowers. The leaves of some plants wilt and fall over prematurely.

CAUSE: Ornithogalum mosaic virus. Infected plants produce small bulbs. This viral disease is transmitted by sap-sucking insects.

WHAT TO DO:
• Knock insects off plants with a water spray.
• Use insecticidal soap, following directions.
• Dig up bulbs, and replant only the largest ones. Discard small, soft, or deformed bulbs.

 Other Problems

PROBLEM: Your hyacinths are growing slowly and have few flowers. The flower clusters are sparse.

CAUSES: Aging plants and overcrowded plants. Young bulbs develop around the original plant in ever-expanding rings. After about five years, the plants at the center of each clump can be crowded out by the surrounding plants. Hybrid hyacinths are bred to produce flower clusters with tightly spaced florets. Newer generations can display flowers with the more open shape of wild hyacinths.

WHAT TO DO:
• Divide hyacinths every five years or when they begin to look overcrowded. Replant 6-inch-diameter groups of young plants taken from the outer edges of each clump. Discard the aging plants at the center of the clumps.

Impatiens

(Impatiens spp.)

Impatiens Pests

PROBLEM: New impatiens shoots and buds have dark spots. The affected leaves or flowers are also deformed.

CAUSE: Tarnished plant bugs (*Lygus lineolaris*). These fast-moving, mottled green or brown bugs are about ¼ inch long. They have a yellow triangle on each side of their bodies, near the back. The young nymphs are yellow-green with five black dots. When they feed, tarnished plant bugs inject toxic saliva into plants, which causes their leaves and

flowers to become deformed. Branch tips may also blacken and die. Adults overwinter either in fallen leaves or in garden debris.

WHAT TO DO:
- Handpick.
- Use insecticidal soap, following directions.
- Remove garden weeds and debris.

PROBLEM: Leaves are stippled and faded. Webbing disfigures leaves and flowers. Plant growth may become stunted.

CAUSE: Spider mites (Family Tetranychidae). These pinpoint-sized, spiderlike pests pierce plant leaves to suck nutrients. The mites feed more during dry spells. Their cobwebs protect eggs and hatchlings. Spider mites overwinter in leaves on the ground and in plant crevices.

WHAT TO DO:
- Dislodge spider mites with a strong stream of water.
- Use insecticidal soap, following label directions. Begin treatment at the pinprick stage.

PROBLEM: New growth is distorted. Clusters of small insects congregate on stems and leaves.

CAUSE: Aphids (*Macrosiphum impatientis; M. impatiensicolens; Aphis impatientis*). These pests are sap-sucking, soft-bodied insects, 1/16 to 3/8 inch long. Aphids range in color from pale tan to light green to nearly black. Aphids can spread disease as they feed. The sticky honeydew they secrete can attract ants, which protect aphids from predators in order to eat their secretions, and it encourages the growth of sooty black mold.

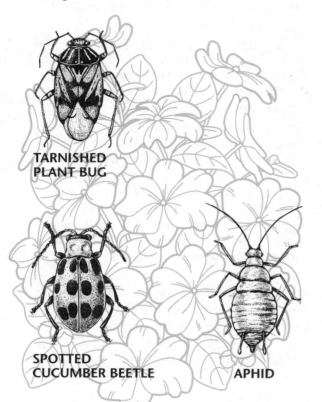

TARNISHED PLANT BUG

SPOTTED CUCUMBER BEETLE

APHID

WHAT TO DO:
- Tolerate light damage.
- Wash aphids off with a stream of water.
- Use insecticidal soap, following directions.
- Attract beneficial insects, like lady beetles and lacewings, by planting small-flowered nectar plants, including yarrow and Queen-Anne's-lace.
- Pour boiling water into anthills not adjacent to plant roots.

PROBLEM: The leaves and flowers of your impatiens are eaten by greenish yellow beetles with black spots.

CAUSE: Spotted cucumber beetles (*Diabrotica undecimpunctata* var. *howardi*). These beetles are about ¼ inch long. As they feed, the beetles can spread diseases.

WHAT TO DO:
- Handpick.
- Plant cucumbers to lure the beetles away.
- Purchase beneficial nematodes (*Steinernema carpocapsae* and *Heterorhabditis heliothidis*) from mail-order suppliers, and apply to the soil. Live nematodes are shipped suspended in gels or sponges.

 Impatiens Diseases

PROBLEM: Plant growth is stunted. Impatiens wilt. The leaves and stems turn yellow. The plants slowly die.

CAUSE: Southern root-knot nematodes (*Meloidogyne incognita* var. *incognita*). Nematodes are actually microscopic worms that live in the soil. They attack roots, causing symptoms above ground that are similar to those of wilt diseases. To check for root-knot nematodes, pull up a wilting plant, and look at its roots. Infested roots will have knots and excessive root branching.

WHAT TO DO:
- Help infested plants resist further damage by watering and fertilizing regularly.
- Turn under compost to introduce nematode-attacking beneficial soil organisms.
- Apply crab or shrimp wastes that contain chitin. Chitin, made from shellfish shells, provides nitrogen and potassium as it breaks down, creating conditions that encourage beneficial soil organisms.
- Solarize the soil. Place clear plastic sheeting over bare soil for three to four weeks to use the sun's energy to heat the soil enough to kill most pests and weed seeds in the top few inches of soil. After removing the plastic, plant crops as usual.
- In regions where nematode problems are severe, grow impatiens in containers.

PROBLEM: Your impatiens plants wilt when soil is moist or when weather is warm. Water won't revive them.

CAUSE: Bacterial wilt (*Pseudomonas solanacearum* and others). These similarly acting soilborne diseases thrive in warm weather. They enter plants through wounds.

WHAT TO DO:
- Remove and destroy infected plants, along with the soil that their roots touch.
- Plant in well-drained soil, and mulch plants with compost.
- Avoid overcrowding or overwatering plants.
- Remove garden debris.

 Other Problems

PROBLEM: Impatiens are not growing well. They may looked bleached, have crisp brown leaves, and wilt in hot sun.

CAUSE: Too much sun. Garden impatiens (*I. wallerana*) grow best in partial to full shade.

WHAT TO DO:
- Transplant them to a shadier location.
- Water plants during hot, dry spells.
- Grow them in humus-rich, moist soil.

Irises

(*Iris* spp. and hybrids)

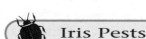

Iris Pests

PROBLEM: Leaves have pinholes or streaks or are chewed. Sawdust appears at the base of rhizomes, which later rot.

CAUSE: Iris borers (*Macronoctua onusta*). These pink caterpillars with brown heads are the larvae of a night-flying moth. The 1-inch-long young caterpillars tunnel through leaves. After reaching the rhizomes, the caterpillars reach lengths of 1½ to 2 inches. The adult moths have a wingspan of 2 inches. The moths have dark purple forewings and yellow-brown hind wings. Iris borer damage often leads to bacterial soft rot disease. The borers do not attack pond-side irises that have their rhizomes fully submerged under water. Borers overwinter in the soil.

WHAT TO DO:
• Remove and destroy infested leaves, and dig up and destroy damaged rhizomes.
• Kill borers in rhizomes by digging up each rhizome and inserting a wire into the tunnel. Dust the infested rhizomes with sulfur (wear a mask) after removing the larvae. Then re-plant the treated rhizomes.
• Purchase beneficial nematodes (*Steinernema carpocapsae* and *Heterorhabditis heliothidis*) from mail-order suppliers. Live nematodes are shipped suspended in sponges or gels. Apply beneficial nematodes as directed, when the borers are present.
• Cover the soil around the rhizomes with fabric weed cloth to keep the borers from reaching the soil; this prevents completion of the borer life cycle.
• Plant resistant iris species, such as Siberian iris (*I. sibirica*) and its many colorfully flow-ered cultivars.

IRIS BORER LARVA

IRIS BORER ADULT

THRIPS

SLUG

PROBLEM: Overnight, irises are reduced to ragged remains of leaves and flowers streaked with shiny slime trails.

CAUSES: Slugs and snails (Order Stylom-matophora). These are ⅛- to 8-inch-long, soft-bodied pests. They can be gray, tan, green, black, yellow, or spotted, and they resemble clams and mussels. Snails have shells; slugs look like snails without shells. At night these pests climb up iris stems to feed. In the morning they leave behind a trail of shiny slime as they climb down to hide under garden debris. Adults lay masses of eggs under mulch and garden debris.

WHAT TO DO:

• Handpick. The best time to begin hunting is two hours after dark.

• Remove mulch and garden debris, which provide these pests with hiding places.

• Sprinkle rings of wood ashes or crushed eggshells around flowerbeds or individual plants.

• Edge plants with a strip of copper, which hits these slimy pests with an electrical shock upon contact.

• Make beer traps from recycled cans sunk to the brim in soil and filled with yeasty beer. Attracted by the scent of beer, slugs and snails will fall into the containers of beer and drown.

• Apply diatomaceous earth (DE). This abrasive dust is made from fossilized shells, called diatoms, which penetrate the pests' skins as they crawl over DE.

PROBLEM: Leaves and flowers have brown or silvery streaks or speckling. They may be distorted.

CAUSE: Thrips (Order Thysanoptera). These extremely tiny, narrow-bodied insects are only ¹⁄₂₅ inch long. Thrips like to hide deep inside the leaf shoots, and they also hide in the flowers of irises. If you suspect that a plant has thrips, pick a damaged shoot or flower and shake it over a clean sheet of white paper. If thrips are present, they will drop onto the paper, and the mites will look like dark specks moving around on the paper.

WHAT TO DO:

• Knock thrips off plants with a strong stream of water.

• Use insecticidal soap, following label directions.

• Spray with neem. This botanical pesticide repels and poisons insect pests but is harmless to beneficial insects.

• Attract beneficial insects, which will reduce thrips populations, by growing small-flowered nectar plants, including alyssum, scabiosa, yarrow, and Queen-Anne's-lace.

• You can also attract beneficials by spraying garden plants with commercial "bug food," which you can order from mail-order sources, or set out shallow pans of sugar-water to attract beneficials.

• Mulch plants to attract beneficial beetles and spiders.

 Iris Diseases

PROBLEM: Leaves die from the tip downward. They turn yellow, then brown, and rot. Affected plants smell foul.

CAUSE: Bacterial soft rot (*Erwinia carotovora*). This soilborne bacterial disease thrives in damp weather. It is spread in splashing rain and by contact with contaminated tools or hands. The bacterium enters plants through injured tissue. Bacterial soft rot often follows damage done by the larvae of night-flying moths called iris borers. Infected rhizomes are dry on the surface, but inside they are filled with wet, foul-smelling, decaying tissue.

WHAT TO DO:

• Remove and destroy infected plants, along with the soil that their roots touch.

• Disinfect tools with rubbing alcohol or a 10 percent solution of household chlorine bleach.

• Wash your hands after handling infected

plants to keep from spreading the disease.
• Dig up and dust rhizomes with sulfur.
• Plant irises in well-drained soil, in raised beds, and in full sun.
• Control iris borers, which can spread disease, by inserting a piece of wire into their tunnels to kill them.

PROBLEM: White strands of fungus form on soil at the base of irises. The leaves turn yellow, and then the plants wilt.

CAUSE: Crown rot, also called southern blight (*Sclerotium rolfsii*). This fungal disease is most common in warm climates, but it can also be brought on by overcrowding plants. The spores can live in soil for many years. When the fungal threads form around the base of plants, they ooze an acidic fluid that kills plant cells on contact.

WHAT TO DO:
• Dig up and discard the infected plants and soil 6 inches beyond their roots.
• Add compost to the soil to increase drainage and to encourage the growth of beneficial soil organisms.
• When planting, space iris plants widely for good air circulation.

PROBLEM: Tiny, tan spots with reddish borders disfigure leaves. The area around the spots is yellow and watery.

CAUSE: Didymellina leaf spot (*Didymellina macrospora*). This fungal disease is at its worst in wet weather. The spores overwinter on plant debris.

WHAT TO DO:
• Cut off and destroy infected plant parts to keep from spreading disease.
• Discard seriously infected plants along with the soil that their roots touch.
• Remove garden debris.
• Apply new mulch.
• Space plants widely for good air circulation.

• Water irises only in the morning; avoid splashing water on plants to keep from giving spores ideal conditions for speading.
• Spray infected plants weekly with sulfur.

PROBLEM: Small, powdery, rust-colored spots on the undersides of leaves turn dark brown. Pale areas are on leaf tops.

CAUSE: Rust (*Puccinia* spp.). This fungal disease thrives in damp weather. The spores spread quickly on wind and in splashing water. As the disease progresses, leaves die and plants stop growing.

WHAT TO DO:
• Remove and discard infected leaves.
• Spray plants with sulfur.
• Avoid overhead watering.
• Grow hybrids, which seem to be less susceptible than native species irises.
• Space or thin plants for adequate air circulation.
• Remove and dispose of old iris leaves in the fall.

 Other Problems

PROBLEM: After several seasons of healthy growth and flowering, clumps of your plants die out in the center.

CAUSE: Overcrowding. Like many perennials, irises reproduce by sending up young plants from the perimeter of the original plant in ever-expanding rings. After about five years, the plants at the center of original clumps can become nutrient-starved by the surrounding plants.

WHAT TO DO:
• Divide irises every five years or when they appear overcrowded. To do so, cut through rhizomes. Replant clumps with several growth points and roots, and discard the aging center of the rhizome clumps.

Lamb's-Ears

(Stachys byzantina)

 Lamb's-Ears Pests

This herb is not usually troubled by pests and is even reported to be deer-resistant.

 Lamb's-Ears Diseases

PROBLEM: The leaves of your lamb's-ears plants wilt and turn brown. The plants rot at the crown.

CAUSES: Crown rot or root rot. These diseases with similar symptoms are caused by various soilborne fungi. They are encouraged by poor soil drainage and wet, warm weather. Infections enter the plants at the soil line.

WHAT TO DO:

• Remove and discard infected plants along with the soil that their roots touch.
• Pull mulch or debris away from plants.
• Avoid overhead watering.

LAMB'S-EARS IS NOT TROUBLED BY MOST COMMON INSECT PESTS

• Allow the soil to dry between waterings.
• Improve soil drainage by incorporating compost or other organic matter into the soil.
• Plant lamb's-ears in raised beds.

PROBLEM: A powdery, white coating covers leaves, flowers, and stems. Affected plants usually do not die.

CAUSE: Powdery mildew (*Erysiphe galeopsidis; Sphaerotheca macularis*). Spores of this fungal disease travel on the wind. Powdery mildew thrives in mild temperatures, and it is also a problem in shady areas and on foggy or cloudy days.

WHAT TO DO:

• Cut off and destroy infected plant parts.
• Apply baking soda spray. Dissolve 1 teaspoon baking soda in 1 quart warm water; add 1 teaspoon insecticidal soap.
• Water plants regularly during droughts.
• Space plants widely for good air circulation.

 Other Problems

PROBLEM: The leaves of your previously healthy lamb's-ears begin to rot during wet or humid conditions.

CAUSE: Lamb's-ears have furry-textured leaves that trap droplets of water. The leaves cannot dry out properly in hot, humid conditions, when they are watered overhead, or during long periods of rainy weather.

WHAT TO DO:

• Avoid overhead watering.
• Plant lamb's-ears in full sun and well-drained soil.

Larkspur

also called Rocket (*Consolida ambigua*)

 Larkspur Pests

PROBLEM: There are tan, winding trails on the leaves of your larkspurs, but the marks do not turn into holes.

CAUSE: Larkspur leafminers (*Phytomyza* spp.). These tiny maggots, which are the larvae of tiny flies, feed inside larkspur leaves. The miners tunnel in groups between the upper and lower surfaces of larkspur leaves, eating as they go. The leafminers emerge from the leaves to pupate in the soil.

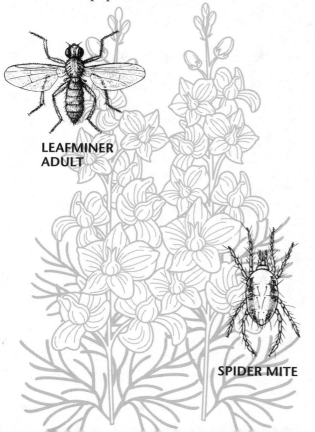

LEAFMINER ADULT

SPIDER MITE

WHAT TO DO:
• Remove and destroy infested leaves promptly.
• Clean up and destroy fallen leaves.
• Treat soil with beneficial nematodes (*Steinernema carpocapsae* and *Heterorhabditis heliothidis*), which you can purchase from mail-order suppliers. Live nematodes are shipped suspended in gels or sponges.

PROBLEM: Plants are distorted. Leaves may turn yellow or brown. Small, pear-shaped insects cluster on plants.

CAUSE: Aphids (Family Aphididae), including delphinium aphid (*Brachycaudus rociadae*) and green peach aphid (*Myzus persicae*). These similar-looking pests are $\frac{1}{16}$- to $\frac{3}{8}$-inch-long, soft-bodied insects. They range in color from pale tan to light green to nearly black. Aphids damage leaves and stems by sucking plant juices. Aphids can transmit plant diseases as they feed. Their sticky secretions, called honeydew, attract sooty mold and ants, which protect aphids from predators in order to eat their secretions.

WHAT TO DO:
• Wash aphids off with a blast of water.
• Use insecticidal soap, following directions.
• Attract beneficial insects, like lady beetles and lacewings, by planting small-flowered nectar plants, including yarrow, dill, and Queen-Anne's-lace. Give the beneficials time to bring the aphids under control.
• Pour boiling water into entry holes of anthills that are not adjacent to larkspur roots.

PROBLEM: The leaves of your larkspurs are chewed ragged. Their stalks wilt and fall over on the ground.

CAUSES: Burdock borers (*Papaipema cataphracta*) and common stalk borers (*P. nebris*). Borers tunnel through main stems of ornamentals like larkspur, eating from the bottom up. Eggs overwinter in weeds and debris.

When young, common stalk borers are thin, ¾-inch-long, dark brown or purple caterpillars with white stripes. As they mature, they become solid brown or purple. Adults are gray or brown moths with white spots on their forewings and 1-inch wingspans.

Burdock borers are 1- to 2-inch-long, pale brown caterpillars with white stripes on their backs and sides. They are the larvae of several species of night-flying cutworm moths (Family Noctuidae).

WHAT TO DO:
• Slit the stem lengthwise and remove the borer. Tape the stem together with masking tape until it heals.
• Pull out and dispose of dying plants.
• Remove debris and weeds, such as ragweed.

PROBLEM: Flower buds and leaves are thickened, curled, and twisted. Brown spots appear in streaks on plant stems.

CAUSE: Cyclamen mites (*Phytonemus pallidus*). These mites are spider relatives that are so tiny (only ¹⁄₁₀₀ inch long) that you can see them only by using a magnifying glass. They are usually found deep in the flower buds, and they also hide in unexpanded leaves. Cyclamen mites are most active during the cool weather of spring and fall. They spread from plant to plant by crawling across leaves.

WHAT TO DO:
• Destroy infested plants.
• Wash your hands and tools after working with infested plants.

• Space plants far enough apart to keep them from touching.

PROBLEM: Leaves appear stippled and faded. Webbing covers leaves. Plants grow slowly and may become stunted.

CAUSE: Spider mites (Family Tetranychidae). These pinpoint-sized, spiderlike pests pierce plant leaves to suck nutrients. The mites feed more during dry spells. Their cobwebs protect eggs and hatchlings. Spider mites overwinter in leaves on the ground, or they find shelter in plant crevices.

WHAT TO DO:
• Dislodge spider mites with a blast of water.
• Use insecticidal soap, following directions. Begin treatment early, at the pinprick stage.
• Attract mite-eating hummingbirds by growing plants with red, trumpet-shaped flowers, like trumpet vine (*Campsis radicans*), wild columbine (*Aquilegia canadensis*), and cardinal flower (*Lobelia cardinalis*).

 Larkspur Diseases

PROBLEM: During cool, wet weather, irregular, shiny black spots appear on tops of leaves that grow near the soil.

CAUSE: Bacterial black spot (*Pseudomonas syringae* pv. *delphinii*). This soilborne bacterial disease travels in splashing water and enters plants through pores. The disease overwinters in soil and debris.

WHAT TO DO:
• Cut off and dispose of damaged leaves.
• Spray with bordeaux mix, a wettable combination of copper sulfate and hydrated lime.
• Remove seriously diseased plants.
• Apply mulch to keep spores from splashing onto plants.
• Water plants early in the morning.
• Avoid wetting leaves when watering.

Lilies

(Lilium spp.)

Lily Pests

PROBLEM: Lilies have abnormally curled leaves. Flowers may become distorted. Small insects cluster on affected plants.

CAUSE: Several species of aphids (Family Aphididae). Aphids are $\frac{1}{16}$- to $\frac{3}{8}$-inch-long, soft-bodied insects. They range in color from pale tan to light green to nearly black. Aphids damage leaves and stems by sucking plant juices. These insects can transmit plant diseases as they feed. Their sticky secretions, called honeydew, attract ants, which protect aphids from predators in order to eat their secretions; and the secretions encourage the growth of sooty mold.

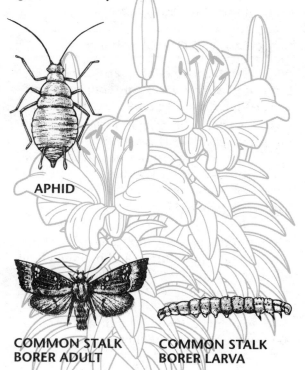

APHID

COMMON STALK
BORER ADULT

COMMON STALK
BORER LARVA

WHAT TO DO:
• Wash aphids off plants with a strong stream of water.
• Use insecticidal soap, following label directions. Be sure to spray the backs of leaves, where aphids hide.
• Attract lady beetles, lacewings, and other beneficial insects by planting small-flowered nectar plants, including yarrow, dill, and Queen-Anne's-lace. Give the beneficials time to bring the aphids under control.
• Pour boiling water into entry holes of anthills that are not adjacent to plant roots.

PROBLEM: Holes suddenly appear in lily leaves. There are slimy black larvae or bright red beetles near damaged leaves.

CAUSE: Red lily leaf beetles (Family Chrysomelidae). This European pest recently invaded the New England states. Although the population is localized, where they exist these pests are a serious threat to lilies. The $\frac{1}{2}$-inch-long adults are bright red with black legs. They lay orange eggs on the undersides of leaves.

WHAT TO DO:
• Handpick.
• Spray with neem. This botanical pesticide repels and poisons insect pests, including red lily leaf beetles, but is harmless to beneficial insects.

PROBLEM: The leaves of your lilies are chewed ragged. Their stalks are wilting and falling over.

CAUSE: Common stalk borers (*Papaipena. nebris*). Young common stalk borers are thin,

¾-inch-long, brown or purple caterpillars with white stripes. As they mature, they become solid brown or purple. The adults are gray or brown moths with white spots on their forewings, and they have wingspans of 1 inch. Borers tunnel through the main stems of ornamentals like lilies, eating from the bottom up. Their eggs overwinter in weeds and garden debris.

WHAT TO DO:
• Slit each infested stem lengthwise and remove the borer. Then tape the stem together with masking tape until the wound heals, then remove the tape.
• Pull out and dispose of infested and dying plants.
• Remove plant debris and weeds, such as ragweed.

PROBLEM: Your lilies have few flowers. Rhizomes have soft necks and small holes. Plants may have white offsets.

CAUSE: Narcissus bulb flies (*Merodon equestris*). These flies look like yellow-and-brown bumblebees. They lay eggs at the base of lily leaves, and their hatching larvae bore into bulbs where they feed.

WHAT TO DO:
• Pull off yellowing foliage.
• When digging bulbs, discard infested ones.

 ### Lily Diseases

PROBLEM: Leaves are mottled with light and dark green. The affected lily plants may grow slowly and become stunted.

CAUSES: Viral diseases are incurable diseases that can distort, stunt, and eventually kill lily plants. Yellowing lower leaves signal a severe infection. Viral diseases are spread via sucking insects, such as aphids.

WHAT TO DO:
• Remove and destroy severely infected plants.
• Spray plants with insecticidal soap to control insects. Be sure to spray the backs of leaves, where pests hide.
• Keep plants well watered and fertilized to help them resist insect attacks.

PROBLEM: The lower leaves of your lilies are limp and turning black. Gray mold develops on the infected plant parts.

CAUSE: Lily Botrytis blight (*Botrytis elliptica*). This fungal disease travels from plant to plant in wind and splashing water or on dirty tools and hands; it spreads rapidly in cool, moist weather. It overwinters in dead leaves and stems. The blight begins as orange to reddish brown leaf spots that are sometimes watersoaked. Flower buds rot or open into distorted flowers with irregular brown flecks. Leaves can blacken and drop. Stems are sometimes infected, but the disease rarely affects bulbs.

WHAT TO DO:
• Remove and destroy all infected plant parts.
• Wash your hands and tools after handling infected plants to keep from spreading the disease.
• Avoid overhead watering.
• Clean up plant debris.
• Incorporate compost or other organic matter into the soil to improve drainage.
• Space plants widely for good air circulation.

PROBLEM: Your lilies suddenly wilt and die. If you dig them up, you discover that their roots are rotten.

CAUSE: Root rot (*Pythium* spp.; *Rhizoctonia solani*). This fungal disease causes plants to stop growing, and the leaves wilt slowly. Root rot also can develop in poorly drained soil or where the soil's pH is too acidic. Fungi build up in the soil, causing this disease.

WHAT TO DO:
• Incorporate compost or other organic matter into the soil to improve drainage.
• Space plants widely for good air circulation.

PROBLEM: Lily plants rot at the base and die. On damp days, threads of fungus grow on the ground around the plants.

CAUSE: Southern blight or crown rot (*Sclerotium rolfsii*). This fungal disease thrives in warm climates. The disease appears first as a white, threadlike fungus at the base of lily plants and then spreads outward across the soil. The threads ooze an acidic fluid that kills plant cells on contact, eventually killing entire plants. The spores survive in the soil for years.

WHAT TO DO:
• Dig up and destroy infected plants and soil 6 inches beyond the roots.
• Improve soil drainage by incorporating compost into the soil.

 Other Problems

PROBLEM: Healthy lily plants blow over in strong wind. They then grow with crooked stalks or break off at the base.

CAUSE: Top-heavy plants. Lilies are naturally tall, thin plants. Their brittle stems are topped with big flowers that act as sails to collect the wind, which can cause the entire plant to topple.

WHAT TO DO:
• Stake tall plants and those that grow in windy sites. When staking, insert the stake near the stem but far enough from the plant to prevent piercing the bulb. Tie the stem of the lily loosely to the stake with inconspicuous green strings.

PROBLEM: After several seasons of lush growth and abundant flowering, your lilies either flower less or stop blooming.

CAUSE: Overcrowding. Lilies will produce new bulbs, from which grow new plants. As each clump of lilies grows in diameter, the plants in the center of the clump become crowded and starved of light and nutrients, causing them to become less productive.

WHAT TO DO:
• Lift and divide lilies every three or four years or when the clumps become crowded. Divide the bulbs in late summer, as the plants are going dormant.
• When dividing lilies, separate the bulbs that grow on the outer edges of each clump. Discard the bloomed-out center plants and replant the young bulbs 1 to 1½ feet apart.

PROBLEM: Your lilies grew well all summer and flowered. The plants did not come back after the winter.

CAUSE: Wet soil; freezing temperatures. Soil that remains wet in winter can cause the roots and bulbs of lilies to rot. If the winter temperatures are too cold, lilies could suffer fatal frost damage.

WHAT TO DO:
• Grow lilies in well-drained but rich soil.
• Make sure water does not stand on the soil in winter.
• In cold climates, protect plant roots in winter with a thick, fluffy organic mulch.

PROBLEM: The leaf tips and edges of your lilies begin to turn brown. The lower leaves are affected first.

CAUSE: Leaf scorch. This condition is most likely to appear in beds with acidic soil. Lilies are most affected during periods of rapid plant growth and temperature fluctuations.

WHAT TO DO:
• Test your garden soil for acidity. Apply limestone as needed to neutralize the soil.

Lily-of-the-Valley

(Convallaria majalis)

Lily-of-the-Valley Pests

PROBLEM: Seemingly overnight, plants are reduced to ragged leaves and flowers streaked with slime trails.

CAUSES: Slugs and snails (Order Stylommatophora). These pests are $\frac{1}{8}$ to 8 inches long. The soft-bodied, gray, tan, green, black, yellow, or spotted pests resemble clams and mussels. Snails have shells; slugs look like snails without shells. At night they climb up the stems of lilies-of-the-valley to feed on leaves. Adults lay masses of clear eggs under debris.

WHAT TO DO:
• Handpick. Begin two hours after dark.
• Remove mulch and garden debris.
• Allow the soil to dry out between waterings.
• Sprinkle ashes or eggshells around plants.

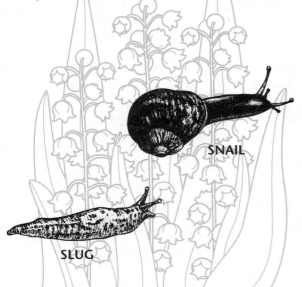

SNAIL

SLUG

• Edge plants with a strip of copper, which hits these pests with an electrical shock.
• Make beer traps from recycled cans sunk to the brim in soil and filled with yeasty beer. Slugs and snails will fall in and drown.
• Dust plants with diatomaceous earth (DE), an abrasive dust made from fossilized shells, called diatoms, which penetrate pests' skin.

Lily-of-the-Valley Diseases

PROBLEM: Plants rot at the base. On damp days, threads of fungus grow on the soil around the plants.

CAUSE: Southern blight, also called crown rot (*Sclerotium rolfsii*). This fungal disease thrives in warm climates. The disease appears first as a white, threadlike fungus at the base of plants. Spores last in the soil for years.

WHAT TO DO:
• Dig up and discard infected plants, along with soil 6 inches beyond their roots.
• Incorporate compost into the soil.
• Space plants widely for good air circulation.

Other Problems

PROBLEM: Your lily-of-the-valley plants appear healthy, but they are producing very few flowers.

CAUSE: Insufficient sunlight. It thrives in part sun but may not bloom in heavy shade.

WHAT TO DO:
• Move into morning or dappled sun.

Lobelias

(*Lobelia* spp.)

 Lobelia Pests

PROBLEM: Lobelia shoots turn yellow and die. The main stems of the plants are chewed off at their bases.

CAUSE: Wireworms (Family Elateridae). These pests are soil-dwelling, wormlike larvae of click beetles. The young larvae are smooth, white worms with dark jaws. As they mature, the larvae turn into ¼- to ¾-inch-long, jointed, dark yellow or brown worms with forked tails. The beetles are gray, brown, or black beetles that flip from their backs to fronts with a loud clicking noise. The larvae eat underground stems and roots. The adults eat leaves but do little damage. The beetles lay eggs in the soil, and the eggs overwinter under ground.

WHAT TO DO:
• Plant vegetable trap crops. Trap wireworms by burying pieces of carrots or potatoes near infested plants. Dig up the vegetables every two or three days, and destroy wireworms feeding on them.
• Apply beneficial nematodes (*Steinernema carpocapsae* and *Heterorhabditis heliothidis*), which you can purchase from mail-order suppliers. Live nematodes are shipped suspended in gels or sponges.
• Grow new plants in well-cultivated beds where grasses have not grown for at least three years.

PROBLEM: New shoots and leaves are distorted. Clusters of small, soft insects are visible on stems or backs of leaves.

CAUSE: Aphids (Family Aphididae). These pests are ¹⁄₁₆- to ³⁄₈-inch-long, soft-bodied insects. They range in color from pale tan to light green to nearly black. Aphids damage leaves and stems by sucking out the plant juices. These insects can transmit plant diseases as they feed. Their sticky secretions, called honeydew, encourage the growth of sooty mold and attract ants, which protect aphids from predators in order to eat their secretions.

WHAT TO DO:
• Wash aphids off plants with a strong stream of water.
• Use insecticidal soap, following directions.
• Attract beneficial insects, like lady beetles and lacewings, by planting small-flowered

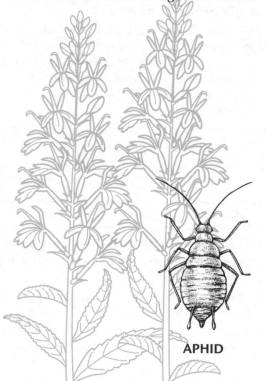

APHID

nectar plants, including yarrow, dill, and Queen-Anne's-lace. Give the beneficials time to bring the aphids under control.
• Pour boiling water into entry holes of anthills that are not adjacent to plant roots.

PROBLEM: Leaves are rolled into tubes tied with webbing. Caterpillars inside the rolls are eating the leaves.

CAUSE: Redbanded leafrollers (*Argyrotaenia velutinana*). These caterpillars are from ½ to ¾ inch long, and they can be pale green, brown, or yellow. The pests hatch from eggs laid by adult moths that are active only after dark. The adult redbanded moths have ¾-inch wingspans and red-striped, brown wings.

WHAT TO DO:
• Handpick.
• Remove and destroy the folded leaves where the caterpillars hide.

PROBLEM: Leaves look bleached, and they have yellow or brown edges. Some leaves and stems are deformed.

CAUSE: Aster leafhoppers, also known as six-spotted leafhoppers (*Macrosteles quadrilineatus*). The ⅛-inch-long adults are black with greenish yellow undersides and black-spotted heads. The adults infect plants with the disease aster yellows (a mycoplasma) as they suck sap from the leaves. Aster leafhoppers overwinter in weeds.

WHAT TO DO:
• Tolerate light damage.
• Attract beneficials, including parasitic flies, wasps, lady beetles, lacewings, and spiders, by growing small-flowered nectar plants, such as yarrow, alyssum, and scabiosa.
• Use insecticidal soap, following directions.
• Spray plants with horticultural oil, which coats plant parts and smothers leafhoppers.

 ## Lobelia Diseases

PROBLEM: The stems of your lobelia plants rot at the soil line. Their lower leaves turn yellow.

CAUSES: Root rot (*Rhizoctonia solani*), stem rot (*Sclerotium rolfsii*), and damping-off (*Pythium debaryanum*). Fungi causes these similar diseases. Often the first symptom is that plants appear to stop growing, and the leaves wilt slowly. Root rot also can develop in poorly drained soil or where the pH is too acidic.

WHAT TO DO:
• Incorporate compost or other organic matter into the soil to improve soil drainage.
• Water plants enough to keep the soil moist but not soggy.
• Space plants widely for adequate air circulation.
• Mulch annually with compost.

PROBLEM: The leaves of your lobelias are developing purplish, yellow, brown, or black spots of various sizes.

CAUSE: Leaf spot (*Septoria lobeliae*; *Cercospora* spp.; *Phyllosticta bridgesii*). Leaf spot, a disease caused by any of these fungi, is most prevalent in moist or humid weather.

WHAT TO DO:
• Tolerate light damage.
• Cut off and destroy infected plant parts to keep from spreading the disease.
• Discard seriously infected plants and the soil that their roots touch.
• Spray infected plants weekly with sulfur.
• Remove garden debris, and apply new mulch.
• Space plants widely for good air circulation.
• Water only in the morning, and avoid splashing plants since spores travel in water.

Lupines

(native American *Lupinus* spp. and hybrids)

Lupine Pests

PROBLEM: Small, pear-shaped insects cluster on leaves, buds, or stems. They have sticky, clear or black, sooty spots.

CAUSE: Aphids (Family Aphididae). These pests are $\frac{1}{16}$- to $\frac{3}{8}$-inch-long, soft-bodied insects. They are pale tan to light green to nearly black. Aphids damage leaves and stems by sucking plant juices. They can transmit plant diseases as they feed. Their secretions, called honeydew, attract sooty mold and ants, which protect aphids from predators in order to eat the secretions.

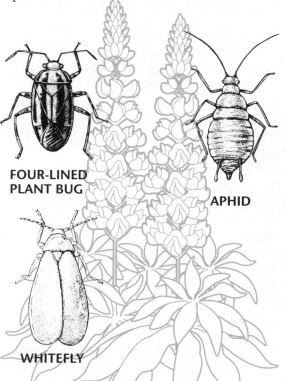

FOUR-LINED PLANT BUG

APHID

WHITEFLY

WHAT TO DO:
• Wash aphids off with a blast of water.
• Use insecticidal soap, following directions.
• Attract beneficial insects, such as lady beetles and lacewings, by planting small-flowered nectar plants, including yarrow, dill, and Queen-Anne's-lace. Give the beneficials time to bring the aphids under control.
• Pour boiling water into entry holes of anthills that are not adjacent to plant roots.

PROBLEM: Leaves and flowers are distorted or dwarfed. They develop yellow, tan, or brown spots in early summer.

CAUSE: Four-lined plant bugs (*Poecilocapsus lineatus*). These sap-sucking pests are $\frac{1}{3}$-inch-long, yellowish green bugs with four black stripes on each wing. In May or June, their eggs hatch into black-spotted red nymphs. Their feeding ends in midsummer. The eggs overwinter in garden debris.

WHAT TO DO:
• Handpick.
• Spray the undersides of lupine leaves with insecticidal soap every third day for two weeks until pests disappear.
• Clean up garden debris in spring and fall.

PROBLEM: Clouds of tiny, white insects fly up when disturbed. Leaves have black mold. Plants grow slowly.

CAUSE: Greenhouse whiteflies (*Trialeurodes vaporariorum*). These pests are tiny, $\frac{1}{25}$-inch-long, flying white insects. Both the $\frac{1}{20}$-inch-long, translucent nymphs and adult flies are sucking insects that weaken plants when they feed in large numbers. They can transmit diseases as they feed. Whiteflies usually disappear after the first frost.

WHAT TO DO:
• Use insecticidal soap, following directions.
• Spray with neem or summer oil, being sure to spray undersides of leaves. Neem is a botanical pesticide that repels and poisons pests but is harmless to beneficial insects. Summer oil smothers pests.
• Water plants well during dry spells.
• Attract predatory wasps and other beneficials with small-flowered nectar plants, like yarrow, dill, and Queen-Anne's-lace.
• Make yellow sticky traps. Coat yellow cardboard or painted boards with petroleum jelly or Tanglefoot (a commercial product for this purpose). Stake the traps near plants.

 Lupine Diseases

PROBLEM: The leaves of your lupines have purplish, yellow, brown, or black spots of various sizes.

CAUSE: Leaf spot. This disease is caused by a variety of different fungi. It is most prevalent in moist or humid weather.

WHAT TO DO:
• Cut off and destroy infected plant parts.
• Discard seriously infected plants and the soil that their roots touch.
• Remove garden debris.
• Apply new mulch.
• Space plants widely for good air circulation.
• Water only in the morning.
• Spray infected plants weekly with sulfur.

PROBLEM: A powdery white coating covers leaves, flowers, and stems. Affected plants usually do not die.

CAUSE: Powdery mildew (*Microsphaera* sp.; *Erysiphe polygoni*). This fungal disease travels

on the wind. It thrives in mild temperatures and in low-light sites.

WHAT TO DO:
• Cut off and destroy infected plant parts.
• Spray with sulfur or baking soda. To make baking soda spray, dissolve 1 teaspoon baking soda in 1 quart warm water; add 1 teaspoon insecticidal soap.
• Water plants regularly during droughts.
• Space plants widely for good air circulation.

PROBLEM: Rust or brown spots mar the undersides of leaves and the stems. Yellow or dark spots mar leaf tops.

CAUSE: Rust (*Puccinia andropogonis* var. *onobrychidis; Uromyces* spp.). This fungal disease travels from plant to plant on wind and in splashing water. It thrives in dampness.

WHAT TO DO:
• Remove and dispose of infected leaves.
• Spray with sulfur.
• Avoid overhead watering.
• Space or thin plants for air circulation.

 Other Problems

PROBLEM: Your lupines are growing abnormally slowly. Or they may be growing but are not blooming.

CAUSES: Poor growing conditions. Some native lupines and Russell hybrid lupines prefer cool summers, humid climates, and acid soil.

Immature plants. Lupines sometimes look their best during their second season.
WHAT TO DO:
• Deadhead flowers.
• Test your soil, and add peat or sulfur as needed to make it neutral or slightly acidic.
• If your climate has dry summers, plant tree lupine (*L. arboreus*), silvery lupine (*L. argenteus*), or a lupine native to your area.
• Divide plants before they become crowded.

Marigolds

(*Tagetes* spp.)

Marigold Pests

PROBLEM: Plants and flowers are eaten. Long, reddish brown insects are inside flowers or under foliage.

CAUSE: European earwigs (*Forficula auricularia*). These pests are about ⅘ inch long, and they have large pincers on their rear end. They feed on marigolds at night and hide inside flowers or under debris during the day.

WHAT TO DO:

• Trap earwigs by placing pieces of garden hose or paper towel tubes on the ground under plants. Earwigs will hide inside. Check the traps in the morning. Empty earwigs from the traps into a pail of soapy water.

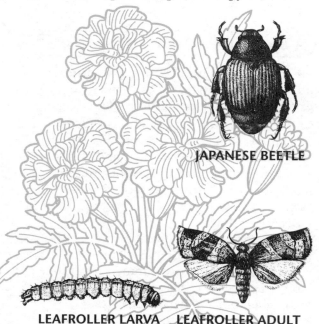

JAPANESE BEETLE

LEAFROLLER LARVA   LEAFROLLER ADULT

PROBLEM: Leaves are chewed between the veins. Some flowers are completely devoured by green-and-copper beetles.

CAUSE: Japanese beetles (*Popillia japonica*). These shiny, ½-inch-long beetles are found throughout the eastern United States, and they are moving westward. Japanese beetles eat marigold leaves and flowers. They emerge in midsummer, and they can do the most damage to marigolds growing in full sun. Their fat, ½-inch-long, white grubs develop in the soil over winter. In the spring, the grubs eat grass roots in lawns.

WHAT TO DO:

• Handpick.
• Collect beetles with a battery-run, hand-held vacuum.
• Put a drop cloth under the plant, and then shake the beetles onto it.
• Use insecticidal soap, following label directions.
• Apply milky disease spores to the soil. Milky disease combines spores of *Bacillus popilliae* and *B. lentimorbus*. Grubs eat the spores, and then they die.
• Plant marigolds in dappled or half-day shade.

PROBLEM: New marigold shoots and buds have small dark spots in them. Leaves and flowers are damaged.

CAUSE: Tarnished plant bugs (*Lygus lineolaris*). These fast-moving, mottled green or brown bugs are about ¼ inch long, with a yellow triangle on each side of their bodies near the back. The young nymphs are yellow-green, and they have five black dots on their bodies. When they feed, tarnished plant bugs inject toxic saliva into plants that causes branch tips, leaves, and flowers to become deformed. Adults overwinter in fallen leaves and can also find shelter in garden debris.

WHAT TO DO:
• Handpick.
• Use insecticidal soap, following label directions.
• Remove garden weeds and debris.

PROBLEM: Leaves are folded or rolled into tubes tied together with webbing. Caterpillars inside tubes feed on leaves.

CAUSES: Leafrollers and leaftiers. Leafrollers, including the redbanded leafroller (*Argyrotaenia velutinana*) and the obliquebanded leafroller (*Choristoneura rosaceana*), along with leaftiers, like the celery leaftier (*Udea rubigalis*), can damage marigolds. These similar caterpillars are from ½ to ¾ inch long, and they can be pale green, brown, or yellow. The pests hatch from eggs laid by adult moths that are active only after dark.

The adult redbanded moths have ¾-inch wingspans and red-striped, brown wings. Obliquebanded adults are brown moths with three darker brown stripes on their front wings and wingspans of ¾ inch.

Celery leaftier moths have brown wings with dark, wavy lines. They have wingspans of ¾ inch.

WHAT TO DO:
• Handpick.
• Remove and destroy the folded leaves where the caterpillars hide.

PROBLEM: Marigold leaves look bleached. They have yellow or brown edges. Leaves and stems are deformed.

CAUSE: Leafhoppers, including the potato leafhopper (*Empoasca fabae*) and the aster leafhopper (*Macrosteles quadrilineatus*). These similar pests are $\frac{1}{10}$- to ½-inch-long, wedge-shaped adults that suck sap from the leaves. Leafhoppers overwinter in weeds.

WHAT TO DO:
• Tolerate light damage.
• Attract parasitic flies, wasps, lady beetles, and other beneficials by planting small-flowered nectar plants, including yarrow, alyssum, and scabiosa.
• Use insecticidal soap, following label directions.
• Spray horticultural oil, a refined oil that coats plant parts and smothers leafhoppers.

PROBLEM: New shoots and young leaves are distorted. Clusters of small, soft insects are visible on stems or leaf backs.

CAUSE: Aphids (Family Aphididae). These pests are $\frac{1}{16}$- to $\frac{3}{8}$-inch-long, soft-bodied insects. They range in color from pale tan to light green to nearly black. Aphids damage leaves and stems by sucking plant juices. These insects can transmit plant diseases as they feed. Their sticky secretions, called honeydew, attract sooty mold and ants, which protect aphids from predators in order to eat their secretions.

WHAT TO DO:
• Wash aphids off plants with a strong stream of water.
• Use insecticidal soap, following label directions.
• Attract beneficial insects, like lady beetles and lacewings, by planting small-flowered nectar plants, including yarrow, dill, and Queen-Anne's-lace. Give the beneficials time to bring the aphids under control.
• Pour boiling water into entry holes of anthills that are not adjacent to plant roots.

PROBLEM: Overnight, marigolds are re-duced to ragged leaves and flowers streaked with shiny slime trails.

CAUSES: Slugs and snails (Order Stylom-matophora). These ⅛- to 8-inch-long, soft-bodied, gray, tan, green, black, yellow, or spotted pests resemble clams and mussels. Snails have shells; slugs look like snails without shells. At night these pests climb up the stems of marigolds to feed on leaves and flowers. In the morning they leave behind a trail of shiny slime as they climb down to hide under garden debris. Adults lay masses of clear eggs under mulch and garden debris.

WHAT TO DO:
• Handpick. The best time to begin hunting is two hours after dark.
• Remove mulch and garden debris.
• Allow the soil to dry out between waterings.
• Sprinkle rings of caustic wood ashes or crushed eggshells around flowerbeds or indi-vidual plants.
• Edge plants with a strip of copper, which hits these slimy pests with an electrical shock upon contact.
• Make beer traps from recycled cans sunk to the brim in soil and filled with yeasty beer. Attracted by the scent of beer, slugs and snails will fall into the traps and drown.
• Dust with diatomaceous earth (DE). This abrasive dust is made from fossilized shells, called diatoms, which penetrate the pests' skin as they crawl over DE.

PROBLEM: Leaves are stippled and faded. Webbing is on leaves. Plants grow poorly, and they may be stunted.

CAUSE: Spider mites (Family Tetranychidae). These pinpoint-sized, spiderlike pests pierce plant leaves to suck nutrients. These mites find marigold leaves tasty, and they feed more voraciously during dry spells. Their cobwebs protect eggs and hatchlings. Spider mites overwinter in leaves on the ground and in plant crevices.

WHAT TO DO:
• Dislodge spider mites with a strong stream of water.
• Use insecticidal soap, following label direc-tions.
• Spray plants with summer oil, a horticul-tural oil that coats plant parts and smothers pests, including spider mites. Begin treat-ment early, at the pinprick stage. By the time webs are visible, it may be too late to save infested marigolds.
• Attract mite-eating hummingbirds by growing plants with red, trumpet-shaped flowers, like trumpet vine (*Campsis radicans*), wild columbine (*Aquilegia canadensis*), and cardinal flower (*Lobelia cardinalis*).

 Marigold Diseases

PROBLEM: Plants rot at the base. Cob-webs develop on lower stems. White strands of fungus form on the soil.

CAUSE: Southern blight (*Sclerotium rolfsii*). This fungal disease thrives in warm climates. The disease appears first as white, threadlike fungus at the base of plants and spreads out-ward across the soil. The threads ooze an acidic fluid that kills plant cells on contact. The spores survive in the soil for years.

WHAT TO DO:
• Dig up infected plants and soil 6 inches beyond the roots and discard it.
• Avoid overwatering and applying excess nitrogen fertilizer.
• Incorporate compost into the soil to in-crease drainage and to add beneficial soil organisms.
• Space plants widely for good air circulation.

PROBLEM: Brown blotches develop on leaves. Fuzzy mold appears on flowers, leaves, and stems. Older flowers rot.

CAUSE: Botrytis blight, also called gray mold (*Botrytis cinerea*). This fungal disease thrives in spring and fall, during periods of cool temperatures and high humidity.

WHAT TO DO:
• Remove and destroy infected flowers and stems.
• Mulch beds with compost to keep rainwater from splashing spores on plants.
• Space plants widely for good air circulation.

PROBLEM: Stunted, yellowing plants have spindly stems. Flowers may be deformed and yellowish.

CAUSE: Aster yellows. This disease is caused by a viruslike organism called a mycoplasma. The disease is spread by wedge-shaped, brown or green, sap-sucking insects called aster leafhoppers (*Macrosteles quadrilineatus*).

WHAT TO DO:
• Remove and destroy infected plants.
• Wash leafhoppers off plants with a strong stream of water.
• Use insecticidal soap, following label directions.
• Attract beneficials by planting small-flowered nectar plants, including scabiosa and alyssum.
• Eliminate weeds from the garden, especially chicory, dandelions, thistles, and plants in the aster family.

PROBLEM: Marigold stems are darkened and are soft at the soil line. Leaves wilt, and they do not revive with watering.

CAUSES: Wilt and stem rot (*Phytophthora cryptogea*). This fungus thrives in cool, wet soils, and it often attacks African marigolds (*T. erecta*).

The dwarf French marigolds (*T. patula*) are resistant to *Phytophthora*, but they may be attacked by a *Fusarium* fungus, which causes similar symptoms.

These soilborne fungi travel to healthy plants in rain, and they can travel on infected tools and hands.

WHAT TO DO:
• Remove and destroy infected plant parts and seriously infected plants.
• Wash your hands and tools after handling infected plants.
• Allow soil to dry out between waterings.
• Grow marigolds in containers of sterile potting soil.

 Other Problems

PROBLEM: Your marigolds flowered early in the summer but stopped blooming during the heat of the summer.

CAUSE: Heat stress. Some marigold species and varieties will bloom well during the shorter, cooler days of spring and late summer but will go into a temporary period of dormancy, called "flagging," during the hottest days of summer. At this time they will produce very few flowers or perhaps stop flowering.

WHAT TO DO:
• Tolerate the temporary dormancy.
• Companion plant marigolds with other annuals, such as geraniums, or perennials, like tickseed. The nonstop all-summer flowering of these other plants will draw attention from the temporary flowerless state of your marigolds.
• In hot climates, plant marigolds in sites that receive afternoon shade or dappled shade.
• Grow signet marigolds, which do not flag during the heat of summer.

Garden Mum

(Chrysanthemum × morifolium, reclassified as *Dendranthema grandiflorum)*

 Garden Mum Pests

PROBLEM: Clusters of small, pear-shaped insects are on leaves, buds, or stems. Young growth may be stunted.

CAUSE: Aphids (Family Aphididae). Adults are sap-sucking, soft-bodied insects, $\frac{1}{16}$ to $\frac{3}{8}$ inch long. Aphids range in color from pale tan to light green to nearly black. They can spread diseases to your garden mums (also popularly called chrysanthemums) as they feed, and their sticky secretions attract ants.

CHRYSANTHEMUM LEAFMINER ADULT

CHRYSANTHEMUM LACE BUG

THRIPS

WHAT TO DO:
• Tolerate light damage.
• Wash aphids off with a blast of water.
• Use insecticidal soap, following directions.
• Attract beneficial insects, like lady beetles and lacewings, by planting small-flowered nectar plants, including yarrow and dill.

PROBLEM: Leaves have tiny yellow or brown spots and can be deformed. Insect droppings may be on leaf backs.

CAUSE: Chrysanthemum lace bugs (*Corythucha marmorata*). These $\frac{1}{8}$-inch-long, brown-speckled, yellow-white bugs have lacy wings. The sap-sucking insects lay their eggs on weeds, especially goldenrod.

WHAT TO DO:
• Handpick.
• Use insecticidal soap, following directions.

PROBLEM: Light tan, winding trails disfigure some of the leaves of your garden mums.

CAUSE: Chrysanthemum leafminers (*Chromatomyia syngenesiae*). These pests are the minute, pale yellow larvae of a tiny fly. The larvae tunnel and feed between the upper and lower leaf surfaces. They overwinter in the soil.

WHAT TO DO:
• Handpick and destroy infested leaves.

• Apply beneficial nematodes (*Steinernema carpocapsae* and *Heterorhabditis heliothidis*), which you can purchase from mail-order suppliers. Nematodes are shipped live.
• Clean up fallen leaves, especially in fall.

PROBLEM: Leaves and flowers have silvery streaks or speckling. The affected plant parts may turn brown.

CAUSE: Thrips (Order Thysanoptera). These extremely tiny, narrow-bodied insects are only $\frac{1}{25}$ inch long. They like to hide deep inside the leaf shoots and flowers of garden mums. Thrips are almost impossible to see on plants without a magnifying glass. If you suspect a plant has thrips, pick a young shoot or damaged flower and shake it over a clean sheet of white paper. If thrips are present, they will drop onto the paper and will look like dark specks moving around on the paper.

WHAT TO DO:
• Knock thrips off with a blast of water.
• Make blue sticky cards. Coat blue cardboard or painted wooden boards with petroleum jelly or Tanglefoot (a commercial product for this purpose), and fasten them to stakes near the plants.
• Use insecticidal soap, following directions.
• Apply neem. This botanical pesticide repels and poisons insect pests but is harmless to beneficial insects.

PROBLEM: Leaves look pale green, due to many tiny, yellow or white spots. Fine webbing may be on the leaves.

CAUSE: Two-spotted spider mites (*Tetranychus urticae*). These pinpoint-sized, red, spiderlike pests pierce leaves and suck nutrients. Mites overwinter in leaves on the ground and in plant crevices; they feed more during dry spells. Cobwebs protect eggs and larvae.

WHAT TO DO:
• Dislodge mites with a blast of water.
• Use insecticidal soap, following directions. Begin treatment at the pinprick stage.

 Garden Mum Diseases

PROBLEM: Plants are stunted and yellowing and have spindly stems. Flowers may be deformed and are yellow-green.

CAUSE: Aster yellows. This disease is caused by a viruslike organism called a mycoplasma. The disease enters plants through feeding holes made by aster leafhoppers (*Macrosteles quadrilineatus*). Once infected, there is no cure. Leafhoppers are winged, wedge-shaped, brown or green insects with triangular heads; they jump rapidly when disturbed.

WHAT TO DO:
• Remove and destroy infected plants.
• Wash leafhoppers off plants with a strong stream of water.
• Use insecticidal soap, following directions.
• Attract beneficial insects to help control leafhoppers by planting small-flowered nectar plants, including scabiosa, alyssum, and yarrow.

PROBLEM: Flowers droop, then decay. Leaves and stems turn brown and become covered with fuzzy, gray mold.

CAUSE: Botrytis blight, also called gray mold (*Botrytis cinerea*). The spores of this fungal disease travel from plant to plant on the wind. It thrives in cool, moist weather.

WHAT TO DO:
• Remove and destroy all infected plant parts.
• Avoid overhead watering.
• Clean up plant debris.
• Improve soil drainage.
• Space plants widely for good air circulation.

PROBLEM: Older leaves develop yellow-brown patches. Leaves turn brown or black and die. Plant growth is stunted.

CAUSE: Foliar nematodes (*Aphelenchoides ritzema-bosi*). The pests that cause this damage are microscopic roundworms that cause diseaselike symptoms. They travel in splashing water and thrive during wet, warm summers. They overwinter in soil debris.

WHAT TO DO:
• Remove and dispose of infected plants and garden debris.
• Do not wet leaves when watering.
• Cover the soil around garden mums with a fabric weed barrier to keep infested soil off plants.

PROBLEM: The leaves of your garden mum plants have yellow, brown, or black spots of various sizes.

CAUSE: Leaf spot. Garden mums are prone to leaf spot caused by many kinds of fungi. Leaf spot infections are most prevalent in mild, moist weather. Leaf spot travels in splashing rain and irrigation water. The spores overwinter in garden debris.

WHAT TO DO:
• Space plants widely for maximum exposure to sun and air.
• Avoid overhead watering.
• Remove and dispose of diseased leaves.
• Destroy seriously infected plants.
• Clean up plant debris.
• Wash your hands and wipe tools with rubbing alcohol to disinfect them after handling plants.

PROBLEM: A powdery, grayish white coating covers leaves, flowers, and stems. Plants usually do not die.

CAUSE: Powdery mildew (*Erysiphe cichoracearum*). This fungal disease is more prevalent in semi-arid regions than in those with high rainfall. Powdery mildew spores travel from plant to plant on wind. The disease thrives in shade, fog, and cloudy weather.

WHAT TO DO:
• Cut off and destroy infected plant parts.
• Apply baking soda spray. Dissolve 1 teaspoon baking soda in 1 quart warm water; add 1 teaspoon insecticidal soap to make the solution stick to leaves.
• Water plants regularly.
• Space plants widely for maximum air circulation.
• Grow plants in full sun.

PROBLEM: The undersides of garden mum flowers turn brown. The flower stems turn black.

CAUSE: Ray blight (*Ascochyta chrysanthemi*). This fungal disease causes buds to blacken without opening and causes infected mature flowers to die.

WHAT TO DO:
• Remove and destroy infected plants.
• Avoid overhead watering.
• Space plants widely for maximum air circulation.
• Examine plants for the disease before buying them.

PROBLEM: Powdery, brown spots are on the undersides of leaves and on stems. Leaves yellow and drop. Plants die.

CAUSE: Rust (*Puccinia tanaceti*). Several fungi cause this disease. Rust spreads from plant to plant on the wind and in rain. It thrives in damp weather.

WHAT TO DO:
• Remove and dispose of infected leaves.
• Spray with sulfur.
• Water early in the day so the plants will dry quickly.

• Space or thin plants widely for good air circulation.

PROBLEM: Leaves have mottling, streaking, or abnormally colored patterns. Leaves curl; plants are stunted.

CAUSES: Viruses. These diseases enter garden mums through feeding holes made by insect pests. Once infected, there is no cure.

WHAT TO DO:
• Destroy infected plants.
• Inspect container plants for visible signs of viruses before purchasing.

PROBLEM: Entire plants or parts of plants turn yellow and wilt. They do not respond to watering.

CAUSES: Wilt (*Fusarium oxysporum* f. *chrysanthemi*). This soilborne fungal disease thrives in warm, wet climates.

Verticillium wilt (*Verticillium albo-atrum*). This soilborne fungal disease favors cool, moist weather.

WHAT TO DO:
• Remove and destroy infected plants and the soil that their roots touch.
• Remove garden debris.
• Improve soil drainage.

 Other Problems

PROBLEM: Plants are growing slowly. They attract an unusual number of pests or have disease problems.

CAUSE: Poor growing conditions. Garden mums grow best in a sunny location with well-drained soil. Healthy plants are better able to fend off pests and diseases.

WHAT TO DO:
• Plant garden mums in full sun.
• Space plants widely for maximum air circulation.

• Divide garden mum clumps every year or two to prevent overcrowding.
• In cold climates, cover plants with several inches of loose, organic mulch after the soil freezes in the fall.

PROBLEM: Your garden mums look green and healthy, but they are too tall and have few flowers.

CAUSE: Lack of shearing. Many garden mum varieties will grow tall and "leggy" if they are not pinched back early in the growing season.

WHAT TO DO:
• Pinch the tops out of the plants when they are 4 to 6 inches tall in late spring, and again in July, making sure to remove all flower buds during the second pinching.

PROBLEM: Your mums grew well all summer and flowered. The plants did not come back after the winter.

CAUSE: Wet soil; freezing temperatures. Soil that remains wet in winter can cause the roots of garden mums to rot. If the winter temperatures are too cold, mums could suffer fatal frost damage.

WHAT TO DO:
• Grow garden mums in well-drained but rich soil.
• Make sure water does not stand on the soil in winter.
• In cold climates, protect plant roots in winter with a fluffy, organic mulch several inches thick.
• Take cuttings in the fall. Plant the cuttings in sandy loam, and overwinter the cuttings in a greenhouse or cold frame or on a cool, sunny windowsill indoors.

Nasturtiums

(*Tropaeolum* spp. and hybrids)

 Nasturtium Pests

PROBLEM: Leaves have small holes in them. Some holes are so small they don't go all the way through the leaves.

CAUSE: Potato flea beetles (*Epitrix cucumeris*). These $\frac{1}{16}$-inch-long, shiny black beetles are most damaging to seedlings in early spring.

WHAT TO DO:
• Use insecticidal soap, following directions.
• Make sticky traps. Coat pieces of white cardboard with petroleum jelly or Tanglefoot (a commercial product for this purpose), and fasten them to stakes put near plants.

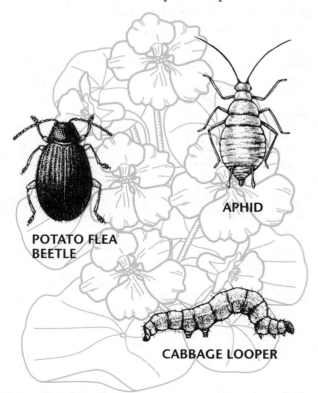

POTATO FLEA BEETLE

APHID

CABBAGE LOOPER

• Apply beneficial nematodes (*Steinernema carpocapsae* and *Heterorhabditis heliothidis*), which you can purchase from mail-order suppliers. Live nematodes are shipped suspended in gels or sponges.
• Dust plants with diatomaceous earth (DE). This abrasive dust is made of fossilized shells, called diatoms, which penetrate pests' skin as they crawl over DE. Wear a dust mask to avoid inhaling particles, and apply DE when plants are wet with dew.
• Watch your garden to see what plants the flea beetles favor. Plant some of these plants some distance from your nasturtiums to lure the beetles away. When they become infested, pull up and destroy the trap plants.

PROBLEM: Nasturtiums have yellowing leaves. Plants droop. Tiny, black insects cluster on stems and leaf undersides.

CAUSE: Bean aphids (*Aphis fabae*). These $\frac{1}{16}$- to $\frac{3}{8}$-inch-long, soft-bodied, dark green or black insects feed in clusters, sucking sap from tender stems and leaf undersides. Aphids can transmit plant diseases as they feed. Their sticky secretions, called honeydew, attract ants and sooty mold; ants protect aphids from predators in order to eat their secretions. Aphids' eggs overwinter on woody shrubs, including *Euonymus* spp. and *Viburnum* spp.

WHAT TO DO:
• Wash aphids off with a blast of water.
• Use insecticidal soap, following directions.
• Attract beneficial insects, like lady beetles

and lacewings, by planting small-flowered nectar plants, including yarrow, dill, and Queen-Anne's-lace. Give the beneficials time to bring the aphids under control.
• Pour boiling water into entry holes of anthills that are not adjacent to plant roots.

PROBLEM: The leaves of your nasturtiums have scalloped edges or holes chewed in the leaves and flowers.

CAUSES: Caterpillars, including cabbage loopers (*Trichoplusia ni*) and imported cabbageworms (*Pieris rapae*). These green caterpillars are tiny. They are difficult to see when they first hatch, but they quickly grow to 1¼ inches long.

Cabbage loopers are the larvae of gray moths with wing markings that make them look like tree bark. The loopers are light green with white stripes on their sides. They raise the center of their bodies up to form a loop.

Imported cabbageworms are the larvae of cabbage white butterflies. These common butterflies have black-tipped and spotted white wings, and they have wingspans of 1½ inches. They are among the first butterflies to lay eggs on nasturtiums leaves in spring. Eggs hatch into tiny, yellowish caterpillars that turn green as they begin to feed. Frequently these caterpillars travel along the central leaf veins, where they are difficult to see. The largest caterpillars have faint yellow stripes down their sides, and they grow to a length of 1½ inches.

WHAT TO DO:
• Handpick.
• Attract beneficial insects with nectar plants, such as dill and Queen-Anne's-lace.
• Companion plant with radishes.
• Apply BTK. *Bacillus thuringiensis* var. *kurstaki* (BTK) is a stomach poison that kills imported cabbageworms.

PROBLEM: There are light tan, winding trails on nasturtium leaves. The marks do not turn into holes.

CAUSE: Serpentine leafminers (*Liriomyza brassicae*). These minute yellow maggots are the larvae of tiny black-and-yellow flies. The leafminers make long, slender, winding trails between the upper and lower surfaces of the leaves. These pests overwinter in debris.

WHAT TO DO:
• Pick and destroy infested leaves.
• Clean up fallen leaves and garden debris.
• Purchase and release beneficial nematodes (*Steinernema carpocapsae* and *Heterorhabditis heliothidis*). These are shipped live from mail-order suppliers.

 Nasturtium Diseases

PROBLEM: The stems of your nasturtium plants rot at the base. The plants turn yellow, then they wilt and die.

CAUSE: Bacterial wilt (*Pseudomonas solanacearum*). This soilborne disease thrives in warm weather. It enters plants through wounds in aboveground tissues. It also enters plants through damaged roots. The disease interferes with the flow of water and nutrients, causing infected plants to wilt and die. Bacterial wilt disease overwinters in debris.

WHAT TO DO:
• Remove and destroy infected plants, along with the soil that their roots touch.
• Plant nasturtiums in well-drained soil, and mulch them with compost.
• Avoid overcrowding or overwatering plants.
• Take care not to damage stems or roots when cultivating.
• Remove and compost garden debris.
• Keep nasturtiums away from susceptible plants, like potatoes, tomatoes, and eggplants.

Pansy

(Viola × wittrockiana)

Pansy Pests

PROBLEM: Overnight, pansies are reduced to ragged remains of leaves and flowers streaked with shiny slime trails.

CAUSES: Slugs and snails (Order Stylommatophora). These ⅛- to 8-inch-long, soft-bodied, gray, tan, green, black, yellow, or spotted pests resemble clams and mussels. Snails have shells; slugs look like snails without shells. At night these pests feed on pansy leaves and flowers. In the morning they leave behind a trail of shiny slime as they leave your pansies to hide under garden debris. Adults lay masses of clear eggs under mulch and garden debris.

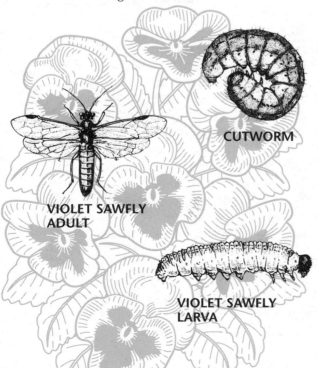

CUTWORM

VIOLET SAWFLY ADULT

VIOLET SAWFLY LARVA

WHAT TO DO:
• Handpick. The best time to begin hunting is two hours after dark.
• Remove mulch and garden debris.
• Allow soil to dry out between waterings.
• Sprinkle barrier rings of wood ashes or crushed eggshells around flowerbeds or individual plants.
• Edge plants with a strip of copper, which hits these slimy pests with an electrical shock upon contact.
• Make beer traps from recycled cans sunk to the brim in soil and filled with yeasty beer. Attracted by the scent of beer, slugs and snails will fall into the traps and drown.
• Dust plants with diatomaceous earth (DE). This abrasive dust is made of fossilized shells, called diatoms, which penetrate the pests' skin as they crawl over DE.

PROBLEM: New shoots and young leaves are distorted. Small, soft insects are visible on stems or leaf undersides.

CAUSE: Aphids (Family Aphididae). These pests are 1/16- to 3/8-inch-long, soft-bodied insects. They range in color from pale tan to light green to nearly black. Aphids damage leaves and stems by sucking plant juices. These insects can transmit plant diseases as they feed. Their sticky secretions, called honeydew, attract ants and sooty mold; ants protect aphids from predators in order to eat the aphids' secretions.

WHAT TO DO:
• Wash aphids off plants with a strong stream of water.
• Use insecticidal soap, following directions.

• Attract beneficial insects, like lady beetles and lacewings, by planting small-flowered nectar plants, including yarrow, dill, and Queen-Anne's-lace. Give the beneficials time to bring the aphids under control.
• Pour boiling water into entry holes of anthills that are not adjacent to plant roots.

PROBLEM: Pansy seedlings are cut off near the ground. You find the plants lying on the ground beside their stems.

CAUSE: Cutworms (Family Noctuidae). These pests are the larvae of several species of night-flying moths with wingspans of 1½ inches. Cutworms are gray or dull brown caterpillars, 1 to 2 inches long. The caterpillars eat their way through seedling stems at night, and they hide in the soil during the day.

WHAT TO DO:
• Handpick the caterpillars after dark.
• Use cutworm collars. To make these collars, use shears to cut 2- to 3-inch-long sections from paper-towel tubes or tin cans. Place these short tubes over seedlings.
• Dust plants with BT granules. "BT" stands for *Bacillus thuringiensis,* an insect-stomach poison that kills caterpillars without harming beneficial insects.

PROBLEM: Your pansies have distorted leaves, which begin to rot. The plants are stunted and produce few flowers.

CAUSE: Violet gall midges (*Phytophaga violicola*). These pests are the larvae of small, dark flies. The adults lay tiny, white eggs in the crevices of unfolding new leaves. The white maggots, which are less than ½ inch long, eat the leaves, causing them to become deformed and rotten. Severely infested plants are stunted.

WHAT TO DO:
• Remove and destroy infested leaves as well as severely deformed plants.
• Use insecticidal soap, following label directions.
• Gather all fallen leaves and destroy them, and compost garden debris.

PROBLEM: Leaves are so eaten that they look skeletonized. There are only veins and remnants of leaf tissue left.

CAUSE: Violet sawflies (*Ametastegia pallipes*). Sawflies are black-and-yellow flies that lay insect eggs into the lower surfaces of leaves. The emerging larvae are about ½ inch long. They are blue-black or olive green, with white spots on their backs and sides. The larvae eat leaves at night, and from May to June they can defoliate entire pansy plants.

WHAT TO DO:
• Knock larvae off plants with a strong spray of water.
• Use insecticidal soap, following label directions.

PROBLEM: Leaves are peppered with tiny tan spots. Affected leaves turn tan and die. Webbing is visible on some leaves.

CAUSE: Two-spotted spider mites (*Tetranychus urticae*). These pinpoint-sized, red, spiderlike pests pierce pansy leaves to suck nutrients, leaving pinprick holes in leaves. Mites overwinter in leaves on the ground, and they also winter in plant crevices. Spider mites feed more during hot, dry spells in midsummer, and they also feed more in enclosed areas with stagnant air. Their cobwebs protect mite eggs and larvae.

WHAT TO DO:
• Dislodge spider mites with a strong stream of water.
• Spray infested plants with insecticidal soap. Begin treatment at the pinprick stage. By the

time the webs appear, it may be too late to save some pansies.
• Water plants regularly during dry spells.
• Space plants widely for adequate air circulation.
• Grow pansies during cool spring or fall weather, which is when they flower best. This is also the time when spider mite outbreaks are less likely to occur.

 ## Pansy Diseases

PROBLEM: Pansy plants are stunted. Often the plants wilt. Leaves and stems turn yellow, and the plants slowly die.

CAUSE: Root-knot nematodes (*Meloidogyne* spp.). Several species of minute, soil-dwelling nematodes, which cause diseaselike symptoms, may attack pansies. These microscopic worms feed inside the roots, causing knotlike swellings as they secrete toxic chemicals, which cause the root cells to enlarge.

WHAT TO DO:
• Help infested plants resist further damage by providing them with regular waterings and regular fertilizer applications.
• Turn under compost.
• Apply crab or shrimp wastes that contain chitin. Chitin, made from shellfish shells, provides nitrogen and potassium as it breaks down, creating conditions that encourage the beneficial soil organisms that attack nematodes.
• Solarize the soil. Clear plastic sheeting placed over bare soil for three to four weeks uses the sun's energy to heat the soil enough to kill most pests and weed seeds in the top few inches of soil. After removing the plastic, plant crops as usual.

PROBLEM: A powdery, gray-white substance covers leaves, stems, and flowers. The covering resists wiping off.

CAUSE: Powdery mildew (*Sphaerotheca macularis*). This common fungal disease weakens pansy plants and makes them unsightly. Infected leaves may shrivel and die. The spores blow from plant to plant on the wind. Unlike many other plant diseases, powdery mildew spores do not require a film of moisture on the leaf to germinate, although they do thrive in high humidity. The disease overwinters on plant debris or on perennials and weeds.

WHAT TO DO:
• Spray infected foliage with baking soda spray. To make the spray, dissolve 1 teaspoon baking soda in 1 quart warm water; add 1 teaspoon insecticidal soap to make the solution stick to leaves.
• Wash leaves on sunny days with a strong spray of water to knock spores off plants.
• Space plants widely, and grow them in full sun.

PROBLEM: Your pansies have patches of gray mold on the fading flowers. Mold is also forming on the leaves.

CAUSE: Botrytis blight, also called gray mold (*Botrytis cinerea*). This common mold appears most often during cool, wet weather. Entire leaves can blacken and drop, and stems are sometimes infected. The spores travel from plant to plant, spreading in splashing water. The blight overwinters in dead leaves and stems.

WHAT TO DO:
• Remove and destroy all infected plant parts.
• Deadhead (remove spent flowers) to keep pansies flowering longer as well as to prevent gray mold from attacking fading flowers.
• Wash your hands and disinfect tools after handling diseased plants to keep from spreading the disease.
• Avoid overhead watering.
• Clean up plant debris.

• Incorporate compost or other organic matter to improve soil drainage and to add beneficial organisms to the soil.
• Space plants widely for adequate air circulation.

PROBLEM: Pansy stems rot at the soil line, and the lower leaves of the affected plants turn yellow.

CAUSE: Root rot, also called damping-off (*Pythium* spp.; *Rhizoctinia solani*). Often the first symptom of this fungal disease is that plants appear to stop growing and the leaves wilt slowly. Root rot also can develop in poorly drained soil or where the pH (acid balance of the soil) is too acidic. Fungi overwinter in the soil.

WHAT TO DO:
• Incorporate compost or other organic matter into the soil to improve soil drainage.
• Water often enough to keep the soil slightly moist.
• Space plants widely for adequate air circulation.
• Mulch pansies annually with compost to add disease-fighting beneficial organisms to the soil.

PROBLEM: Leaves have brown blotches with distinct black margins. The flower petals may be misshapen.

CAUSE: Anthracnose (*Colletotrichum violae-tricoloris*). The spores of this fungal disease are produced when the weather warms in spring. They are spread in splashing water and require a film of water on a leaf in order to germinate and infect the plant. This fungal disease overwinters in seeds and on crop debris.

WHAT TO DO:
• Remove and dispose of infected plant parts.
• Water early in the day and avoid wetting foliage.

• Remove plant debris from the garden.
• Space pansies widely for adequate air circulation.

PROBLEM: Spots of various colors and sizes are on leaves. Scabby spots with black edges form on stems and leaves.

CAUSES: Leaf spot; spot anthracnose.

Leaf spot, which causes the multicolored spots to blemish leaves, can be caused by several fungi.

Spot anthracnose (*Sphaceloma violae*), a more serious fungal disease, causes the scabby spots. This disease sometimes kills infected pansies.

WHAT TO DO:
• Remove and destroy leaf spot–infected leaves.
• For anthracnose-infected violets, remove and destroy the entire plant.
• Clean up and compost debris in the fall.

 Other Problems

PROBLEM: Your pansies grew and bloomed in spring but began to wilt and stopped blooming in early summer.

CAUSE: Heat stress. Pansies grow and flower best in cool temperatures. As the heat and humidity of midsummer approaches, they will begin to die out.

WHAT TO DO:
• In areas where summers are hot, start pansies in early spring and again in late summer.
• Replace pansies with heat-loving annuals when they begin to deteriorate in early summer.
• In the Deep South, pansies set out in fall can grow and bloom all winter long.

Penstemons

(*Penstemon* spp. and hybrids)

Penstemon Pests

PROBLEM: Flowers and buds have small holes. Blossoms may be chewed, and dark-colored droppings may be present.

CAUSE: Tobacco budworms (*Heliocoverpa virescens*). These are caterpillar larvae of night-flying moths. The adults have light green wings with four light-colored stripes on them and wingspans of 1½ inches. They lay eggs on the backs of leaves that hatch into 1⅓-inch-long, striped, green larvae.

WHAT TO DO:
• Handpick.
• Spray infested penstemons with *Bacillus*

thuringiensis var. *kurstaki* (BTK). "BT" stands for *Bacillus thuringiensis*, an insect-stomach poison that kills caterpillars without harming beneficial insects. *B.t.* var. *kurstaki* (BTK) kills tobacco budworms.

PROBLEM: New shoots and young leaves are distorted. Clusters of small, soft insects are on stems or leaf undersides.

CAUSE: Aphids (Family Aphididae). These pests are ¹⁄₁₆- to ⅜-inch-long, soft-bodied insects. They range in color from pale tan to light green to nearly black. Aphids damage leaves and stems by sucking plant juices. These insects can transmit plant diseases as they feed. Their sticky secretions, called honeydew, attract ants and sooty mold; ants protect aphids in order to eat their secretions.

WHAT TO DO:
• Wash aphids off with a blast of water.
• Use insecticidal soap, following directions.
• Attract beneficial insects, like lady beetles and lacewings, by planting small-flowered nectar plants, including yarrow, dill, and Queen-Anne's-lace. Give the beneficials time to bring the aphids under control.
• Pour boiling water into entry holes of anthills that are not adjacent to plant roots.

Penstemon Diseases

PROBLEM: Leaves turn yellow; plants wilt and die. There may be yellowish or white fungal strands at plant bases.

CAUSES: Crown or stem rot, also called

APHID

southern blight (*Sclerotium rolfsii*); Texas root rot (*Phymatotrichum omnivorum*). These diseases, which have similar symptoms, are usually brought about by poor soil drainage.

Texas root rot is most common in heavy, alkaline soils, and it can be quite fast acting. Infected plants can collapse and die, and they tend to die in clumps. Texas root rot occurs primarily during the summer and early fall in Texas and other southern states.

WHAT TO DO:
• Remove diseased plants plus 6 inches of soil beyond the root zone, and discard all of it.
• Incorporate compost into the soil to improve drainage and to reduce rot by introducing beneficial soil organisms.
• Wipe tools with rubbing alcohol after working with diseased plants to keep from spreading the disease to other plants.
• Keep mulch away from the base of plants.
• Allow soil to dry out between waterings.
• Space plants widely for air circulation.
• Substitute resistant perennials, like bee balm, foxglove, iris, and lily.

PROBLEM: Rusty or brown spots mar stems and the undersides of leaves. Pale yellow or dark areas disfigure leaf tops.

CAUSE: Rust (*Puccinia* spp.). The spores of this fungal disease travel from plant to plant on the wind and in splashing water.

WHAT TO DO:
• Remove and dispose of infected leaves.
• Spray infected foliage with sulfur.
• Avoid overhead watering.
• Water in the morning.
• Space or thin plants for air circulation.

PROBLEM: The leaves of your penstemons have purplish, yellow, brown, or black spots of various sizes.

CAUSE: Leaf spot. This disease is caused by a variety of different fungi. It is most prevalent in moist or humid weather.

WHAT TO DO:
• Tolerate light damage.
• Cut off and destroy infected plant parts. Discard seriously infected plants and the soil that their roots touch.
• Spray infected plants weekly with sulfur.
• Remove garden debris.
• Apply new mulch.
• Space plants widely for good air circulation.
• Water only in the morning, and avoid splashing plants.

 Other Problems

PROBLEM: Some penstemons do not thrive following winter. Others do not live through the winter.

CAUSE: The particular species or hybrid of penstemon you are growing is not adapted to your climate or soil. Penstemons, depending on the species, can be native to North America or South America. Some are very tender, such as Hartweg penstemon (*P. hartwegii*) and gloxinia penstemon (variants of *P. hartwegii* or *P. hartwegii* and *P. cobaea* and its hybrids). Others may be short-lived in warm-winter climates while being long-lived in colder areas, such as common beardtongue (*P. barbatus*) and its hybrids and foxglove penstemon (*P. digitalis*). Most of these native perennials prefer full sun. Their soil preferences can vary from acid to alkaline, depending on the species. All need good drainage, and some are drought-tolerant.

WHAT TO DO:
• Grow penstemons that are native to your area or hybrids that can tolerate your climate.
• Divide penstemons after four to six years in the garden, when the older plants in clumps start to decline.

Peonies

(*Paeonia* spp. and hybrids)

Peony Pests

PROBLEM: Leaves are chewed between the veins. Some flowers are devoured. You see green-and-copper beetles.

CAUSE: Japanese beetles (*Popillia japonica*). These shiny, ½-inch-long beetles are found throughout the eastern United States and are moving westward. Japanese beetles eat peony leaves and flowers. They emerge in mid-summer and can do great damage, focusing on plants growing in full sun. Their fat, ½-inch-long, white grubs develop in the soil over winter and in the spring eat grass roots.

WHAT TO DO:
- Handpick.
- Collect beetles with a battery-run, hand-held vacuum.
- Put a drop cloth under peony plants and shake the beetles onto it; destroy the collected beetles.
- Use insecticidal soap, following directions.
- Spray plants with neem. Neem is a botanical pesticide that repels and poisons insect pests but is harmless to beneficial insects.
- Apply milky disease to the soil. Milky disease combines spores of *Bacillus popilliae* and *B. lentimorbus*. Grubs eat the spores and die.

PROBLEM: Buds do not open, or they open partially. Brown edges or streaks mar light-colored buds and flowers.

CAUSE: Flower thrips (*Frankliniella tritici*). These extremely tiny, narrow-bodied insects are only ½₀ inch long. Young thrips are lemon yellow. Adults are light brown with orange undersides. Thrips hide deep inside peony flowers and are almost impossible to see on plants without using a magnifying glass. If you suspect that a plant has thrips, pick a damaged flower and shake it over a clean sheet of white paper. If thrips are present, they will drop onto the paper and will look like dark specks. These pests injure only peony flowers, and their feeding can ruin the flowers.

WHAT TO DO:
- Destroy infested buds and flowers.
- Use insecticidal soap, following directions.

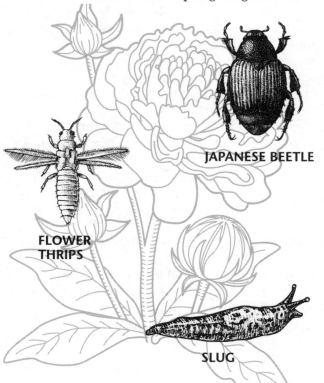

JAPANESE BEETLE

FLOWER THRIPS

SLUG

• Keep plants adequately watered and mulched to keep soil moist but not soggy.
• Apply loose, organic mulch to attract beneficial spiders.
• Attract other beneficial insects by planting nectar and pollen plants, such as alyssum, yarrow, and scabiosa.
• Purchase lacewings and beneficial nematodes from mail-order suppliers, and release these beneficials in the garden.

PROBLEM: Young peony shoots are eaten in spring. Large holes in leaves or flowers are edged in slimy streaks.

CAUSES: Slugs and snails (Order Stylommatophora). These ⅛- to 8-inch-long, soft-bodied, gray, tan, green, black, yellow, or spotted pests resemble clams and mussels. Snails have shells; slugs look like snails without shells. At night these pests feed on peony leaves and flowers. In the morning they leave behind a trail of shiny slime as they climb down to hide under garden debris. Adults lay masses of clear eggs under mulch and garden debris.

WHAT TO DO:
• Handpick. The best time to begin hunting is two hours after dark.
• Remove mulch and garden debris.
• Allow the soil to dry out between waterings.
• Sprinkle barrier rings of wood ashes or crushed eggshells around flowerbeds or individual plants.
• Edge plants with a strip of copper, which hits these slimy pests with an electrical shock upon contact.
• Make beer traps from recycled cans sunk to the brim in soil and filled with yeasty beer. Attracted by the scent of beer, the pests will fall into the traps and drown.
• Dust plants with diatomaceous earth (DE). This abrasive dust is made from fossilized shells, called diatoms, which penetrate the pests' skin as they crawl over DE.

PROBLEM: Leaves and flowers are distorted. They develop small yellow, tan, or brown spots in early summer.

CAUSE: Four-lined plant bugs (*Poecilocapsus lineatus*). These sap-sucking pests are ⅓-inch-long, yellowish green bugs with four black stripes on each wing. In May or June their eggs hatch into bright red nymphs with black-dotted chests. Their feeding ends in midsummer. Their eggs overwinter in garden debris.

WHAT TO DO:
• Handpick.
• Spray insecticidal soap on the undersides of leaves every third day for two weeks until pests disappear.
• Clean up garden debris in spring and fall.

PROBLEM: The leaves and stems of your peonies have small bumps and sticky, clear spots. Ants are on the plants.

CAUSES: Oystershell scale (*Leidosaphes ulmi*); San Jose scale (*Quadraspidiotas perniciosus*). These ⅛-inch-diameter insects suck plant juices from peonies. Adult scale look like immobile bumps and produce a sticky secretion, called honeydew, that attracts ants and sooty mildew.

WHAT TO DO:
• Scrape scale off leaves and stems with a plastic scouring pad.
• Attract parasitic wasps and other beneficial insects by growing small-flowered nectar plants, such as scabiosa, yarrow, dill, and Queen-Anne's-lace.
• Pour boiling water into anthills that are not next to roots.

Peony Diseases

PROBLEM: Your peonies are not thriving, and growth is stunted. They may wilt easily, even when watered, and die.

CAUSE: Root-knot nematodes (*Meloidogyne* spp.). Several species of minute, soil-dwelling nematodes may attack peonies. These microscopic worms feed inside the roots and secrete chemicals that cause root cells to enlarge, causing knotlike swellings and diseaselike symptoms above ground.

WHAT TO DO:
• Drench the soil around diseased plants with neem. Neem is a botanical pesticide that repels and poisons insect pests but is harmless to beneficial insects.
• Once nematodes have infected your peonies, help the plants resist further damage by providing them with regular waterings and fertilizer applications.
• Turn under compost.
• Apply crab or shrimp wastes that contain chitin. Chitin, made from shellfish shells, provides nitrogen and potassium, creating conditions that encourage the beneficial soil organisms that attack nematodes.
• Solarize the soil. Clear plastic sheeting placed over bare soil for three to four weeks uses the sun's energy to heat the soil enough to kill most pests and weed seeds in the top few inches of soil. After removing the plastic, plant crops as usual.
• In regions where nematode problems are severe, grow flowers in containers.

PROBLEM: Young leaves have small, yellowish, water-soaked spots that become dark or tan. Centers of spots fall out.

CAUSE: Bacterial leaf spot (*Pseudomonas syringae* pv. *aptata*). This disease attacks peonies in warm spring weather. The bacterium travels from plant to plant in rain and wind and is carried on contaminated tools and hands. The bacterium overwinters in plant debris and infected seeds.

WHAT TO DO:
• Remove and destroy infected plant parts.
• Allow the soil to dry between waterings.
• Mulch with compost, which introduces beneficial soil microorganisms that help control disease bacteria.

PROBLEM: Leaves have brown blotches with distinct black margins. The flower petals may be misshapen.

CAUSE: Anthracnose (*Gloeosporium* spp.). The spores of this fungal disease spread when the weather warms in spring and when the air is damp. Spores travel from plant to plant in splashing water and require a film of water on a leaf in order to germinate and infect plants. This fungal disease overwinters in seeds and plant debris left in the garden.

WHAT TO DO:
• Remove and dispose of infected plant parts.
• Spray with bordeaux mix. Bordeaux mix is a wettable combination of copper sulfate and hydrated lime in powdered form.
• Water early in the day, and avoid wetting foliage.
• Remove plant debris from the garden.
• Space peonies widely for adequate air circulation.
• Mulch to keep spore-laden mud from splashing on plants.

PROBLEM: Your peonies have patches of gray mold beginning to form on the fading flowers and on the leaves.

CAUSES: Botrytis blight, also called gray mold or late blight (*Botrytis cinerea*); early bud rot (*B. paeoniae*). These similar-acting fungal diseases appear most often during cool, wet weather. Infected new shoots die as they emerge or when they are a few inches high.

Their bases may be black and rotted, with portions covered by gray mold. The disease spores travel from plant to plant in splashing water. The blight overwinters in dead leaves and stems.

WHAT TO DO:
• Remove and destroy infected plant parts.
• Spray shoots in early spring with bordeaux mix. Repeat spraying two or three times at ten-day intervals. Bordeaux mix is a wettable combination of copper sulfate and hydrated lime in powdered form.
• Deadhead (remove spent flowers) to keep peonies flowering longer as well as to prevent gray mold from attacking fading flowers.
• Wash hands and tools after handling diseased plants to keep from spreading disease.
• Avoid overhead watering.
• Clean up plant debris.
• Incorporate compost into the soil to improve soil drainage and to introduce beneficial organisms.
• Space plants widely for good air circulation.

PROBLEM: Shoots wilt and turn dark. Flowers, leaves, or stems shrivel and brown. Affected plants are easy to pull.

CAUSE: Phytophthora blight (*Phytophthora cactorum*). This long-lived, soilborne fungal disease is often brought on by poorly drained soil. Phytophthora blight thrives in cool, wet weather and travels from plant to plant in splashing water or on dirty tools or hands.

WHAT TO DO:
• Remove and destroy infected plants parts. If roots are decayed, remove and destroy the entire plant.
• Clean up and destroy all plant debris.
• Wash your hands and sterilize tools with rubbing alcohol after working with infected plants to avoid spreading disease.
• Avoid excessive watering and overhead watering.

• Space plants widely for good air circulation.
• Grow plants in well-drained soil.

 Other Problems

PROBLEM: Peonies seem to be healthy and growing, but they do not produce flower buds, or buds do not develop.

CAUSES: Peonies are planted too deeply; plants lack sufficient winter chilling; immature plants; plants need dividing; too much shade; too much fertilizer.

Peonies that are planted deeply will send up stems and leaves but will rarely bloom.

The plants need to go dormant and experience freezing conditions in winter in order to grow properly. In a mild-winter area, they may exhaust themselves by continuing to grow during winter.

Peonies do not mature and bloom for about three years after planting.

Old clumps of peonies can become overgrown and stop blooming. If they are divided, the new plantings will thrive and bloom.

Peonies need to be grown in full sun in order to bloom well. They will bloom to some extent in partial shade, but in full shade they will produce leaves and no flowers.

Too much nitrogen causes plants to produce more leaves and few flowers.

WHAT TO DO:
• When planting, make sure the "eyes" (buds at tops of roots) are facing up and are covered by no more than 1 to 1½ inches of soil.
• Divide clumps of plants in late summer, and space divisions with three to five eyes about 3 feet apart.
• If they are growing in shade, move them to a sunny site.
• Fertilize peonies in the spring with composted manure or a high-potassium fertilizer, such as greensand.
• Substitute tree peonies (*P. suffruticosa*).

Petunia

(Petunia × hybrida)

 Petunia Pests

PROBLEM: In late spring, you find brick red, soft-bodied grubs with black spots munching on leaf tips and flowers.

CAUSE: Colorado potato beetles (*Leptinotarsa decemlineata*). These common pests of potatoes also attack related plants, including petunias. The pests are ½-inch-long, yellowish orange beetles with ten black stripes on their backs. The beetles overwinter in leaf

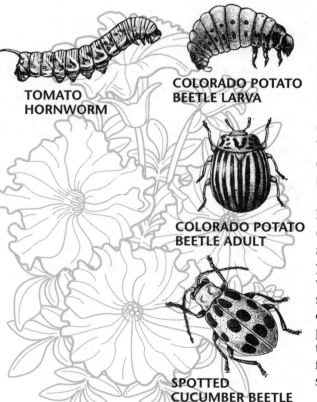

TOMATO HORNWORM

COLORADO POTATO BEETLE LARVA

COLORADO POTATO BEETLE ADULT

SPOTTED CUCUMBER BEETLE

litter; in spring they lay clusters of bright yellow eggs on leaf undersides. The many nymphs, which grow up to ½ inch long, are fat and yellow with black dots along their sides. Both the nymphs and adults cause great damage as they eat petunia leaves and flowers.

WHAT TO DO:
• Remove leaves with egg masses on their backs.
• Handpick beetles and larvae.
• Apply straw mulch to the ground around petunias to deter this pest.
• Spray BTSD on plants, or sprinkle granules on plants. *Bacillus thuringiensis* is an insect-stomach poison that kills caterpillars without harming beneficial insects. *B.t.* var *san diego* (BTSD) kills beetle grubs.
• Remove leaves, mulches, and petunia plant debris after hard freezes in the fall, and cultivate beds to kill overwintering beetles.

PROBLEM: Greenish yellow beetles with 12 black spots are eating your petunia leaves and flowers.

CAUSE: Spotted cucumber beetles (*Diabrotica undecimpunctata* var. *howardi*). These greenish yellow beetles with 12 black spots on their wings are about ¼ inch long. As their name suggests, they are especially fond of eating cucumber plants. They also like to feed on petunias, and they can spread viral and bacterial wilt diseases from plant to plant as they feed. Their petunia-eating larvae, called southern corn rootworms, are ½- to ¾-inch-long, white, segmented grubs with brown heads and patches on the first and last segments.

WHAT TO DO:
• Handpick beetles and grubs.
• Apply milky disease spores. Milky disease combines spores of *Bacillus popilliae* and *B. lentimorbus*. Grubs eat the spores and die.
• Apply beneficial nematodes (*Steinernema carpocapsae* and *Heterorhabditis heliothidis*), which you can purchase from mail-order suppliers. Live nematodes are shipped suspended in sponges or gels. Follow label instructions for application, and release nematodes when pest larvae are present.

PROBLEM: Leaves of young petunia plants are covered with tiny holes. You can see small, black beetles on them.

CAUSE: Potato flea beetles (*Epitrix cucumeris*). These $\frac{1}{16}$-inch-long, shiny black beetles are called flea beetles because they jump like fleas when disturbed. These pests are found throughout the United States and are most damaging in early spring, when high numbers can kill seedlings.

WHAT TO DO:
• Apply beneficial nematodes (*Steinernema carpocapsae* and *Heterorhabditis heliothidis*), which you can purchase from mail-order suppliers. Live nematodes are shipped suspended in gels or sponges. Follow label instructions, and apply beneficial nematodes when pests are present.
• Make white sticky traps. Coat white cardboard or painted wooden boards with petroleum jelly or Tanglefoot (a commercial product for this purpose), and fasten them to stakes near petunia plants. Replace traps when they become covered with potato flea beetles.
• Spray infested plants with insecticidal soap. Be sure to spray soap on the backs of leaves,

where pests often hide, as well as the tops.
• Sprinkle diatomaceous earth (DE) around petunia plants. This abrasive dust is made from fossilized shells, called diatoms, which penetrate pests' skin as they crawl over DE. Wear a dust mask to avoid inhaling particles, and apply DE when petunia plants are wet with dew.
• Watch your garden to see what plants the flea beetles favor. Plant some of their favorite plants some distance from your petunias to lure the beetles away. When the trap plants become infested with flea beetles, pull them up and destroy them.

PROBLEM: Young petunias are eaten in spring. The large holes in the leaves or flowers are streaked with slime.

CAUSES: Slugs and snails (Order Stylommatophora). These $\frac{1}{8}$- to 8-inch-long, soft-bodied, gray, tan, green, black, yellow, or spotted pests resemble clams and mussels. Snails have shells; slugs look like snails without shells. At night these pests feed on petunia leaves and flowers. In the morning they leave behind a trail of shiny slime as they climb down your petunias to hide under garden debris during the day. Adults lay masses of clear eggs under mulch and garden debris.

WHAT TO DO:
• Handpick. The best time to begin hunting is two hours after dark.
• Remove mulch and garden debris.
• Allow the soil to dry out between waterings.
• Create barriers by sprinkling wood ashes or crushed eggshells around flowerbeds or individual plants.
• Edge plants with a strip of copper, which hits these slimy pests with an electrical shock upon contact.

• Sprinkle diatomaceous earth (DE) around plants. This abrasive dust is made from fossilized shells, called diatoms, which penetrate the pests' skin as they crawl over DE. Wear a dust mask to avoid inhaling particles, and apply DE when the petunia plants are wet with dew.

• Make beer traps from recycled cans sunk to the brim in soil and filled with yeasty beer. Attracted by the scent of beer, slugs and snails will fall into the traps and drown.

PROBLEM: Large holes appear in petunia leaves. Caterpillars and black specks of excrement may be visible on them.

CAUSES: Caterpillars, including tomato hornworms (*Manduca quinquemaculata*) and yellow woollybears (*Spilosoma virginica*), sometimes feed on petunias.

Tomato hornworms are 1- to 4-inch-long, bright green caterpillars with eight diagonal white stripes on their sides and a fleshy, pointed, black "horn" on their tail ends. The caterpillars are the larvae of the large hummingbird moth. They have fuzzy, orange abdomens, narrow wings, and wingspans of 4 to 5 inches.

Yellow woollybear caterpillars can actually be yellow, rusty red, or even white. They are 2 inches long and covered with fuzzy, thick hairs. These caterpillars are the larvae of moths with 1½-inch wingspans. The white, velvety-textured moths have tiny black dots on their wings and abdomen. The woollybear caterpillars eat petunia leaves and flowers.

WHAT TO DO:

• Handpick.

• Apply *Bacillus thuringiensis* (BT). This insect-stomach poison targets and kills caterpillars without harming beneficial insects. Follow directions, and apply when caterpillars are present.

 Petunia Diseases

PROBLEM: Young seedling collapse at the soil line, fall over, and die. Their main stems are darkened at the soil.

CAUSE: Damping-off (*Rhizoctonia solani*). This soil-dwelling fungus primarily attacks seedlings started indoors and those growing in heavy, wet soil outdoors. Stem injuries are likely sites of infection; but because the fungi live in soil, roots are also vulnerable. The disease overwinters in garden debris and in soil.

WHAT TO DO:

• Use sterile seed-starting mix for seeds started indoors, and plant seeds in clean containers. Keep seedlings within 2 inches of a plant light if seeds are started indoors, and circulate air by running a fan if needed.

• Outdoors, plant seeds in moist, well-drained garden soil that is fortified with compost.

• Use high-nitrogen fertilizers sparingly until seedlings have well-developed roots.

PROBLEM: Masses of short, thick stems with misshapen leaves are developing on petunia stems near the soil line.

CAUSE: Bacterial fasciation (*Clavibacter fascians*). Petunias infected with this soilborne bacterial disease become stunted and produce few flowers. The disease can overwinter in the soil from year to year.

WHAT TO DO:

• Remove damaged leaves and severely damaged plants.

• Solarize the soil before replanting it with healthy petunias. Clear plastic sheeting placed over bare soil for three to four weeks uses the sun's energy to heat the soil enough to kill most disease organisms in the top few inches of soil. After removing the plastic, plant crops as usual.

PROBLEM: Strands of odd-looking, orange, stringy organisms are woven throughout your petunia plants.

CAUSE: Dodder (*Cuscuta* spp.). These unusual strands are actually parasitic plants that have no leaves or chlorophyl. Dodder sucks nutrients from plants to which it attaches itself with tiny suckers. The parasitic plants can eventually kill host plants and then send out long stems to attach to nearby plants. Dodder seeds can be carried into the garden on contaminated hay or straw mulch.

WHAT TO DO:

• Remove and destroy dodder and the plants that it attacks. If you just remove the visible strings, the dodder will regrow from small pieces left on host plants.

PROBLEM: Growth is stunted. Plants wilt, turn yellow, and slowly die, although no pests or diseases are visible.

CAUSE: Southern root-knot nematodes (*Meloidogyne incognita* var. *incognita*). These minute pests are most often a problem in the South and Midwest, and they are especially severe in areas with sandy or peaty soils. The nematodes are actually microscopic worms that live in the soil and attack roots, causing symptoms above ground that are similar to wilt diseases. To check for root-knot nematodes, pull up a wilting plant and look at the roots. If nematodes are present, the roots will have knots and excessive root branching.

WHAT TO DO:

• Help infested plants resist further damage by providing them with regular waterings and fertilizer applications.
• Turn under compost to introduce beneficial soil organisms.
• Apply crab or shrimp wastes that contain chitin. Chitin, made from shellfish shells, provides nitrogen and potassium as it breaks down, creating conditions that encourage the beneficial soil organisms that attack nematodes.
• Solarize the soil. Clear plastic sheeting placed over bare soil for three to four weeks uses the sun's energy to heat the soil enough to kill most pests and weed seeds in the top few inches of soil. After removing the plastic, plant petunias as usual.
• In regions where nematode problems are severe, grow petunias and other flowers in containers.

PROBLEM: Your petunia leaves are mottled with yellow. Leaf blades are distorted, and there are few or no flowers.

CAUSE: Cucumber mosaic virus. This viral disease is spread via feeding insects, including aphids. It overwinters in weeds, such as ground cherry, milkweed, and pokeweed.

WHAT TO DO:

• Remove and destroy infected plants.
• Control aphids by spraying infested plants with insecticidal soap.

 Other Problems

PROBLEM: Spots ranging from white to bronze appear on leaf undersides. Leaves have a silvery appearance.

CAUSE: Pollution damage. An air pollutant called peroxyacyl nitrate forms when sunlight reacts with smog. This chemical damages petunias grown in smoggy urban areas. The symptoms are similar to damage caused by mites or thrips.

WHAT TO DO:

• Remove damaged leaves.
• Replace severely affected plants.

Phlox

(Phlox spp.)

 Phlox Pests

PROBLEM: White or light green spots are on young leaves. Leaves, shoots, and flowers may be stunted or deformed.

CAUSE: Phlox plant bugs (*Lopidea davisi*). These bugs eat young leaves and buds. Both the ¼-inch-long, yellow-green bugs with black-striped backs and their smaller red or orange nymphs eat phlox plants.

WHAT TO DO:
• Handpick bugs and nymphs.
• Spray infested plants with insecticidal soap.
• Spray infested plants with summer oil, a horticultural oil that coats plant parts and smothers pests.
• Spray infested plants with neem. This botanical pesticide repels and poisons insect pests but is harmless to beneficial insects.

PROBLEM: Leaves appear very pale green and stippled, due to tiny, yellow or white spots. Webbing may be present.

CAUSE: Spider mites (Family Tetranychidae). These pinpoint-sized, spiderlike pests pierce plant leaves to suck nutrients, leaving pinpricks in leaves. Mites feed more voraciously during dry spells. Their cobwebs protect eggs and hatchlings. These pests overwinter in leaves on the ground and in plant crevices.

WHAT TO DO:
• Dislodge mites with a blast of water.
• Spray infested plants with insecticidal soap.
• Spray infested plants with summer oil, a horticultural oil that coats plant parts and smothers pests. Begin treatment early, at the pinprick stage. By the time webs are visible, it may be too late to save the plants.
• Attract mite-eating hummingbirds by growing plants with red, trumpet-shaped flowers, like trumpet vine (*Campsis radicans*), wild columbine (*Aquilegia canadensis*), and cardinal flower (*Lobelia cardinalis*).

 Phlox Diseases

PROBLEM: Phlox plants have swollen stems. The shoots and leaves are curled, wrinkled, and deformed.

CAUSE: Nematodes, including fern nema-

SPIDER MITE

PHLOX PLANT BUG

todes (*Aphelenchoides fragariae*), stem and bulb nematodes (*Ditylenchus dipsaci*), and root-knot nematodes (*Meloidogyne* spp.). Fern nematodes affect leaves. Stem and bulb nematodes and root-knot nematodes are similar, wormlike, microscopic organisms ¹⁄₅₀ to ¹⁄₁₀ inch long that invade and feed on roots, causing diseaselike symptoms above ground. Their toxic secretions cause infested tissues to swell into recognizable knots. Infected plants become stunted, weakened, and susceptible to diseases. These pests travel on dirty tools, hands and feet, splashing water, or wind.

WHAT TO DO:
• Remove and destroy infested plants and surrounding garden debris.
• Incorporate compost into beds to introduce beneficial soil organisms into the soil.
• Water to keep soil moist but not soggy.

PROBLEM: Phlox plants wilt and die. Stems may blacken and decay at the base, and crowns may rot.

CAUSES: Crown rot and root rot. These diseases are caused by various soilborne fungi. The potentially fatal infections are common in poorly drained soils.

WHAT TO DO:
• Remove and destroy infected plants and the soil that their roots touch.
• Remove and compost garden debris.
• Pull mulch away from the bases of healthy plants to increase air circulation.

PROBLEM: A powdery, gray-white coating covers leaves, flowers, and stems. Plants usually do not die.

CAUSE: Powdery mildew (*Erysiphe cichoracearum* and *Sphaerotheca macularis*). Unlike many other plant diseases, powdery mildew spores do not require a film of moisture on the leaf to germinate. But they do thrive in the high humidity that results when plants are crowded or grown in shady locations. The disease overwinters on plant debris or on perennials and weeds. Phlox are very susceptible to powdery mildew, but susceptibility does vary with species and cultivars.

WHAT TO DO:
• Cut off and destroy infected plant parts.
• Water well during dry spells, since powdery mildew is often a sign of a thirsty plant.
• Spray a 2 percent solution of horticultural oil, which smothers disease organisms.
• Water with fermented compost tea every two to four weeks.
• Do not plant the susceptible species *P. paniculata* and the cultivar 'Anja'. Instead grow resistant plants, such as thick leaf phlox (*P. carolina*) and wild blue phlox (*P. divaricata*), both of which perform well in the heat and humidity of southern gardens.
• Space plants widely for good air circulation.
• Grow phlox in a sunny site.

PROBLEM: Leaves die and drop off, beginning at the base of plants and progressing upward.

CAUSE: Leaf drop, also called leaf blight or rust. The spores of this fungal disease travel from plant to plant on the wind and in splashing water. It thrives in damp weather and inhibits the plants' ability to take up water. It occurs on older phlox plants. The plants need to be divided every few years.

WHAT TO DO:
• Remove and dispose of infected leaves.
• Spray with sulfur.
• Avoid overhead watering.
• Space or thin plants widely for circulation.
• Divide clumps of phlox every three to five years. Replant shoots from the outer edges.

Poppies

(*Papaver* spp.)

 Poppy Pests

PROBLEM: Small, pear-shaped insects cluster on leaves or stems. Leaves may have a clear, sticky or black coating.

CAUSE: Aphids (Family Aphididae). These pests are $\frac{1}{16}$- to $\frac{3}{8}$-inch-long, soft-bodied insects. They range in color from pale tan to light green to nearly black. Aphids damage leaves and stems by sucking plant juices. These insects can transmit plant diseases as they feed. Their sticky secretions, called honeydew, attract ants and sooty mold; ants protect aphids from predators in order to eat their secretions.

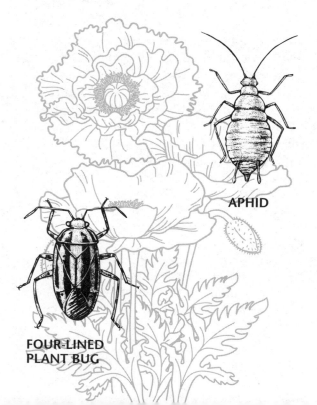

APHID

**FOUR-LINED
PLANT BUG**

WHAT TO DO:
• Wash aphids off plants with a strong stream of water.
• Use insecticidal soap, following directions.
• Attract lady beetles, lacewings, and other beneficial insects by planting small-flowered nectar plants, including yarrow, dill, and Queen-Anne's-lace. Give the beneficials time to bring the aphids under control.
• Pour boiling water into entry holes of anthills that are not adjacent to plant roots.

PROBLEM: Leaves and flowers are distorted or dwarfed. They develop yellow, tan, or brown spots in early summer.

CAUSE: Four-lined plant bugs (*Poecilocapsus lineatus*). These sap-sucking pests are $\frac{1}{3}$-inch-long, yellowish green bugs with four black stripes on each wing. In May or June their eggs hatch into bright red nymphs with black-dotted chests. Their feeding ends in midsummer. The eggs overwinter in garden debris.

WHAT TO DO:
• Handpick.
• Spray insecticidal soap on undersides of leaves every third day for two weeks until pests disappear.
• Clean up garden debris in spring and fall.

PROBLEM: Leaves look bleached and have yellow or brown edges. Some leaves and stems are deformed.

CAUSE: Aster leafhoppers, also known as six-spotted leafhoppers (*Macrosteles quadrilineatus*). The $\frac{1}{8}$-inch-long adults are black with greenish yellow undersides and black-spotted heads. The adults infect plants with the disease aster yellows (a mycoplasma) as they suck sap from the leaves. Aster leafhoppers overwinter in weeds.

WHAT TO DO:
• Tolerate light damage.
• Use insecticidal soap, following directions.
• Spray plants with horticultural oil. This refined oil smothers leafhoppers.
• Attract parasitic flies, wasps, lady beetles, lacewings, spiders, and other beneficials by planting small-flowered nectar plants, like yarrow, alyssum, and scabiosa.

 ## Poppy Diseases

PROBLEM: Small, black, water-soaked spots appear on leaves, stems, and flowers. Plants brown and lose leaves.

CAUSE: Bacterial blight (*Xanthomonas papavericola*). This bacterial disease enters plants through their pores and creates leaf spots that are wet, black, and ringed in white. Flowers darken. Infected plants can fall over and die. The disease travels in infected seeds.

WHAT TO DO:
• Dig out and destroy infected plants and the soil that their roots touch.
• Avoid overhead watering, or water early in the day so that plants dry before evening.
• Solarize the soil. Clear plastic sheeting placed over bare soil for three to four weeks uses the sun's energy to heat the soil enough to kill most diseases in the top few inches of soil. Remove plastic; plant poppies as usual.
• Plant certified disease-free seed.

PROBLEM: Plants wilt, but they do not respond to watering. Their leaves turn yellow, and the plants eventually die.

CAUSE: Verticillium wilt (*Verticillium alboatrum*). This soilborne fungal disease spreads during periods of cool, moist weather. It tar-

gets poppies growing in poorly drained soil. Disease spores survive in the soil for years.

WHAT TO DO:
• Remove and dispose of infected plants.
• Add compost to the soil to introduce beneficial organisms and to improve drainage.

PROBLEM: A powdery, gray-white coating covers leaves, flowers, and stems. Plants usually do not die.

CAUSE: Powdery mildew (*Erysiphe polygoni*). Unlike many other plant diseases, powdery mildew spores do not require a film of moisture on the leaf to germinate. They do thrive in the high humidity that results when plants are crowded or grown in shady locations. The disease overwinters on plant debris or on perennials and weeds.

WHAT TO DO:
• Cut off and destroy infected plant parts.
• Water well during dry spells since powdery mildew is often a sign of a thirsty plant.
• Spray a 2 percent solution of horticultural oil, which coats plant parts and smothers disease organisms.
• Water with disease-fighting fermented compost tea every two to four weeks.
• Space or thin plants widely for circulation.
• Grow poppies in full sun.

 ## Other Problems

PROBLEM: Your perennial poppies do not last more than a year or two.

CAUSE: Unsuitable growing conditions. Perennial poppies need to go dormant during long, cold winters. They are short-lived in warm-winter climates, where they become weakened by the longer-than-optimum growing seasons.

WHAT TO DO:
• Grow perennial poppies as annuals.
• Grow Iceland poppies (*P. nudicaule*).

Purple Coneflowers

(Echinacea spp.)

Purple Coneflower Pests

PROBLEM: Leaves are chewed between the veins. Some flowers are devoured. You see green-and-copper beetles.

CAUSE: Japanese beetles (*Popillia japonica*). These shiny, ½-inch-long beetles eat leaves and flowers. They emerge in midsummer and can do great damage, focusing on plants growing in full sun. Their fat, ½-inch-long, white grubs develop in the soil over winter. In the spring they eat grass roots in lawns.

WHAT TO DO:
• Handpick.
• Spray infested plants with insecticidal soap.
• Spray infested plants with neem. This botanical pesticide repels and poisons insect pests but is harmless to beneficial insects.
• Apply milky disease spores to the soil. This combination of *Bacillus popilliae* and *B. lentimorbus* kills grubs when they eat it.

Purple Coneflower Diseases

PROBLEM: Some plants wilt and do not revive with watering. Affected plants eventually die.

CAUSE: Texas root rot (*Phymatotrichum omnivorum*). This fungal disease is most common in heavy, alkaline soils, and it can be quite fast acting. Texas root rot occurs primarily during summer and early fall in southern states.

WHAT TO DO:
• Remove diseased plants and destroy them.
• Incorporate compost to improve soil drainage and to introduce beneficial soil organisms.

PROBLEM: A powdery white coating covers leaves, flowers, and stems. Plants usually do not die.

CAUSE: Powdery mildew (*Erysiphe cichora-*

JAPANESE BEETLE

cearum). This common fungal disease weakens plants and makes them unsightly. Infected leaves may shrivel and die. The disease spores may overwinter on plant debris or on perennial garden plants and weeds. The spores thrive in the high humidity that results when plants are crowded or grown in shady locations.

WHAT TO DO:
• Remove and destroy severely infected plant parts or plants.
• Spray with baking soda. To make baking soda spray, dissolve 1 teaspoon baking soda in 1 quart warm water; add 1 teaspoon insecticidal soap to make the solution stick to leaves.
• Grow purple coneflowers in full sun.
• Space new plants and thin old clumps of plants, putting them far enough apart for adequate air circulation.
• Water the plants regularly during dry spells.

 Other Problems

PROBLEM: Clumps that grew well and flowered for several years are beginning to grow slowly and flower less.

CAUSE: Overcrowding. Purple coneflowers reproduce by sending up new plants from the base of original plants. As clumps increase in diameter, older plants at the center of clumps are crowded by new plants surrounding them.

WHAT TO DO:
• Divide coneflowers every three or four years in the spring (or in the fall in milder climates). Plant groups of three or more plantlets taken from the outer edges of clumps, and discard older plants in the centers.

PROBLEM: Your purple coneflowers are taller than they should be. They have thin, weak stems.

CAUSES: Too much shade; too much fertil-izer. These prairie plants crave full sunshine and lean soil. Growing them in the shade and giving them nitrogen-rich fertilizers can cause them to produce weak, spindly stems and few flowers.

WHAT TO DO:
• Transplant coneflowers to a sunny site with well-drained soil.
• Stop fertilizing purple coneflowers.

PROBLEM: Plants have spindly stems, flower poorly, and may attract numbers of pests or have repeated infections.

CAUSE: Poor growing conditions. Wet soil due to overwatering, poor drainage, or long periods of rainy weather will cause purple coneflower to produce limp stems and leaves that are targeted by insects and many diseases. These conditions also make plants susceptible to potentially fatal fungal infections.

WHAT TO DO:
• If your purple coneflowers are growing in soggy soil, allow the soil to dry out between waterings.
• Incorporate organic matter, such as compost or leaf mold, into the soil to improve drainage.
• Move plants. If your purple coneflowers are growing in the shade, trim off the stems, lift the roots, and replant them in full sun and in well-drained garden soil of average fertility.

PROBLEM: Your coneflower plants are green and healthy-looking, but they are not blooming.

CAUSE: Too much nitrogen fertilizer. Providing more high-nitrogen fertilizer than plants need will cause them to produce lush foliage and few or no flowers.

WHAT TO DO:
• Avoid excessive use of high-nitrogen fertilizer.

Roses

(*Rosa* spp. and hybrids)

 Rose Pests

PROBLEM: New growth wilts. Canes exude sap. Holes are visible in stems or in the cut ends of canes after pruning.

CAUSES: Borers, including the larvae of small carpenter bees called pith borers (*Ceratina* spp.), the larvae of rose stem girdlers (*Agrilus aurichalceus*), and the larvae of rose stem sawflies (*Hartigia trimaculata*).

Carpenter bees are ⅓ inch long and are black with a metallic sheen. They burrow into rose canes to nest. If you cut an infested stem open lengthwise, you will see six or more yellowish, curved maggots.

Rose stem girdlers are the larvae of a greenish beetle. The white, ¾-inch-long larvae make spiral burrows just beneath the bark of canes, causing canes to swell and split. Rose stem girdlers more often attack species roses, such as *R. rugosa* and *R. hugonis*, than hybrid garden roses.

Rose stem sawflies are wasplike insects that lay eggs in holes they make in canes. White larvae hatch and bore through the canes.

WHAT TO DO:
• Prune off infected canes below the infestations and dispose of them.
• Seal pruned cuts with the liquid white glue commonly used on paper.
• Insert a sharp wire into the tunnel to kill borers.

PROBLEM: Rose leaves have large holes in them, or they are skeletonized. The undersides of the leaves look rasped.

CAUSE: Bristly rose slugs (*Cladius difformis*). These night-feeding pests are the brown-headed, pale green larvae of a sawfly. The ½- to ¾-inch-long, sluglike, bristly larvae first rasp tissue from the undersides of leaves and then eat holes all the way through them. The adults lay eggs in leaf tissue. Maturing larvae spin cocoons on leaves and twigs. They overwinter in the soil.

WHAT TO DO:
• Handpick, wearing gloves to protect your hands from the bristles.
• Wash bristly rose slugs off roses with a strong stream of water.
• Use insecticidal soap. Follow label directions when spraying.

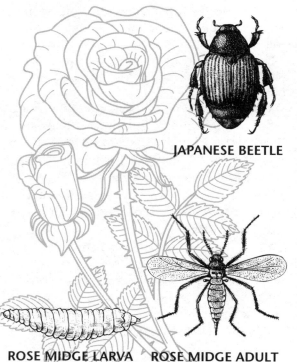

JAPANESE BEETLE

ROSE MIDGE LARVA   **ROSE MIDGE ADULT**

PROBLEM: Your roses have chewed leaves, buds, and blossoms. Leaves may be skeletonized and covered with webs.

CAUSES: Caterpillars, including fall webworms (*Hyphantria cunea*) and rose budworms (*Pyrrhia umbra*).

Fall webworms are the fuzzy, golden larvae of white moths with brown spots and 2-inch wingspans. Webworms eat rose leaves in summer and then overwinter in cocoons attached to tree bark or garden debris.

Rose budworms are the larvae of the bordered sallow moth, a brown moth with striped wings and a wingspan of 1½ inches. The leaf-eating caterpillars can be green with black spots and stripes or have white markings on their backs.

WHAT TO DO:
• Handpick caterpillars.
• Spray infested plants with *Bacillus thuringiensis* (BT), an insect-stomach poison.
• Attract parasitic wasps and other beneficial insects by growing small-flowered nectar plants, such as alyssum, scabiosa, and yarrow.

PROBLEM: Pastel roses have brown edges or streaked blossoms and buds. Buds do not open or open only partially.

CAUSE: Flower thrips (*Frankliniella tritici*). These extremely tiny, narrow-bodied insects are only ¹⁄₂₀ inch long. Young thrips are lemon yellow; adults are light brown with orange undersides. Thrips hide deep inside the flowers and are almost impossible to see without using a magnifying glass. If you suspect a rose has thrips, pick a damaged flower and shake it over a clean sheet of white paper. If thrips are present, they will drop onto the paper and will look like dark specks.

WHAT TO DO:
• Pick off and destroy infested buds and flowers.

• Spray infested plants with insecticidal soap.
• Spray infested plants with sulfur.
• Keep plants adequately watered and mulched to keep soil moist but not soggy.
• Use loose, organic mulch to attract beneficial spiders.
• Attract beneficial insects by planting small-flowered nectar plants, such as alyssum, yarrow, and scabiosa.
• Purchase lacewings and beneficial nematodes from mail-order suppliers, and release them in the garden to supplement native populations.

PROBLEM: Leaves, flowers and buds are chewed between veins and have a brown, lacy look.

CAUSES: Japanese beetles (*Popillia japonica*) and rose chafers (*Macrodactylus subspinosus*).

Japanese beetles are shiny, metallic, green-and-copper, ½-inch-long beetles that skeletonize leaves and feed on flowers and buds. Japanese beetles are found east of the Mississippi River.

Rose chafers are ⅓- to ½-inch-long, tan beetles with reddish brown heads; they eat rose flowers.

WHAT TO DO:
• Handpick.
• Collect beetles with a battery-operated, hand-held vacuum.
• Put a drop cloth under the plant and shake the beetles onto it; drown collected beetles in soapy water.
• Spray foliage with neem, a botanical insecticide that kills pests without harming beneficial insects.
• For long-term control of Japanese beetle grubs, which overwinter in lawns, apply beneficial nematodes (*Steinernema carpocapsae* and *Heterorhabditis heliothidis*), which you can purchase from mail-order suppliers. Live nematodes are shipped suspended in sponges or

gels. Follow label instructions for application, and release nematodes when pest larvae are present.
• Apply milky disease spores to the soil. This combination of *Bacillus popilliae* and *B. lentimorbus* kills grubs when they eat it.

PROBLEM: Small, green or pinkish, pear-shaped insects are on plants. Leaves may have a clear or black coating.

CAUSE: Rose aphids (*Macrosiphum rosae*). These pests are $\frac{1}{16}$- to $\frac{3}{8}$-inch-long, soft-bodied insects that damage leaves and stems by sucking plant juices. Aphids can transmit plant diseases as they feed. Their sticky secretions, called honeydew, attract ants and sooty mold; ants protect aphids from predators in order to eat their secretions.

WHAT TO DO:
• Wash aphids off plants with a strong stream of water.
• Use insecticidal soap, following label directions.
• Attract beneficial insects, like lady beetles and lacewings, by planting small-flowered nectar plants, including yarrow, dill, and Queen-Anne's-lace. Give the beneficials time to bring the aphids under control.
• Pour boiling water into entry holes of anthills that are not adjacent to plant roots.

PROBLEM: Buds and shoot tips turn black and shrivel. You see tiny, white maggots on buds or on stem tips.

CAUSE: Rose midges (*Dasineura rhodophaga*). The adults are $\frac{1}{20}$-inch-long, reddish or yellowish brown flies. They lay small eggs in flower buds and unfolding leaves. The tiny hatchling maggots devour buds and young leaves. A week after hatching they turn from white to orange and grow to $\frac{1}{12}$ inch in length. The maggots then fall to the ground to pupate.

WHAT TO DO:
• Remove and destroy all infested plant parts daily until no more are seen.

PROBLEM: Roses have wilted leaves and stunted growth. There are small gray or white bumps on the canes.

CAUSE: Scale (Order Homoptera). These $\frac{1}{10}$-inch-long insects look like oval, waxy bumps. Both the stationary adults and their similarly sized, fuzzy, mobile nymphs suck plant juices and produce sticky honeydew that encourages the growth of sooty mold.

WHAT TO DO:
• Scrape scale off canes with a nylon scouring pad.
• Kill scale by dabbing them with a cotton swab dipped in rubbing alcohol.
• Prune off heavily encrusted canes.
• Wash black sooty mold off plants with water.
• Spray summer oil when crawlers (young, mobile scale) are present. This horticultural oil coats plant parts, smothering pests.
• Attract beneficial insects by planting small-flowered nectar plants, like alyssum, scabiosa, and yarrow.

PROBLEM: Leaves appear pale green and stippled, with tiny yellow or white spots. Webbing may appear on leaves.

CAUSE: Spider mites (Family Tetranychidae). These pinpoint-sized, spiderlike pests pierce plant leaves to suck nutrients, leaving pinprick holes in leaves. Spider mites feed more voraciously during dry spells. Their cobwebs protect eggs and hatchlings. These pests overwinter in leaves on the ground and in plant crevices.

WHAT TO DO:
• Dislodge spider mites with a strong stream of water.
• Spray infested plants with insecticidal soap.
• Spray infested plants with summer oil, a

horticultural oil that coats plant parts and smothers pests. Begin treatment early, at the pinprick stage. By the time webs are visible, it may be too late to save the plants.
• Attract mite-eating hummingbirds by growing plants with red, trumpet-shaped flowers, like trumpet vine (*Campsis radicans*), wild columbine (*Aquilegia canadensis*), and cardinal flower (*Lobelia cardinalis*).

PROBLEM: **Edges of leaves are notched or scalloped. There may be holes in flower buds, and eaten buds may not open.**

CAUSES: Fuller rose beetles (*Asynonychus godmani*) and rose curculios (*Merhynchites bicolor*).

Adult fuller rose beetles are ⅓-inch-long weevils with short snouts and a white stripe across on each wing. These pests chew holes along the edges of rose leaves at night, while their brown-headed, white or pale yellow larvae pupate in the soil and eat rose roots.

Rose curculios are ¼-inch-long, bright red, weevil-like insects with black undersides and black mouthparts. Rose curculios specialize in eating holes in rosebuds, and they lay their eggs in rose hips in the fall. The white, maggotlike pupae eat their way out of the hips and drop to the ground to over-winter in garden debris. Wild roses can also host rose curculios.

WHAT TO DO:
• Tolerate light damage.
• Collect and destroy flower buds infested with rose curculios or hips infested with their larvae. To collect either pest, spread a cloth on the ground under the plant and shake the branches over the cloth, and destroy the weevils that fall to the cloth.
• Apply beneficial nematodes (*Steinernema carpocapsae* and *Heterorhabditis heliothidis*) to the soil around roses. You can purchase these from mail-order suppliers; live nematodes are shipped suspended in gels or sponges. Follow label instructions, and apply when pests are present.

Rose Diseases

PROBLEM: **Black spots with uneven edges spread across canes and tops and backs of leaves. Spotted leaves drop.**

CAUSE: Black spot (*Diplocarpon rosae*). Spores of this fungal disease travel from plant to plant in splashing water, on the wind, and on work gloves and tools. They are also carried by feeding insects. Black spot is most active where summers are warm and wet.

WHAT TO DO:
• Remove and destroy infected leaves, along with seriously infected plants and garden debris.
• Spray with liquid sulfur or baking soda spray at least twice monthly for as long as warm, humid weather continues. Reapply after rain. Do not apply sulfur during very humid or very hot (85°F or higher) weather because it may damage leaf tissue. (To make baking soda spray, dissolve 1 teaspoon baking soda in 1 quart warm water; add 1 teaspoon insecticidal soap to make the solution stick to leaves.)
• Prune out inward-growing shoots to open the center of rose bushes to air and sun.
• Avoid splashing water on the foliage when watering.
• Mulch roses with disease-fighting compost.
• Grow roses in full sun, and space them far enough apart for adequate air circulation.
• In winter, cut back seriously infected canes to 8 inches.
• Grow resistant roses, such as 'Iceberg', 'Olympiad', and 'Queen Elizabeth'.

PROBLEM: **Rosebuds droop, turn dark, and rot. Flowers, leaves, and stems may be covered with gray mold.**

CAUSE: Botrytis blight (*Botrytis cinerea*). The

spores of this fungal disease blow from plant to plant on the wind. The blight spreads rapidly in humid weather.

WHAT TO DO:
- Remove and dispose of infected plant parts.
- Avoid overhead watering.
- Plant roses in well-drained soil.
- Space plants far enough apart for adequate air circulation.
- Remove and compost garden debris.

PROBLEM: In summer, purplish spots appear on canes. In winter, tan spots develop on canes mulched with soil.

CAUSE: Brown canker (*Cryptosporella umbrina*). The spores of this fungal disease enter plants through cuts and wounds on the canes. Infected plants can eventually die.

WHAT TO DO:
- In winter, while roses are dormant, prune infected canes 5 inches below the diseased part and destroy the prunings. Seal cuts with wood glue (available at hardware stores).
- Disinfect pruners between cuts with rubbing alcohol.
- Spray roses during the dormant season with bordeaux mix, a wettable combination of copper sulfate and hydrated lime.
- Mulch with compost or dried leaves in the winter rather than using potentially infected soil.

PROBLEM: New leaves curl, or leaves and stem tips turn reddish and become covered with gray-white coating.

CAUSE: Powdery mildew (*Sphaerotheca pannosa* var. *rosae; S. macularis;* and *Phyllactinia corylea*). Several fungi can cause the disease symptoms called powdery mildew. The spores infect leaves under the humid conditions that result when plants are crowded or grown in shady locations. The disease overwinters on garden debris or on perennials and weeds.

WHAT TO DO:
- Remove and destroy severely infested plant parts or plants.
- Spray infected roses with liquid sulfur or baking soda spray. (To make baking soda spray, dissolve 1 teaspoon baking soda in 1 quart warm water; add 1 teaspoon insecticidal soap to make the solution stick to leaves.)
- Water plants regularly during dry spells.
- Grow roses in full sun.
- Space them far enough apart for adequate air circulation.
- Remove inward-growing shoots to open the center of the bush to air and sun.
- Plant resistant roses, such as 'Iceberg', 'Olympiad', and 'Queen Elizabeth'.

PROBLEM: Bright-orange spots on the backs of leaves appear, followed by yellow or dark splotches on tops.

CAUSE: Rust (*Phragmidium* spp.). The spores of this fungal disease travel on wind and in water. Rust thrives in mild, moist weather and is at its worst in spring and early summer.

WHAT TO DO:
- Remove and destroy infected roses and plant debris.
- Spray with liquid sulfur every week when weather is mild and humid.
- Avoid splashing water on the foliage.
- Mulch with compost.
- Plant in full sun.
- Space plants widely for air circulation.
- Prune out inward-growing shoots to open the centers of bushes to air and sun.
- Plant resistant roses, such as 'Iceberg' and 'Olympiad'.

PROBLEM: Mottling, streaking, or oddly shaped patterns develop on leaves. Foliage curls and plants are stunted.

CAUSES: Viruses, such as rose mosaic, rose streak, rose yellow mosaic, and rose leaf curl, cause one or more of these symptoms. Viral diseases such as these are spread by sap-sucking insects, like aphids and leafhoppers.

WHAT TO DO:
• Remove and destroy infected plants.
• Use insecticidal soap to control aphids and leafhoppers, which spread viral diseases.

 Other Problems

PROBLEM: Rose leaves have crisp, dry edges. Some brown and drop. Buds and flowers droop, and plants may wilt.

CAUSE: Drought stress. If roses dry out a few times during the season, they can recover. But a drought that lasts several days or weeks can ruin flowers and leaves and severely stress plants, making them susceptible to pests and diseases.

WHAT TO DO:
• Water regularly during hot, dry spells.
• In areas with long, hot summers, grow roses in afternoon shade or dappled shade.
• Incorporate organic matter into the soil to increase its moisture retention.
• Mulch to reduce water evaporation from the soil.

PROBLEM: Your rose plants are growing and appear healthy, but they flower sparsely.

CAUSE: Lack of sunlight. Like many flowering shrubs, roses need six hours or more of full sun daily to bloom well.

WHAT TO DO:
• Move plants to a site with full sun for best flowering in all but the hottest climates.
• In hot climates, grow roses in a site that receives morning sun and afternoon shade.

PROBLEM: Your roses grew well and flowered last season, but they did not come back after the winter.

CAUSE: Frost damage. Some rose cultivars are less hardy than others, while species roses are generally dependably hardy.

WHAT TO DO:
• In Zone 5 (to –20°F) and areas that are colder, apply several inches of protective mulch, such as straw, evergreen boughs, salt hay, or compost, after ground freezes in fall.
• In cold climates, grow tough, species roses and old-fashioned shrub roses.

PROBLEM: Plants are not growing well. They may attract an unusual number of pests or have repeated infections.

CAUSES: Poor growing conditions; poor nutrition. Roses that grow in the shade or in wet, poorly drained soil will have fewer flowers. Stressed plants will also produce weak, succulent stems and leaves that are targeted by insects and many diseases. Roses are heavy feeders.

WHAT TO DO:
• Lift and replant roses in a well-drained site that receives full sun.
• Grow roses in humus-rich garden soil.
• Water with diluted fish emulsion or manure tea several times during the flowering season.
• Mulch plants with compost.

Sedums

(*Sedum* spp. and hybrids)

Sedum Pests

PROBLEM: Small, pear-shaped insects cluster on leaves or stems. Leaves may have a clear or black, sooty coating.

CAUSE: Aphids (Family Aphididae). These pests are ⅟16- to ⅜-inch-long, soft-bodied insects. They range in color from pale tan to light green to nearly black. Aphids damage sedum leaves and stems by sucking juices from the plants. These insects can transmit plant diseases as they feed, and their sticky secretions, called honeydew, attract ants and sooty mold; ants protect aphids from predators in order to eat their secretions.

WHAT TO DO:
• Wash aphids off sedums with a strong stream of water.
• Use insecticidal soap, following directions.
• Attract beneficial insects, like lady beetles and lacewings, by growing small-flowered nectar plants, including yarrow, dill, and Queen-Anne's-lace. Give the beneficials time to bring the aphids under control.
• Pour boiling water into entry holes of anthills that are not right next to plant roots.

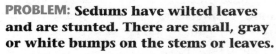

PROBLEM: Sedums have wilted leaves and are stunted. There are small, gray or white bumps on the stems or leaves.

CAUSE: Scale (Order Homoptera). Both greedy scale (*Hemiberlesia rapax*) and white peach scale (*Pseudaulacaspis pentagona*) are sap-sucking insects that can infest sedums. These ⅟10-inch-long insects look like oval, waxy bumps. Both the stationary adults and their similarly sized, fuzzy, mobile nymphs suck plant juices and produce sticky honeydew that encourages the growth of sooty mold and can attract ants.

WHAT TO DO:
• Scrape scale off the stems and fleshy leaves of sedums with a nylon scouring pad.
• Kill scale by dabbing them with a cotton swab dipped in rubbing alcohol.
• Prune off heavily encrusted stems.
• Wash black sooty mold off sedums with water.

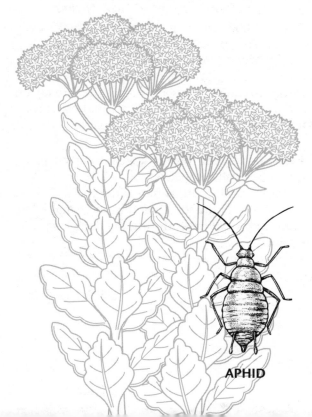

APHID

• Spray with summer oil when crawlers (young, mobile scale) are present. This horticultural oil coats plant parts, smothering scale.

• Attract beneficial insects by planting small-flowered nectar plants, like alyssum, scabiosa, and yarrow.

• Pour boiling water into anthills that are not right next to plant roots.

 ## Sedum Diseases

PROBLEM: **Dark brown spots are at the base of sedum stems. Plant roots rot. Plants wilt, turn yellow, and then die.**

CAUSE: Root rot, also called stem rot (*Rhizoctonia solani; Colletotrichum* spp.; and *Phytophthora* spp.). This fungal infection thrives in humid, rainy weather and is more a serious threat for sedums growing in poorly drained soil. Sedums grow best in dry climates and well-drained soil.

WHAT TO DO:
• Remove and dispose of infected plants.
• Allow the soil to dry between waterings.
• Space plants widely, and pull mulch away from base of sedums to increase air circulation around the plants.
• Grow sedums in well-drained soil.

PROBLEM: **Sedums rot at the base and die. Cobwebs develop on lower stems, and strands of fungus form on soil.**

CAUSE: Southern blight (*Sclerotium rolfsii*). This fungal disease thrives in warm climates. The disease appears first as a white, thread-like fungus at the base of sedum plants; then it spreads outward across the soil. The threads ooze an acidic fluid that kills plant cells on contact. Spores stay in soil for years.

WHAT TO DO:
• Dig up and discard infected plants and soil

6 inches beyond the plants' roots.
• Avoid overwatering plants, and withhold high-nitrogen fertilizer.
• Add compost to soil to increase drainage and to add beneficial soil organisms.
• Space plants widely for good air circulation.

PROBLEM: **Powdery, bright orange spots on the backs of leaves are followed by yellow or dark splotches on tops.**

CAUSE: Rust (*Puccinia rydbergii* and *P. umbilici*). The spores of this fungal disease travel from plant to plant on wind and in water. Rust thrives in mild, moist weather and is at its worst in spring and early summer.

WHAT TO DO:
• Destroy infected sedums and plant debris.
• Spray with liquid sulfur every week when weather is mild and humid.
• Avoid splashing water on the foliage.
• Mulch with compost.
• Grow sedums in full sun.
• Space plants widely for air circulation.

 ## Other Problems

PROBLEM: **Clumps of sedums which previously grew normally now look limp and fall open in the center.**

CAUSES: Clumps of sedums normally begin to die out in the center when they are several seasons old.

The soil they grow in may be too fertile. Like many succulents, sedums grow best in well-drained, lean soil and in a site in full sun.

WHAT TO DO:
• Divide clumps of sedums that are three to five years old and that begin to thin out in the center or otherwise look overcrowded.
• Move plants where there is well-drained soil and full sun.

Snapdragon

(Antirrhinum majus)

 Snapdragon Pests

PROBLEM: Leaves are folded or rolled into tubes and tied with webbing. Caterpillars inside rolls eating leaves.

CAUSES: Leafrollers and leaftiers. Leafrollers, including the redbanded leafroller (*Argyrotaenia velutinana*) and the obliquebanded leafroller (*Choristoneura rosaceana*), along with leaftiers, like the celery leaftier (*Udea rubi-*

galis), can all damage snapdragons. All these caterpillars are from ½ to ¾ inch long and can be pale green, brown, or yellow. The pests hatch from eggs laid by adult moths that are active only after dark.

The adult redbanded moths have ¾-inch wingspans and red-striped, brown wings.

Obliquebanded adults are brown moths with three darker brown stripes on their front wings. Obliquebanded moths have wingspans of ¾ inch.

Celery leaftier moths have brown wings with dark, wavy lines and wingspans of ¾ inch.

WHAT TO DO:

• Handpick.

PROBLEM: New growth is distorted. Small, soft-bodied insects cluster on the stems and leaves of your snapdragons.

CAUSE: Aphids (Family Aphididae), including the melon aphid (*Aphis gossypii*). These pests are $\frac{1}{16}$- to $\frac{3}{8}$-inch-long, soft-bodied insects. Aphids range in color from pale tan to light green to nearly black. They damage snapdragon leaves and stems by sucking juices from the plants. These insects can transmit plant diseases as they feed. Their sticky secretions, called honeydew, attract ants and sooty mold; ants protect aphids from predators in order to eat their secretions.

WHAT TO DO:

• Wash aphids off with a blast of water.
• Use insecticidal soap, following directions.
• Attract beneficial insects, like lady beetles and lacewings, by growing small-flowered

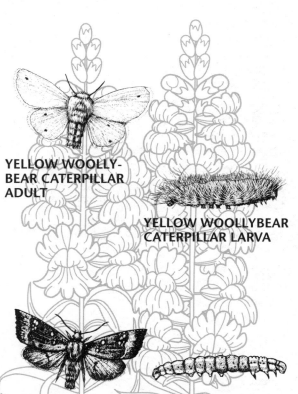

YELLOW WOOLLY-BEAR CATERPILLAR ADULT

YELLOW WOOLLYBEAR CATERPILLAR LARVA

COMMON STALK BORER ADULT

COMMON STALK BORER LARVA

nectar plants, including yarrow, dill, and Queen-Anne's-lace. Give the beneficials time to bring the aphids under control.

• Pour boiling water into entry holes of anthills that are not right next to plant roots.

PROBLEM: Leaves are stippled and faded. Webbing may be on leaves and flowers. Plants may be stunted.

CAUSE: Spider mites (Family Tetranychidae). These sap-sucking pests may become a serious problem during hot, dry weather, when they can reproduce very rapidly. They attack snapdragons, sucking juice from plant cells on the undersides of leaves, leaving pinprick holes. They move from leaf to leaf on their tiny webbing. The mites are so small that they are very difficult to see unless you use a magnifying glass. You can confirm a suspected mite outbreak by tapping a damaged leaf over a sheet of white paper; if mites are present, you should be able to see them as tiny specks. Mites are not actually insects (which all have six legs) but instead are related to spiders (which have eight legs).

WHAT TO DO:
• Dislodge mites with a blast of water.
• Spray infested plants with insecticidal soap.
• Spray infested plants with summer oil, a horticultural oil that coats plant parts and smothers pests. Begin treatment early, at the pinprick stage. By the time webs are visible, it may be too late to save the plants.
• Attract mite-eating hummingbirds by growing plants with red, trumpet-shaped flowers, like trumpet vine (*Campsis radicans*), wild columbine (*Aquilegia canadensis*), and cardinal flower (*Lobelia cardinalis*).

PROBLEM: Snapdragon leaves are riddled with holes in summer and autumn. You see caterpillars on leaves.

CAUSE: Yellow woollybear caterpillars (*Spilosoma virginica*). These 2-inch-long caterpillars are the larvae of Virginia tiger moths, which have a black-spotted abdomen and white wings. These hairy, grayish yellow caterpillars with black lines like to eat leaves, buds, and flowers of snapdragons. Woollybears are most active in July and August. They overwinter in clustered cocoons in garden debris and under rocks and soil.

WHAT TO DO:
• Handpick caterpillars.
• Spray BTK when caterpillars are feeding. "BT" stands for *Bacillus thuringiensis*, an insect-stomach poison that kills caterpillars without harming beneficial insects. *B.t.* var. *kurstaki* (BTK) kills these caterpillars.
• Remove hiding places, such as mulch and garden debris.
• Cultivate the soil lightly in fall to expose cocoons, and collect and destroy them.

PROBLEM: The leaves of your snapdragons are chewed and ragged-looking. Their stalks wilt and fall over.

CAUSE: Common stalk borers (*Papaipema nebris*). These ¾- to 1½-inch-long worms are dark brown with several brown or purple lengthwise stripes down their backs. Stalk borers feed inside flower stalks, causing plants to become twisted or bent over. The borers move from plant to plant, causing considerable damage. The eggs overwinter on grasses. In the spring, eggs hatch and young borers tunnel into grasses before moving to garden plants. The worms are the larvae of grayish brown moths with white spotted wings and wingspans of 1 inch.

WHAT TO DO:
• Cut open stalks of distorted plants, and remove and destroy the borer. Then tape the cut closed with masking tape until it heals.

• Control nearby weeds, especially great ragweed (*Ambrosia trifida*), and destroy any weed debris around the garden in fall.

PROBLEM: Small, green caterpillars attack seedpods. They move to leaves to feed, then return to the pods to feed.

CAUSE: Verbena bud moth larvae (*Endothenia hebesana*). These wormlike larvae are yellow-green with a black head, about ½ inch long. They tunnel into new snapdragon shoots and seedpods. They are the larvae of small, purplish brown moths. They pupate halfway inside the pod, in a brown case projecting from the black-ringed hole in the pod. They overwinter as larvae in plant stems or seedpods.

WHAT TO DO:
• Cut off and destroy wilting shoots containing the caterpillars.
• Remove and destroy infected seedpods.

 Snapdragon Diseases

PROBLEM: Snapdragons are stunted. The affected plants wilt, turn yellow, and begin to slowly die.

CAUSE: Southern root-knot nematodes (*Meloidogyne incognita* var. *incognita*). These minute pests are most often a problem in the South and Midwest and are especially severe in areas with sandy or peaty soils. The nematodes are actually microscopic worms that live in the soil and attack roots, causing diseaselike symptoms above ground that are similar to wilt diseases.

WHAT TO DO:
• Once nematodes have infected your snapdragons, help the plants resist further damage by providing them with regular waterings and fertilizer applications.
• Turn under compost.
• Apply crab or shrimp wastes that contain chitin. Chitin, made from shellfish shells, provides nitrogen and potassium as it breaks down, creating conditions that encourage beneficial soil organisms.
• Solarize the soil. Clear plastic sheeting placed over bare soil for three to four weeks uses the sun's energy to heat the soil enough to kill most pests and weed seeds in the top few inches of soil. After removing the plastic, plant crops as usual.
• Grow flowers in containers.

PROBLEM: Small, brown blisters appear on backs of leaves, often in concentric circles. The tops of leaves are yellow.

CAUSE: Snapdragon rust (*Puccinia antirrhini*). Spores of this fungal disease are spread by the wind. They germinate and infect plant leaves during warm, rainy weather. They favor temperatures between 70° and 75°F.

WHAT TO DO:
• Spray infected plants with sulfur.

PROBLEM: Circular, brown-bordered, yellowish spots are on leaves. Oval, gray-white, sunken spots are on stems.

CAUSE: Snapdragon anthracnose (*Colletotrichum antirrhini*). This fungal disease is primarily a problem in the eastern part of the United States. The spores are spread from plant to plant by wind-splashed rain. The stem cankers it causes can grow to the point where they girdle plants at their bases, causing them to wilt permanently.

WHAT TO DO:
• Allow the soil to dry out between waterings.
• Remove and destroy all infected plants in fall.
• When planting, space plants widely to provide good air circulation.

PROBLEM: Large, circular, dark brown or black spots with concentric ridges are on tips and margins of leaves.

CAUSE: Snapdragon leaf spot (*Phyllosticta antirrhini*). This fungal disease is found mainly in the eastern and north-central United States. The spores travel from plant to plant in splashing water and can infect plants during periods of damp weather. The disease overwinters in infected plant debris.

WHAT TO DO:
- Pull up and destroy infected plants.
- Avoid wetting leaves when watering.
- Remove and compost garden debris.

PROBLEM: Snapdragons rot at the base and die. Cobwebs develop on lower stems. Strands of fungus form on soil.

CAUSES: Southern blight (*Sclerotium rolfsii*). This fungal disease thrives in warm climates. The disease appears first as a white, thread-like fungus at the base of snapdragon plants and then spreads outward across the soil. The threads ooze an acidic fluid that kills plant cells on contact. Spores survive in the soil for years.

Root rots, such as root rot (*Rhizoctonia solani*), Texas root rot (*Phymatotrichum omnivorum*), and black root rot (*Thielaviopsis basicola*). Root rots are diseases caused by various soilborne fungi. These potentially fatal infections are usually brought on by poorly drained soils and warm climates.

WHAT TO DO:
- Remove and destroy infected plants and the soil that their roots touch.
- Allow the soil to dry between waterings.
- Remove and compost garden debris.
- Pull mulch away from the bases of healthy plants to increase air circulation.

 Other Problems

PROBLEM: Leaves have crisp, dry edges. Some leaves turn brown and drop. Affected plants die in midsummer.

CAUSE: Drought stress. If plants dry out a few times during the season, they can recover. But a drought that lasts several days or weeks, especially if combined with extreme heat, can kill snapdragons.

WHAT TO DO:
- Water plants regularly during hot, dry spells.
- Grow snapdragons in light shade in southern zones.
- Add organic matter, such as compost or leaf mold, to the soil to increase its ability to retain moisture.
- Mulch to reduce moisture evaporation from the soil.

PROBLEM: Your snapdragon plants are growing and appear healthy, but they flower sparsely.

CAUSE: Lack of sunlight. Like many flowering annuals, snapdragons need six hours or more of full sun daily to bloom well.

WHAT TO DO:
- Grow snapdragons in full sun for best flowering.
- Set out new plants in a sunny location.

PROBLEM: Your snapdragons grew well and flowered during summer but in September suddenly wilted and died.

CAUSE: Frost damage. Although snapdragons grow and bloom well in the cool temperatures of spring and fall, freezing night temperatures can kill them.

WHAT TO DO:
- To prolong flowering, cover plantings with old sheets or floating row covers when the weather report predicts overnight freezes. Cover the plantings with these synthetic, spunbonded fabrics or the sheets, and bury the edges of the material in the soil.

Sunflowers

(*Helianthus* spp.)

Sunflower Pests

PROBLEM: Sunflower leaves turn yellow or brown. You see small, soft-bodied insects clustered on stems or leaves.

CAUSE: Aphids (Family Aphididae). These pests are $\frac{1}{16}$- to $\frac{3}{8}$-inch-long, soft-bodied insects. They range in color from pale tan to light green to nearly black. Aphids damage sunflower leaves and stems by sucking juices from the plants. These insects can transmit plant diseases as they feed. And their sticky secretions, called honeydew, attract ants and sooty mold; ants protect aphids from predators in order to eat their secretions.

WHAT TO DO:
• Wash aphids off with a strong stream of water.
• Use insecticidal soap, following label directions.
• Attract beneficial insects, like lady beetles and lacewings, by growing small-flowered nectar plants, including yarrow, dill, and Queen-Anne's-lace. Give the beneficials time to bring the aphids under control.
• Pour boiling water into entry holes of anthills that are not right next to plant roots.

PROBLEM: The first, emerging leaves of your sunflower seedlings are eaten. You see striped beetles on the foliage.

CAUSE: Sunflower beetles (*Zygogramma exclamationis*). These beetles closely resemble Colorado potato beetles, with cream-yellow-striped bodies. The adult beetles emerge from hibernation in spring and feed during the day on newly emerged seedlings. They then mate and lay eggs. Their yellow-green, $\frac{3}{8}$-inch-long larvae feed at night, defoliating maturing plants and causing them to produce few flowers.

WHAT TO DO:
• Use floating row covers to protect seedlings from feeding insects. Cover the plants with these synthetic, spunbonded fabrics, and bury the edges of the row cover in the soil.
• Spray insecticidal soap on plants when nymphs appear.

TARNISHED PLANT BUG

YELLOW WOOLLYBEAR CATERPILLAR ADULT

YELLOW WOOLLYBEAR CATERPILLAR LARVA

PROBLEM: Leaves are riddled with holes in summer and autumn. Fuzzy caterpillars feed in groups on leaf undersides.

CAUSE: Yellow woollybear caterpillars (*Spilosoma virginica*). These 2-inch-long caterpillars are the larvae of Virginia tiger moths, which are moths with a black-spotted abdomen and white wings. The hairy, gray-yellow caterpillars with black lines like to eat leaves, buds, and flowers of sunflowers. Woollybears are most active in July and August. They overwinter in clustered cocoons in garden debris and under rocks and clods of soil.

WHAT TO DO:
• Handpick caterpillars.
• Spray BTK when caterpillars are feeding. "BT" stands for *Bacillus thuringiensis*, an insect-stomach poison that kills caterpillars without harming beneficial insects. *B.t.* var. *kurstaki* (BTK) kills woollybears and their relatives.
• Remove hiding places, like garden debris.
• Cultivate the soil lightly in fall.

PROBLEM: The new shoots and buds of your sunflowers are damaged. Some of the flowers are misshapen.

CAUSE: Tarnished plant bugs (*Lygus lineolaris*). These fast-moving, mottled green or brown bugs are about ¼ inch long; they have a yellow triangle on each side of their bodies near the back. The young nymphs are yellowish green and have five black dots on their bodies. Tarnished plant bugs are very active in early spring and may increase during the summer. When they feed, they inject toxic saliva into plants that causes leaves and flowers to be deformed. Adults overwinter in fallen leaves and garden debris.

WHAT TO DO:
• Handpick.
• Spray larvae with insecticidal soap.
• Use floating row covers to exclude feeding insects. Cover young plants, and bury the edges of the row cover in the soil.

 Sunflower Diseases

PROBLEM: Powdery, white or grayish spots cover the leaves and stems of your sunflowers. Spots spread to the flowers.

CAUSE: Powdery mildew (*Erysiphe cichoracearum*). This common fungal disease weakens plants and makes them unsightly. Infected leaves may shrivel and die. The disease spores may overwinter on plant debris or on perennial garden plants and weeds, or they may blow into the garden on wind currents. Unlike many other plant diseases, powdery mildew spores do not require a film of moisture on the leaf to germinate. They do, however, thrive in high humidity.

WHAT TO DO:
• Destroy infested plant parts or plants.
• Spray with liquid sulfur or baking soda spray. (To make baking soda spray, dissolve 1 teaspoon baking soda in 1 quart warm water; add 1 teaspoon insecticidal soap to make the solution stick to leaves.)
• Water plants regularly during dry spells.
• Grow sunflowers in full sun.
• Space widely for adequate air circulation.

PROBLEM: Brown pustules develop on the undersides of leaves. The rusty-looking leaves dry up and fall off.

CAUSE: Rust (*Puccinia* spp.; *Coleosporium helianthi;* and *Uromyces* spp.). Spores of this fungal disease are spread by the wind. They germinate and infect sunflower plants during warm, rainy weather, favoring temperatures between 70° and 75°F.

WHAT TO DO:
• Remove and destroy infected leaves.
• If many leaves get pustules, spray sulfur.

Sweet Peas

(*Lathyrus* spp.)

 ## Sweet Pea Pests

PROBLEM: Leaves are folded or rolled into tubes and tied with webbing. Caterpillars are eating the rolled leaves.

CAUSES: Leafrollers and leaftiers. Leafrollers, including the redbanded leafroller (*Argyrotaenia velutinana*) and the obliquebanded leafroller (*Choristoneura rosaceana*), along with leaftiers, like the celery leaftier (*Udea rubigalis*), can damage sweet peas. These

LEAFROLLER ADULT

LEAFROLLER LARVA

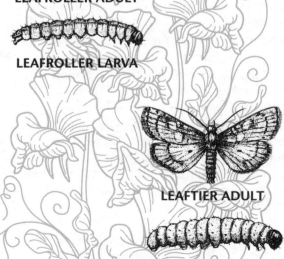

LEAFTIER ADULT

LEAFTIER LARVA

similar-looking caterpillars are from ½ to ¾ inch long and can be pale green, brown, or yellow. The pests hatch from eggs laid by adult moths that are active only after dark.

The adult redbanded moths have ¾-inch wingspans and red-striped, brown wings. Obliquebanded adults are brown moths with three darker brown stripes on their front wings. Obliquebanded moths have wingspans of ¾ inch.

Celery leaftier moths have brown wings with dark, wavy lines and wingspans of ¾ inch.

WHAT TO DO:
• Handpick. Infestations of these caterpillars are usually light, so you can usually control them easily by handpicking the folded leaves where the caterpillars hide.

 ## Sweet Pea Diseases

PROBLEM: Masses of short, thick stems with misshapen leaves are developing at the base of your sweet peas.

CAUSE: Bacterial fasciation (*Clavibacter fascians*). This soilborne bacterial disease lives from year to year in infected plant debris and in the soil.

WHAT TO DO:
• Remove and destroy diseased plants.
• Solarize soil before replanting. Clear plastic sheeting placed over bare soil for three to four weeks uses the sun's energy to heat the soil enough to kill most diseases in the top few inches of soil. After removing the plastic, plant crops as usual.

PROBLEM: White spots are on sweet pea leaves and shoots. Leaves wither and drop. Stalks dry up before blossoming.

CAUSE: Anthracnose, also called blossom and shoot blight (*Glomerella cingulata*). This fungal disease is common in all areas of the United States except the Pacific Northwest. It often infects plants that are already weakened by drought or infertile soil. The fungus overwinters in infected woody plants, especially apples and privet.

WHAT TO DO:
• Grow sweet peas in cool seasons.
• Keep plants well watered and fertilized.
• Clean up and destroy plant debris at the end of the growing season.
• Do not plant sweet peas near apple trees or privet hedges.

PROBLEM: Your sweet peas have patches of gray mold forming on their fading flowers and on the leaves.

CAUSE: Botrytis blight (*Botrytis cinerea*). The spores of this fungal disease blow from plant to plant on the wind. The blight, which is not usually found in dry climates, spreads rapidly in humid weather.

WHAT TO DO:
• Remove and dispose of infected plant parts.
• Avoid overhead watering.
• Plant sweet peas in well-drained soil.
• Space plants far enough apart for adequate air circulation.
• Remove and compost garden debris.

PROBLEM: Seedlings collapse at the soil line, fall over, and die. Main stems are darkened at the soil line.

CAUSE: Damping-off (*Rhizoctonia solani*; *Pythium* spp.). This common soil-dwelling fungus primarily attacks seedlings started indoors and those growing in heavy, wet soil outdoors. Stem injuries are likely sites of infection; but because the fungi live in soil, roots are also vulnerable.

WHAT TO DO:
• Use sterile seed-starting mix for seeds started indoors, and plant seeds in clean containers. Keep seedlings within 2 inches of a plant light if seeds are started indoors, and provide circulating air by running a fan if needed.
• Outdoors, plant seeds in moist, well-drained garden soil that is fortified with compost.
• Use high-nitrogen fertilizers sparingly until seedlings have well-developed roots.

PROBLEM: Powdery, white or gray spots cover leaves and stems of sweet peas, and the spots spread to the flowers.

CAUSE: Powdery mildew (*Microsphaera alni*; *Erysiphe polygoni*). This common disease, caused by a couple of different fungi, weakens plants and makes them unsightly. Infected leaves may shrivel and die. The disease spores may overwinter on plant debris or on perennial garden plants and weeds, or they may blow into the garden on wind currents. Unlike many other plant diseases, powdery mildew spores do not require a film of moisture on the leaf to germinate. They do, however, thrive in the high humidity that results when plants are crowded or grown in shady locations.

WHAT TO DO:
• Remove and destroy severely infested plant parts or plants.
• Spray with liquid sulfur or baking soda spray. (To make baking soda spray, dissolve 1 teaspoon baking soda in 1 quart warm water; add 1 teaspoon insecticidal soap to make the solution stick to leaves.)
• Grow the plants in full sun.
• Space them far enough apart for adequate air circulation.
• Water sweet peas regularly during dry spells.

Tulips

(*Tulipa* spp. and hybrids)

Tulip Pests

PROBLEM: New shoots and leaves are distorted. Clusters of small, soft insects cling to tulip stems or leaf undersides.

CAUSE: Aphids (Family Aphididae). These pests are $\frac{1}{16}$- to $\frac{3}{8}$-inch-long, soft-bodied insects. They range in color from pale tan to light green to nearly black. Aphids damage tulip leaves and stems by sucking juices from the plants. These insects can transmit plant diseases as they feed, and their sticky secretions, called honeydew, attract ants and sooty mold; ants protect aphids from predators in order to eat their secretions. Tulip bulb aphids (*Dysaphis tulipae*) are powdery white aphids that infest the base of plants and feed on both foliage and bulbs. They even eat stored bulbs. Infested tulip plants become stunted and can die.

WHAT TO DO:
• Wash aphids off tulips with a strong stream of water.
• Use insecticidal soap, following directions.
• Attract beneficial insects, like lady beetles and lacewings, by growing small-flowered nectar plants, such as yarrow, dill, and Queen-Anne's-lace. Give the beneficials time to bring the aphids under control because these flowers will bloom after the tuilps have finished, but the beneficials will help next season's tulips.
• Pour boiling water into entry holes of anthills that are not right next to plant roots.
• When purchasing bulbs, inspect them for clusters of aphids under the bulb coat.
• Destroy seriously infected bulbs.

PROBLEM: You planted tulip bulbs in the fall, as recommended, but the plants did not come up in the spring.

CAUSE: Wet soil or rodents. Sometimes tulip bulbs rot during mild, wet winters. But more often, hungry rodents, like squirrels, chipmunks, mice, or voles, dig the bulbs up or burrow into the soil and eat them.

WHAT TO DO:
• When planting, add sharp, crushed rock in holes around bulbs to discourage digging rodents, or wrap bulbs in chicken wire.
• Plant tulips in well-drained soil.

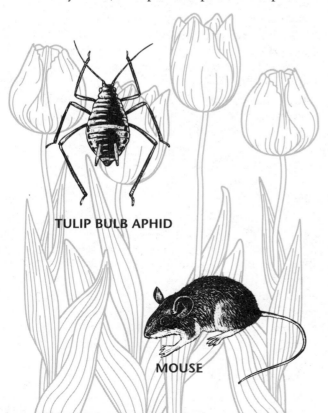

TULIP BULB APHID

MOUSE

• Do not mulch in winter, because mulches attract mice and voles looking for shelter.

PROBLEM: Tulips grow slowly. Leaves yellow; flowers may not appear. Bulbs may rot in the ground or in storage.

CAUSE: Bulb mites (*Rhizoglyphus echinopus*). These pests are minute, white, spiderlike mites, from $\frac{1}{25}$ to $\frac{1}{50}$ inch long. Bulb mites infest healthy and rotting bulbs. They cause bulbs growing in the ground, as well as those in storage, to turn brown and rot.

WHAT TO DO:
• Dispose of rotting or soft bulbs.
• Attract beneficials by planting small-flowered nectar plants, like alyssum and scabiosa.

PROBLEM: Leaves are peppered with tiny, tan spots, turn totally tan, and die. Webbing is visible on some leaves.

CAUSE: Two-spotted spider mites (*Tetranychus urticae*). These pinpoint-sized, red, spiderlike pests pierce tulip leaves to suck nutrients, leaving pinprick holes in leaves. Mites overwinter in leaves on the ground and in plant crevices. Spider mites feed more during hot, dry spells and in enclosed sites with stagnant air. Their cobwebs protect mite eggs and larvae.

WHAT TO DO:
• Dislodge mites with a blast of water.
• Use insecticidal soap, following directions. Begin treatment at the pinprick stage.
• Water plants regularly during dry spells.
• Space plants widely for air circulation.

 Tulip Diseases

PROBLEM: New leaves are small and show unusual crinkling and have patches of yellow and brown streaks.

CAUSE: Cucumber mosaic virus. Feeding insects, such as aphids, and infected seeds spread the disease. Yellowing lower leaves signal a severe infection.

WHAT TO DO:
• Remove and destroy infected plants.
• Do not grow tulips near cucumbers and their relatives or gladiolus.
• Spray insecticidal soap to control insects.
• Keep plants well watered and fertilized to help them resist insect attacks.

PROBLEM: Leaves are mottled and streaked with light and dark green. Flower petals have bleached streaks.

CAUSE: Tulip breaking virus. This incurable disease can distort, stunt, and eventually kill tulip plants. Yellowing lower leaves signal a severe infection. Sap-sucking insects, like aphids, spread the disease, which also infects lilies.

WHAT TO DO:
• Destroy severely infected plants.
• Spray insecticidal soap to control insects.
• Keep plants well watered and fertilized to help them resist insect attacks.
• Do not plant near disease-prone lilies.

 Other Problems

PROBLEM: Plants bloom well for one or two years, then become small and bloom poorly or don't come up at all.

CAUSE: Short-lived plants. Many tulip hybrids and cultivars are naturally short-lived, gradually dying out after two or more seasons of flowering. And tulips, which need to go dormant in several months of cold winter temperatures, are stressed and short-lived when grown in warm-winter areas.

WHAT TO DO:
• Grow the small-flowered species tulips, which will live longer and reproduce to naturalize over the years.
• In warm climates plant bulbs every fall.

Verbenas

(*Verbena* spp. and hybrids)

Verbena Pests

PROBLEM: New leaves and shoots are distorted and coated with a shiny substance and may have black, sooty spots.

CAUSE: Aphids (Family Aphididae). These pests, including the common green peach aphid (*Myzus persicae*), are $\frac{1}{16}$- to $\frac{3}{8}$-inch-long, soft-bodied insects that damage leaves and stems by sucking plant juices. They range in color from tan, green, and brown to black. These insects cause buds and young growth to be stunted, curled, or distorted. Aphids can transmit plant diseases as they feed. Their secretions, called honeydew, attract mold and ants, which protect aphids in order to eat their secretions.

WHAT TO DO:

• Tolerate light damage.
• Wash aphids off with a blast of water.
• Use insecticidal soap, following directions.
• Attract beneficial insects, like lady beetles and lacewings, by planting small-flowered nectar plants, including yarrow and dill.
• Purchase beneficial "bug food" products from mail-order sources, or put out shallow pans of sugar-water to attract beneficials.
• Purchase beneficial green lacewings and aphid midges from mail-order sources, and release them in your garden. Give the beneficials time to bring the aphids under control.
• Pour boiling water into entry holes of anthills that are not adjacent to plant roots.
• Reduce fertilizer applications because aphids prefer tender new growth.
• Grow verbenas in full sun to prevent the weak growth that aphids target.

PROBLEM: Leaves are pale green and stippled with tiny yellow or white spots. Leaves are wrapped in webbing.

CAUSE: Spider mites (Family Tetranychidae). These sap-sucking pests may become a serious problem during hot, dry weather, when they can reproduce very rapidly. The mites are so small they are very difficult to see unless you use a magnifying glass. Mites are not actually insects (which all have six legs). They are related to spiders (which have eight legs). They attack verbenas, sucking juice

APHID

from plant cells on the undersides of leaves, leaving pinprick holes in leaves. They move from leaf to leaf on webbing, causing overall yellowing of leaves and distorted growth.

WHAT TO DO:

• Dislodge mites with a blast of water.
• Spray infested plants with insecticidal soap.
• Spray summer oil, a horticultural oil that smothers pests. Begin treatment early, at the pinprick stage. By the time webs are visible, it may be too late to save the plants.
• Attract mite-eating hummingbirds by growing plants with red, trumpet-shaped flowers, like trumpet vine (*Campsis radicans*), wild columbine (*Aquilegia canadensis*), and cardinal flower (*Lobelia cardinalis*).

PROBLEM: There are light tan, winding trails on the surfaces of verbena leaves. The markings do not penetrate leaves.

CAUSE: Verbena leafminers (*Agromyza artemisiae*). These pests are the larvae of tiny flying insects called midges. The minute, white, wormlike larvae tunnel and eat between the upper and lower surfaces of leaves. They overwinter in garden debris.

WHAT TO DO:

• Pick and destroy infested leaves.
• Clean up and compost fallen leaves.
• Apply beneficial nematodes (*Steinernema carpocapsae* and *Heterorhabditis heliothidis*), which you can purchase live from mail-order suppliers; release them when pests are present.

PROBLEM: Verbena plants have sticky leaves. You see small, white insects flying when the foliage is disturbed.

CAUSE: Whiteflies (Family Aleyrodidae). These tiny insects, only ½5 inch long, weaken plants by sucking sap, and they also transmit viruses from plant to plant as they feed. Whiteflies lay pinpoint-sized eggs on the

backs of leaves; the eggs hatch into ½0-inch-long nymphs. Both the nymphs and adult flies feed on verbenas. They usually disappear after the first frost.

WHAT TO DO:

• Use insecticidal soap, following directions.
• Spray with neem or summer oil, being sure to spray undersides of leaves. Neem is a botanical pesticide that is harmless to beneficial insects. Summer oil smothers pests.
• Collect whiteflies with a hand-held vacuum.
• Water plants well during dry spells.
• Attract beneficial insects by planting small-flowered nectar plants, like yarrow and dill.
• Coat yellow cardboard or painted wooden boards with petroleum jelly or Tanglefoot (a commercial product for this purpose), and fasten them to stakes near plants.
• Space widely for good air circulation.

 Verbena Diseases

PROBLEM: A powdery, white coating covers leaves, flowers, and stems. Plants usually do not die.

CAUSE: Powdery mildew (*Erysiphe cichoracearum*). This common disease, caused by a couple of different fungi, weakens verbena plants and makes them unsightly. Infected leaves may shrivel and die. The disease spores thrive in humid conditions and reproduce rapidly when they land on moist leaves. Spores overwinter on plant debris.

WHAT TO DO:

• Destroy infested plant parts or plants.
• Spray with liquid sulfur or baking soda spray. (To make baking soda spray, dissolve 1 teaspoon baking soda in 1 quart warm water; add 1 teaspoon insecticidal soap.)
• Water plants regularly during dry spells.
• Grow verbenas in full sun.
• Space widely for adequate air circulation.

Veronicas

also called Speedwells (*Veronica* spp. and hybrids)

Veronica Pests

PROBLEM: Clusters of small, pear-shaped insects on veronica leaves, buds, or stems produce a clear, sticky coating.

CAUSE: Foxglove aphids (*Aulacorthum solani*). Foxglove aphids, like their many aphid relatives, are soft-bodied, sap-sucking insects, $\frac{1}{16}$ to $\frac{3}{8}$ inch long. Aphids range in color from pale tan to light green to nearly black. These pests can transmit diseases as they feed. The sticky honeydew they excrete attracts ants and black mold; ants protect aphids from predators in order to eat their honeydew.

WHAT TO DO:
• Tolerate light damage.
• Wash aphids off plants with a strong stream of water.
• Spray infested plants with insecticidal soap.
• Attract beneficials, like lady beetles and lacewings, by planting small-flowered nectar plants, including yarrow and dill.
• Pour boiling water into anthills that are not adjacent to plant roots.
• Pinch off the top shoots of foxglove plants in fall, since foxglove aphids overwinter only on foxgloves.

PROBLEM: Leaves of veronicas have holes chewed in them. You see spiny, black caterpillars with orange markings

CAUSE: Chalcedon checkerspot butterflies (*Euphydryas chalcedona*). These butterflies have black wings with yellow spots. Their spiny caterpillars are black with small, orange markings. These caterpillars eat the foliage and can cover it with silken webs as they feed.

WHAT TO DO:
• Handpick caterpillars.
• Spray BTK when caterpillars are feeding. "BT" stands for *Bacillus thuringiensis*, an insect-stomach poison that kills caterpillars without harming beneficial insects. *B.t.* var. *kurstaki* (BTK) kills the larvae of chalcedon checkerspot butterflies.
• Remove pests' hiding places, such as mulch and garden debris.
• Cultivate the soil lightly in fall to expose

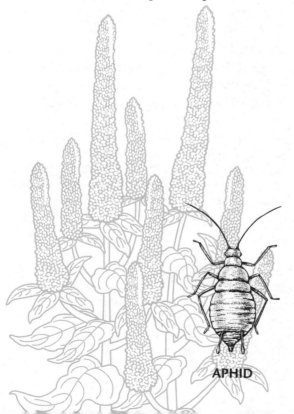

APHID

the overwintering cocoons, and collect and destroy them.

 Veronica Diseases

PROBLEM: Leaves have yellowish spots. The spots darken and develop a yellow halo. Spots begin to enlarge or merge.

CAUSE: Leaf spot. These disease symptoms are caused by a variety of fungi. The spores infect veronica leaves during wet or humid weather. They overwinter on plant debris left in the garden.

WHAT TO DO:
• Cut off and dispose of infected leaves.
• Plant veronicas in full sun.
• Space plants widely or thin them for adequate air circulation.
• Avoid overhead watering, and do not splash water on foliage.
• Water early in the day so foliage will dry before evening.

PROBLEM: Angular, yellow or pale green spots are on leaf tops. White, gray, tan, or purplish mold develops on leaf backs.

CAUSE: Downy mildew (*Peronospora grisea*). Cool, damp weather encourages this disease. The tops of the plants, where rain and dew accumulate, and the bottom leaves that touch damp soil are where you will see the most damage. If you look on the backs of the leaves opposite the discolored patches, you will see gray fuzz. The disease makes veronicas unsightly, but it is rarely fatal.

WHAT TO DO:
• Remove diseased growth when you see signs of infection.
• Space plants widely for adequate air circulation.
• Avoid overhead watering or splashing water on foliage.

• Water early in the day so foliage will dry before evening.

PROBLEM: Brown pustules develop on the undersides of veronica leaves. The rusty-looking leaves dry up and fall off.

CAUSE: Rust (*Puccinia* spp.). Spores of this fungal disease are spread by the wind. They germinate and infect veronica plants during warm, rainy weather. The disease is at its worst when temperatures are between 70° and 75°F.

WHAT TO DO:
• Remove and destroy infected leaves.
• If many leaves have brown pustules, infected plants may be saved by spraying them immediately with sulfur.

PROBLEM: A powdery, white coating covers leaves, flowers, and stems. Plants usually do not die.

CAUSE: Powdery mildew (*Sphaerotheca macularis*). This common disease, caused by a couple of different fungi, weakens veronica plants and makes them unsightly. Infected leaves may shrivel and die. The disease spores may blow into the garden on wind currents. They overwinter on plant debris or on perennial garden plants and weeds. Powdery mildew thrives in the high humidity that results when plants are crowded or grown in shady locations.

WHAT TO DO:
• Destroy infested plant parts or plants.
• Spray with liquid sulfur or baking soda spray. (To make baking soda spray, dissolve 1 teaspoon baking soda in 1 quart warm water; add 1 teaspoon insecticidal soap to make the solution stick to leaves.)
• Grow veronicas in full sun.
• Space widely for adequate air circulation.
• Water the plants regularly during dry spells.

Violets

(*Viola* spp.)

Violet Pests

PROBLEM: Young violets are eaten in spring. Large holes in leaves or flowers are streaked with a slimy substance.

CAUSES: Slugs and snails (Order Stylommatophora). These ⅛- to 8-inch-long, soft-bodied, gray, tan, green, black, yellow, or spotted pests resemble clams and mussels. Snails have shells; slugs look like snails without shells. At night these pests feed on violet leaves and flowers, leaving behind a trail of shiny slime. They hide in debris.

WHAT TO DO:
• Handpick two hours after dark.
• Remove mulch and garden debris.
• Allow soil to dry between waterings.

• Create barriers by sprinkling wood ashes or crushed eggshells around flowerbeds.
• Edge plants with a strip of copper, which hits these pests with an electrical shock.
• Sprinkle diatomaceous earth (DE) around plants. This abrasive dust is made of fossilized shells, called diatoms, which penetrate the pests' skin as they crawl over DE.
• Make beer traps from recycled cans sunk to the brim in soil and filled with yeasty beer. Slugs and snails will fall in and drown.

PROBLEM: Your violets have distorted leaves that begin to rot. The plants are stunted, and they produce few flowers.

CAUSE: Violet gall midges (*Phytophaga violicola*). These pests are the larvae of small, dark flies. The adults lay tiny, white eggs in the crevices of unfolding new leaves. The white maggots, which are less than ½ inch long, eat the leaves. Infested plants can be stunted.

WHAT TO DO:
• Destroy infested plant parts.
• Spray infested plants with insecticidal soap.

Violet Diseases

PROBLEM: Spots of various colors and sizes appear on leaves. Black-edged scabby spots form on stems or leaves.

CAUSES: Leaf spot; spot anthracnose.

Leaf spot, which causes the multicolored spots, can be caused by several fungi.

Spot anthracnose (*Sphaceloma violae*), a more serious fungal disease, causes scabby spots.

WHAT TO DO:
• Destroy leaf spot–infected plant parts.

SNAIL

SLUG

Yarrows

(Achillea spp.)

Yarrow Pests

PROBLEM: Leaves and flowers have brown or silvery streaks or speckling. They may be distorted.

CAUSE: Thrips (Order Thysanoptera). These extremely tiny, narrow-bodied insects are only ⅟₂₅ inch long. Thrips like to hide deep inside the leaf shoots and flowers of yarrows.

WHAT TO DO:
• Knock thrips off with a blast of water.
• Spray infested plants with insecticidal soap.
• Spray infested plants with neem. This botanical pesticide is harmless to beneficials.

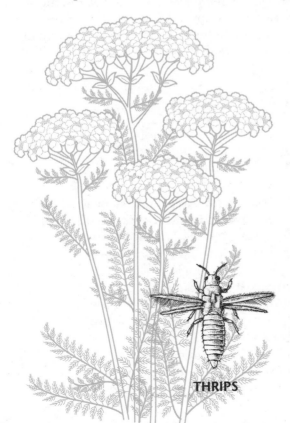

THRIPS

• Attract beneficials by growing small-flowered nectar plants, like alyssum and scabiosa.
• Spray garden plants with commercial "bug food," which you can order from mail-order sources, or set out shallow pans of sugar-water to attract beneficials.
• Mulch plants to attract beneficial spiders.

Yarrow Diseases

PROBLEM: A powdery, white coating covers leaves, flowers, and stems. Plants usually do not die.

CAUSE: Powdery mildew (*Erysiphe cichoracearum*). This common fungal disease weakens yarrows and makes them unsightly. The spores thrive in the high humidity. The spores overwinter on plant debris.

WHAT TO DO:
• Destroy infested plant parts or plants.
• Spray with liquid sulfur or baking soda spray. (To make baking soda spray, dissolve 1 teaspoon baking soda in 1 quart warm water; add 1 teaspoon insecticidal soap.)
• Grow yarrow plants in full sun.

PROBLEM: A portion of a plant or the whole plant wilts, turns yellow, and dies. Stems darken; roots rot.

CAUSE: Root and stem rot (*Rhizoctonia solani*). This potentially fatal infection is caused by various soilborne fungi. It often attacks plants growing in poorly drained soils.

WHAT TO DO:
• Destroy sick plants and surrounding soil.
• Remove and compost garden debris.

Zinnias

(Zinnia spp.)

 ## Zinnia Pests

PROBLEM: Leaves are chewed between the veins. Some flowers are devoured. You see green-and-copper beetles.

CAUSE: Japanese beetles (*Popillia japonica*). These shiny, ½-inch-long beetles are found throughout the eastern United States and are moving westward. They emerge in mid-summer and can do great damage. Their fat, ½-inch-long, white grubs develop in the soil.

WHAT TO DO:
• Handpick.

• Collect beetles with a hand-held vacuum.
• Use insecticidal soap, following directions.
• Apply milky disease spores. This disease combines spores of *Bacillus popilliae* and *B. lentimorbus*. Grubs eat the spores and die.
• Plant zinnias in dappled or half-day shade.

 ## Zinnia Diseases

PROBLEM: Leaves, stems, and flowers develop reddish brown spots with gray centers that turn brown and dry.

CAUSE: Zinnia blight (*Alternaria zinniae*). This fungal disease develops during warm, moist weather and spreads from plant to plant in splashing water or on dirty tools. The blight overwinters in the soil and on seeds.

WHAT TO DO:
• Cut off and destroy infected plant parts.
• Remove garden debris.
• Apply new mulch.
• Space plants widely for good air circulation.
• Water only in the morning.
• Grow zinnias in new locations.

PROBLEM: Powdery, white or grayish spots cover zinnia leaves, stems, and flowers, especially in late summer.

CAUSE: Powdery mildew (*Erysiphe cichoracearum*). This fungal disease weakens plants and makes them unsightly. The disease thrives in high humidity. Mildew disease spores overwinter on plant debris.

WHAT TO DO:
• Pick and destroy infected leaves.
• Water plants in the morning.
• Grow the resistant *Z. angustifolia*.

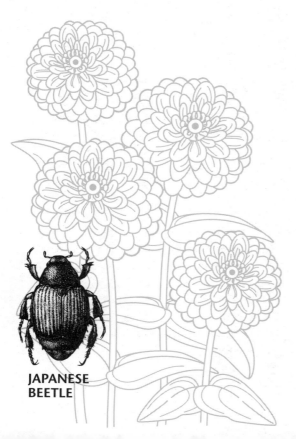

JAPANESE BEETLE

The Pest Finder

PEST	PROBLEMS	SUSCEPTIBLE PLANTS	WHAT TO DO
Aphids	Distorted leaves, buds, flowers; sticky, clear honeydew on leaves; yellowed leaves; ants on leaves and stems	Vegetable, herb, fruiting, and flowering plants	Wash aphids from leaves with strong spray of water; attract beneficial insects by planting the small-flowered nectar plants alyssum, dill, and Queen-Anne's-lace; purchase beneficial insects from mail-order sources; spray insecticidal soap
Apple maggot flies	Brown, winding tunnels in fruit; premature fruit drop	Fruits from apple and crabapple trees; blueberries	Grow varieties that ripen late; remove dropped fruit daily; trap females with red sticky balls (coat balls with Tanglefoot or petroleum jelly)
Armyworms	Leaves of young plants are eaten	Vegetable seedlings and mature plants	Handpick; apply *B.t.* var. *kurstaki* (BTK), a stomach poison that kills armyworms
Asparagus beetles	Holes chewed in spears; leaves stripped from stems	Asparagus plants	Cover plants with floating row covers (bury edges in soil) in early spring; handpick; spray with pyrethrins
Black vine weevils	Leaf edges notched; roots eaten	Berry plants; flowering plants	Handpick; apply parasitic nematodes to soil in late spring and in summer
Cabbage loopers	Holes chewed in leaves; plants defoliated; caterpillar excrement on leaves	Vegetable plants in the cabbage family; tomatoes	Handpick; cover plants with floating row covers (bury edges in soil); apply *B.t.* var. *kurstaki* (BTK); attract pest-eating birds to the garden
Cabbage maggots	Leaves yellow and wilt; roots have brown tunnels	Vegetable plants in the cabbage family; onions; garlic	Apply floating row covers (bury edges in soil); apply parasitic nematodes; remove plant debris
Colorado potato beetles	Holes chewed in leaves; leaves skeletonized; plants defoliated; flowers eaten	Potato plants	Handpick; apply floating row covers (bury edges in soil); attract beneficial insects by planting the small-flowered nectar plants alyssum and dill; attract pest-eating birds; apply *B.t.* var. *san diego* (BTSD); apply neem (*azadirachtin*)
Cucumber beetles	Small, ragged holes appear in leaves	Vegetable and ornamental flowering plants	Handpick; apply floating row covers (bury edges in soil); apply beneficial nematodes

(continued)

PEST	PROBLEMS	SUSCEPTIBLE PLANTS	WHAT TO DO
Cutworms	Leaves eaten; small plants chewed off at soil line	Vegetable and flower seedlings	Handpick; apply cutworm collars; apply BT
Flea beetles	Leaves appear peppered with fine shotholes	Vegetable plants, especially members of cabbage and tomato families; flowering plants	Cover seedlings with floating row covers (bury edges in soil); collect beetles in hand-held vacuum; spray insecticidal soap; apply parasitic nematodes to soil; delay planting
Fruit flies	Maggotlike larvae tunnel in fruit; fruit drops prematurely	Fruiting plants: blueberries; currants; plums; cherries; peaches; walnuts	Remove fallen fruit; hang yellow sticky traps (coat yellow boards with Tanglefoot or petroleum jelly); spray summer oil; attract beneficial insects by growing the small-flowered nectar plants alyssum and dill; cultivate soil to kill larvae
Imported cabbageworms	Holes chewed in leaves; leaves skeletonized; plants defoliated, flowers eaten	Vegetable plants in the cabbage family;	Handpick; cover plants with floating row covers (bury edges in soil); apply *B.t.* var. *kurstaki* (BTK); attract pest-eating birds to the garden
Japanese beetles	Holes chewed in flowers and leaves; turfgrass roots eaten	Vegetable, fruiting, and flowering plants; turfgrass	Handpick; collect beetles in hand-held vacuum; spray insecticidal soap; cover plants with floating row covers (bury edges in soil); pheromone traps (put traps where they will lure beetles *away* from garden plants); apply parasitic nematodes or milky disease spores to soil
Lacebugs and Tarnished plant bugs	Yellow or brown patches or speckled leaf surfaces; spots of excrement on leaf undersides	Vegetable, fruiting, and flowering plants	Handpick; collect in vacuum; hang white sticky traps (coat white boards with Tanglefoot or petroleum jelly); apply insecticidal soap; cover plants with floating row covers (bury edges in soil); attract beneficial insects by planting the nectar plants alyssum and dill; remove weeds
Leafrollers and Leaftiers	Leaves rolled into tubes and tied with webbing; caterpillars inside the rolls eat leaves	Ornamental flowering plants	Handpick; crush caterpillar-infested leaves; remove garden debris
Mealybugs	Leaves turn yellow and drop; sticky, white, woolly specks and black mold are on leaves	Herbs, fruiting plants, or ornamental flowering plants	Knock mealybugs off with a strong stream of water; apply insecticidal soap; attract beneficial insects, such as native parasitic wasps, by planting nectar plants like alyssum and dill
Mexican bean beetles	Leaves are skeletonized	Bean plants	Handpick; apply floating row covers (bury edges in soil); apply neem (*azadirachtin*)

PEST	PROBLEMS	SUSCEPTIBLE PLANTS	WHAT TO DO
Onion maggots	Leaves yellow and wilt; roots have brown tunnels	Onions; garlic; leeks	Apply floating row covers (bury edges in soil); apply parasitic nematodes; remove plant debris
Scale	Leaves are yellowed or distorted; clear, sticky honeydew on leaves; small, bumplike scale on leaves or stems	Fruiting and flowering plants; fruit trees	Scrape scale off branches with plastic scouring pad; dab scale with rubbing alcohol; prune infested growth; plant the small-flowered nectar plants alyssum and dill to attract beneficial insects; apply horticultural oil; spray with pyrethrins at crawler stage
Slugs and Snails	Large holes chewed in leaves and stems; plants may be defoliated; shiny slime trails are on foliage	Tender-leaved plants, including vegetable, herb, and flowering plants	Handpick; make traps from recycled cans sunk in soil and filled with yeasty beer; encircle plants with copper strips; sprinkle abrasive diatomaceous earth (DE) around plants
Spider mites	Leaves, flowers, or fruits are yellow, bronze, or speckled; some plants have webs on undersides of leaves; leaves drop prematurely	Vegetable, herb, fruiting, and flowering plants; fruit trees	Knock mites off plants with a strong stream of water; apply horticultural oil; attract beneficial insects by growing the small-flowered nectar plants alyssum and dill; spray insecticidal soap or pyrethrins
Thrips	Plants are stunted; leaves are distorted; flowers are damaged and have a silvery sheen	Vegetable, flowering, and fruiting plants; fruit and nut trees	Knock thrips off plants with a strong spray of water; spray insecticidal soap; encourage beneficial insects by growing the small-flowered nectar plants alyssum and dill; apply horticultural oil; hang blue or yellow sticky traps (coat colored boards with Tanglefoot or petroleum jelly); spray neem; weed garden
Tomato hornworms	Holes chewed in leaves; leaves skeletonized; plants defoliated; flowers eaten	Tomatoes, peppers, and flowering plants	Handpick; cover plants with floating row covers (bury edges in soil); apply *B.t.* var. *kurstaki* (BTK); companion plant with radishes; attract pest-eating birds to the garden
Whiteflies	Tiny white insects fly up when disturbed; leaves have spots of sticky, clear honeydew; plants grow poorly	Vegetable, herb, and flowering plants	Attract beneficial insects by growing the small-flowered nectar plants alyssum and dill; collect flies with hand-held vacuum; hang yellow sticky traps (coat yellow boards with Tanglefoot or petroleum jelly); spray insecticidal soap; spray summer oil

The Disease Finder

DISEASE	PROBLEMS	SUSCEPTIBLE PLANTS	WHAT TO DO
Anthracnose (Fungus)	Leaves have irregular brown or yellow spots that darken and enlarge; leaves drop early; fruits have dark, sunken spots; infected fruits rot	Vegetable plants; herbs; fruiting plants; flowering plants	Mulch; pick ripe fruits promptly; destroy infected plants; spray with bordeaux in spring; space plants widely; rotate crops
Bacterial spot (Bacteria)	Leaves have purplish brown spots with yellow rings; fruits are sunken and have scabby spots or crack	Vegetable plants, especially peppers; flowering plants, including annuals	Pull up and dispose of infected plants; plant disease-free seeds
Bacterial wilt (Bacteria)	Leaves and stems wilt and collapse, then leaves turn dry, brown	Vegetable plants; herbs; flowering plants	Destroy infected plants; cover seedlings with floating row covers (bury edges in soil); rotate plantings
Black rot (Fungus)	Leaves have red to brown spots; fruits have purple to brown spots; fruits shrivel, then cling to plant	Vegetable plants; fruiting plants	Destroy diseased plant parts; spray bordeaux mix on fruiting plants; rotate plantings
Black spot (Fungus)	Leaves have black spots with fringed margin; leaves fall early	Rose plants	Destroy infected plant parts; spray sulfur or baking soda; avoid wetting foliage; mulch with compost; site plants in full sun; space plants widely
Blossom-end rot (soil calcium deficiency)	Fruits are leathery; skin at blossom end turns brown	Vegetable plants	Mulch; drench soil with seaweed solution weekly while fruits form
Brown rot (Fungus)	On fruit, brown spots enlarge, followed by gray spores; fruit rots and shrivels	Fruiting plants, especially peaches	Remove and destroy infected fruit; prune tree to open up center; spray sulfur
Damping-off (Fungus)	Stems rot at soil; seedlings fall over; poor germination	Vegetable plants; flowering plants	Use sterile containers and potting mix; provide strong light for seedlings started indoors
Downy mildew (Fungus)	Leaves have yellow spots with corresponding fluffy fungus spots on undersides	Vegetable plants; herbs; fruiting plants; flowering plants	Destroy infected plant parts; drench soil with compost tea; spray baking soda or bordeaux; avoid wetting foliage; space plants widely; protect seedlings with floating row covers (bury edges in soil)

DISEASE	PROBLEMS	SUSCEPTIBLE PLANTS	WHAT TO DO
Early blight (Fungus)	Leaves have brown spots with concentric rings; leaves drop early	Vegetable plants	Plant in full sun; space plants widely; grow in raised beds; rotate crops
Fusarium wilt (Fungus)	Leaves curl and stems wilt; leaves drop early	Vegetable plants; herbs; flowering plants	Add lime to raise soil alkalinity to pH 6.5–7.5; destroy infected plants; avoid overwatering; cover seedlings with floating row covers (bury edges in soil); place clear plastic sheeting over soil for 3–4 weeks
Late blight (Fungus)	Leaves have brown spots with yellow haloes; white fungi grow on undersides; fruits and tubers shrivel and rot	Vegetable plants; flowering plants	Pull up and destroy infected plants; improve soil drainage; plant disease-free seeds and starts; space plants widely; rotate plants; spray flowering plants with bordeaux
Mosaic (Virus)	Leaves and fruit are mottled with spots or streaks of yellow, white, or brown; leaves distort; plants stunted	Vegetable plants; herbs; fruiting plants; flowering plants	Destroy infected plants; plant seeds early in season; attract beneficial insects by planting small-flowered nectar plants, like yarrow; cover seedlings with floating row covers (bury edges in soil)
Powdery mildew (Fungus)	Leaves have a powdery coating; plant distorts; fruits have webbing, cracking, or powdery coating	Vegetable plants; herbs; fruiting plants; flowering plants	Destroy infected leaves; spray sulfur or bordeaux; space plants widely; rotate plants
Rust, Cedar apple rust, White pine blister rust (Fungi)	Leaves and stems have red to orange powdery spots and streaks	Vegetable plants; herbs; fruiting plants; flowering plants	Destroy infected foliage; compost garden debris; space plants widely; for apples: remove cedar trees from property; spray with sulfur
Scab (Fungus)	On fruit and leaves, velvety green or brown spots become raised, corky; fruit and leaves drop early	Vegetable plants; fruiting plants and nut plants	Compost old leaves in the fall; prune for good air circulation; spray copper or bordeaux
Soft rot (Bacteria)	Water-soaked spots on fruits enlarge and become sunken, sometimes with a foul odor; plants are yellowed, stunted	Vegetable plants; flowering plants	Destroy diseased plant parts; disinfect tools with bleach; compost debris; space plants widely; plant in well-drained soil; dust flower storage roots with sulfur
Verticillium wilt (Fungus)	Leaves have yellow patches that turn brown; leaves and stems droop	Vegetable plants; herbs; flowering plants	Destroy diseased plant parts; fertilize; space widely; grow in containers; rotate plantings

Sources

INFORMATION SOURCES

Bio-Integral Resource Center (BIRC)
Box 7414
Berkeley, CA 94707
(510) 524-2567

This organization publishes information on the latest least-toxic solutions to pest problems. It is also a clearinghouse for sources of least-toxic products and services. Members receive the newsletter IPM Practitioner.

Cooperative Extension Service
You can find your Cooperative Extension office listed under "government offices" in the phone book. Contact these offices for information on obtaining their publications on all aspects of pest control, including excellent photographic pest guides. The Cooperative Extension office is a governmental agency, associated with the land-grant university in each state.

SOURCES OF GARDENING, PEST-CONTROL, AND DISEASE-CONTROL PRODUCTS

Note: *Many of the following mail-order sources sell beneficial insects and other products described in this book for least-toxic, garden pest–management.*

Arbico Environmentals
P.O. Box 4247 CRB
Tucson, AZ 85738

Gardener's Supply Co.
128 Intervale Road
Burlington, VT 05401

Gardens Alive!
5100 Schenley Place
Lawrenceburg, IN 47025

Harmony Farm Supply
P.O. Box 460
Graton, CA 95444

The Natural Gardening Company
217 San Anselmo Avenue
San Anselmo, CA 94960

Peaceful Valley Farm Supply
P.O. Box 2209
Grass Valley, CA 95945

Smith & Hawken
Two Arbor Lane
Box 6900
Florence, KY 41022-6900

Worm's Way Garden Center and Home Brewing Supply
7850 North Highway 37
Bloomington, IN 47404-9477

MAIL-ORDER SOURCES FOR BENEFICIAL INSECTS AND MITES

Applied Bionomics Ltd.
11074 West Saanich Road
Sidney, B.C.
Canada V8L 5P5

Beneficial Insectary
14751 Oak Run Road
Oak Run, CA 96069

Better Yield Insects
1302 Highway 2, No. 3
Belle River, Ontario
Canada N0R 1A0

Biofac Crop Care
P.O. Box 87
Mathis, TX 78368

Buena Biosystems
P.O. Box 4008
Ventura, CA 93007

Foothill Agricultural Research
510½ West Chase Drive
Corona, CA 91720

Hydro-Gardens
P.O. Box 25845
Colorado Springs, CO 80936

The LadyBug Company (Bio-Control Products)
8706 Oro-Quincy Highway
Berry Creek, CA 95916

Nature's Control
P.O. Box 35
Medford, OR 97501

Rincon-Vitova Insectaries
P.O. Box 1555
Ventura, CA 93002

Recommended Reading

BOOKS

Carr, Anna. *Good Neighbors: Companion Planting for Gardeners*. Emmaus, PA: Rodale Press, 1985.

———. *Rodale's Color Handbook of Garden Insects*. Emmaus, PA: Rodale Press, 1979.

Ellis, Barbara W., and Fern Marshall Bradley, eds. *The Organic Gardener's Handbook of Natural Insect and Disease Control*. Emmaus, PA: Rodale Press, 1992.

Gilkeson, Linda, Pam Peirce, and Miranda Smith. *Rodale's Pest and Disease Problem Solver*. Emmaus, PA: Rodale Press, 1996.

Hart, Rhonda Massingham. *Bugs, Slugs and Other Thugs*. Pownal, VT: Storey Publishing, 1991.

MacNab, A. A., A. F. Sherf, and J. K. Springer. *Identifying Diseases of Vegetables*. University Park, PA: The Pennsylvania State University College of Agriculture, 1983.

Michalak, Patricia S., and Linda A. Gilkeson. *Rodale's Successful Organic Gardening: Controlling Pests and Diseases*. Emmaus, PA: Rodale Press, 1994.

Nancarrow, Loren, and Janet Hogan Taylor. *Dead Snails Leave No Trails*. Berkeley, CA: Ten Speed Press, 1996.

Olkowski, William, Sheila Darr, and Helga Olkowski. *Common-Sense Pest Control*. Newtown, CT: Taunton Press, 1991.

Pleasant, Barbara. *The Gardener's Bug Book*. Pownal, VT: Storey Publishing, 1994.

———. *The Gardener's Guide to Plant Diseases*. Pownal, VT: Storey Publishing, 1995.

Smith, Miranda, and Anna Carr. *Rodale's Garden Insect, Disease & Weed Indentification Guide*. Emmaus, PA: Rodale Press, 1988.

Westcott, Cynthia. *The Gardener's Bug Book*. 4th ed. Garden City, NY: Doubleday & Company, 1973.

———. *Westcott's Plant Disease Handbook*. 5th ed. rev. by R. Kenneth Horst. New York, NY: Van Nostrand Reinhold Co., 1990.

Also useful are The Disease Compendium Series *by The American Phytopathological Society. Titles in the series include:* Beet Diseases and Insects, Corn Diseases, Pea Diseases, Peanut Diseases, Potato Diseases, Rose Diseases, *and* Strawberry Diseases.

PERIODICALS

Common Sense Pest Control Quarterly
Bio-Integral Resource Center (BIRC)
P.O. Box 7414
Berkeley, CA 94707

IPM Practitioner
Bio-Integral Resource Center (BIRC)
P.O. Box 7414
Berkeley, CA 94707

Organic Gardening
Rodale Press, Inc.
33 East Minor Street
Emmaus, PA 18098

Index

You can find solutions to your plants' problems two ways: Either look up your plant, or look up the solution. Solutions are indexed only once, but all solutions are given in the plant entries whenever appropriate. Page references in *italic* indicate tables; **boldface** references indicate illustrations.

A

Abelmoschus esculentus, 48–49, **48**
Achillea, 327, **327**
Actinidia, 164–65, **164**
Ageratum, 188–89, **188**
Agrobacterium radiobacter, 140
Alcea rosea, 252–53, **252**
Allium, 36–37, **36**, 42–43, **42**, 50–51, **50**
Almond, 124–27, **124**
Aloysia triphylla, 122
Alternaria blight, 32, 47
Alternaria leaf blight, 21
Alternaria leaf spot, 17, 236–37, 249
Anemone, 192–94, **192**
Anethum graveolens, 104
Angular leaf spot, 31–32
Animals, 7, 127, 165, 228, **228**
Anthracnose, *332*
  bean and, 5–6
  blackberry and, 139
  cucumber and, 32
  pansy and, 287
  peony and, 292
  persimmon and, 177
  raspberry and, 139
  sweet pea and, 319
  tomato and, 82
  watermelon and, 86–87
Anthriscus cerefolium, 102
Antirrhinum majus, 312–15, **312**
Ants, 27–28, 102, 157
Aphids, 15, *329*
  artemisia and, 195, **195**
  asparagus and, 3
  aster and, 196, **196**

astilbe and, 199
bachelor's-button and, 202, **202**
basil and, **92**, 93
beet and, 8
begonia and, **206**, 207
blackberry and, 136
black-eyed Susan and, 210–11
broccoli and, 10
cabbage and, 15
calendula and, **98**, 99
canna and, 217, **217**
caraway and, 100–101, **100**
cherry and, 146
chervil and, 102, **102**
cleome and, 217, **217**
columbine and, 220, **220**
coreopsis and, 224
corn and, 27–28
cosmos and, 226
currant and, 154
daylily and, 232, **232**
dill and, 104
fennel and, 105
filbert and, 162, **162**
forget-me-not and, 241, **241**
foxglove and, 324, **324**
garden mum and, 278
geranium and, 244, **244**
gladiolus and, 250
gooseberry and, 154
hardy geranium and, 246–47
hazelnut and, 162, **162**
hyacinth and, 256, **256**
impatiens and, 258–59, **258**
kale and, 39
larkspur and, 264
lettuce and, 44, **44**
lily and, 266, **266**
lobelia and, 270–71, **270**
lovage and, 108, **108**
lupine and, 272, **272**
marigold and, 275
mint and, 110
nasturtium and, 282–83, **282**
oregano and, 111
pansy and, 284–85
parsley and, 112

pea and, 54–55
pecan and, 174
penstemon and, 288, **288**
plum and, 178, **178**
poppy and, 300, **300**
raspberry and, 136
rose and, 306
rosemary and, 115, **115**
rutabaga and, **68**, 69
sedum and, 310, **310**
snapdragon and, 312–13
spinach and, 70, **70**
strawberry and, 181
sunflower and, 316
tomato and, **78**, 79
tulip and, 320, **320**
turnip and, **84**, 85
verbena and, 322, **322**
veronica and, 324, **324**
walnut and, 185
Apium, 24–25, **24**
Apple, 128–31, **128**
Apple maggot flies, 128, *128*, *329*
Apple scab, 130
Apricot, 132–35, **132**
Aquilegia, 220–21, **220**
Arachis hypogaea, 170–71, **170**
Armyworms, 8–9, 16, *329.* *See also* Fall armyworms
Artemisia, 195, **195**
Artemisia dracunculus var. *sativa,* 120
Asclepias tuberosa, 214, **214**
Asparagus, 2–3, **2**
Asparagus beetles, 2–3, **2**, *329*
Asparagus miners, 2
Aster, 196–97, **196**
Aster leafhoppers
  aster and, 196, **196**
  baby's-breath and, 200, **200**
  black-eyed Susan and, 210, **210**
  coreopsis and, 224, **224**
  lobelia and, 271
  marigold and, 275
  poppy and, 300–301
Aster yellows
  anemone and, 193

baby's-breath and, 201
bachelor's-button and, 204
carrots and, 21
coreopsis and, 225
cosmos and, 227
delphinium and, 235
garden mum and, 279
marigold and, 277
parsnip and, 53
potato and, 63
sweet alyssum and, 190
Astilbe, 198–99, **198**
Azadirachtin, 4

B

Baby's-breath, 200–201, **200**
Bachelor's-button, 202–5, **202**
Bacillus thuringiensis, 9, 40, 60
Bacterial black spot, 235, 265
Bacterial blight, 126, 301
Bacterial crown gall, 139–40
Bacterial fasciation, 296, 318
Bacterial leaf spot, 134, 168,
  208–9, 245, 249, 292
Bacterial soft rot, 257, 261–62
Bacterial spot, 58–59, *332*
Bacterial wilt, *332*
  caraway and, 101
  coriander and, 103
  cucumber and, 32
  dianthus and, 237
  impatiens and, 259
  melon and, 47
  nasturtium and, 283
  pumpkin and, 89
  sage and, 119
  tomato and, 81–82
  winter squash and, 89
Bactericides, 140
Baking soda as fungicide, 45
Barriers, 26, 127, 130, 228
  for birds, 26, 54
  for cutworms, 4, 56
  floating row covers as, 2
  for slugs and snails, 95, 152, 193
Basal rot, 229
Basil, 92–93
Bay, 94
Bean, 4–5, **4**
Bean aphids, 282

Bean leaf beetles, **4**, 5
Bean mosaic, 5
Bee balm, 95
Beet, 8–9, **8**
Beet curly top, 237, 249
Beetles, 48
Begonia, 206–9, **206**
Beneficial insects, 3
  aphid midges, 217
  attracting, 211
  flies, 143, 210
  lacewings, 3
  lady beetles, 3
  Macrocentrus ancylivorus, 167
  mealybug destroyers, 222
  minute pirate bugs, 181
  mites, 125
  spiders, 210
  wasps, 3, 128–29, 167
Beneficial nematodes, 2
Beta vulgaris, 8–9, **8**, 76–77, **76**
Birds as pest predators, 10, 276
Birds as pests. *See specific plants*
Blackberry, 136–41, **136**
Black cherry aphids, 146
Black-eyed Susan, 210–11, **210**
Black fruit spot, 173
Black heart, 25
Black knot, 179
Black leg, 17, 23, 235
Blackline virus, 185–86
Black pecan aphids, 174
Black root rot, 181, 315
Black rot, 16, 75, 90, 159–60,
  332
Black scale, **94**, **115**, 116
Black spot, 307, *332*
Black vine weevil, 198, **198**, 206,
  206, *329*
Black walnut curculios, 184
Blanching, 23, 25, 43
Bleeding heart, 212–13, **212**
Blister beetles, 34, **34**, 56, **56**, 79,
  192, **192**
Blossom and shoot blight, 319
Blossom blight, 49, 73, 126–27
Blossom-end rot, 58, 83, *332*
Blueberry, 142–45, **142**
Blueberry maggot flies, 142
Blue mold, 71

Blue mold rot, 36–37
Blue stem, 141
Bolting, 19, 37, 45, 71
Borage, 96
Bordeaux mix, 126, 130
Borers, 132, **132**, 250–51, 304
Boron deficiency, 9, 11, 53, 77
Botryosphaeria stem canker, 144
Botrytis, 7, 45, 117, 140
Botrytis blight
  blueberry and, 144–45
  forget-me-not and, 241
  garden mum and, 279–80
  gladiolus and, **250**, 251
  hyacinth and, 257
  marigold and, 277
  pansy and, 286–87
  peony and, 292–93
  rose and, 307–8
  sweet pea and, 319
  zonal geranium and, 249
Botrytis bunch rot, 160
Botrytis rot, 165
Bottom rot, 45
Brassica spp.
  broccoli, 10–11, **10**
  brussels sprouts, 12–13, **12**
  cabbage, 14–17, **14**
  cauliflower, 22–23, **22**
  Chinese cabbage, 18–19, **18**
  kale, 38–39, **38**
  kohlrabi, 40–41, **40**
  rutabaga, 68–69, 68
  turnip, 84–85, **84**
Bristly rose slugs, 304
Broccoli, 10–11, **10**
Brown ambrosia aphids, 210–11
Brown canker, 308
Brown rot, 126–27, 134–35,
  148–49, 168, *332*
Brown rot gummosis, 152
Brussels sprouts, 12–13, **12**
BT, 40
BTK, 9
BTSD, 60
Bulb mites, 228, 251, 256, **256**,
  321
Bunching onion, 42–43
Burdock borers, 265
Butterfly weed, 214, **214**

C

Cabbage, 14–17, **14**
Cabbage aphids, 10, 15, 39
Cabbage loopers, *329*
　broccoli and, 10, **10**
　cabbage and, 14–15, **14**
　kale and, 38, **38**
　kohlrabi and, 40, **40**
　nasturtium and, **282**, 283
　zonal geranium and, **246**, 247
Cabbage maggots, 11, 15, 22, 65, 68, 84, *329*
Calcium deficiency, 25, 45, 58, 83, *332*
Calendula, 98–99
Candytuft, 215, **215**
Cane blight, 140
Cankers, 53, 135, 168–69
Canna, 216, **216**
Canna bud rot, 216
Capsicum spp., 56–59, **56**
Caraway, 100–101
Carnation collar blight, 236–37
Carnation latent disease, 237
Carnation mottle virus, 237
Carnation ringspot virus, 237
Carnation streak virus, 237
Carrot, 20–21, **20**
Carrot rust fly larvae, 20, **20**, 24, **24**, 52, **52**, 100, 112
Carrot weevil larvae, 20
Carum carvi, 100–101
Carya illinoinensis, 174–75, **174**
Catalina cherry moths, 163
Caterpillars, 110, 188, 247, 296, 305
Cauliflower, 22–23, **22**
Cedar apple rust, 130, *333*
Celery, 24–25, **24**
Celery leaftiers, 188–89, 246, 275, 312, 318
Celosia cristata, 218, **218**
Centaurea, 202–5, **202**, 238, **238**
Cercospora blight, 3
Cercospora leaf blight, 21
Cercospora leaf spot
　asparagus and, 3
　beans and, 6–7
　beet and, 9
　calendula and, 99
　lavender and, 106
　swiss chard and, 77
　watermelon and, 87
　zonal geranium and, 249

Chalcedon checkerspot butterflies, 324–25
Cherry, 146–49, **146**
Cherry fruit flies, 146–47, **146**
Cherry fruitworms, 142–43, 147
Cherry leaf spot, 149
Cherry slugs, 147–48
Chervil, 102
Chinese cabbage, 18–19, **18**
Choanephora wet rot, 73
Chrysanthemum, 278–81, **278**
Chrysanthemum lace bugs, 196–97, **196**, 278, **278**
Chrysanthemum leafminers, 278–79, **278**
Cilantro, 103
Citrullus lanatus, 86–87, **86**
Citrus, 150–53, **150**
Citrus mealybugs, **150**, 151
Citrus red mites, 150–51
Citrus scab, 152
Citrus thrips, 151
Cleome, 217, **217**
Clubroot, 11
Cockscomb, 218, **218**
Codling moth larvae, 128–29, *128*
Codling moths, 184, **184**
Coleus, 219, **219**
Colorado potato beetles, 60, **60**, 239, **239**, 294, **294**, *329*
Columbine, 220–21, **220**
Columbine borers, 220–21
Columbine leafminers, **220**, 221
Common stalk borers
　bachelor's-button and, 202–3
　columbine and, 220–21, **220**
　cosmos and, 226–27, **226**
　dahlia and, 230
　delphinium and, 234–35, **234**
　gladiolus and, 250–51
　larkspur and, 265
　lily and, 266–67, **266**
　potato and, 61
　snapdragon and, **312**, 313–14
Consolida ambigua, 264–65, **264**
Convallaria majalis, 269, **269**
Copper spray, 87, 130
Copper sulfate, 126
Coral bells, 222–23, **222**
Coreopsis, 224–25, **224**
Coriander, 103

Corn, 26–29, **26**
Corn earworms, **26**, 27, 80, 188
Cornflower, 202–5, **202**
Corn rootworms, **26**, 27
Corn smut, 28
Corylus, 162–63, **162**
Cosmos, 226–27, **226**
Cotton root rot, 253
Cottonycushion scale, 126, 133–34, 151
Cranberry fruitworms, 142
Cranesbill, 244–45, **244**
Crocus, 228, **228**
Crop rotation, 6, 49
Crown gall, 139–40, 160, 201
Crown rot
　ageratum and, 189
　anemone and, 194
　bachelor's-button and, 205
　delphinium and, 235
　dusty miller and, 238
　forget-me-not and, 241
　hosta and, 255
　iris and, 262
　kiwi and, 165
　lamb's-ears and, 263
　lily and, 268
　lily-of-the-valley and, 269
　penstemon and, 288–89
　phlox and, 299
Crumbly berry virus, 140
Cucumber, 30–33, **30**
Cucumber beetles, *329*
Cucumber mosaic, 33, 45, 59, 71, 249, 297, 321
Cucumis, 30–33, **30**, 46–47, **46**
Cucurbita, 72–73, **72**, 88–90, **88**
Currant, 154–55, **154**
Currant borers, 154
Currant fruit flies, 154–55, **154**
Cutworms, *330*
　anemone and, 192–93, **192**
　asparagus and, 2, **2**
　bachelor's-button and, **202**, 203
　beans and, 4, **4**
　celery and, 24, **24**
　corn and, 26
　cucumber and, 30, **30**
　delphinium and, 234, **234**
　dianthus and, 236, **236**
　flowering tobacco and, 239, **239**

lettuce and, 44, **44**
pansy and, **284**, 285
pea and, 54, **54**
pepper and, 56–57, **56**
sweet alyssum and, 190, **190**
Cyclamen mites, 234, 265

D

Daffodil, 229, **229**
Dahlia, 230–31, **230**
Damping-off, *332*
  basil and, 93
  broccoli and, 11
  dusty miller and, 238
  kale and, 39
  kohlrabi and, 41
  lettuce and, 44–45
  lobelia and, 271
  pansy and, 287
  pepper and, 58
  petunia and, 296
  sweet alyssum and, 191
  sweet pea and, 319
Daucus carota var. *sativus,* 20–21, **20**
Daylily, 232–33, **232**
DE (diatomaceous earth), 5
Delphinium, 234–35, **234**
Delphinium aphids, 264
Dendranthema grandiflorum,
  278–81, **278**
Diamondback moths, 215
Dianthus, 236–37, **236**
Diatomaceous earth, 5
Dicentra, 212–13, **212**
Didymellina leaf spot, 262
Digitalis, 242–43, **242**
Dill, 104
Diospyros, 176–77, **176**
Disease finder, *332–333*
Disinfecting practices, 106, 233,
  250
Dodder, 297
Downy mildew, *332*
  bachelor's-button and, 204
  broccoli and, 11
  brussels sprouts and, 13
  cauliflower and, 23
  Chinese cabbage and, 19
  coriander and, 103, **103**
  cucumber and, 32
  flowering tobacco and, 240

grape and, 160
hardy geranium and, 245
kale and, 39
lemon balm and, 107
veronica and, 325
Dry rot, 6, 228, **250,** 251
Dusty miller, 238, **238**

E

Early blight, 35, 62, 81, *333*
Early bud rot, 292–93
Eastern filbert blight, 163
Eastern red cedar, 130
Echinacea, 302–3, **302**
Egg-based rodent repellent, 228
Eggplant, 34–35, **34**
European apple sawflies, 129
European corn borers, 26–27, **26,**
  226–27, 230, **230,** 250–51
European earwigs, 230, 274
European red mites, 129–30, 156,
  178
Eutypa dieback, 135, 160–61

F

Fall armyworms, 12, **12,** 39, 40,
  40, 64–65, **64**
Fall webworms, 305
Fennel, 105
Fern nematodes, 298–99
Fertilizer, 11, 83, 153
  excessive, 97, 153, 233, 249,
    293, 302
Filbert, 162–63, **162**
Filbert bud mites, 162–63
Filbertworms, 163
Fire blight, 131, 173
Flathead borers, 130
Flea beetles, *330*
  beet and, 8, **8**
  blueberry and, 144
  Chinese cabbage and, 18, **18**
  eggplant and, 34, **34**
  flowering tobacco and, 239–40
  forget-me-not and, 241, **241**
  grape, 157
  melons and, 46
  nasturtium and, 282, **282**
  petunia and, 295
  potato and, 60
  radish and, 64, **64**
  rutabaga and, 68–69, **68**

spinach and, 70–71
sweet potato and, 74, **74**
swiss chard and, 76–77, **76**
tomato and, 78, **78**
turnip and, 84–85, **84**
Floating row covers, 2
Florida wax scale, 254–55
Flossflower, 188–89, **188**
Flowering tobacco, 239–40, **239**
Flower thrips, 290–91, **290,** 305
Foeniculum vulgare, 105
Foliar nematodes, 280
Foot rot, 67
Forget-me-not, 241, **241**
Four-lined plant bugs
  coreopsis and, **224,** 225
  hardy geranium and, 244, **244**
  lupine and, 272, **272**
  mint and, 110
  peony and, 291
  poppy and, 300, **300**
Foxglove, 242–43, **242**
Foxglove anthracnose, 242
Foxglove aphids, 324, **324**
Fragaria, 180–83, **180**
French tarragon, 120
Frost damage. *See specific plants*
Fruit drop, 177
Fruit flies, *330*
Fruittree bark borers, 126
Fuller rose beetles, 307
Fungicides, 45
  baking soda, 45
  bordeaux mix, 126, 130
  copper, 130
  sulfur, 127, 130
  summer oil, 161
  washing soda, 155
Fusarium basal rot, 43, 51, 204
Fusarium root rot, 6
Fusarium wilt, *333*
  asparagus and, 3
  astilbe and, 199
  basil and, 93
  dianthus and, 237
  foxglove and, 243
  French tarragon and, 120, *120*
  lavender and, 106, **106**
  lemon balm and, 107
  oregano and, 111
  parsley and, 113

Fusarium wilt (*continued*)
  rhubarb and, 66–67
  rosemary and, 116–17
  sage and, 119
  salad burnet and, 97, **97**
  sweet potato and, 75
  thyme and, 121, **121**
  tomato and, 81
Fusarium yellows, 11, 16
Fusicoccum canker, 144

G

Garden mum, 278–81, **278**
Garlic, 36–37, **36**
Geranium, hardy (*Geranium* spp.),
  244–45, **244**
Geranium, zonal (*Pelargonium* spp.),
  246–49, **246**
Geranium aphids, 246–47
Germination. *See specific plants*
Gladiolus, 250–51, **250**
Gladiolus thrips, 250, 252, **252**
Gooseberry, 154–55, **154**
Granulosis virus, 184
Grape, 156–61, **156**
Grape berry moths, 156–57, **156**
Grape flea beetles, 144, 157
Grape mealybugs, 157
Grape phylloxera, 158
Grape root borers, 158
Grasshoppers, **76**, 77, 92, 96, **96**,
  142, 143, 195, **195**
Gray leaf spot, 82
Gray mold
  ageratum and, 189
  bean and, 7
  blackberry and, 140
  blueberry and, 144–45
  forget-me-not and, 241
  garden mum and, 279–80
  grape and, 160
  hyacinth and, 257
  lettuce and, 45
  marigold and, 277
  pansy and, 286–87
  peony and, 292–93
  raspberry and, 140
  rosemary and, 117
  strawberry and, 181–82
  zonal geranium and, 249

Greasy spot, 152
Greedy scale, 310–11
Greenhouse whiteflies, 272–73
Green peach aphids, 70, **70**, 217,
  217, 241, 246–47, 264, 322
Growing condition problems. *See
  specific plants*
Gummosis, 149, 169
Gummy stem blight, 87
Gypsophila paniculata, 200–201, **200**

H

Hand removal of pests, 2, 89, 94,
  98, 129, 132, 192, 260, 313
Hardiness zone map, **346**
Harlequin bugs, 16
Hazelnut, 162–63, **162**
Hazelnut twig blight, 163
Heart rot, 53, 77
Hedeoma pulegioides, 114
Helianthus, 316–17, **316**
Hemerocallis, 232–33, **232**
Hemispherical scale, 203
Heuchera, 222–23, **222**
Hickory shuckworms, 174
Hollyhock, 252–53, **252**
Hollyhock thrips, 252
Horticultural oils, 61, 126, 129–30,
  148, 164
Hosta, 254–55, **254**
Humidity problems, 153, 237,
  263, 273
Hyacinth, 256–57, **256**

I

Iberis sempervirens, 215, **215**
Impatiens, 258–59, **258**
Imported cabbageworms, *330*
  broccoli and, 10, **10**
  brussels sprouts and, 12
  cabbage and, 14, **14**
  cauliflower and, 22, **22**
  kale and, 38, **38**
  kohlrabi and, 40–41, **40**
  nasturtium and, 283
Imported currantworms, **154**,
  155
Insecticidal soap, 3
Ipomoea batatas, 74–75, **74**
Iris, 260–62, **260**

Iris borers, 260, **260**
Iron deficiency, 145, 153

J

Japanese beetles, *330*
  aster and, **196**, 197
  astilbe and, 198, **198**
  basil and, 92
  blackberry and, 136–37
  canna and, 216, **216**
  cosmos and, **226**, 227
  dahlia and, 230–31, **230**
  grape and, **156**, 158–59
  hollyhock and, 252–53, **252**
  kiwi and, 164, **164**
  marigold and, 274, **274**
  okra and, 48, **48**
  peony and, 290, **290**
  purple coneflower and, 302,
    302
  raspberry and, 136–37
  rhubarb and, 66, **66**
  rose and, **304**, 305–6
  zinnia and, 328, **328**
Juglans, 184–86, **184**
Juniperus virginiana, 130

K

Kale, 38–39, **38**
Kiwi, 164–65, **164**
Kohlrabi, 40–41, **40**

L

Lacebugs, *330*
Lactuca sativa, 44–45, **44**
Lamb's-ears, 263, **263**
Larger canna leafrollers, 216, **216**
Larkspur, 264–65, **264**
Larkspur leafminers, 235, 264
Late blight, 62, 82, 292–93, *333*
Lathyrus, 318–19, **318**
Laurus nobilis, 94
Lavender, 106
Leaf blight, 197, 299
Leaf-curl plum aphids, 202
Leaf drop, 299
Leafhoppers
  bean and, 5
  grape and, **156**, 159
  lettuce and, 44
  marigold and, 275

peanut and, 170, **170**
potato and, 61
Leafminers
butterfly weed and, 214, **214**
delphinium and, **234**, 235
larkspur and, 264, **264**
lovage and, 108, **108**
oregano and, 111
Leafrollers, *330*
ageratum and, 188–89, **188**
marigold and, **274**, 275
snapdragon and, 312
sweet pea and, 318, **318**
zonal geranium and, 246, **246**
Leaf scorch, 268
Leaf spot
aster and, 197
cleome and, 217
cockscomb and, 218
columbine and, 221
coral bells and, 223
flowering tobacco and, 240
garden mum and, 280
hollyhock and, 253
lobelia and, 271
lupine and, 273
pansy and, 287
parsnip and, 53
penstemon and, 289
strawberry and, 182
veronica and, 325
violet and, 326
Leaftiers, *330*
ageratum and, 188–89, **188**
marigold and, 275
snapdragon and, 312
sweet peas and, 318, **318**
zonal geranium and, 246
Leather rot, 182
Leek, 42–43, **42**
Lemon balm, 107
Lemon verbena, 122
Lesser canna leafrollers, 216
Lesser peach tree borers, 167
Lettuce, 44–45, **44**
Lettuce mosaic, 45
Levisticum officinale, 108
Life cycle. *See specific plants*
Light problems. *See specific plants*
Lilium, 266–68, **266**

Lily, 266–68, **266**
Lily botrytis blight, 267
Lily-of-the-valley, 269, **269**
Lime for insect and disease control, 126
Lobelia, 270–71, **270**
Lobularia maritima, 190–91, **190**
Lodging, 29, 227, 268
Lovage, 108
Lupine, 272–73, **272**
Lycopersicon lesculentum, 78–83, **78**

M

Magnesium deficiency, 65
Maize chlorotic dwarf virus, 29
Maize dwarf mosaic, 28–29
Malus, 128–31, **128**
Marigold, 49, 274–77, **274**
Meadow spittlebugs, 138
Mealybugs, *330*
begonia and, 206–7, **206**
citrus and, **150**, 151
coleus and, 219, **219**
coral bells and, 222, **222**
rosemary and, 116
zonal geranium and, 248
Melanose, 152–53
Melissa officinalis, 107
Melon, 46–47, **46**
Melon aphids, 207, 312–13
Mentha, 110, 114
Mexican bean beetles, 4, **4**, *330*
Mice, 26, 54
Milky disease, 48
Mint, 110
Misshapen fruits, 33, 87, 90
Mist flower, 188–89, **188**
Moisture. *See specific plants*
Monarch butterfly larvae, 214
Monarda, 95
Mosaic viruses, *333*
bean and, 5
blackberry and, 140
corn and, 28–29
cucumber and, 33
daffodil and, 229
dill and, 104
flowering tobacco and, 240
hyacinth and, 257
lettuce and, 45

melon and, 47
pea and, 55
pepper and, 59
petunia and, 297
raspberry and, 140
rose and, 309
spinach and, 71
tomato and, 82
tulip and, 321
zonal geranium and, 249
Mulching, 9, 17, 73, 215
Mummyberry, 145
Myosotis, 241, **241**

N

Narcissus, 229, **229**
Narcissus bulb flies, 229, **229**, 267
Narcissus flower streak, 229
Narcissus mosaic, 229
Narcissus yellow stripe, 229
Narcussus white streak, 229
Nasturtium, 282–83, **282**
Navel orangeworms, 124, **124**
Needleblight, 3
Neem, 4, 292
Negro bugs, 144
Nematodes
beneficial, 2
harmful, 209, 231, 298–99 (*see also* Root-knot nematodes)
Nicotiana alata, 239–40, **239**
Nitrogen deficiency, 9, 29, 153
Northern corn leaf blight, 28
Nutrient deficiencies, 67, 122. *See also specific nutrients; specific plants*
Nutrient excesses, 25, 53

O

Obliquebanded leafrollers
ageratum and, 188–89
apricot and, 134
marigold and, 275
snapdragon and, 312
sweet peas and, 318
zonal geranium and, 246
Ocimum basilicum, 92–93
Okra, 48–49, **48**
Omnivorous leaftiers, 203–4
Onion, 50–51, **50**

Onion maggots, 36, **36**, 42, 50, **50**, *331*
Orange rust, 141
Oregano, 111
Oregon swallowtail larvae, 120
Oriental fruit moth larvae, 124–25, **124**, 132–33, **132**, 147
Oriental fruit moths, 166–67, **166**
Origanum, 109, 111
Ornithogalum mosaic, 257
Oystershell scale, 291

P

Paeonia, 290–93, **290**
Pansy, 284–87, **284**
Papaver, 300–301, **300**
Parsley, 112–13
Parsleyworms
    caraway and, 100, **100**
    carrot and, 20, **20**
    dill and, 104, **104**
    fennel and, 105
    parsley and, 112–13, **112**
    parsnip and, 52, **52**
    rue and, 118, *118*
Parsnip, 52–53, **52**
Parsnip webworms, 52–53
Pastinaca sativa, 52–53, **52**
Pea, 54–55, **54**
Peach, 166–69, **166**
Peach leaf curl, 169
Peach scab, 169
Peach tree borers, **132**, **166**, 167
Peach twig borers, **124**, 125, 166–67
Pea enation mosaic, 55
Peanut, 170–71, **170**
Peanut leaf spot, 171
Pear, 172–73, **172**
Pear leaf blight, 173
Pear psyllids, 172, **172**
Pear sawflies, 147–48, 172, **172**
Pear scab, 173
Pear slugs, 147–48, 172, **172**
Pea stunt, 55
Pecan, 174–75, **174**
Pecan downy spot, 175
Pecan nut casebearers, 174–75
Pecan scab, 175
Pecan weevils, **174**, 175

Pelargonium, 246–49, **246**
Pelargonium leaf curl, 249
Pelargonium rust, 249
Pennyroyal, 114
Penstemon, 288–89, **288**
Peony, 290–93, **290**
Pepper, 56–59, **56**
Pepper-based rodent repellent, 228
Pepper weevils, 57
Persimmon, 176–77, **176**
Pest finder, *329–31*
Petroselinum crispum, 112–13
Petunia, 294–97, **294**
Phaseolus, 4–5, **4**
Pheromone lures, 125
Phlox, 298–99, **298**
Phlox plant bugs, 298, **298**
Phomopsis blight, 35
Phomopsis cane spot, 161
Phomopsis fruit rot, 161
Phomopsis leaf spot, 161
Phosphorus deficiency, 29
Phytophthora blight, 293
Phytophthora crown rot, 67
"Picnic beetles," 139
Pierce's disease, 161
Pink root, 42–43, 50–51
Pisum sativum, 54–55, **54**
Plum, 178–79, **178**
Plum curculios, **128**, 129, **132**, 133, **142**, 143, **146**, 148, **178**, 179
Plume moth caterpillars, 247
Pollination difficulties, 29, 33, 73, 90, 105
Pollution damage, 231, 297
Poppy, 300–301, **300**
Potassium deficiency, 11
Potato, 60–63, **60**
Potato flea beetles, 239–40, 241, **241**, 282, **282**, 295
Potato leafhoppers, 61, 275
Potato stalk borers, **60**, 61
Poterium sanguisorba, 97
Pot marigold, 98–99
Powdery mildew. *See specific plants*
Prunus
    amygdalus, 124–27, **124**
    armeniaca, 132–35, **132**
    persica, 166–69, **166**
    species (cherry), 146–49, **146**

species (plum), 178–79, **178**
Pumpkins, 88–90, **88**
Purple blotch, 51
Purple coneflower, 302–3, **302**
Pyrethrins, 138
Pyrus, 172–73, **172**
Pythium root rot, 6, 238

R

Radish, 64–65, **64**
Raphanus sativus, 64–65, **64**
Raspberry, 136–41, **136**
Raspberry cane borers, 137
Raspberry crown borers, **136**, 137
Raspberry fruitworms, 137–38
Ray blight, 280
Recommended reading, 335
Redbanded leafrollers
    ageratum and, 188–89
    lobelia and, 271
    marigold and, 275
    snapdragon and, 312
    sweet peas and, 318
    zonal geranium and, 246
Redberry mites, 138
Red clover vein mosaic, 55
Red lily leaf beetles, 266
Rednecked cane borers, **136**, 138
Red stele root rot, 182
Rheum rhabarbarum, 66–67, **66**
Rhizoctonia root rot, 6
Rhubarb, 66–67, **66**
Rhubarb curculios, 66
Ribes, 154–55, **154**
Ring spot, 63
Rocket, 264–65, **264**
Root and stem rot, 327
Root-knot nematodes
    carrot and, 21
    dahlia and, 231
    daylily and, 233
    lavender and, 106
    okra and, 49
    pansy and, 286
    parsley and, 113
    peanut and, 170–71
    peony and, 292
    pepper and, 57–58
    phlox and, 298–99
    sweet potato and, 75

Root rot, 97, **97**
  asparagus and, 3
  bachelor's-button and, 204
  basil and, 93
  bean and, 6
  beet and, 9
  begonia and, 209
  blackberry and, 141
  bunching onions and, 43
  dusty miller and, 238
  flowering tobacco and, 240
  French tarragon and, 120, *120*
  hosta and, 255
  lamb's-ears and, 263, **263**
  lavender and, 106, **106**
  leek and, 43
  lemon balm and, 107
  lily and, 267–68
  lobelia and, 271
  onion and, 51
  oregano and, 111
  pansy and, 287
  parsley and, 113
  pea and, 55
  phlox and, 299
  raspberry and, 141
  rhubarb and, 66–67
  rosemary and, 116–17
  sage and, 119
  sedum and, 311
  snapdragon and, 315
  sweet alyssum and, 191
  sweet potato and, 75
  thyme and, 121, **121**
  tomato and, 81
  walnut and, 186
Rose, 304–9, **304**
Rose aphids, 306
Rose budworms, 305
Rose chafers, 159, 305–6
Rose curculios, 307
Rose leaf curl, 309
Rosemary, 115–17
Rose midges, **304**, 306
Rose mosaic, 309
Rose scale, 138–39
Rose stem girders, 304
Rose stem sawflies, 304
Rose streak, 309
Rose yellow mosaic, 240, 309

Rosmarinus officinalis, 115–17
Rubus, 136–41, **136**
Rudbeckia, 210–11, **210**
Rue, 118
Rust, *333*
  anemone and, 193–94
  artemisia and, 195
  asparagus and, 3
  bachelor's-button and, 205
  bean and, 6
  bee balm and, 95, **95**
  black-eyed Susan and, 211
  butterfly weed and, 214
  coral bells and, 223
  corn and, 28
  dianthus and, 237
  dusty miller and, 238
  garden mum and, 280–81
  hardy geranium and, 245
  hollyhock and, 253
  iris and, 262
  lemon balm and, 107, **107**
  lupine and, 273
  mint and, 110
  penstemon and, 289
  phlox and, 299
  rose and, 308
  sedum and, 311
  sunflower and, 317
  veronica and, 325
Rutabaga, 68–69, **68**
Ruta graveolens, 118

S

Sage, 119
Salad burnet, 97
Salvia officinalis, 119
San Jose scale, 133, 148, 150, **150**,
  173, 176, **176**, 291
Sap beetles, 139
Scab, *333*
  apricot and, 135
  beet and, 9
  melons and, 47
  potato and, 62
  radish and, 65
Scale, *331*
  almond and, 126
  apricot and, 133–34
  bachelor's-button and, 203

  bay and, 94, **94**
  blackberry and, 138–39
  bleeding heart and, 212
  blueberry and, 143
  cherry and, 148
  citrus and, 150, **150**, 151
  hosta and, 254–55
  kiwi and, 164–65, **164**
  peony and, 291
  persimmon and, 176, **176**
  raspberry and, 138–39
  rose and, 306
  rosemary, **115**, 116
  sedum and, 310–11
Scallions, 42–43
Scurf, 75
Sedum, 310–11, **310**
Septoria leaf spot, 82, 155
Serpentine leafminers, 214, 283
Shothole borers, 126
Shothole disease, 127, 135, 149,
  169
Six-spotted leafhoppers. *See* Aster
  leafhoppers
Slugs, *331*
  anemone and, **192**, 193
  astilbe and, **198**, 199
  baby's-breath and, 200–201, **200**
  bean and, 5
  bee balm and, 95
  begonia and, 207–8
  bleeding heart and, 212–13, **212**
  calendula and, 98
  Chinese cabbage and, 18–19,
  18
  delphinium and, **234**, 235
  hosta and, 254, **254**
  iris and, 260–61, **260**
  lily-of-the-valley and, 269, **269**
  marigold and, 276
  pansy and, 284
  parsley and, 113
  peony and, **290**, 291
  petunia and, 295–96
  potato and, 61
  sage and, 119, **119**
  spinach and, 70, **70**
  violet and, 326, **326**
  zonal geranium and, 248
Smut, 28, 51

Snails, *331*
  anemone and, 193
  astilbe and, 199
  baby's-breath and, 200–201, **200**
  bee balm and, 95
  begonia and, 207–8
  calendula and, 98
  citrus and, **150**, 151–52
  delphinium and, 235
  hosta and, 254, **254**
  iris and, 260–61
  lily-of-the-valley and, 269, **269**
  marigold and, 276
  pansy and, 284
  parsley and, 113
  peony and, 291
  petunia and, 295–96
  sage and, 119
  violet and, 326, **326**
  zonal geranium and, 248
Snapdragon, 312–15, **312**
Snapdragon anthracnose, 314
Snapdragon leaf spot, 314–15
Snapdragon rust, 314
Soft rot, 24–25, *333*
Soft scale, 164–65, **164**
Soil drainage problems. *See specific plants*
Soil solarization, 43
Solanum, 34–35, **34**, 60–63, **60**
Sources, 334
Southern bacterial wilt, 81–82
Southern blight
  ageratum and, 189
  anemone and, 194
  bachelor's-button and, 205
  dusty miller and, 238
  iris and, 262
  lily and, 268
  lily-of-the-valley and, 269
  marigold and, 276
  okra and, 49
  penstemon and, 288–89
  pepper and, 58
  rhubarb and, 67
  sedum and, 311
  snapdragon and, 315
  strawberry and, 183
Southern corn leaf blight, 28
Southern corn rootworms, 294–95

Southern root-knot nematodes
  cockscomb and, 218
  coleus and, 219
  impatiens and, 259
  petunia and, 297
  snapdragon and, 314
  sweet alyssum and, 190–91
  zonal geranium and, 248–49
Speedwell, 324–25, **324**
Spider mites, *331*
  ageratum and, 189
  almond and, 125–26
  cockscomb and, 218, **218**
  daylily and, 232, **232**
  dianthus and, 236, **236**
  impatiens and, 258
  larkspur and, **264**, 265
  lemon verbena and, 122, **122**
  marigold and, 276
  oregano and, 111
  peanut and, 170, **170**
  phlox and, 298, **298**
  rose and, 306–7
  rosemary and, 115–16, **115**
  sage and, 119
  snapdragon and, 313
  strawberry and, 180–81, **180**
  sweet marjoram and, 109
  thyme and, 121
  tomato and, 79–80
  verbena and, 322–23
  zonal geranium and, **246**, 247
Spinach, 70–71, **70**
Spinach blight, 71
Spinach flea beetles, 70–71
Spinach leafminers, 8, **8**, 70, **70**, 76, **76**
Spinacia oleracea, 70–71, **70**
Spot anthracnose, 287, 326
Spotted cucumber beetles
  canna and, 216, **216**
  coreopsis and, **224**, 225
  cosmos and, **226**, 227
  cucumber and, **30**, 31
  impatiens and, **258**, 259
  melon and, 46–47
  petunia and, 294–95, **294**
  pumpkin and, 89
  watermelon and, 86, **86**
  winter squash and, 89

Spring dwarf nematodes, 209
Squash
  summer, 72–73, **72**
  winter, 88–90, **88**
Squash bugs, 30–31, 72–73, **72**, 88, **88**
Squash vine borers, 31, 46, **46**, 72, **72**, 88–89, **88**
Stachys byzantina, 263, **263**
Steel blue flea beetles, 144
Stem and bulb nematodes, 256–57, 298–99
Stem blight, 145
Stem nematodes, 229
Stem rot
  bachelor's-button and, 205
  bleeding heart and, 213, **212**
  coral bells and, 223
  dianthus and, 237
  dusty miller and, 238
  penstemon and, 288–89
  rhubarb and, 67
  sedum and, 311
  sweet alyssum and, 191
Stewart's bacterial wilt, 28
Stink bugs, 48, **48**, 167
Storage rot, 165
Strawberry, 180–83, **180**
Strawberry bud weevils, 139
Strawberry crown borers, 180
Strawberry root weevils, 180, **180**, 222, **222**
Striped cucumber beetles, **30**, 31, 46–47, **46**, **88**, 89
Sulfur
  deficiency, 37
  as fungicide, 127, 130, 131
Summer squash, 72–73, **72**
Sunburn, 177
Sunflower, 316–17, **316**
Sunflower beetles, 316
Sunscald, 59, 177
Superior oil, 148
Sweet alyssum, 190–91, **190**
Sweet marjoram, 109
Sweet pea, 318–19, **318**
Sweet potato, 74–75, **74**
Sweet potato flea beetles, 74, **74**
Sweet potato weevils, 74
Swiss chard, 76–77, **76**

T

Tagetes, 274–77, **274**
Tarnished plant bugs, *330*
  dahlia and, **230**, 231
  gladiolus and, 251
  impatiens and, 258, **258**
  marigold and, 274–75
  peach and, 167–68
  strawberry and, 181
  sunflower and, **316**, 317
  swiss chard and, 76, **76**
Tarragon, 120
Temperature-related problems. *See specific plants*
Texas root rot, 253, 288–89, 302, 315
Thrips, *331*
  begonia and, **206**, 208
  blueberry and, 143–44
  bunching onions and, 42
  daylily and, 232–33, **232**
  foxglove and, 242, **242**
  garden mum and, **278**, 279
  hollyhock and, 252, **252**
  iris and, **260**, 261
  leek and, 42
  lettuce and, 44, **44**
  onion and, 50, **50**
  yarrow and, 327, **327**
Thyme, 121
Tipburn, 45
Tobacco budworms, 188, 247, 288
Tobacco mosaic virus, 59, 82
Tomato, 78–83, **78**
Tomato fruitworms, 80, 188
Tomato hornworms, **56**, 57, 78–79, **78**, **294**, 296, *331*
Tomato ringspot virus, 140
Transplanting problems, 43, 114, 213, 293
Traps, 5, 21, 77, 127, 189, 230
  sticky, 71, 92, 128, 129, 157, 233
Tropaeolum, 282–83, **282**
Tulip, 320–21, **320**
Tulip breaking virus, 321
Tulip bulb aphids, 320, **320**
Turnip, **84**, 84–85
Twig girdlers, 176
Two-spotted spider mites, 321
  apple and, 129–30

blackberry and, 139
garden mum and, 279
hollyhock and, 253
pansy and, 285–86
plum and, 178, **178**
raspberry and, 139

V

Vaccinium, 142–45, **142**
Vacuuming pests, 13
Verbena, 322–23, **322**
Verbena bud moth larvae, 314
Verbena leafminers, 323
Veronica, 324–25, **324**
Verticillium wilt, *333*
  blackberry and, 141
  caraway and, 101
  coriander and, 103
  eggplant and, 35
  foxglove and, 243
  garden mum and, 281
  mint and, 110
  poppy and, 301
  raspberry and, 141
  rhubarb and, 67
  strawberry and, 183
  tomato and, 80–81
Viola, 326, **326**
  × *wittrockiana,* 284–87, **284**
Violet, 326, **326**
Violet gall midges, 285, 326
Violet sawflies, **284**, 285
Viral diseases
  bean and, 5
  daffodil and, 229
  dianthus and, 237
  garden mum and, 281
  lily and, 267
  pepper and, 59
  rose and, 309
  strawberry and, 183
  summer squash and, 73
  zonal geranium and, 249
Vitis, 156–61, **156**

W

Walnut, 184–86, **184**
Walnut anthracnose, 186
Walnut aphids, 185
Walnut blight, 186

Walnut caterpillars, 185
Walnut husk flies, 185
Walnut husk maggots, 185
Washing soda as fungicide, 155
Water as pest control, 3, 8, 101
Watering practices, 3, 7, 245
Watermelon, 86–87, **86**
Watermelon fruit blotch, 87
Weeds, 11, 39, 151
Weevils
  astilbe and, 198, **198**
  begonia and, 206, **206**
  blackberry and, 139
  carrot and, 20
  coral bells and, 222, **222**
  pecan and, **174**, 175
  pepper and, 57
  raspberry and, 139
  strawberry and, 180, **180**
  sweet potato and, 74
Western filbert blight, 163
Whiteflies, *331*
  ageratum and, 189
  basil and, 92, **92**
  begonia and, 208
  brussels sprouts and, **12**, 13
  calendula and, 98–99, **98**
  coleus and, 219, **219**
  kale and, 38–39
  lupine and, 272–73, **272**
  rosemary and, 116
  rue and, 118, *118*
  verbena and, 323
  zonal geranium and, 247–48
White peach scale, 310–11
White pine blister rust, 155, *333*
White rot, 37
Wilt, 177, 281
Wilt and stem rot, 277
Winter squash, 88–90, **88**
Wireworms, 20–21, 62, 244–45, 270

Y

Yarrow, 327, **327**
Yellow woollybear caterpillars, 296, **312**, 313, **316**, 317

Z

Zea mays, 26–29, **26**
Zinnia, 328, **328**
Zinnia blight, 328

USDA Plant Hardiness Zone Map

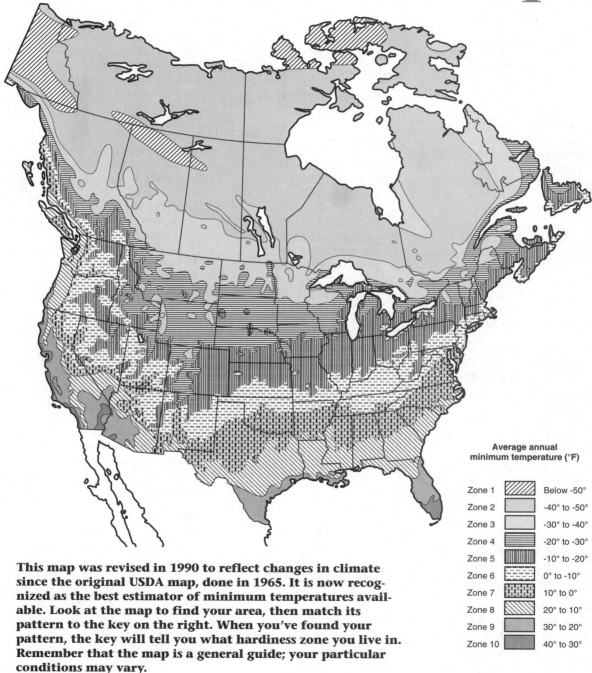

Average annual minimum temperature (°F)

Zone 1		Below -50°
Zone 2		-40° to -50°
Zone 3		-30° to -40°
Zone 4		-20° to -30°
Zone 5		-10° to -20°
Zone 6		0° to -10°
Zone 7		10° to 0°
Zone 8		20° to 10°
Zone 9		30° to 20°
Zone 10		40° to 30°

This map was revised in 1990 to reflect changes in climate since the original USDA map, done in 1965. It is now recognized as the best estimator of minimum temperatures available. Look at the map to find your area, then match its pattern to the key on the right. When you've found your pattern, the key will tell you what hardiness zone you live in. Remember that the map is a general guide; your particular conditions may vary.